AF538923

# Trends for Youth Entrepreneurship

# Trends for Youth Entrepreneurship

**Dr. S. K. Panneer Selvam**
Assistant Professor, Department of Education
Bharathidasan University, T.N

**RANDOM PUBLICATIONS**

**NEW DELHI (INDIA)**

**Trends for Youth Entrepreneurship**

ISBN 978-93-5111-534-2



Published in 2015 in India by

**RANDOM PUBLICATIONS**

4376-A/4B, Gali Murari Lal, Ansari Road
New Delhi-110 002
Phone : +9111-43580356, 011-43142548, 011-23289044
e-mail : sales@randompublications.com
info@randompublications.com
randomexports@gmail.com

Reprinted 2021

*Type Setting by :* Shah Computer Graphics, Delhi-110094
*Printed at :* Replika Press Pvt. Ltd.

# Contents

1



2

## 4



## 5

## 21



## 22

# Topics and Contributors

1. From Macro-Level Spillovers to Micro-Level Dynamic Capabilities: A Knowledge-Based Model of New Ventures' Internationalization

   *Antonia Mercedes García-Cabrera, María Gracia García-Soto, Sonia María Suárez-Ortega & Arístides Olivares-Mesa*
   *Universidad de Las Palmas de Gran Canaria, Canada*

2. Entrepreneurship & Economic Development through LLP: A New Paradigm

   *Bharat, Panjab University, Chandigarh*
   *Shivangi, Center for Environmental Planning and Technology University, Ahmedabad*

3. Indian Jute Industry: Its Crises - Need for Entrepreneurial Interventions

   *Manish Ur Rahman, Debasish Sarkar*
   *Goenka College of Commerce and Business Administration, Kolkata*

4. Special Economic Zone (SEZ) & Institution Building for Entrepreneurship

   *Paramasivan S Vellala*
   *Nirma University, Ahmedabad*

5. Family Business in India: Survival for Three Generations or Beyond

   *S S Khanka, National Institute of Financial Management, Faridabad*

6. An Array of Environment for Intrapreneurship Development: An Empirical Study of Some Selected Companies in Lucknow, India

   *Surendra Kumar*
   *Babu Banarasi Das National Institute of Technology & Management, Lucknow*

16. Evaluation of Entrepreneurship Development Preparedness of Tripura Vis-À-Vis Entrepreneurial Framework Conditions

    *Subrata Debnath*
    *Tripura State Electricity Corporation Limited, Tripura*

17. Harnessing the Achievement Oriented Youth for Entrepreneurial Growth

    *Yavnika Khanna*
    *K. J Somaiya Institute of Management Studies and Research, Mumbai*

18. Trust, Network, and Market: Start-up Strategies of SMEs in Indian ICT industry

    *Anirban Sengupta*
    *Bharat Ratna Dr B.R. Ambedkar University, Delhi*

19. Small and Medium Enterprise (SME) Artisan Clusters: Opportunities and Challenges

    *Nandita Verma, Ashish Pareek & B P Saraswat*
    *Maharshi Dayanand Saraswati University, Ajmer*

20. Role of Rural Entrepreneurship in Development of SME sector in Assam with special reference to Nalbari District

    *Biju Mani Das, Don Bosco College of Engineering and Technology, Guwahati*
    *Rosy Sarma, Lalit Chandra Bharali College, Guwahati*

21. Networks, Micro and Small Enterprises (MSE's) and Performance in Kenya

    *Jared O. Ongong'a & Evance O. Abeka*
    *Maseno University, Kenya*

22. Small and Medium Enterprise (SME) Development in Vietnam

    *Rajkumar Phatate, Institute of Management Technology, Nagpur*

23. Challenges of Pharmaceutical Entrepreneurship in India: The SME Sector

    *Abhijeet Chatterjee, Shantanu Chakravarty, J K Patel Institute of Management, Baroda*
    *Jayarajsinh Jadeja, The M S University of Baroda, Baroda*

24. Challenges faced by Small Scale Entrepreneurs

    *Vijaykumar P Sinkar.*
    *Sinkar Consultancy & Management Services, Pune*

# 1

# From Macro-Level Spillovers to Micro-Level Dynamic Capabilities: A Knowledge-Based Model of New Ventures' Internationalization

***Abstract***

This paper explores the following relevant question: what are the environmental and internal knowledge-based factors that influence the propensity of new ventures to launch international expansion at or near their inception? Hence, this study contributes to the literature on born-global firms by introducing a multilevel approach that encompasses the internal dynamic capabilities and the external environmental conditions of the new venture within the entrepreneurship research field. We empirically test the effect of these potential determinants on the adoption of a born-global strategy by comparing this type of strategy with two other strategic options: international entrepreneurial firms that adopt a slower pace of internationalization and the decision to focus in the domestic market. Therefore, we act in response to the lack of integrative models and empirical research in this domain and extend the existing knowledge on international new ventures. The literature on knowledge based view and born global was used as a basis for drawing up the hypotheses, which were tested with data from 242 Spanish manufacturing SMEs representing manufacturing industries of a diverse technological content. Our results show that entrepreneurial spillovers and export spillovers of the firms' region of origin, as well as several dynamic capabilities are determinants of the adoption of a fast and committed internationalization.

## Introduction

Zahra and George (2002:261) define international entrepreneurship as "the process of creatively discovering and exploiting opportunities that lie outside a firm's domestic markets in pursuit of competitive advantage". To refer to this type of new venture, the term *born global* –BG– has been coined, as well as *instant exporter* and *international new venture* –INV- (*e.g.*, Karra *et al.*, 2008; Knight and Cavusgil, 2004). These BG firms are a sub-set of SMEs (Gabrielsson *et al.*, 2008) with the distinct feature of early and fast international expansion.

Literature examining BGs relates internationalization to personal-, firm- industry- or macro-level factors. Most research works have analyzed personal level factors, such as demographic and cognitive characteristics of entrepreneurs (Keupp and Gassmann, 2009). However, Gassmann and Keupp (2007:352) consider that "[...] focus on those cognitive characteristics neither explains why some SMEs are able to internationalize rapidly and early, whereas others are not, although all of them are founded by entrepreneurs". By contrast, the research on firm-level factors is rather limited (Keupp and Gassmann, 2009; Gassmann and Keupp, 2007). Finally, we have found a truly limited amount of empirical research exploring the role of environmental factors on new venture internationalization -*e.g.*, Zahra and George (2002) note the lack of industry-level factors and De Clercq *et al.* (2008) the lack of macro level factors.

Those partial studies do not satisfy the expectations of the researchers who emphasize the relevance of finding a comprehensive theoretical framework that would permit the explanation of this complex phenomenon (Jantunen *et al.*, 2008; Weerawardena *et al.*, 2007; Zhou, 2007; Spence and Crick, 2006; Zahra *et al.*, 2005). Addressing these concerns and following Gassmann and Keupp's (2007) recommendation, this paper introduces a multilevel knowledge-based approach to explain the accelerated internationalization of BGs. This approach is justified on the relevance that knowledge has reached for the development of both entrepreneurial activities (*e.g.*, West III and Noel, 2009) and successful international business (*e.g.*, Gassman and Keupp, 2007; Knight and

Cavusgil, 2004). Specifically, the proposed model is based on two sets of factors: (1) the environmental conditions of the firm, as external sources of knowledge –i.e., knowledge spillovers– and (2) firm dynamic capabilities both to capture existing knowledge in the environment and to generate new knowledge internally.

Then, this study contributes to the existing knowledge in several ways. First, it introduces a multilevel knowledge-based approach to explain new ventures' internationalization, combining a perspective based on aggregated data from the territory with a micro-level perspective to find the determinants of the entrepreneur decision. Second, we empirically test the effect of these variables on the adoption of a BG strategy but looking at it together with other strategic alternatives: international entrepreneurial firms that adopt a slower pace internationalization process and firms deciding to remain focused on serving local markets. Third, the limited literature that has studied the influence that the environment can have on the decision to internationalize the new venture, has approached its study from a cross-national comparative perspective that takes as its premise the spatial homogeneity of the variables under study (*e.g.*, De Clercq *et al.*, 2008; Spence and Crick, 2006). In our research, however, we believe that such sub-national differences exist and may be relevant, so that is why we study them and their influence on early internationalization of BGs.

Fourth, we study a new source of knowledge spillover, international entrepreneurship spillover and we try to extend existing literature by suggesting that INVs may result from previous new ventures funding by opportunity driven entrepreneurs.

## Theoretical Background

As opposed to *traditional firms,* BGs are entrepreneurial firms conceived from inception as a project with the capacity to offer products targeting a global market (Karra *et al.*, 2008). For this sub-set of international entrepreneurial SMEs, size and age are no longer prerequisites for doing international business (Gabrielsson *et al.*, 2008). Nevertheless, there is no widespread definition of a born-global firm. When referring to this kind of firm, many authors emphasize three dimensions: speed, scale and scope of internationalization (Oviatt and McDougall, 1994).

First, speed of internationalization is the period of time between the inception and the moment when a firm initiates international operations. The original definition by Knight and Cavusgil (1996) required that exports should start within 3 years from inception. Second, scale of internation alization relates to the extent of a firm's international operations and it is usually measured by the proportion of international sales related to total sales. The definition of BG by Knight and Cavusgil (1996) requires an export volume greater than 25% of total sales. In Zahra *et al.*'s (2000) opinion, this last figure is too high for young ventures that are early in their internationalization, so they used a minimum of 5%. Nevertheless, we consider appropriate the criteria established by Knight and Cavusgil (1996) –i.e., 3 years from inception and 25% of total sales– because of two main reasons: (a) it has been used in many different empirical contexts; and (b) it helps ensuring adequate identification of firms as BGs by its strong commitment to early international operations.

Finally, scope of internationalization is related to the narrow or broad range of targeted geographic markets because BGs operate in multiple countries from their very outset (Oviatt and McDougall, 1994). According to Kuivalainen *et al.* (2007), the ambiguity associated with the term "multiple countries" (scope), which ignores their locations and possible institutional distances between them, makes it difficult to conceptualize the BG firm precisely. Thus, it has been customary in the literature to omit this third criterion to qualify a new company as a BG (*e.g.*, Jantunen *et al.*, 2008; Gassman and Keupp, 2007; Knight and Cavusgil, 2004). Thus, in our study the *scope* criterion was not taken into account.

## Knowledge resources and international entrepreneurship

Knowledge resources include the understanding of how to attain growth and competitive position in global markets (Maskell and Malmberg, 1999), how to get technology and new product development (Gabrielsson *et al.*, 2008; Gassmann and Keupp, 2007), how to handle export procedures and paperwork (*e.g.*, Greenaway *et al.*, 2004), etc. Because knowledge resources per se could be complementarily acquired from internal and external sources, we study both sources of relevant knowledge to new ventures' internationalization.

## Knowledge spillovers and new ventures' internationalization

Knowledge spillovers allow firms to acquire knowledge from other economic players without having to pay for it in a formal market transaction (Acs *et al.*, 1994). As this paper is focused on international entrepreneurship, we are especially interested in two types of knowledge from the environment: export knowledge and international entrepreneurial knowledge.

## Export spillovers

Export spillover is a particular type of spillover that may affect export decision of existing and new domestic firms (Greenaway *et al.*, 2004). Due to the fact that *spillovers* mean free transfer of knowledge across economic players, these are especially crucial for small and new ventures, which often lack internal export knowledge or experience (Acs *et al.*, 1994). Specifically, foreign direct investment (henceforth, FDI) and international trade could be sources of export spillovers (Andersson and Johansson, 2008; De Clercq *et al.*, 2008). Those spillovers take place when knowledge useful for operating abroad (*e.g.*, export process, foreign markets) transfers from one economic actor to another (Acs *et al.*, 1994). For example, when a new venture comes in contact with existing exporters and MNEs in its territory, it gains information about how to become a successful exporter (Burpitt and Rondinelli, 2000). Additionally, demonstration and imitation effects may exist that lead new ventures to use MNEs and exporters as role model for their own decision to engage in exporting (Powell and DiMaggio, 1991). Finally, spillover effects from imports relate to technology transfer between domestic producers and foreign suppliers, and to knowledge about foreign producers' countries (De Clercq *et al.*, 2008). H1a. The greater the export spillovers in a particular territory (inward FDI, outward FDI, export and import), the more likely new ventures founded within that territory will become BG firms.

## International entrepreneurship spillovers

The institutional endowment of a region also includes the entrepreneurial spirit (Maskell and Malmberg, 1999); this spirit consists of a set of factors such as the predominant type of entrepreneurial motivation in that location, for examplenecessity and opportunity entrepreneurship (Acs *et al.*, 2008). Opportunity entrepreneurship implies pull motives to start up a new venture such as wealth, status or independence, while necessity entrepreneurship, occurs, for example, when unemployment forces people into self-employment –i.e., push motives– (Hessel *et al.*, 2008). This distinction is relevant as opportunity differs from necessity entrepreneurship in the growth aspirations for the new firm (Acs *et al.*, 2008). For example, opportunity driven entrepreneurs are more committed to international activities (Hessels *et al.* 2008). Then, those possess a superior set of motivations and knowledge, such as increase-wealth motivations (Hessels *et al.*, 2008), growth aspirations and willingness to deal with an early and fast internationalization (Hessels *et al.*, 2008;

Karra *et al.*, 2008), as well as abilities to identify international opportunities (Karra *et al.*, 2008). Thus, we could assume that these opportunity driven entrepreneurs are more skilled and have a superior knowledge base.

Then, concerning macro-level analysis, we argue that opportunity entrepreneurship in a territory represents a source of knowledge spillovers that may affect the local new founders' decision to start up an INV. So we understand *international entrepreneurship spillover* as those spillovers that allow the entrepreneur to acquire knowledge from previous entrepreneurs. The positive influence these nearby opportunity driven entrepreneurs have on the internationalization of new ventures may be generated by information spillovers –i.e., diffusion of information– and by skilled and specialized labour pool with entrepreneurship specific knowledge. First, positive publicity on those who have obtained personal wealth through entrepreneurial actions is likely to influence entrepreneurial motivations and intent (Levie and Autio, 2008) of new entrepreneurs. Here, opportunity driven new ventures may act as role model for aspirant entrepreneurs. Second, when new entrepreneurs come in contact with existing opportunity driven entrepreneurs, they can learn from them instrumental skills required to start up an INV, and cognitive abilities to manage the complex process of international opportunity recognition and assessment.

When new entrepreneurs exposes to stories of the discovery and exploitation of entrepreneurial opportunities, they get access to examples that they can found useful to understand what is possible and what is feasible (Levie and Autio, 2008). H1b. The greater the international entrepreneurship spillovers in a particular territory, the more likely new ventures founded within that territory will become BG firms.

## Firm's dynamic capabilities and new ventures' internationalization

"Dynamic capabilities are the routines through which the firm learns from different sources" (Weerawardeba *et al.*, 2007:298). In the particular case of SME aspiring to accelerated internationalization, these firms must develop the strategic set of capabilities needed to achieve their international goals at o near the firm's inception (Weerawardeba *et al.*, 2007), such as market and technological knowledge capabilities.

**Market knowledge related capabilities.** One of the environmental factors influencing the emergence of the BG phenomenon is the increasingly global nature of demand. Globalization is related to the increasing homogenization of buyer preferences around the globe, which has made international business easier by simplifying product development and positioning in foreign markets (Knight and Cavusgil, 2004). The similarity of the markets makes demand uniform at a global level (Jantunen *et al.*, 2008), but it is the new venture's understanding of such market characteristics the prerequisite for the development of effective marketing-mix strategies and competitive positioning in multiple markets. To this respect, "market-focused learning capability is characterized by the acquisition and dissemination of market information" (Weerawardena *et al.*, 2007:300).

H2a. SME's capability to position homogeneous products in global markets increases its likelihood of becoming a BG.

**Technological knowledge related capabilities**. Technological knowledge management requires two capabilities proposed by Zahra and George (2002): the potential technological knowledge capability and the realized technological knowledge. The first one includes the ability to identify and acquire externally generated knowledge and the second one is related to the ability to develop and improve routines that facilitate the integration between existing and newly acquired knowledge. Along this line, firm innovation has been considered a measure of realized technological knowledge capability because it represents the application of acquired and generated knowledge and its materialization in new products (Díaz-Díaz *et al.*, 2006). Based on this distinction, we first focus on innovation capability right below, and afterwards we will focus on the potential influence that technological knowledge capability may exert on the early and fast internationalization of new ventures. *Innovation related capabilities*. Gassmann and Keupp's (2007) findings provide a picture of BGs' limited set of competitive strategic options as compared to those available for MNEs: either focusing on a niche market for the product where the SME can charge high prices, or serving a large market, if the product is both highly specialized and homogeneous. In both cases, the high value added of its products and/or services generates a margin for the SME which is big enough to absorb the potential transaction costs associated with international expansion. However, these two strategies are feasible only if the product has a unique competitive advantage over competitors which stems from the SME's specialized knowledge (Gabrielsson *et al.*, 2008; Gassmann and Keupp, 2007).

The underlying variable that leads to the product's distinctiveness is innovation, which may be considered a dynamic knowledge capability that represents the application of technological or non-technological knowledge and its materialization to obtain new and unique products (Weerawardena *et al.*, 2007; Díaz-Díaz *et al.*, 2006). H2b. SME's capability to innovate in new products increases its likelihood of becoming a BG.

Nevertheless, the new venture, due to its youth and small size, usually lacks key knowledge resources necessary to develop the innovations (Weerawardena et al., 2007); then entrepreneurs may search for and attempt to acquiretechnological knowledge resources that belong to others. External knowledge includes explicit technological knowledge resources, usually legally protected via patens, and tacit technological knowledge resources, not directly acquirable in the markets (Díaz-Díaz *et al.*, 2006). The internal development of certain capabilities may permit to capture tacit and/or explicit knowledge resources (Lefebvre *et al.*, 1998) without having to pay a high price for them, such as: (1) the ability to gather tacit knowledge from hiring R&D qualified personnel which can, to some degree, substitute the lack of experience within the new venture with new human resources experience; and (2) the ability to resort to long-term external collaboration–i.e., networking capabilities such as joint-ventures, sharing in capital and other non-equity alliances. While informal networks may provide access to resources and information, formal networks can help entrepreneurial firms learn new capabilities because they are generative of both tacit and explicit knowledge that is helpful for the venture (West III and Noel, 2009); in addition, formal networks facilitate knowledge integration and application in new products (Lefebvre *et al.*, 1998). Thus, new venture's capabilities to capture and integrate externally developed knowledge may compensate for the lack of resources and facilitate BG's early internationalization.

H2c. SME's capability to hire R&D qualified personnel increases its likelihood of becoming a BG. H2d. SME's capability to establish R&D alliances increases its likelihood of becoming a BG.

## Methodology

### Data and Sampl

We examine new Spanish manufacturing firms. We combine firm-level data, which is obtained from the Survey on Business Strategies (SBS) conducted by Fundación SEPI1, with territorial data at the autonomous community2 (AC) level, which are obtained from different public sources of information. Generally, for each territorial independent variable, each firm of the analyzed sample is assigned the value of its AC in the year of its foundation, as a measure of the level of knowledge in the particular AC where the firm was born and is developing. The study analyzes the sample of firms that answered the SBS in 2006 (2,023 firms), but considering all available data of each firm down to 1999.

Thus, we conduct a cross-sectional study of firms in 2006, but with a longitudinal analysis of each firm through its historical data. Considering the objective of our study, we only examine the subsample that meets the following criteria: (1) *Small and medium-sized firms* (SME), firms with less than 250 employees in 2006; (2) *young firms*, firms up to ten years of age, as firms up to the age of 12 years have survived the liability of newness (Zahra *et al.*, 2000); and (3) *independent firms*, firms not integrated in a corporate group, with an equity no equity on the firm by any foreign company. This last criterion guarantee the firm is established and managed by entrepreneurs (Zahra *et al.*, 2000). Following all the above criteria, our final sample size is 242 young, independent, small and medium sized Spanish manufacturing firms.

**Measurement of variables SME's international status**. Our dependent variable has value 0 if the SME is a domestic firm; 1 if the SME has international activities, but it cannot be considered a BG because does not meet BG criteria; and 2 BG firms. Following Jantunen *et al.* (2008), firms are classified as purely domestic firms although they had had export sales if they have turned their focus solely to domestic markets (they have not exported in the last three years, 2004-2006). Following the above criteria, 151 SMEs in our sample are domestic firms, 65 international firms and 26 BG firms.

**Knowledge spillovers**. (1) *Export spillovers* are measured using the AC stock of inward and outward FDI and import and export levels. Stocks of FDI in a certain year is calculated summing the time series of FDI flows up to that particular year (DataInvex, Secretaría de Estado de Comercio). Import and export levels are measured as the total import/export value of the firm's AC in its year of foundation (STACOM, Spanish government, ICEX). All variables are divided by GDP to eliminate the effect of size of the different ACs; (2) *International entrepreneurship spillover* is measured through the level of Improvement-driven opportunity entrepreneurial activity based on GEM's opportunity-TEA index.

**Firm's dynamic capabilities**: (1) *Market knowledge capabilities* are measured through the firm's capability to position homogeneous products in global markets, using a dummy variable coded 1 if firm's products are highly standardized, and 0 if firm's products are mostly designed specifically for each client; (2) *Innovation capabilities* are measured through the firm's capability to innovate in new products, using a dummy variable, which takes the value of 1 if the firm has obtained, in any of the years analyzed (1999-2006), any new products, and the value 0 otherwise; and (3) *Potential technological knowledge capability* are measured through three dimensions identified from items in the SBS by Díaz-Díaz *et al.* (2006) that refer to capabilities to acquire and integrate external technological knowledge: (i) Hiring R&D qualified personnel capability–*e.g.*, engineers, personnel with business experience in R&D–, (ii) horizontal and complementary networking capability–*e.g.*, joint venture, non-equity alliances with Universities and/ or Research Centers, etc., and (iii) vertical networking capability, with customers and suppliers. Each capability is a dummy variable coded 1 if the firm has answered "yes" to any of the statement related with each dimension in any of the years analyzed, and 0 otherwise.

**Control variables**. The sample is already controlled for key potential influencing factors on internationalization, like not belonging a corporate group and age. Nevertheless, industry and size of the firm have also traditionally been considered as factors that may have an impact on internationalization strategy, and those are our additional control variables. *Previous size* is measured using the logarithm of total number of employees in the year before the first year with cxport sales, and each firm that has never exported is assigned the total number of employees in 2006. *Industry* is measured with a dummy variable coded 1 for the firm which is in a high-tech industry or in a medium to high-tech industry (e.g., chemicals, optical equipment, electronic equipment, etc.) and 0 otherwise.

## Results

Table 1 presents the basic statistics of the independent variables and the correlations between them. Table 1 also presents the test to know if there are significant differences between the three categories of the dependent variable - SME's international status- for each individual independent variable. We did not introduce in the multinomial logistic regression those independents variables that showed no relationship with the dependent one (Inward IDE/GDP). With respect to multi co linearity, in the multinomial logistic regression solution, is detected by examining the standard errors for the beta coefficients, existing a potential problem when they are higher that 2.0 (Naderi *et al.*, 2009). None of the independent variables in this analysis had a standard error larger than 2.0, which suggest the absence of multi co linearity in the data.

**Table 1. Descriptive statistics and correlations**

| | International status | 1 | 2 | 3 | 4 | 5 | 6 | 7 | 8 | 9 | 10 | 11 | 12 |
|---|---|---|---|---|---|---|---|---|---|---|---|---|---|
| 1. Previous size | 7.634** | 1 | | | | | | | | | | | |
| 2. Industry | 10.253** | .016 | 1 | | | | | | | | | | |
| 3. Inward FDI | 0.498 | -.104 | -.025 | 1 | | | | | | | | | |
| 4. Outward FDI | 2.616† | -.061 | -.034 | .541*** | 1 | | | | | | | | |
| 5. Export | 6.312** | -.113† | -.022 | -.037 | .026 | 1 | | | | | | | |
| 6. Import | 2.427† | -.177** | .015 | .640*** | .339*** | .505** | 1 | | | | | | |
| 7. Opportunity TEA | 6.190** | -.068 | .035 | .515*** | .210** | .103 | .614*** | 1 | | | | | |
| 8. Position products in markets | 6.216* | .095 | -.126† | -.161* | -.053 | .001 | -.176** | -.115† | 1 | | | | |
| 9. Innovation | 37.685*** | .188** | .260*** | -.051 | -.034 | .219** | .143* | .149* | .074 | 1 | | | |
| 10. Hiring personnel | 18.103*** | .226*** | .329*** | -.099 | -.073 | .051 | -.098 | -.013 | -.027 | .238*** | 1 | | |
| 11. Horizontal networking | 11.210** | .144* | .158* | -.013 | -.020 | .059 | -.029 | -.001 | -.118† | .378*** | .291*** | 1 | |
| 12. Vertical networking | 14.414** | .145* | .328*** | .016 | -.054 | .050 | .114† | .175** | -.047 | .541*** | .310*** | .490*** | 1 |
| **Mean** | **0.48** | **3.11** | **.16** | **5.98** | **7.78** | **17.52** | **19.80** | **6.02** | **.50** | **.25** | **.13** | **.15** | **.16** |
| **SD** | **0.68** | **.71** | **.37** | **9.01** | **19.22** | **7.59** | **8.64** | **1.19** | **.50** | **.43** | **.33** | **.36** | **.36** |

Levels of significance: †p < .1, *p < .05, **p < .01, ***p < .001.

Table 2 shows the results of multinomial logistic regression model for international status of the SME. Concerning knowledge spillovers, first, export spillovers from outward FDI have a significant effect on the international status of the SME, but only if we compare BGs with international firms. The negative sign of the coefficient shows that the particular explanatory factor reduces the likelihood of being in the category compared with the category of reference, BG firms in our case. Thus, that is exactly the same of saying that the variable increases the likelihood of being BG. Second, spillover from exports has a significant and positive effect on the likelihood of being a BG, both comparing this group with domestic firms and with international firms. Third, spillovers effects from imports are not significant. All these results in mind, along with the absent relationship between inward FDI and the dependent variable (see table 1), we can affirm that H1a is partially supported, as the likelihood of a SME to be a BG increases, the greater the spillover effects from outward FDI and export levels in the firm's territory. Opportunity entrepreneurship has a significant and positive effect on early and fast internationalization but only when is compared with domestic firms, partially supporting H1b.

Table 2. Multinomial regression(a)

| Variables | Domestic | | International | |
|---|---|---|---|---|
| | Beta coefficients | Standard errors | Beta coefficients | Standard errors |
| Independent term | 11.341 *** | (2.291) | 3.649 | (2.237) |
| ***Control variables*** | | | | |
| Previous size (Log) | -.939 † | (.358) | -.157 | (.337) |
| Industry | -.907 | (.715) | .240 | (.675) |
| ***Knowledge Spillovers*** | | | | |
| Outward FDI/GDP | .006 | (.016) | -.124 ** | (.045) |
| Export/GDP | -.074 † | (.041) | -.078 † | (.044) |
| Import/GDP | -.007 | (.047) | .079 | (.054) |
| Opportunity TEA | -.525 † | (.276) | -.070 | (.277) |
| ***Firm's Dynamic capabilities*** | | | | |
| Position homogeneous products in global market | -1.474 ** | (.574) | -1.024 † | (.574) |
| Products innovation | -1.549 ** | (.605) | -1.041 † | (.603) |
| Hiring R&D qualified personnel | -1.282 † | (.704) | -.551 | (.672) |
| R&D horizontal networking | -.888 | (.713) | -.102 | (.680) |
| R&D vertical networking | .373 | (.766) | -.247 | (.735) |
| ***Pseudo $R^2$ Nagelkerke*** | | 41.5% | | |
| ***Likelihood Ratio Test*** | | 325.165*** | | |
| ***Pearson Chi-square*** | | 485.021 | | |
| ***% correct*** | | 73.4% | | |

Levels of significance: †p < .1, *p < .05, **p < .01, ***p < .001.
(a) BGs category is the reference.

Relating to firm's dynamic capabilities, first, firms's capability to position homogeneous products in global markets has a significant and positive effect on the likelihood of being BG, both comparing BGs with domestic firms and with international firms. Hence H2a is supported. Second, firm's capability to innovate in new products is also significant and has a positive influence on the likelihood of being BG, both comparing with the domestic firms and with international firms. Hence, H2b is also supported. Third, firm's capacity to hire R&D qualified personnel has a significant and positive effect on early and fast internationalization when BGs are compared with domestic firms, which gives support to H2c. Finally, H2d is supported as neither R&D horizontal and complementary networking capacity nor R&D vertical networking capacity is significant.

## Discussion and Conclusions

Our results indicate that export spillovers from a great export activity in a particular territory have a positive influence on the decision of a new venture to internationalize soon after its inception. Exporters in a territory may be a role model (Powell and DiMaggio, 1991) as well as a source of reliable information on the advantages of exporting and on export-related processes (Burpitt and Rondinelli, 2000) to encourage new entrepreneurs to undertake the early internationalization. Besides, the existence of outward FDI represents another source of export spillovers, but only when compared with SMEs internationalizing following a slow pace. This result may indicate that, as BGs' early and commitment internationalization may include the possibility of making foreign direct investment, some SMEs follow the role model represented by Spanish MNEs located in their territories. SMEs facing gradual internationalization, however, usually begin just exporting, so not benefiting from the spillover effect generated by the national MNEs. In this regard, it should be taken into consideration that in our sample all firms are young, so those following the gradual process may have not thought about FDI yet.

Moreover, the effect of inward FDI turned out to be independent of the SMEs' international status. This is not a new result in the literature, as it is evidenced in the review by Rojec *et al.* (2009), who suggest that those results may be justify based on the following arguments: (1) a foreign MNE may be effective at ensuring its technology advantages do not spill over, so it may be able to prevent leakages to domestic firms; (2) positive spillovers may only affect a subset of firms due to the firms' heterogeneity problem, meaning that FDI spillovers depend on firms absorptive capacity. This may be suggesting, in sub-national level studies like the present one, the need to consider the uneven levels of technological development or the minimum stock of human capital to ensure the capacity of absorption of knowledge brought by foreign MNEs (Andersson and Johansson, 2008).

Regarding international entrepreneurship spillovers, the results show that they increase the likelihood of a new venture to follow a BG strategy comparing with firms opting to compete only in the local market. However, no significant difference was found if we compare BGs with the rest of international firms.

This may be because in the territories with high levels of opportunity-driven entrepreneurship, knowledge and role models that represent the BGs already established in that territory may positively influence not only the decision of the new entrepreneurs, but also those of others that have already established their firms in recent years, and due to the contagion effect and their relationships with such BGs, also choose to start international activities. With regard to dynamic capabilities, our results support that firm's capacities to position homogeneous products in global markets, as well as those related to product innovation clearly determine the choice of a BG strategy. These results confirm the relevance that dynamic capabilities, focused on learning and generating idiosyncratic knowledge within the new venture, have on the possibility that a SME, with few resources, internationalizes at or near the inception.

Regarding the potential technological knowledge capabilities, our results depart significantly from the assumptions made. First, firm's capability to hire R&D qualified personnel only influences the choice of a BG strategy only when it is compared with the strategy based on competing locally. This may be because the recruitment of staff with technological knowledge to facilitate the uptake and application of that knowledge generated in the environment to undertake the development of innovations may be developed by any SME that decides to internationalize. In this regard, we highlight again that all firms in our sample are relatively young and therefore still do not have a relevant pool of technological knowledge.

Second, firm's capabilities of establishing technological alliances with other economic actors were not significant in explaining the decision to undertake the early internationalization. This may be due to two circumstances. The first deals with the use of embeddings in social, not inter-firm, networks. Indeed, some authors have highlighted that SMEs need to be continuously updating their knowledge by inter-firm relations must be relativized (Gassmann and Keupp, 2007). In Gassmann and Keupp's (2007), although BGs rely on inter-firm collaborations to update their knowledge and to get access to resources, yet these inter-firm collaborations are characterized by social embeddeness, not by formal agreements, joint ventures or strategic alliances, such as those discussed in our empirical research.

## References


1. Acs, Z.J.; Audretsch, D.B.; Feldman, M. (1994). R&D spillovers and recipient firm size. *The Review of Economics and Statistics*, 76(2), 336–340.
2. Acs, Z.J.; Desai, S.; Hessels, J. (2008). Entrepreneurship, economics development and institutions. *Small Business Economics*, 31(3), 219-234.
3. Andersson, M.; Johansson, B. (2008). Innovation ideas and regional characteristics: product innovations and export entrepreneurship by firms in Swedish regions. *Growth and Change*, 39(2), 193-224.
4. Burpitt, W.J.; Rondinelli, D.A. (2000). Small firm's motivations for exporting: To earn and learn? *Journal of Small Business Management*, 38, 1-14.
5. De Clercq, D.; Hessels, J.; van Stel, A. (2008). Knowledge spillovers and new ventures' export orientation. *Small Business Economics*, 31, 283-303.

6. Díaz-Díaz, N.L.; Aguiar-Díaz, I.; De Saá-Pérez, P. (2006). Technological knowledge assets in industrial firms. *R&D Management*, 36(2), 189-203.
7. Gabrielsson, M.; Kirpalani, V.H.M.; Dimitratos, P.; Solberg, C.A.; Zucchella, A. (2008). Born globals: propositions to help advance the theory. *International Business Review*, 17(4), 385-401.
8. Gassmann, O.; Keupp, M.M. (2007). The competitive advantage of early and rapidly internationalizing in the biotechnology industry: A knowledge-based view. *Journal of World Business,* 42, 350-366.
9. Greenaway, D.; Sousa, N.; Wakelin, K. (2004). Do domestic firms learn to export form multinationals? *European Journal of Political Economy*, 20(4), 1027- 1043.
10. Hessel, J.; van Gelderen, M.W.; Thurik, A.R. (2008). Drivers of entrepreneurial aspirations at the country level: The role of start-up motivations and social security. *International Entrepreneurship and Management Journal*, 4(4), 401- 417.
11. Jantunen, A.; Nummela, N.; Puumalainen, K.; Saarenketo, S. (2008). Strategic orientation of born globals - Do they really matter? *Journal of World Business*, 43, 158-170.
12. Karra, N.; Phillips, N.; Tracey, P. (2008). Building the born global firm. Developing entrepreneurial capabilities for international new venture success. *Long Range Planning*, 41, 440-458.
13. Keupp, M.M.; Gassmann, O. (2009). The past and the future of international entrepreneurship: A review and suggestions for developing the field. *Journal of Management*, 35(3), 600-633.
14. Knight, G.A.; Cavusgil, S.T. (1996). The born global firm: a challenge to traditional internalization theory. In S.T. Cavusgil and Madsen, T. (Eds.), *Advances in International Marketing* (11-26). Greenwich, CT: JAL Press.
15. Kuivalainen, O.; Sundqvist, S.; Servais, P. (2007). Firm's degree of bornglobalness, international entrepreneurial orientation and export performance. *Journal of World Business*, 42, 523-267.
16. Lefebvre, E.; Lefebvre, L.A.; Bourgault, M. (1998). R&D-related capabilities as determinants of export performance. *Small Business Economics*, 10, 365-377.
17. Levie, J.; Autio, E. (2008). A theoretical grounding and test of the GEM model. *Small Business Economics*, 31, 235-263.
18. Maskell, P.; Malmberg, A. (1999). Localised learning and industrial competitiveness, *Cambridge Journal of Economics*, 23, 167-185.
19. Naderi, H.; Abdullah, R.; Aizan, H.T.; Sharir, J.; Kumar, V. (2009). Self esteem, gender and academic achievement of undergraduate students. *American Journal of Scientific Research,* 3, 26-37.

20. Oviatt, B.; McDougall, P. (1994). Toward a Theory of International New Ventures. *Journal of International Business Studies*, 25(1), 45-64.
21. Powel, W.W.; DiMaggio, P.J. (1991). *The new institutionalism in organizational analysis*. Chicago: University of Chicago Press.
22. Rojec, M.; Knell, M.; Damijan, J.P. (2009). Why is there so little evidence on knowledge spillovers from foreign direct investment? *Paper presented at the EIBA Annual Conference*. Valencia. España.
23. Spence, M.; Crick, D. (2006). A comparative investigation into the internationalisation of Canadian and UK high-tech SMEs. *International Marketing Review*, 23(5), 524-548.
24. Weerawardena, J.; Mort, G.S.; Liesch, P.W.; Knight, G. (2007). Conceptualizing accelerated internationalization in the born global firm: a dynamic capabilities perspective. *Journal of World Business*, 42, 294-306.
25. West III, G.P.; Noel, T.W. (2009). The impact of knowledge resources on new venture performance. *Journal of Small Business Management*, 47(1), 1-22.
26. Winter, S. (2003). Understanding dynamic capabilities. *Strategic Management Journal*, 24, 991-995.
27. Zahra, S.A.; George, G. (2002). International entrepreneurship: the current status of the field and future research agenda. In M. A. Hitt, M.A., Irelands, R.D., Camp, S.M. and Sexton, D.L. (Eds), *Strategic entrepreneurship: creating a new mindset* (255-288). Oxford: Blackwell Publisher.
28. Zahra, S.A., Ireland, R.D.; Hitt, M.A. (2000). International expansion by new ventures firms: International diversity, mode of market entry, technological learning, and performance. *Academy of Management Journal*, 43, 925-950.
29. Zahra, S.A.; Korri, J.S.; Yu, J. (2005). Cognition and international entrepreneurship: implications for research on international opportunity recognition and exploitation. *International Business Review*, 14(2), 129-146.
30. Zhou, L. (2007). The effects of entrepreneurial proclivity and foreign market
31. Knowledge on early internationalization. *Journal of World Business*,42,281- 293.

# 2

# Entrepreneurship & Economic Development through LLP: A New Paradigm

***Abstract***

The essence of entrepreneurship lies in the perception and exploitation of new opportunities in the realm of business... it always has to do with bringing about a different use of national resources in that they are withdrawn from their traditional employ and subjected to new combinations. Entrepreneurs provide a spark to the engine of a nation's economy. The role played by the entrepreneurs in the advancement of an economy has been acknowledged internationally and India is no exception to that. Entrepreneurship and economic development are intimately interrelated. Amid the growth of the Indian economy the concept of Limited Liability Partnership got the statutory mandate of the Indian Parliament with the enactment of the Limited Liability Partnership Act, 20083. The concept of LLP is an alternative to the existing models of corporate vehicles. The need and rationale for introducing the LLP has been explained as under: With the growth of Indian economy, the role played by its entrepreneurs as well as its technical and professional manpower has been acknowledged internationally. It was felt opportune that entrepreneurship, knowledge and risk capital combine provide a further impetus to India's economic growth. In this background, a need had been felt for a new corporate form that would provide an alternative to traditional partnership with unlimited personal liability on the one hand, and, the statute based governance of the limited liability company on the other, in order to enable professional expertise and entrepreneurial initiative to combine organize and operate in flexible, innovative and efficient manner. The LLP *avtar* provides the benefit of organizational flexibility as in case of a traditional partnership with glittering feature of limited liability and the corporate personality of a company. The happiness for the LLPs is blowing with full volume. There is bound to be phenomenal increase in the number of LLPs and they are bound to dominate all areas of business and professional domain. The present day business world is full of competition and with the growth of economy, the role played by the entrepreneurs is internationally acknowledged.

The progress of Indian economic development from 1947 to the present provides further evidence that individuals do respond to incentives in their pursuit of self-survival and accumulation of wealth. India can do more, to further advance its economic development. Indeed, one of the more recent microeconomic approaches to economic growth is the promotion of entrepreneurial activities.

Entrepreneurial efforts have been found to generate a wide range of economic benefits, including new businesses, new jobs, innovative products and services, and increased wealth for future community investment *(Kayne, 1999)*. The following narrative explains in considerable depth how entrepreneurial activities have succeeded in several countries and how it can now be used to further India's economic development.

Following an extensive study of entrepreneurship in 21 countries, Reynolds, Hay, Bygrave, Camp and Autio (2000) concluded that successful entrepreneurial activity is strongly associated with economic growth. Their research was subsumed under the "Global Entrepreneurship Monitor", a joint research initiative conducted by Babson College and London Business School and supported by the Kauffman Center for Entrepreneurial Leadership. Their findings, based on surveys of the adult population of each country, in-depth interviews of experts on entrepreneurship in each country, and the use of standardized national data, supported their conceptual model depicting the role of the entrepreneurial process in a country's economic development. The following Global Entrepreneurship Monitor Conceptual Model is as under:

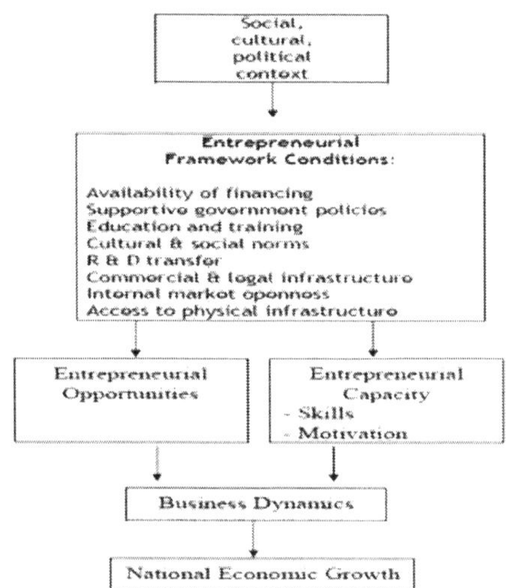


The Global Entrepreneurship Monitor Conceptual Model suggests that the social cultural- political context within a country must foster certain "General National Framework Conditions," which can generate not only the opportunities for entrepreneurship but also the capacity for entrepreneurship – in particular, the skills and motivation necessary to succeed. Together, the entrepreneurship opportunities, on the one hand, and the skills and motivation, on the other, lead to business dynamics that yield creative destruction, a process in which new firms are created and older, less efficient firms are destroyed. The overall result for a country is economic growth. Amid the growth of the Indian economy the concept of Limited Liability Partnership (LLP) got the statutory mandate of the Indian Parliament with the enactment of the Limited Liability Partnership Act, 2008. The concept of limited liability partnership is an alternative to the existing models of corporate vehicles.

## LLP– A New Dimension to Entrepenurship

To carry on business is a fundamental right enshrined in the Indian Constitution. Among all the business organizations like Sole Proprietorship, Partnership, Joint Hindu family business etc. the concept of corporate personality is prevalent only in case of the company. Till yester-years, corporate personality was the unique feature of the company. But now with the legislative sanction to the Limited Liability Partnership Act, 2008 another form of business vehicle enjoys the attribute of corporate personality.

***Entrepreneurship is the key driver of economic development***

An entrepreneur can be regarded as a person who has the initiative skill and motivation to set up a business or enterprise of his own and who always looks for high achievements. He is the catalyst for social change and works for the common good. He looks for opportunities, identify them and seize them mainly for economic gains. An action oriented entrepreneur is a highly calculative individual who is always willing to undertake risks in-order to achieve their goals.

The *avtar* of Limited Liability Partnership is analyzed as a new corporate vehicle that provides the benefit of organizational flexibility to its members as in case of a traditional partnership with glittering feature of limited liability and the corporate personality of a company. Limited Liability Partnership is a corporate business vehicle that enables professional expertise and entrepreneurial initiative to combine and operate in flexible, innovative and efficient manner, providing benefits of limited liability while allowing its members the flexibility for organizing their internal structure as a partnership.

The salient features of the Limited Liability Partnership Act 2008 inter alia are as follows:-

i. The Limited Liability Partnership shall be a body corporate and a legal entity separate from its partners. Any two or more persons, associated for carrying on a lawful business with a view to profit, may by subscribing their names to an incorporation document and filing the same with the Registrar, form a Limited Liability Partnership. The Limited Liability Partnership will have perpetual succession;
ii. The mutual rights and duties of partners of a Limited Liability Partnership *inter se* and those of the Limited Liability Partnership and its partners shall be governed by an agreement between partners or between the Limited Liability Partnership and the partners subject to the provisions of the Limited Liability Partnership Act 2008. The act provides flexibility to devise the agreement as per their choice. In the absence of any such agreement, the mutual rights and duties shall be governed by the provisions of proposed the Limited Liability Partnership Act;
iii. The Limited Liability Partnership will be a separate legal entity, liable to the full extent of its assets, with the liability of the partners being limited to their agreed contribution in the Limited Liability Partnership which may be of tangible or intangible nature or both

tangible and intangible in nature. No partner would be liable on account of the independent or un-authorized actions of other partners or their misconduct. The liabilities of the Limited Liability Partnership and partners who are found to have acted with intent to defraud creditors or for any fraudulent purpose shall be unlimited for all or any of the debts or other liabilities of the Limited Liability Partnership;

iv. Every Limited Liability Partnership shall have at least two partners and shall also have at least two individuals as Designated Partners, of whom at least one shall be resident in India. The duties and obligations of Designated Partners shall be as provided in the law;

v. The Limited Liability Partnership shall be under an obligation to maintain annual accounts reflecting true and fair view of its state of affairs. A statement of accounts and solvency shall be filed by every Limited Liability Partnership with the Registrar every year. The accounts of Limited Liability Partnerships shall also be audited, subject to any class of Limited Liability Partnerships being exempted from this requirement by the Central Government;

vi. The Central Government has powers to investigate the affairs of a Limited Liability Partnership, if required, by appointment of competent Inspector for the purpose.

vii. The compromise or arrangement including merger and amalgamation of Limited Liability Partnerships shall be in accordance with the provisions of the Limited Liability Partnership Act 2008;

viii. A firm, private company or an unlisted public company is allowed to be converted into Limited Liability Partnership in accordance with the provisions of the Act. Upon such conversion, on and from the date of certificate of registration issued by the Registrar in this regard, the effects of the conversion shall be such as are specified in the Limited Liability Partnership Act. On and from the date of registration specified in the certificate of registration, all tangible (moveable or immoveable) and intangible property vested in the firm or the company, all assets, interests, rights, privileges, liabilities, obligations relating to the firm or the company, and the whole of the undertaking of the firm or the company, shall be transferred to and shall vest in the Limited Liability Partnership without further assurance, act or deed and the firm or the company, shall be deemed to be dissolved and removed from the records of the Registrar of Firms or Registrar of Companies, as the case may be;

ix. The winding up of the Limited Liability Partnership may be either voluntary or by the Tribunal to be established under the Companies

Act, 1956. Till the Tribunal is established, the power in this regard has been given to the High Court;

x. The Limited Liability Partnership Act 2008 confers powers on the Central Government to apply provisions of the Companies Act, 1956 as appropriate, by notification with such changes or modifications as deemed necessary. However, such notifications shall be laid in draft before each House of Parliament for a total period of 30 days and shall be subject to any modification as may be approved by both Houses;

xi. The Limited Liability Partnership Act has incorporated the concept of whistle blowing.

xii. The Indian Partnership Act, 1932 shall not be applicable to Limited Liability Partnerships.

The above stated points help to a great extent to clear the concept of the Limited Liability Partnership and give an insight to this form of business organization.

## LLP Vs Partnership Firm and Company

As compared to the other form of popular business organizations opcrating in the scene, Limited Liability Partnership has an edge over the others. Limited Liability Partnership combincs the advantages of ease of running a Partnership and separate legal entity status and limited liability aspect of a Company.

## LLP, Entrpreneurship and Economic Development

In India, where over 30 crore people are living below the poverty line, it is simply impossible for any government to provide means of livelihood to everyone. Such situations surely demand for a continuous effort from the society, where the people are encouraged to come up with their entrepreneurial initiative.

The rapidly developing economy of India has '*Indian Inc*' as a key driver in the efforts to achieve the 2020 dream of making India a developed nation.

India being a member of the extended global economic village has not remained untouched with the meltdown and economic recession. While G20 summit has been held to evolve policies for walking out of shadow of economic recession, *Indian Inc* apprehends further slowdown and losses in the running of the industries. There is a concern that in the upcoming months, there would be a reporting of various industries being on the verge of insolvency or turning insolvent and a timely action is to be taken to avoid loss of production, loss to government revenue and employment as also the locking up of invertible funds of banks and financial institutions.

The need and rationale for introducing the Limited Liability Partnership has been explained as under: *With the growth of Indian economy, the role played by its entrepreneurs as well as its technical and professional manpower has been acknowledged internationally. It was felt opportune that entrepreneurship, knowledge and risk capital combine provide a further impetus to India's economic growth. In this background, a need had been felt for a new corporate form that would provide an alternative to traditional partnership with unlimited personal liability on the one hand, and, the statute based governance of the limited liability company on the other, in order to enable professional expertise and entrepreneurial initiative to combine organize and operate in flexible, innovative and efficient manner.*

Entrepreneurship helps in the process of economic development in the following ways:

***(1) Employment Generation:***

Growing unemployment particularly educated unemployment is the problem of the nation. The available employment opportunities can cater only 5 to 10% of the unemployed. Entrepreneurs generate employment both directly and indirectly. Directly, self employment as an entrepreneur and indirectly by starting many industrial units they offer jobs to millions. Thus entrepreneurship is the best way to fight the evil of unemployment.

***(2) National Income:***

National Income consists of the goods and services produced in the country and imported. The goods and services produced are for consumption within the country as well as to meet the demand of exports. The domestic demand increases with increase in population and increase in standard of living. The export demand also increases to meet the needs of growing imports due to various reasons. An increasing number of entrepreneurism is required to meet this increasing demand for goods and services. Thus entrepreneurship increases the national income.

***(3) Balanced Regional Development:***

The growth of industry and business leads to a lot of public benefits like transport facilities, health, education, entertainment etc. When the industries are concentrated in selected cities, development gets limited to these cities. When the new entrepreneurism grow at a faster rate, in view of increasing competition in and around cities, they are forced to set up their enterprises in the smaller towns away from big cities. This helps in the development of backward regions.

***(4) Dispersal of economic power:***

Industrial development normally may lead to concentration of economic powers in a few hands. This concentration of power in a few hands has its own evils in the form of monopolies. Developing a large number of entrepreneurism helps in dispersing the economic power amongst the population. Thus it helps in weakening the harmful effects of monopoly.

***(5) Better standards of living:***

Entrepreneurism plays a vital role in achieving a higher rate of economic growth. Entrepreneurers are able to produce goods at lower cost and supply quality goods at lower price to the community according to their requirements. When the price of the commodities decreases the consumers get the power to buy more goods for their satisfaction. In this way they can increase the standard of living of the people.

***(6) Creating innovation:***

An entrepreneur is a person who always looks for changes. Apart from combining the factors of production, he also introduces new ideas and new combination of factors. He always tries to introduce newer and newer technique of production of goods and services. An entrepreneur brings economic development through innovation.

## Conclusion

*Limited Liability Partnership is the basis, Entrepreneurship is a cause and Economic development is the effect.* Entrepreneurial activity and the resultant financial gain are always of benefit to a country. The importance of entrepreneurship in economic development is like that of entrepreneurship in any community. The role of entrepreneurship on economic growth, market expansion, commercializing innovation, and reducing unemployment is an open secret. Indian Entrepreneurs – *Dhirubhai Ambani, Azim H. Premji, N.R.Narayana Murthy* are the lively examples of the same. Entrepreneurship development is the key factor to fight against unemployment, poverty and to prepare ourselves for globalization in order to achieve overall Indian economic progress. Entrepreneurial activities are a way to economic growth. The present day business world is full of competition and with the growth of economy, the role played by the entrepreneurs is internationally acknowledged. With 3062 Limited Liability Partnerships registered by December 13, 2010, the happiness for the Limited Liability Partnerships is blowing with full volume. There is bound to be phenomenal increase in the number of Limited Liability Partnerships and they are bound to dominate all areas of business and professional domain. In short, the development of the entrepreneurship is inevitable in the economic development of the country especially through the new paradigm of Limited Liability Partnership.

## Reference

1. Act VI of 2009, which was passed by the *Upper House* on October 24, 2008, by the *Lower House* on December 12, 2008 and received the assent of the President of India on January 07, 2009.
2. Economic Development in India: The Role of Individual Enterprise, *Anil K. Lal* and *Ronald W. Clement*, Asia-Pacific Development Journal Vol. 12, No. 2, December 2005 at 91.
3. *Ibid*
4. Source: Reynolds, Paul D., Michael Hay, William D. Bygrave, S. Michael Camp, and Erkko Autio, 2000. Global Entrepreneurship Monitor: 2000 Executive Report (Kansas City, Kauffman Center for Entrepreneurial Leadership), at 6.
5. *Supra Note 2 at 92.*
6. Act VI of 2009, which was passed by the *Upper House* on October 24, 2008, by the *Lower House* on December 12, 2008 and received the assent of the President of India on January 07, 2009.

# 3

# Indian Jute Industry: Its Crises - Need for Entrepreneurial Interventions

***Abstract***

India is the largest producer of *raw jute* in the world. But the past glory of the Indian jute industry has faded out and it is suffering from stagnancy in recent times. An attempt has been made in this paper to find out the reasons behind the present stagnancy through a detailed observation of the existing market trend and the production cum marketing chain of *raw jute*. The problems of this labour-intensive agro-based industry have been identified through a field work carried out all over the jute producing districts of West Bengal. We found that the industry is run entirely on indigenous and traditional technological knowhow.

Further it is suffering from an utter imperfectness as far as the cumbersome production cum marketing chain is concerned. This ultimately shoots up the cost of *raw jute*, making the industry less competitive in the national and international market. We conclude that the industry is in a desperate need of entrepreneurial interventions for modern technological and marketing innovativeness at various levels to strategize a whole new alternative approach. This would streamline the *raw jute* production cum marketing based on cost and time effective measures. Finally a model of a

'Central Jute Hub' has been conceptualized which would possibly become the nerve center of future *raw jute* production in India.

## Introduction

Jute is a natural fibre with golden and silky shine, hence called 'The Golden Fibre'. It is the second most important vegetable fibre after cotton, in terms of usage, global consumption, production, and availability, produced from plants in the genus *Corchorus*, family Malvaceae. Jute fibre is lignin-cellulose fibre that is partially a textile and partially wood fibre. The industrial term for jute fibre is *'raw jute'*, is off-white to brown and 1-4 meters (3-12 feet) long. For its ecofriendly nature jute and jute derivatives are used for various purposes all over the world; some of which include sacks, jute pulps for paper making, yarns, clothing, and handicrafts. Jute sticks are used as fuel and leaves as manure.

## World Vis a Vis West Bengal's Jute Industry

Jute has been used since ancient times in Africa and Asia to provide cordage and weaving fiber from the stem and food from the leaves but currently its production is centered on the Indian subcontinent where Bangladesh is the largest exporter of *raw jute* and India is the largest producer as well as the largest consumer of jute products in the world. Apart from India and Bangladesh, countries like Thailand, Myanmar, Indonesia, Mexico, Brazil etc also produce a large quantity of jute. India, especially Bengal (Both West Bengal and Bangladesh) region holds the global leadership from historic times. The first jute mill in India was established at Rishra, on the River Hooghly near Calcutta in 1855. By 1940 Indian jute mills possessed 68,415 looms (57%) of the world total (Stewart, 1998, p. 16) and Bengal held a near-monopoly on world jute cultivation (Sen, 1999, p.13). During independence of India in 1947 a geographic demarcation was created by 'Partition' that divided eastern province of Bengal into two parts. It placed an artificial barrier between the jute-growing eastern districts (that fell under the then East Pakistan) and the jute mills that had come up in the west (which came under West Bengal, India) around Calcutta (Bose,1993,p.44). As 81% of existing jute cultivation was in what became East Pakistan, while all of the mills were in West Bengal (Ghosh,1999, p.63) the result was a sharp decline of supply of *raw jute* to Indian mills, and a subsequent increase in the price. After the liberation of Bangladesh from Pakistan in 1971, most of the Pakistan owned Jute mills were taken over by the government of Bangladesh. As the finest of jute producing lands went to Bangladesh a vacuum was created in India's *raw jute* production. To revive the Indian jute industry Jute Corporation of India Limited (JCI) was set up in 1971 for the welfare of the jute growers. It expanded its networking in almost all the states which are important for the production of jute. But its primary role remained restricted to the procurement of *raw jute* from farmers, overlooking the production process.

Though jute growing areas in India include states like West Bengal, Bihar, Assam, Meghalaya, Tripura, Orissa, and Andhra Pradesh, a striking feature of India's jute cultivation has been the significant inter-state variations in respect of all the three dimensions, viz., production, area coverage and yield. The Bengal region (*West Bengal and Bangladesh*) is the largest producer of the *Tossa* variety globally. West Bengal retained its status as the leading jute producing state in the country by producing more than 70% of *raw jute* and harbours 59 jute mills among 76 in India. The factors endowing advantage to the state of West Bengal for jute production include climatic conditions (i.e. temperature 20 to 40°C, 5–8 cm of weekly rainfall during the sowing period and relative humidity 70–80%) are conducive here, large number of water bodies available for retting, concentration of jute mills, and dynamic cropping pattern adopted in the state. Districts like Jalpaiguri, Coochbehar, North Dinajpur, Murshidabad, Malda in north Bengal and Nadia, Hooghly, West Midnapur and North (24) Parganas in south are known for major jute production. Despite its glorious past and eco-friendly branding, the jute Industry in West Bengal is not witnessing successes owing to the causes like cheap and convenient synthetic alternatives, fierce competition from jute producing countries like Bangladesh, volatile jute policies, labor-intensiveness, obsolete machinery, lack of industry oriented research and development etc. The study aims to identify recent trend of jute industry and the production chain of *raw jute*, its dependence on natural parameters and factors that are making *raw jute* costly and to find out the scope of interventions for making *raw jute* market competitive. In section 2 we have pointed out in detail the methodology used whereas section 3 focuses on the recent trend of jute industry and existing production chain in West Bengal. Section 4 highlights the results and observations arising from primary data analysis and our survey. Section 5 discusses the scope of interventions to shake-off nature dependence and make *raw jute* market competitive through alternative marketing model and the proposed 'Central Jute Hub'.

## Methodology

The study is based both on secondary and primary data sources. Data of India as well as West Bengal's *raw jute* production, productivity in recent years were drawn from various secondary sources like JCI, office of Jute commissioner to analyze existing production environment. In addition to that we carried out a field survey during the 2009-10 seasons to collect data from districts like Jalpaiguri, Coochbehar, North Dinajpur, Murshidabad, Malda ,Nadia, Hooghly, 24 (N) Parganas which are considered as jute hubs of West Bengal by JCI. According to this network there are 8 regional centers namely Barasat (North 24 Parganas), Berhampur (Murshidabad), Bethuadohari (Nadia), Coochbehar, Krishna Nagar (Nadia), Malda, Sheorafully (Hooghly) and Siliguri (Jalpaiguri and North Dinajpur)) in West Bengal. We have surveyed each regional centre and drawn one representative sample (Berachapa (Barasat), Jalangi (Berhampur), Bethuadohari, Alipurduar (Coochbehar), Hilli (Malda), Chapadanga (Sherofully), Belacoba and Islampur (Siliguri)) from each of the regional centers comprising of 15 cultivators at random. In total 120 farmers were personally interviewed along with number of JCI officials, local agriculturists, and microbiologists to know the prevailing mode of *raw jute* production process, their pros and cons, together with the possible scope of interventions. Statistical data analysis software is used to analyze the data collected from field. We have conceptualized the alternative model for the marketing of *raw jute* and 'Central Jute Hub' based from our field observations, existing institutional frameworks and the contemporary needs of jute industry.

## Recent trend analysis of jute industry

Jute is a nature based industry that runs on traditional knowledge in West Bengal which is one of the nerve centres of world *raw jute* production. To assess the present scenario we have studied the recent demand-supply trend of *raw jute* in West Bengal. Further an attempt has been made to identify the factors influencing the existing production chain.

## Supply trend of *raw jute* in recent years

We have taken into consideration the trend of production scenario of Indian jute industry in new millennium. It appears from figure-3 that the total area used for *raw jute* cultivation has not changed as such over last 5 years and so is the total production of *raw jute*. Figure-4 states that the present trend in the case of productivity also shows an element of stagnancy. Hence a pattern of overall stagnancy is observed in the supply side of *raw jute*. Now to find out the cause we studied the trend of demand of jute products in the present day market.

## Demand scenario of *raw jute* in recent years

Now the consumption pattern of the *raw jute* has also been studied closely. The demand curve (Figure-5) shows no exceptional trend except only a little ripple towards the end of the decade. There is no remarkable trend of increasing demand for jute products in the market that may usher in the increased production of *raw* jute.

Hence we observed a sense of stagnancy in both the demand and supply side of the jute industry in West Bengal, and found that the industry is suffering from demand constraint problem. Fierce competition from the other synthetic alternatives in the international market, the outdated production machinery and cumbersome production process are also factors hindering jute industry to become market competitive. Hence, there is no significant factor in the supply side that may affect and help the increase of the productivity of jute products.

This in turn again affects the demand of the jute product thus creating a vicious circle and the jute industry as a whole suffers from an overall stagnancy. Now the demand of jute products in the market can be increased only by making the jute products more cost effective so that it can compete against the other available alternatives in the market in terms of price.

In order to break this stagnancy in the demand side, the cost of the *raw jute* must be curbed down so that the jute products become more cost effective than other alternatives in the present day market. In order to achieve that, the productivity, on the one hand must be increased; while on the other, the production cost of the *raw jute* must also be reduced. Hence what we are basically looking forward is to increase the productivity of *raw jute*, with minimum cost, in order to make the jute products more cost effective in the present day market. Thus we enter into a detail study of the production chain of the *raw jute* in West Bengal.

## Existing production process of *raw jute* in West Bengal

The existing production chain of *raw jute* follows a decentralized mode where the journey starts from sowing of jute seeds in the farm and ends up in the marketing of *raw jute* in local market. Intermediate steps like retting and stripping play very crucial roles in determining the quality of the product and its ultimate market price. The steps in the present production process are as follows:

### Cutting and Bundling of the jute plants

Jute is harvested between 90 to 130 days from its initial plantation.

When they are between 8-15 ft high and close to the ground level they are left in field for 1-3 days for the leaves to shed so that they may work as natural manure in the fields. Harvested plants are then bundled off and carried to the nearby retting field.

### Retting of jute plants

The most important single factor for determining *raw jute* quality and its market value is 'retting'. It is a microbiological process where various fungi, aerobic and anaerobic bacteria are involved and takes around 15-20 days to complete. During the process jute bundles are kept standing in water, 30 cm deep, and later placed side by side in retting water, usually in 2 to 3 layers and are tied together. They are covered with water-hyacinth or any weed that does not release tannin and iron but farmers also place covers of jute bags, clay, hay etc. The float is then weighed down with seasoned logs or concrete blocks or stones etc and are kept submerged (at least 10 cm below the surface of the water) in water. Gently flowing, fairly deep, clear and soft water and temperature around 34oC is ideal for retting of the jute plant. Traditional retting known as `stem retting' requires sufficient clean water. Jute cultivation has gradually shifted towards marginal land as sufficient clean water is scarce.

Ribbon retting, dry retting and chemical retting are the alternative ways. They have the following advantages over conventional retting: (1) it requires lesser volume of water and less time, (3) it produces lesser environmental pollution, and (4) it produces improved quality fibre.

### iii. Extraction of jute fibre:

It is a process by which jute fibers are extracted from the stalk one by one. It takes 2-4 days of work and requires some labor-force. Farmers beat the ends of the jute sticks with some rigid tool made of wood to fracture that part of the stem and then strips the fibrous part in back and forth movement and the stalk is then left out.

### iv. Drying of *raw jute* fibres:

Extracted fibers are washed in clean water. After squeezing excess water, fibers are hung on bamboo railings for sun drying for 2-3 days. Dry fibers are stored intermediately for 1-2 days and finally transported to the selling point.

### *v.* Grading and Pressing of *raw jute*:

Jute fibers are categorized as per grades (TD1-7). Grade wise bundles are then subjected to machine press to convert them into Bales. The bales are intermediately stored in the warehouse for sale to local markets.

## Results and Observations

Analysis of the primary data collected by the earlier stated process draws our attention to some important facts as discussed below.

### Factors influencing production of *raw jute*

The paper attempts to find out factors that may have significant influence in the production of *raw jute* and could make the production process cheaper than before. As jute is totally a nature based agro-industry we have analyzed the importance of natural parameters at first and then tried to identify the factors that are responsible for making *raw jute* production costly from our field survey.

### Natural parameters affecting production of *raw jute*

From data analysis it emerges that the two most important natural parameters that influence the production of *raw jute* are rainfall and temperature. Rainfall is required for cultivation and also acts as a supplement to the water availability for the retting of *raw jute*. Table-4 shows the output of the regression analysis to find the dependency of retting duration, in number of days, on rainfall and temperature. Table-5 shows the regression coefficients where the significance of the temperature denoted by the variable temp_C is below .05. This suffices that temperature is an important factor for a jute plant to thrive. The significance level for rainfall, denoted by the variable rain_mm is .373 which indicates that rainfall is also a very important parameter for jute production.

Overall from our field study it is found that the existing production chain depends on indigenous knowledge and practices which are nature dependent, cumbersome and not cost-effective. Traditional retting and fiber extraction methods with faulty practices, downgrades the quality of *raw jute* fetching even lesser rewards to the producers. Retting also causes transient water pollution (asphyxiation to native flora and fauna, exerts stress on local water table, generates foul smell etc) and gives stress on native water table. Again uncertainty of the monsoon on which retting process is heavily dependent brings uncertainty in retting duration.

### Parameters affecting cost of *raw jute*

Parameters which are influencing the total cost of the farmers to produce *raw jute* are also being analysed. The cost components are mainly cultivation cost, cutting cost, retting cost and carrying cost which sum up to form the total production cost. An important issue that came out from this primary data analysis is that there is a huge gap between the selling price of the jute farmers and the buying price of the jute mill owners.It is observed that the market for *raw jute* is basically unorganized, volatile and dominated by intermediaries who do not add value to the production processes. This marketing imperfection was studied and from field work it was observed that per quintal average production cost of *raw jute (TD-5 variety)* hovers around Rs-1270/- which in turn was sold by farmers at approximately Rs-2230/- in the primary market. But the jute mills purchase it approximately around Rs 3000-3500 per quintal making *raw jute* 35 to 57 % costlier, owing to this indirect form of marketing.

That is, though the SP (of jute farmers) = CP + MUF
The BP (of jute mill owners) = CP + MUF + MUB

Where, SP = Selling Price, BP = Buying Price, CP = Cost Price of the raw jute incurred by the farmers, MUF = Mark Up enjoyed by the farmers, MUB = Mark Up enjoyed by the intermediaries.

Now the presence of this MUB in the cost price of the jute mill owners is solely responsible for creating the above stated gap.

Hence this multi-layered marketing i.e. too much hand-offs is adding an unnecessary cost to the commodity for its procurers and reducing the competitive edge of jute and jute products in the market at home and abroad. In this context the present marketing chain prevailing in West Bengal needs to be stated here.

## Existing marketing chain of *raw jute* in West Bengal:

The *Raw jute* after production is taken to the Jute Mills for further processing and the only way to reach the destination is through the following intermediate steps.

### Primary Market

Farmers sell raw jute in local hats or primary markets where local *pariahs* or sub-brokers and other intermediate small buyer buy them. Farmers seldom sell to JCI. This market is largely unorganized, volatile and doesn't abide by any single controllable factor.

### Secondary Market

This market is primarily dominated by large Pariahs, Mahajons, brokers and stockiest or JCI. Farmers hardly get an access to sell their products to this market. Number of links in secondary market could differ so is the price of the commodity making *raw jute* a costly commodity.

## Jute Mills

Jute mills are the ultimate destination of *raw jute* purchased from Godown owners, stockists, large buyers or JCI authorities. Farmers never get an access to directly merchandising their products to mills that may fetch them higher returns. The entire journey from primary market to jute mills takes approximately 30 days.

Apart from this a parallel network is run by the JCI. Through this network the JCI procures raw jute from the farmers with minimum support price and sell them to the jute mill owners at the Jute Baler's Association. But this network is hardly used by the farmers to sell their product because the Minimum Support Price (MSP) provided by the JCI is much lower in comparison to the local *Pharias*.

For example, in the year 2009 – 10 the MSP provided by JCI was Rs. 1250 per quintal for average TD-5 verity whereas from survey it is evident that the farmers fetched Rs 2230 per quintal by selling it to the local *Pariahs*.

## Discussion

Thus the imperfections in the Production cum marketing of raw jute need serious entrepreneurial interventions at various levels as discussed below:

## Selective interventions for making *raw jute* production efficient

The total production consumes approximately 150 days including 90 to 120 days for cultivation and 30 days for processing on an average. Minimization of this time span needs intervention into each of these stages of production of *raw jute*. This could be accomplished as:

## Mechanical intervention in jute fibre extraction

In different countries mechanical decorticators are used for jute fiber extraction as they are time-labor efficient and convenient to use. With a mechanical decorticator tons of *raw jute* fiber could be extracted in minutes instead of several days, saving time as well as labor. Research organizations in India are experimenting with small to large size 'high speed mechanical jute ribbon extractors'(JCI 2010) which could completely decorticate jute fiber leaving jute sticks intact which fetch high value in market. Proper implementation of this technology could help industry by saving significant production time and cost.

## Biological interventions in Cultivation and Retting process

Future of raw jute fiber (*Corchorus* and *Hibiscus)* lies mainly through quality improvement for diversified and value-added uses. Modern biotechnological methods and tools in combination with traditional approaches through markerassisted selection have the potential to achieve product specific quality improvements in future. Genetical manipulation is a very important approach to achieve the targeted quality improvement. Assemblage of genes on the jute chromosomes is very poorly understood. Developing linkage map of different jute species would help in preparing an integrated map using molecular map data on the species. High lignin content of these fibers is responsible for color instability, which is a distinct disadvantage in the dyed products. Isolation of a lignified phloem fiber deficient (dlpf) mutant of jute suggests its usefulness to engineer low-lignin jute variety. The germplasm accession of jute available in India has a narrow genetic base, which is the basic detriment for any attempt to improve its fiber quality. Germplasm collection from far unexplored regions of the country, particularly the exotic types from the centres of origin must be given top priority. Molecular characterization of genes governing economically important traits like tolerance/ resistance to biotic and abiotic stress, fiber quality (strength, fineness, cellulose and lignin content), fiber development, and efficiency of retting microbes would ultimately lead to precision molecular breeding. Furthermore, functional genomics that includes identification of conserved domains, targeted disruption, complementation, cloning followed by constitutive, tissue specific enhanced expression, should be applied for the improvement of fiber quality. Being a strong adjunct to molecular techniques, bioinformatics would be helpful to construct database for germplasm accessions of jute based on morphological and molecular characterization done by different DNA markers and EST sequences. With concerted efforts to pyramid genes for productivity, fiber quality and resistance to stress along with location specific crop husbandry, the targeted national or even international level of jute may be achieved, for which bioinformatics should be of significant help. All these techniques not only could boost qualitative production but possibly reduce significant cultivation time which is now taking nearly three months. Development of improved retting practices especially ribbon retting with a combination of chemical, biochemical, microbiological or enzymatic method is needed. Development of a potential pectinolytic microbial culture should be helpful for jute industry in the processing of jute fiber with improved quality.

Furthermore, the presence of active microbial population showed great promise of active inoculums to accelerate retting and improve the fiber quality. These microbes could be absorbed in several substrates like wheat or rice bran. It can be dehydrated using freeze dryer and could be used in retting in stagnant water under controlled condition (Banik and Ghosh pp.151-156; 2008). The process could significantly cut down retting time from normal 18-20 days to 6-8 days. It can also save huge volume of water, space, shake off labor intensiveness and dependence on the whimsical monsoon. Controlled environment ribbon retting or large scale microbial retting tank for commercial purpose could become a viable option.

## Alternate Marketing Model

Now as discussed earlier the farmers prefer to sell their product to the local *Pariahs* instead of the JCI procurement units only because they make more profit there. This subsequently owes to an overwhelming increase in the cost price of *raw jute* incurred by the mill owners.

To solve this problem we suggest the JCI to intervene here and play a more meaningful role in this context. The JCI must fix the Minimum Support Price at a level which may encourage the farmers to sell their products to JCI instead of the local *Pariahs*. Such a level of Minimum Support Price must exceed the mark reached by the farmers when they sell it to the local *Pariahs*. At the same time it is also of vital importance that the mark set up by the JCI is not too high for that too might make the *raw jute* costly for the mill owners. This trade off needs careful handling and periodic revisions so that the price of *raw jute* remains reasonable at both the ends. The parameters to be considered for the fixation of such a Just Price of *raw jute* are as follows:

(i) Cost of production of *raw jute*

(ii) Percentage of mark up of the farmers by selling *raw jute* to the local *Pariahs*.

(iii) Percentage of mark up of the local *Pariahs* by selling *raw jute* to the jute mill owners.

(iv) Prices of the substitutable commodities.

Not only this but the JCI should enjoy a full monopoly and monopoly power as far as *raw jute* is concerned. The JCI should be the only buyer of *raw jute* from the farmers as well as the only seller of *raw jute* to the jute mill owners. By using the JCI Pipeline only, we will be able to keep the local *Pariahs* at bay and avoid too much hand-offs of *raw jute* before they reach the mills.

Hence, in these two ways - (i) by fixing an optimum price of raw *jute* using pure market economics and (ii) by replacing the existing unorganized market imperfections by organised market perfection, we can put forward an alternate marketing strategy to curb the market imperfections as far as *raw jute* is concerned. Continuing from the above discussion here we present a wholesome component diagram of the jute industry on the basis of our modified model.

We envision a 'Central Jute Hub' (Figure9) as an alternative approach of *raw ju*te production- cum -marketing. It will stress on integration of both the processes and sub processes under a single roof to minimize labor-cost and save time. Further selective technological intervention would be incorporated to make the processes efficient. Procurement of *raw jute* by the mills would be streamlined with the help of organized institutional structure like the JCI. All these strategies would help the farmers fetch maximum return and jute mills to buy *raw jute* cheaper, easily bypassing the cumbersome marketing chain. The proposed 'Central Jute Hub' would include features like 'High speed mechanical jute ribboner', artificial tank and controlled environment for ribbon retting, facilities for quick drying of jute fibers, godowns for intermediate storage of dry fibers along with facilities for pressing and qualitative grading. All these would quicken the entire process; make it cost effective and less labor-intensive.

Procurement units of JCI could be incorporated within 'Central Jute Hub' for direct purchase of *raw jute* from farmers and sell them directly to jute mills. This would make *raw jute* market streamlined, organized and less volatile. We propose an authoritative power to be handed over to JCI for proper synchronization of all processes of 'Central Jute Hub'. The central jute hub would be eco-efficient too as it would minimize the huge stress on local water table exerted by traditional retting process. It can also reduce the transient water pollution caused by the same and minimize carbon footprint by reducing transportation needs. The hub would also include the capacity for waste management within its fold. All these measures would make Central Jute Hub' the nerve centre of future *raw jute* production- cum- marketing that in turn would help jute industry to become time saving and market efficient.

## Conclusions

We conclude that the jute industry in West Bengal is going through an overall stagnancy in recent decades owing to its lesser market competitiveness against the available cheap alternatives. Raw jute production runs on indigenous knowledge and is too much dependent on natural parameters like temperature and rainfall making it vulnerable in the hands of nature. The production –cummarketing chain is time and cost consuming making *raw jute* costly. Selective entrepreneurial interventions at various stages of production- cum- marketing have been suggested through this paper which would help it to shake-off all its imperfectness and become time and cost efficient along with empowering the institutions like JCI and reinstate the lost glory of West Bengal's Jute Industry.

## References

1. Banik. and Ghosh (2008), Phenolytic activity of microorganisms in pilling of jute; pp 151-156; Indian journal of fibre & Textile Research;
2. Bose, S. (1993). Peasant Labour and Colonial Capital: Rural Bengal Since 1770. Cambridge University
3. Press Cambridge (United Kingdom).Commission for agricultural cost and price report on price policy of raw jute for the 2009-10 seasons
4. Ghosh, T. (1999). Income and productivity in the jute industry across the 1947 divide. A case for labour history, pages 54–81.
5. Sen, S. (1999). Women and Labour in Late Colonial India: The Bengal Jute Industry. Cambridge University Press.
6. Stewart, G. T. (1998). Jute and Empire: The Calcutta Jute Wallahs and the Landscapes of Empire. Manchester University Press

# 4

# Special Economic Zone (SEZ) & Institution Building for Entrepreneurship


### *Abstract*

Encouraged by the phenomenal success of Special Economic Zones (SEZs) in the People's Republic of China which first used this model to attract Foreign Direct Investment (FDI), Technological Transfers and Managerial Expertise, developing countries such as India, Indonesia, Iran, Malaysia, North Korea, South Korea, Philippines, Russia etc uses SEZ driven economic growth to accelerate the rate of GDP in their respective countries. SEZs are specially designated geographical areas within the country that possess special economic regulations which normally incorporate calibrated fiscal and monetary policy mix of liberalized trade regime like decontrol, deli cense and deregulations that attract huge investment from domestic as well as FDI to take advantage of the favorable trade policies. These policies are normally announced by the government in the EXIM (Export Import) and Foreign Trade Policies periodically to boost the investment of the nation. These SEZs contain special measures that are conducive to FDI and the units operating in the SEZ get tax incentive and the opportunity to pay lower tariffs. The ultimate goal of forming SEZ is to incorporate vibrant institutional building to accelerate economic activities through pro entrepreneurial policies. A single SEZ can contain multiple Free Trade Zones (FTZ), Export Processing Zone (EPZ), Free Zones (FZ), industrial Estates (IE), Free Ports and urban Enterprise Zones etc. SEZs are normally implemented through a variety of institutional structures like fully public, fully private and on Public-Private Partnership (PPP) models. This paper will make an empirical analysis of SEZ to understand the economies of scale in SEZ and the institutional building for entrepreneurship that can accelerate economic growth of a nation.

Developing countries in their search for rapid economic growth use SEZ growth model followed by the huge and phenomenal success of SEZs in the People's Republic of China which first used this model to attract Foreign Direct Investment (FDI), Technological Transfer and in Skill Formation. Government of India announced a scheme of establishing SEZ in its EXIM Policy of March, 2000. Subsequently the SEZ Act was enacted in the year 2005 which came in to enforcement with effect from 10th Feb.2006 and has been indeed a milestone in the celebrated growth story of Indian Economy. The growth of SEZs was the strongest evidence of China's robust economic growth, increase in trade and investment. The Chinese zones are probably the best examples of selective application of new policies within a defined geographical boundary and successful results encouraged wider application of specific foreign trade, export-import policies and other macroeconomic policies such as fiscal and monetary policy framework. The remarkable economic gains have been largely shaped by the active involvement of expatriate Chinese resources from Hong Kong, Macao and Taiwan. India smelled the success story from China and introduced similar economic growth model in the year 2000 which culminated in SEZ Act, 2005 which was a landmark legislation passed by the Indian Parliament.

The economic gains include huge turnaround in the exports, acceleration of employment and India slowly becoming the investment destination for global investors.

**Objectives of the Study:** The general objective of this study is to critically examine the contribution of SEZ in providing the legal and institutional support for vibrant economic development of our country. Besides covering the critical success factors of successful SEZs the study also throws light into the major issues and challenges in setting up SEZs, the cost-benefit analysis and future course of strategy for vibrant SEZ which can boost the balanced regional economic growth and Indian can continue to clock higher growth trajectory which can usher in a new direction of inclusive outlook.

**Methodology:** Field survey at Nangunery SEZ, Tamil Nadu is undertaken to address various issues and the study is also based on the secondary data which have collected from Ministry of Commerce. Publication of Government and NGOs, information received from websites and well known economic and political journals, Books etc.

## Organization of the Study

This research paper is organized as follows. Section-I deals with the Introduction, General Literature Review and Rationale Section-II incorporates the Legal and Institutional Framework, and finally Section-III deals with the Major Issues and Challenges

## Section – I Introduction, General Literature and Rationale

**Introduction:** SEZ is a specially designated and demarcated area within the country that possess special economic regulation different from the rest of the country which are conducive to Foreign Direct Investment (FDI) and the units operating in the SEZ get the tax incentive and the opportunity to pay lower tariffs. SEZs are usually set up with the objective of incorporating vibrant institutional building to accelerate business activities in colossal proportions, guaranteed global investors a large number of concessions – tax exemptions.

According to Aseem Shrivastava (2007) "SEZs is a specially demarcated area of land , owned and operated by a private developer, deemed to be foreign territory for the purposes of trade, duties and tariffs with the intent of increasing exports. Within the SEZ., production can be carried out by investing companies utilizing a large number of concessions – tax exemptions, guaranteed infrastructure and the relaxation of labour and environmental standards". SEZs are duty free economic enclaves where nation's trade-distorting policies – the existing labour laws, tax rates for different slabs of income, tariff rates etc are allegedly relaxed to attract the domestic and huge FDI . In other words, we can define SEZs as a specifically designed and demarcated geographical region that has liberal economic – trade, fiscal and monetary policies than a country's existing economic laws to attract additional foreign capital, generate additional employment, establish industrial units having export potential and setting up business service providers to remove the infrastructure deficit.

The salient features of SEZs are

- Duty free imports of capital goods
- Liberal access to foreign exchange

- Encouragement to FDI
- Simplified "Single – Window – Clearance"
- Tax Incentives and Low tariff regime
- Flexible labour laws
- Big Push to infrastructure investment
- Better coordination among business service providers
- Employment generation

SEZs are expected to attract FDI, earning foreign exchange, export growth, employment generation, transfer of technology, backward and forward domestic linkages and regional development. SEZs will work as an engine for economic growth supported by quality infrastructure completed by an attractive fiscal package, both at the Centre and at the State levels, with minimum possible regulations. To instill confidence in investors and signal government's commitment for stable SEZ policy regime thereby generating greater economic activity and employment through setting of many small scale units in the SEZs Minimum Area Requirements for setting up a SEZ are as follows:

| Type of SEZ | Minimum Land Requirement |
|---|---|
| Multi Sector SEZ | 1000 hectares |
| Sector Specific SEZ | 100 hectares |
| FTWz | 40 hectares |
| IT/ITes/HandicraftsSEZ/Bio-Techchnology/Non-Conventional Energy/Gems and Jewellery Sectors | 10 hectares |

(Source: Department of Commerce, Government of India)

## General Literature Review

Khanna Shivank (2007) visualized a situation when government faced a dilemma of whether a nation has to pursue policies of LPG or should continue with State control, they are forced to create pockets of free market economies to make economic growth gains that could stop economic collapse and yet continue their absolute State control.

Soumitra Bose (2007) noted that Specially Enclosed Zones for forming capital through production or servicing within a nation-state and without the encumbrances of law of the native land is what gets called as SEZ.

Lauren Fulton (2007) made it clear the goal of setting up SEZs. SEZs are designed to increase economic growth and lure foreign investment with incentives such as tax exemptions andindustrial business parks.

Surveying the ability of the SEZ in attracting huge amount of FDI in China, Wong(1987) concluded that the Shenzen SEZ itself attracted little over half of China's total FDI. Wong's study reflect the major issues of setting up of SEZ in China such as absence of vocational training institutes in skill formation, the inflated rise in the price of land and rent etc.

Underlining the role of private players in the SEZ, Rajiv Kumar (2007), former Chief Economist of CII made it clear that "the decision to allow private players in SEZ was welcome decision and this would give a boost to both investment and employment in India in near future."

Underlining the need for an appropriate legal framework for effective regulatory control of SEZs to provide a long-term and stable policy framework with a minimum regulatory regime and to provide an expeditious single window clearance facility a Central Act for SEZ has been found to be necessary in line with international practice (Embasy, 2005).

SEZs promises huge investment on infrastructure which further attract large amount of FDI. Normally even under the reformist Government doing business in India is a nightmare, with investors strangled by red tape and confronted by infrastructure deficit that cannot ensure regular electricity and water supplies and transport routes that are sometimes impossible (Bruce London, 2006).

Indicating the crucial areas for better performance studies made by CII throws enough light. "The SEZ performance in attracting investment and promoting export competitiveness seems to be directly related with location, infrastructure facilities, quality of governance and the incentive packages"(CII, 2006).

While converting the EPZs into SEZs it came to the light that in the erstwhile EPZs technological transfer never happened. "The substantial gains from technological gains had not occurred in the earlier period since EPZs were generally isolated from the domestic economy (Warr, 1988).

Comparing China's outstanding success in SEZs to that of moderate success in India (Amit Abhyankar,, 2006) summarizes the findings of the study as follows'

(i) The SEZs in China were mostly public funded in which economic gains prospects assumed far more significance than financial viability consideration of PPP (Public Private Partnership) model which India largely adopted.

(ii) In China SEZs are the only routes through which FDI can enter while in India Foreign Investors cannot be confined to SEZs only. Besides India has not equivalent to Hong Kong or Taiwan where industries had a pressing need to relocate and China served as a ready relocation base.

(iii) While China continues to score because it has bundled an attractive tax environment with world class infrastructure and a liberal labour environment, India has strong labour unions organically linked to political parties. Further buckling under the pressure game deployed by the Left parties during the UPA-I regime when the SEZ Bill was introduced, Union Government has axed the section 50(b) from the Bill which would have empowered the states to ease labour laws in SEZS

(iv) India has some advantages over China in larger English speaking work-force, and edge in knowledge based industries like software, IT-enabled services, medical services, drugs and pharmaceuticals and agro-based industries.

**Rationale**: Following are the expected benefits and rationale behind the willingness of the governments to establish SEZs in rapid pace.

(i) Pace of Economic Growth: SEZs are vehicle for accelerating economic growth. The expansion of industrial unit will enhance the industrial output and GDP of the country and their export will enhance the GNP of the nation

(ii) Employment Generation: Employment opportunities will increase as a result of large number of the industrial units and service unit within the SEZ and in the whole supply chain management around the SEZ notified area through the establishment of ancillary units. As on 31st December, 2009, the total employment in the SEZ sector is estimated at 4,90, 358 persons.

(iii) Foreign Direct Investment: Huge FDI can be attracted on account of the special tax and other tariff incentives offered in the SEZ. China and India turned out to be the most favored FDI destinations for MNCs

(iv) Boost to Local Infrastructure: SEZ is playing a significant role as Big-Push factor in transforming the infrastructure deficit Indian Economy into infrastructure conglomerates which will act as catalyst and trigger more FDIs.

(v) Skill Formation: Exclusive SEZs for automobiles or IT sector will boost the need for skill formation and the urgent need for vocational training institutes which will impart skill to the unskilled labour force.

(vi) Rural Upliftment through Employment Generation: Many SEZs recruit people from rural areas and provide them training for operations in the SEZs. Some of the examples are:

a. Gem and Jewellery SEZ in Hyderabad
b. Textile units in Mahindra SEZ in Chennai
c. New SEZs like NOKIA, Flextronics in Chennai
d. Appache SEZ, Brandix Apparel SEZ, in Andhra Pradesh
e. Rajiv Gandhi Technological Park in Chandigarh

(vii) Huge Export Promotion: The goods manufactured in the SEZs adhere to benchmark international quality and therefore enhanced the exports of a nation which will have positive impact on the accumulation of the nation's foreign exchange reserves. A double digit share of total exports can justify the existence of SEZ and at present it is about 5%

| Year | Total Exports | Exports from SEZ | Percentage |
|---|---|---|---|
| 2000-01 | 203571 | 8552 | 4.20% |
| 2001-02 | 209018 | 9190 | 4.40 |
| 2002-03 | 255137 | 10053 | 3.90 |
| 2003-04 | 283637 | 13853 | 4.90 |
| 2004-05 | 362879 | 18309 | 5.10 |
| 2005-06 | 445658 | 22500 | 5.00 |

Government of India has set up seven SEZs across the nation and the export performance since 2004-05 is as follows:

(1) Kandla Special Economic Zone (KSEZ) (Rs.Crores)

| Year | Target | Exports |
|---|---|---|
| 2004-05 | 1275.00 | 1060.14 |
| 2005-06 | 1270.00 | 1101.18 |
| 2006-07 | 1275.00 | 1517.00 |
| 2007-08 | 1500.00 | 1938.85 |
| 2008-09 | Target not fixed | 2420.38 |
| 2009-10 (Apr-Dec) | Target not fixed | 1589.26 |

(Source: Department of Commerce, Government of India)

(2) Santacruz Special Economic Zone (SEEPZ) (Rs. Crore)

| Year | Target | Exports |
|---|---|---|
| 2004-05 | 9790.00 | 8298.59 |
| 2005-06 | 9950.00 | 9192.22 |
| 2006-07 | 10000.00 | 12047.67 |
| 2007-08 | 11000.00 | 11268.53 |
| 2008-09 | Target not fixed | 10078.81 |
| 2009-10 (Apr-Dec) | Target not fixed | 7515.48 |

(Source: Department of Commerce, Government of India)

(3) Noida Special Economic Zone (NSEZ) (Rs.Crore)

| Year | Target | Exports |
|---|---|---|
| 2004-05 | 1920.00 | 4266.00 |
| 2005-06 | 5100.00 | 5670.76 |
| 2006-07 | 5700.00 | 6893.00 |
| 2007-08 | 7000.00 | 16843.36 |
| 2008-09 | Target not fixed | 16295.65 |
| 2009-10 (Apr-Dec) | Target not fixed | 13109.67 |

(Source: Department of Commerce, Government of India)

(4) Madras Special Economic Zone (MSEZ) (Rs. Crores)

| Year | Target | Exports |
|---|---|---|
| 2004-05 | 1295.00 | 1376.91 |
| 2005-06 | 1650.00 | 1858.80 |
| 2006-07 | 1700.00 | 2383.98 |
| 2007-08 | 2500.00 | 3046.53 |
| 2008-09 | Target not fixed | 3985.41 |
| 2009-10 (Apr-Dec) | Target not fizod | 3963.56 |

(Source: Department of Commerce, Government of India)

(5) Cochin Special Economic Zone (CSEZs) (Rs.Crores)

| Year | Target | Exports |
|---|---|---|
| 2004-05 | 375.00 | 462.90 |
| 2005-06 | 550.00 | 696.01 |
| 2006-07 | 800.00 | 802.70 |
| 2007-08 | 1250.00 | 4661.00 |
| 2008-09 | Target not fixed | 11332.24 |
| 2009-10 (Apr-Dec) | Target not fized | 12688.34 |

(Source; Department of Commerce, Government of India)

(6) Falta Special Economic Zone (FSEZ) (Rs.Crores)

| Year | Target | Exports |
|---|---|---|
| 2004-05 | 1030.00 | 569.15 |
| 2005-06 | 700.00 | 524.95 |
| 2006-07 | 700.00 | 998.70 |
| 2007-08 | 1500.00 | 1029.87 |
| 2008-09 | Target not fixed | 961.28 |
| 2009-10 (Apr-Dec) | Target not fixed | 728.18 |

(Source; Department of Commerce, Government of India)

(7): Viskhapatnam Special Economic Zone (VSEZ):

| Year | Target | Exports |
|---|---|---|
| 2004-05 | 545.00 | 579.27 |
| 2005-06 | 700.00 | 612.71 |
| 2006-07 | 700.00 | 749.79 |
| 2007-08 | 800.00 | 746.47 |
| 2008-09 | Target not fixed | 747.86 |
| 2009-10 (Apr-Dec) | Target not fixed | 649.92 |

(Source: Department of Commerce, Government of India

## Section – II Legal and Institutional Framework

SEZs have been implemented using a variety of institutional structure across the world ranging from fully public, fully private and PPP (Public Private Partnership) model.

(i) Fully Public: Government Developer, Government Operator and Government Regulator

(ii) Fully Private: Private Developer, Private Operator and Government Regulator – The success story of Mundra SEZ Gujarat and the Nokia SEZ, Chennai are an excellent example of this model.

(iii) PPP Model: Under this model, the institutional set up of developing and operation rest with equal ownership from private and public partnership and the regulatory rest with the government – Majority of the IT SEZ in India are set up under this model.

To regulate, control and govern the Government of India has passed the Special Economic Zones Act, 2005 in the Parliament which came into force from 10th February, 2006.

Guidelines for Notifying Special Economic Zone: - The Central Government while notifying any area as SEZ or additional area to be included in the SEZ and discharging its functions under this Act shall be governed by the following;

(a) Generation of additional economic activity;

(b) Promotion of exports of goods and services;

(c) Promotion of investment from domestic and foreign sources

(d) Creation of employment opportunities;

(e) Development of infrastructure facilities;

(f) Maintenance of sovereignty and integrity of India, the security of the State and friendly relations with foreign States

The Act has provided the following institutional set up for establishing, supervising and regulating the economic activities within the SEZ.

### Board of Approval

- Perhaps this is the apex institution set up by the SEZ Act, 2005 to govern the SEZs effectively for the maximum possible benefits of the nation. The Board shall consists of –

(a) An officer not below the rank of an Additional Secretary to GOI

(b) Two officers, not below the rank of Joint Secretary to GOI

(c) One Officer to be nominated by Department of Economic Affairs of GOI

(d) Such number of officers, not exceeding ten, below the rank of the Joint

Secretary to be nominated by Ministries dealing with commerce, industrial policy and promotion, science and technology, SSIs and agro and rural industries, home affairs, defence, environment, and forests, low overseas Indian Affairs and Urban Development.

(e) A nominee of the concerned State Government

(f) Director General of Foreign Trade or his nominee

(g) Development Commissioner

(h) A Professor in the IIM

Duties, Powers and Functions of Board of Approval:

The Board has the duty to promote and ensure orderly development of SEZs and without prejudice to the generality of the provisions contained in sub-section

(1), the powers and functions of the Board shall include –

a) Granting of approval or rejecting proposal or modifying such proposals for establishment of the SEZs.
b) Granting approval of authorized operations to be carried out in the SEZ by the Developer.
c) Granting of approval to the Developer or Units for foreign collaborations and foreign direct investments.
d) Granting of approval or rejecting of proposal for providing infrastructure facilities in SEZ or modifying such proposals.
e) Granting notwithstanding anything contained in the Industries Act, 1951, a licence to an industrial undertaking.
f) Suspension of the letter of approval granted to a Developer and appointment of an Administrator.
g) Disposing of appeals preferred under sub section (4) of section 15.

## Development Commissioner

The Central Government may appoint any of its officers not below the rank of Deputy Secretary to the GOI as the Development Commissioner of one or more SEZs. The functions of Development Commissioner are as follows

(a) Guide entrepreneurs for setting up of Units in the SEZs
(b) Ensure and take suitable steps for effective promotion of exports from the SEZs
(c) Ensure proper co-ordination with the Central Government or State Government Departments concerned or agencies with respect to or for the purpose of clauses (a) and (b) as stated above.
(d) Monitor the performance of the Developer and the Units in a SEZ
(e) Discharge such other functions as may be assigned to him by the Central Government under this Act or any other law for the time being in force and
(f) Discharge such other function as may be delegated to him by the Board

## Single Window Clearance

The Central Government by notification constitutes a Committee for every SEZ to be called Approval Committee to exercise the powers and perform the functions specified in section 14 of the SEZ Act, 2005. Every Approval Committee shall consist of the following persons:

(a) The Development Commissioner – Chairperson, ex officio;
(b) Two officers nominated by the Central Government.
(c) Two members of Central Government to be nominated by Departments dealing with Revenue.
(d) One officer of the Central Government to be nominated by Department of Economic Affairs.
(e) Two officers nominated by the State Government concerned.
(f) A representative of the concerned Developer – Special invitee.

Powers and functions of Approval Committee: The Approval Committee may discharge the functions as follows.

(a) Approve the import or procurement of goods from the Domestic Tariff Area in the SEZ for carrying on the authorized operations by a Developer.
(b) Approve the providing of services by a service provider from outside India or from the Domestic Tariff Area, for carrying on the authorized operations by the Developer in the SEZ.
(c) Monitor the utilization of goods or services or warehousing or trading in the SEZ.
(d) Approve, modify or reject proposals for setting up Units for manufacturing or rendering services or warehousing or trading in the SEZ.

(e) Allow, on receipt of approval under clause ( c ) of sub section (2) of section 9, foreign collaborations and foreign direct investment for setting up a unit.

(f) Monitor and supervise compliance of conditions subject to which the letter of approval or permission, if any, has been granted to the Developer or entrepreneur and

(g) Perform such other functions as may be entrusted to it by the Central Government or the State Government concerned, as the case may be

## Setting up of International Financial Services Centre

The Central Government may approve the setting up of an International Financial Services Centre in a SEZ and prescribe the requirements for setting up and operations of such Centre:

## Special Fiscal Provisions for Sez

Every Developer and the entrepreneur shall be entitled to the following exemptions and concessions, namely":

(a) Exemptions from any duty of Customs, under the Customs Act, , 1962 or the Customs Tariff Act, 1975.

(b) Exemptions from any duty of excise, under the Central Excise Act, 1944 on goods brought from Domestic Tariff Area to a SEZ or unit to carry on the authorized operations by the Developer or entrepreneurs.

(c) Exemptions from service tax under Chapter V of Finance Act, 1994 on taxable services provided to a Developer or Unit to carry on the authorized operations in a SEZ.

(d) Exemption from the Securities Transaction Tax leviable under section 98 of Finance Act, 2004 in the case the taxable securities transactions are entered into by a non-resident through the International Financial Services Centre.

(e) Exemption from the levy of taxes on the sale or purchase of goods other than newspapers under the Central Sales Tax Act, 1956

## Setting up of Sez Authority

The Central Government shall, by notification in the Official Gazette, constitute, for every SEZ established by it before the commencement of this Act of which may be established by it after such commencement by the Central Government, an Authority to be called ........(name of the SEZ)

Authority to exercise the powers conferred on, and discharge the functions assigned to it under this Act.

Such an Authority shall consist of -

(a) The Development Commissioner of the SEZ over which the Authority exercises its jurisdiction – Chairperson, ex officio;

(b) Two officers of the Central Government to be nominated by it having knowledge of or experience in dealing with matters relating to SEZ – Members, ex officio.

(c) An Officer of the GOI in the Ministry or Department dealing with Commerce on matters relating to SEZ – Member, ex officio.

(d) Not more than two persons, being entrepreneurs or their nominee, to be nominated by the Central Government – Members, ex officio

## Functions

Subject to the provisions of the SEZ Act, 2005, the Authority can undertake such measures as it thinks fit for the development, operation and management of the SEZ for which it is constituted and can discharge the following functions

- The development of infrastructure in the SEZ
- Promoting exports from the SEZ
- Reviewing the functioning and performance of the SEZ
- Levy user or service charges or fees or rent for the use of properties belonging to the Authority

## VII: Apart from the above institutional building the Act has also amended several other Acts and incorporated them with several schedules as follows.

1. **FIRST SCHEDULE:** (Enactments related to Mica Mines, Rubber, Tea, Salt, Sugar, Textiles, Coal Oil Tobacco Jute Spices Cess Act etc,
2. **SECOND SCHEDULE:** Several modifications to the Income Tax Act, 1961
3. **THIRD SCHEDULE:** Amendments to the following Enactments
   (a) Amendments to the Insurance Act, 1938
   (b) Amendments to the Banking Regulation Act, 1949
   (c) Amendment to the Indian Stamp Act, 1899

**THE SPECIAL ECONOMIC ZONES RULES, 2006:** In exercise of the powers conferred by section 55 of the Special Economic Act, 2005, the

Central Government has also made the Special Economic Zones Rules, 2006, which consist of the following chapters.

1.Chapter – I consists of the definitions of various concepts such as Act, Authorised Officer, Advance Licence, custodian, drawback, duty entitlement etc.

2.Chapter – II Procedure for establishment of SEZ

3.Chapter – III Procedure for establishment of a unit within the SEZ

4.Chapter – IV Terms and conditions subject to which entrepreneur and developer shall be entitled to exemptions, drawbacks and concessions

5.Chapter – V Conditions subject to which goods may be removed from SEZ to the Domestic Tariff Area

6.Chapter – VI Foreign Exchange Earning – Requirements and Monitoring

7.Chapter – VII Appeal

8. Chapter – VIII Miscellaneous

## Section – III – Issues and Challenges of SEZ Growth Model

Some of the major issues and challenges which emerge in the development of

SEZ can be summarized as follows.

(i) Land Acquisition and Displacing Agricultural Land
(ii) Labour Issues
(iii) Fiscal Issues - Revenue Loss due to Tax Heavens
(iv) Challenge to Democracy and ideological confusion - the story of Nandigram
(v) Social Issues
(vi) Regional Disparities
(vii) Issues related to Food Security
(viii) Resettlement and Rehabilitation Policy
(ix) Space for Small Scale Sector
(x) Environmental issues

### (i) Land Acquisition and Displacing of Agricultural Land:

Establishment of Multi-Product SEZ usually require huge land and a large scale farmland acquisition will lead to displacement of farmers from agriculture and they will become landless. The forceful procurement of land for establishment of SEZs looks like a form of 'crony capitalism" ,doing business through undeserved tax-breaks and other benefits at the cost of agricultural productivity, will be counterproductive. According to a study done by G.K.Pillai of SEZ in Tamil Nadu "At Sriperumputhur near Chennai, government acquired 700 hectares of land in 2002 much before the SEZs came and farmers who were displaced were paid Rs.5 lacs per acre of land as per the market price at that time. These 700 hectares of land had about 15000 farmers. After the SEZ cam there the land now fetches almost Rs.80 lacs per acre and almost 15000 farmers living outside the SEZ without any job in hand."

### (ii) Labour issues

All industrial units in the SEZs have been declared as "Public Utility Service" under the provisions of the Industrial Disputes Act, 1947 and a 45 day strike notice period is now legally required. State laws can dilute the central labour legislation in SEZs. For example, the Delhi Government has exempted SEZs from most labour legislation and there is a ban on the formation of trade unions. In Andhra Pradesh, the labour department has been dissuaded from conducting inspections in SEZs. Further new employment sectors operating within the SEZs such as Call Centres, BPOs, the Visual Media and Telecommunications are not covered by any explicit employment regulations. Many dalits are still landless labourers in India. Landless labourers work all over India just for some rice or wages below the Minimum Wage. Dalit women are paid even less than a dollar.

Many of these workers may end up on bonded labour in the SEZ (WTO, 2007). Liberalizing of labour laws under section 49 of the SEZ Act would adversely impact the social security and the livelihoods of the large labour force in the unorganized sector.

### (iii) Fiscal issues and revenue loss

The SEZ Act, 2005 offers various fiscal and non fiscal incentives and facilities for attracting both domestic and foreign investment. Department of Revenue, GOI is against providing blanket tax sops to all SEZs and also to all types of industrial and service units operating in SEZs without some conditions. It has estimated that over a five year period 2005-10 there is a revenue loss to the tune of Rs.1,75,847 crores due to various tax exemptions/fiscal incentives given to the SEZs and to the units operating in the SEZs.

### (iv) Challenges to Democracy and Ideological Confusion - Nandigram Vs. Nanguneri

It is a sad and shameful story of the degeneration of SEZ history itself when the author of this paper has made the field survey at Nanguneri SEZ at Tirunelveli in the southernmost district of Tamil Nadu. This Nanguneri SEZ was officially notified long back but nothing physically came in the operation of this particular SEZ. The field survey shows that only the land price has been shooted in and around Nanguneri SEZ. The political turmoil the TN State facing is which governments brought SEZs and in the subsequent rival war between the ruling and opposition parties the people of Nanguneri remain ed mutue watch-dog of democracy as the Nanguneri never transformed into a development zone.

Rather people in this small town live in abject poverty, unemployment, malnutrition, and the whole are looks like an abandoned piece of land in the name of SEZ.

Nandigram is in the opposite direction of the Nanguneri, but experimenting the very same story of Nanguneri. Nandigram represents an increasing frequency of constitutional breakdown in the country with a ruling party taking the law into its own hands and making the state machinery stand by mute witness to the excesses of the cadres of the ruling party. The issuing of the notice on Dec.28, 2006 by the Haldia Development Authority identifying 25000 acres of land for acquisition provoked a reaction. The violence started on Jan,3m 2007 with a clash between the police and protestors. To prevent the police and the local administration from entering the area, the people set up blockades. Clashes with the pro government groups started and some of them had to move to the nearby Khejuri town, a stronghold of the ruling party. Subsequence events dominated the newspapers in the country for many months to come with attacks, counter attacks etc. became the order of the day at Nandigram. The issue is not just the viability of the SEZ by about democratic functioning in the State.

### (v) Social issues

Most of the workforces in SEZs consist of young women, with little or no knowledge of and experience with trade unions. Their stay in any one company seldom exceeds three years and in countries with high unemployment, their main pre occupation is to keep their jobs.

## (vi) Regional Disparities

Most of the formally approved SEZs came in the southern region leaving East and North very little. The following chart show regional distribution of Formal Approvals.

REGION-WISE DISTRIBUTION OF FORMAL APPROVAL OF SEZs

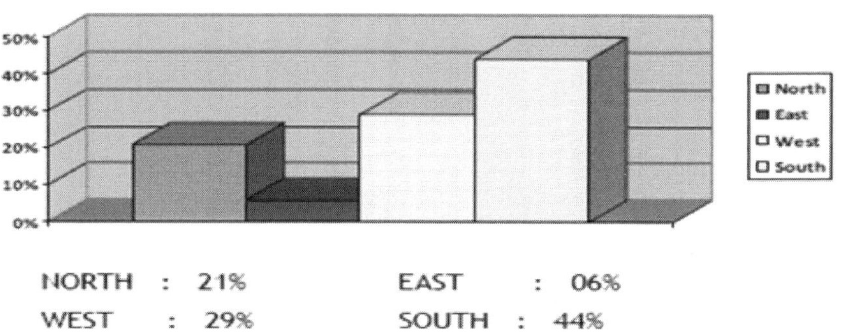


## (vii) Issues related to Food Security

All across the country agricultural land is shrinking. Many states lost huge hectares of agricultural land to mining, power projects, real estates residential project, SEZs establishments etc. This will adversely impact the agricultural production and productivity which will have ultimate bearing on the food security for a nation which has to feed a billion plus population.

## (viii) Resettlement and Rehabilitation Policy

The government promises humane displacement followed by relief and rehabilitations. However the reality does not match the promise. An estimated 40 million people (of whom nearly 40% are adivasis and 25% are dalits) have lost their land since industrialization and urbanization started in India. New large projects like setting up of power plant, airports or the expansion of existing airports, the expansion of the highway network etc are likely to displace millions of the rural people.

## (ix) Space for SSIs

Another interesting issue is related to the position of SSIs within the demarcated area of SEZs. Central Government has recently notified that SEZ will have to mandatorily reserve one-tenth of production space for establishing SSIs and in many SEZs this notification has not been implemented in letter and spirit. SSIs have huge employment and export potential and therefore SEZs should not overlook the role played by SSIs.

**(x) Environmental issues:** The transformations of land into SEZ involve environmental cost that cannot be overlooked in the looming threat of global warming perspective. Settings up of an exclusive SEZ involve the following three environmental cost benefit analysis (Ray & Das, 2009).

(i) Cost of Development (Cd)

(ii) The Benefit of preserving the environment by not developing the area (Bp) and

(iii) Direct Benefit of the SEZ (Bd)

A SEZ can be developed if

Bd – Cd > Bp and

We should not develop a SEZ if

Bd-Cd < Bp

## Conclusion

Thus the SEZ model of development accelerate the economic growth, generate additional employment, promotes exports, attracts FDI, but there are areas of concern which have to be addressed by the policy makers before aggressively moving ahead with the SEZ model of economic growth.

There is no doubt that entrepreneurs are getting institutional support in establishing their business but government must ensure that there exist both positive and negative externality in SEZ model of economic growth and therefore should make the policy framework accordingly. As former FM, P.Chidambaram has stated "SEZs per se will distort land, capital and labour costs, which will encourage relocation or shifting of industries in clever ways that can't be stopped. This will be further aggravated by the proliferation of a large number of SEZs in and around metros".

## References

1. Abhyankar Amit (2006), "Special Economic Zones: Indian Scenario."
2. Arunachalam P "*Special Economic Zones in India: Principles, Problems and Prospects.*"
3. Arunachalam P "*Social, Political Economic and Environmental Concerns of Special Economic Zones in India : An International Experience*".
4. Balasubramaniyam R " Special Economic Zones in India: The Major Issues and Challenges'.

5. Bruce London, (2006)www.economistuk.com/discussion/viewtopic.php.
6. Confederation of Indian Industry, "Special Economic Zones – Engine for Growth" May, 2006.
7. C.K.Hebbar & Yathish Kumar "Special Economic Zone: India's Sustainable Model?
8. C.R.Bijoy "Special Economic Zones: Profits at any Cost.
9. Goswamy Bhaskar " Diversion of Agriculture Land and Impact on Food Security.
10. Khanna Shivank (2007). What is Special Economic Zone?.
11. Kumar Arun "Nandigram: Another Symbol of Challenge to Democracy in India".
12. Kumar Arun "Special Economic Zones in India: Growth and Blood".
13. Kumar Rajive (2007) SEZs: Opening Doors, others Policy.
14. Mathew C.J. "Cochin Special Economic Zone (CSEZ) : An overview.
15. Mathew P Gisha 'Special Economic Zones: A Changing Scenario.
16. Prajapati Pradeep "Special Economic Zones (SEZs) in India; Matter of More Worry than Think".
17. Shrivastava Aseem (2007) War Zones – The Present and Future of India's SEZs.
18. Special Economic Zone Act, 2005.
19. Special Economic Zone Rules, 2006.
20. V.K.Shobana & R.Rajamant "An overview of SEZs in India".Wong, Edy L (1987).

# 5

# Family Business in India: Survival for three Generations or Beyond

***Abstract***

Historically, family as a social institution has been one of the oldest surviving business units in India, as anywhere else, constituting above 75% in terms of ownership. Most of the researches in family business are limited to western economies. However, the research interest in family business is recent and stray outputs have started appearing in developing countries or Asia in general. Whatsoever research has so far been conducted in family business in India is scattered and our knowledge about the subject has been far from satisfactory. No comprehensive picture is still clear on most aspects of family business. As such, currency is generally given to assumptions and general predilections family business in the country. One of the general assumptions held is the most of the family businesses in India survive for three generations and only a few go beyond thus, supporting the age-old saying, "shirt sleeve to shirt sleeve in three generations." It is in this context that the present paper makes a modest attempt to examine the survival issue of family business in India. The main foci of paper will be to examine the reality or myth about survival of family business in India up to three generations or beyond. Accordingly, the paper has been presented in two parts. Part I gives the theoretical perspective of family business in India and part II presents the empirical evidences based on some case studies on family business in India.

## Introduction

"Govern a family business as you cook a small fish – very gently." – ***Chinese Proverb*** "The saga of three generations of family business is in the first generation the scruffy and astute patriarch works hard and makes money. Born into money, the second generation does not want more money. It wants power; it goes after it with the single-mindedness of a Joseph Kennedy, and Buddenbrook's son becomes a senator. Born into money and power, what else is left for the third generation to do but to dedicate itself to art? So, the aesthetic but physically weak grandson plays the violin. But the signs of decline are visible and that this is end of the Buddenbrook's family."

**Thomas Mann:** Buddenbrook (the greatest book about a family business) Family and business have been coeval since time immemorial. While family is one of the oldest surviving social system (Goode 1982), family business is the oldest surviving economic system. Business history is witness to the fact that most countries have family businesses playing significant roles in their economies. Family businesses constitute the largest size in terms of ownership; contribute significantly to the gross national production (GNP), total industrial employment, and total exports of the country. Though estimates do vary from country to country, these are above 60 per cent in the majority of the cases.

About a third of the companies listed in Fortune 500 are family businesses (Lee 2004: 46-53). For example, even in the US, the most professionalized business nation, more than 80 per cent of all enterprises are family-owned businesses which create its 40 per cent of GDP. Coming to the Indian case, according to the 'Report of the Monopolies Enquiry Commission, Government of India (1965), 75 largest business houses in India controlled 1536 companies accounting for 47 per cent of assets and 44 per cent of paid up capital of all non-governmental and non-banking companies. According to Dutta (1997), more than 70 per cent of the hundred largest corporations and 99.9 per cent of all enterprises in India are either family-owned or controlled. Not surprisingly, this has had a significant impact on the conduct and development of business in the country. This clearly indicates that family business has come to occupy a significant place in Indian industry. In most of the countries, much of retail trade, small industry, and all type of services are in the hands of the family, from the corner store to the most high-tech manufacturing items (Anonymous 1996).

Family businesses exist all over the world for centuries –from shoemakers to confectioners to farmers. Over 80 per cent of world business is controlled by families. They employ around 50 per cent of world work force and contribute around 40 to 50 per cent in the world GDP. The world's oldest documented family business is a construction company, named; 'Kongo Gumi' of Japan founded in 578 AD and is currently managed by the 40th generation. Prince Shotoku brought the Kongo family members to Japan from Korea more than 1400 years ago to build the Buddhist Shitennoji Temple, which still stands in Japan.

Over the centuries, Kongo Gumi participated in the construction of many famous buildings, including the sixteenth-century Osaka castle. The Kongo family still continues to build and repair religious temples. Presently, Toshitaka is its president and his son Masakazu Kongo who is 51-year old, is waiting in the wings to succeed Toshitaka. Some of the largest family business firms worldwide are:

**Wal-Mart** (USA): Revenues $245 billion, *Sam Walton Family*

**Samsung Group** (South Korea): Revenues $98.7 billion, *Lee Family*

**Flat Group** (Italy): Revenues $54.7 billion, *Agnell Family*

**McCain Foods** (Canada): Revenues $ 3.5 billion, *McCainFfamily*

**Tata Group** (India): Revenues $7.9 billion, *Tata Family*

Following is an overview of significant place assumed by family business by now worldwide:

Over 75 per cent of all registered companies in the industrialized world are family businesses (OECD).

One-third of fortune 500 has families at their helm.

70 per cent firms in the United Kingdom are family owned.

Of Italy's 100 top countries, 43 are family owned.

Family owned firms employ about 50-60 per cent of the work force in the industrialized world.

In India too, 95 per cent of the registered firms are family owned.

Companies with founding family participation performed better than non-family businesses (*Study of Standard and Poor's 500*).

In India too, the highest creator of wealth are family-owned businesses. Fifteen out of the twenty largest industrial houses in 1997 derived from the Vaishya or Bania trading castes. Eight of them were Marwaris (Anonymous 1997: 218). But, the sad picture is that only 15 to 20 per cent of family businesses survive till the third generation and around 5 per cent go to the fourth generation (Sue 1986:36). Researchers report that family businesses are found to split up like amoeba as they grow, and vary few of them, around 5 per cent survive beyond three generations. Thus, they support the age-old saying, "shirt sleeve to shirt sleeve in the three generations" (Carlock and Ward 2001, McCulloch 2004: 20-22).

Professor Pulin Garg at the Indian Institute of Management, Ahmedabad (IIMA), used to tell his students, *"Haveli ki umar saath saal"* (The life of a family is sixty years) (*http://*gurucharandas.org). Most discussions in this area of survival of family business are based on research on advanced countries like US. However, in most developing countries including India, this area still remains a black box. The reason being the academics and industry observers were puzzled to witness the recent amoebic type break up in the second generation of the Ambani family, the largest private sector group worth over US $ 20 billion. Even the anecdotal evidence is highly limited to a few biographical sketchcs only (Tripathy 2004, Piramal 1998) and consultant impressions (Dutta 1997, Sampath 2001).

Indian industry is largely dominated by family businesses. Family businesses have always been a matter of great curiosity as they are distinctively different from other forms of businesses such as public enterprises, joint sector enterprises, and cooperatives in more than one term such as their entrepreneurial, managerial and organizational behaviours and styles. This is because of the fact that their behaviours and styles are influenced by the emotions of family members, inter-personal pressures of relatives and owners, and most importantly, the conflicting interest of family and business. Then, such uniqueness on these aspects leads the family business to exhibit distinct operational characteristics and also unique set of problems and challenges. It is against this backdrop, the present paper makes a modest attempt to discuss the nature of family business in India and also unfold the unique challenges and problem of management succession considered important in family owned businesses. Also given are suggestions towards the end of the paper to make family business more effective in India.

## Family Business Defined

Family business has been as common in the Indian economy like elsewhere in the world, it is perceived in a common sense. Various terms like 'family-owned,' family controlled,' 'family managed,' 'business houses,' and 'industrial houses' are used to refer to family business. Thus, the term family business conjures up different meanings to different people. While some view it as traditional business, others consider it as community business, and still others mean it as home-based business. As such, there are various definitions of family business given looking at the different aspects of family business. For the convenience of understanding, all definitions have been broadly classified into two types based on the structure and process involved in family business.

**Structured Definitions:** These definitions are given based on ownership and/ or management of family business. A few such definitions are:

"Ownership control by the members of a single family." – Barry. "Majority ownership by a single family and direct involvement by at least two members in its operation." - Rosenblatt, de Mik, Anderson, and Johnson. "Single family effectively controls firm through the ownership of greater than 50 per cent of the voting shares; a significant portion of the firm's senior management is drawn from the same family." -Leach et al.

**Process Definitions:** These definitions are based on how the family is involved in the business. Following are some of such important definitions of family business:

"Family business is a firm which has been closely identified with at least two generations of a family and when this link has had a mutual influence on company policy and on the interests and objectives of the family." - R. G. Donneley (1964: 93-105)

""Family businesses are those where policy and decision are subject to significant influence by one or more family units. This influence is exercised through ownership and sometime through the participation of family members in management. It is the interaction between two sets of organizations, family and business, that establishes the basic character of the family business and defines its uniqueness." - P. Davis

Some researchers argue that a broad definition of a family business should incorporate some degree of control over strategic decisions by the family and the intention to leave the business in the family. Shanker and Astrachan (1996) note that the criteria used to define a family business can include: Percentage of ownership; Voting control; _Power over strategic decisions; Involvement of multiple generations; and _Active management of family members. In an effort to resolve the definitional ambiguity surrounding family business research, Litz (1995: 71-81) suggests that a business can be defined as a family business when its ownership and management are concentrated within a family unit. Furthermore, he argues that to be considered a family business; the business' members must strive to achieve, maintain, and/or increase intraorganizational family-based relatedness.

In sum and substance, a family business can simply be defined as a business one that includes two or more members of a family with financial control of the company. In other words, a family business is one actively owned and/or managed by more than one member of the same family.

## Characteristics

The definitions of family business given above indicate the following characteristics of family business:

1. A group of people belonging to one or more families run one business enterprise.
2. Position in family business is influenced by the relationship the family members enjoy among themselves.
3. Family exercises control over business in the form of ownership or in the form of management of the firm where family members are employed on key positions.
4. Family exercises the influence on the firm's policy direction in the mutual interest of family and business.
5. The succession of family business goes to the next generation.
6. Family business in India is largely caste-related.
7. Every caste enjoys a dominant culture which gets duly reflected in their family businesses also.

## Types of Family Businesses

Having defined and outlined the salient characteristics of family business, we can now profitably classify family businesses into various types as follows:

**Family-Owned Business:** This is a family business in which a controlling size of ownership either in the form of shareholding or any other is owned either by the family or a member of the family member. Most of the family businesses especially when these are small in size fall this type of family businesses.

**Family-Owned and Managed Business:** In this type of family business, a controlling size of ownership, be in the form of shares or other form of ownership, rests with the members of a single extended family or with a single member of the family but greatly influenced by other members of the family.

Such a controlling ownership confers the family permission to devise and decide the objectives, methods for achieving them, and policies for implementing the methods. One or more family members exercise the ultimate control over the management of the family business.

**Family-Owned and Led Business:** This type of family business is, to a great extent, similar to that of above i. e. 'Family-owned and managed' business.

Nonetheless, it is different from above one in the sense that at least one member of the family is a member of the board of directors of the company / business. This enables him / her to exert influence over the business's direction, culture, and strategies.

**Family Business in India: A Historical Perspective:** Family business in India had been in practice since long, of course, with its changing nature and structure over the period. India enjoys a rich and glorious history of family-owned business. The origin of family business in India is traced back to the *bazaar system* in the ancient times. Initially, family business in India started in the form of trading and money lending involving the hustle and bustle of the *bazaar.* It was also confined to certain communities, notably the Jains and Marwaris especially in the northern India. Its industry form is relatively of recent origin, going back largely to the British rule and the First World War.

Here is one such instance to it. Cawasji Davar set up the first cotton mill, or say, the first manufacturing enterprise in Bombay (now Mumbai) in 1854. Consequent upon this, some trading communities started textile mills in Mumbai and Ahmedabad during the last half of the 19th Century. The trading communities emerged as Aggarwals and Guptas in the North, the Chettiars in the South, the Parsees, Gujarati Jains and Banias, Muslim Khojas and Memons in the West, and Marwaris all over India. Nowadays Aggarwals are mostly referred to as Marwaris. Here is an interesting legend of how Aggarwal families emerged as most dominating and successful in business in India (Roy 2008: 84).

## The Agrawals

The Agrawals claim descent from the legendary king Agrasena of Agroha.

According to the legend, Agroha was a prosperous city and hundred thousand traders lived in the city during its heydays. An insolvent community person as well as an immigrant wishing to settle in the city would be given a rupee and a brick by each inhabitant of the city. Thus, the person would have hundred thousand bricks to build a house and hundred thousand rupees to start a new business. Gradually, the city of Agroha declined and finally gutted in a huge fire. The residents of Agroha, i.e. the Agrawals, moved out of Agroha and spread to other parts of India. In his book, *'Agarwalon ki utpatti,'* Bhartendu Harishchandra categorized Agrawals into four branches: Marwaris, Deswal, Purabiya, and Pachihiye. Nowadays, Agrawal families are mostly referred to as 'Marwaris.'

Jamshedji Tata started his various business enterprises like cotton mill in Nagpur, the Taj Hotel in Mumbai, his famous steel plant in Jamshedpur, and several real-state developments. These enterprises, in turn, prompted other people to join the business foray. A number of families, such as Birlas, Bangurs, Khaitans and Goenkas started their business in Kolkata and developed the city as a centre for commerce.

Initially family businessmen were engaged in small-size businesses requiring small investments managed by themselves only. But, once they entered into manufacturing sector, they felt the need for more and heavy investments not manageable by themselves. At the same time, they also knew that once they allow someone to join business, their control over management of the business will weaken which they, however, did not want. In such a case, family businesses inducted their family members or relatives or friends in the business by allotting them blocks of shares while making sure that the majority control and, in turn, the management of the business remained with the promoting family itself. This is how corporate management was born embedded by a combination of joint stock principle and family control over business. Because stock markets were yet to gain sufficient momentum, on the one hand, and the joint family system was also intact, on the other, business families were holding control over their business empires built up through the ingenious device, popularly known as the 'managing agency system.' The managing agency system continued till 1970 as an instrument of maintaining family control over business enterprise. As such, all critical decisions about the business were taken by the promoting families, euphemistically termed managing agents. This system of corporate management got so rooted in due course of time that hardly any industrial firm remained out of its orbit. In other words, this indicates that all businesses were controlled and managed by a few families in the country. R. K. Hazari, a well-known industrial economist, had concluded after an exclusive analysis that most of the prominent industrial firms on the contours of Indian business during the 1950s, were in the hands of just 18 Indian families and two British houses. However, the period of 1950s experienced certain changes with some developments shaking and disturbing the business environment, in general, and family business, in particular. The consequence was the earlier tranquil situation that the family business was enjoying in the country got greatly disturbed especially by four major developments as mentioned below:

1. With a resolution to accelerate the pace of economic development during the post-Independence period to solve the problem of unemployment and poverty stalking the land, the Government invited private sector to partake of new opportunities available for business and industrial development, of course, amidst a myriad of restrictions imposed on the freedom of enterprise.
2. The Governments, both at Central and State levels, set up various financial institutions to provide finance to private sector enterprises in the country.
3. The joint family system, once the bedrock of the Indian social structure in India, started experiencing severe strains and threats and, in turn, increasingly losing its place in the social structure. For such a sorry state of situation, thanks to *inter alia* growing urbanization and ever increasing westernization in the country.
4. The right of possession of private property and its inheritance has been one of the major factors in encouraging family business in India.

In lump sum, these changes, in turn, caused changes in family business in the country. With increase in the magnanimous size of infrastructural projects in the country, business families were no longer capable enough to mobilize the required resources including finance from their own resources. As a result, financial control of business started gradually shifting from promoting families to financial institutions. Also the business families started splitting and cracking.

To quote, the Dalmias were the first prominent business house in the country to break up after freedom. The pace of splitting family businesses started accelerating in the country beginning with 1970 and since then, it has been increasingly growing. Business history is replete with increasing number of families splitting in the country over the period. Birlas, Modis, Sarabhais, Bangurs, Singhanias, Mafatlals, Shrirams, Thapars, Walchands,

Goenkas and the most recently, the Ambanis are the illustrious family businesses in our country who have experienced split in their businesses. Nonetheless, it is worth mentioning that inspite of various changes like losing financial control over business and growing splits in businesses, the family control over management of business still remains impaired in the hands of promoting families. This is indicated by the fact that the management of as many as 461 out of 500 most valuable companies is still under family control in our country. One of the significant changes in family business in India is induction of professionals to manage the affairs of business. Tatas, Birlas, Reliance, Wipro, and Murugappa Group are some of the illustrative family businesses employing professional managers to look after the management issues of their businesses. With increase in size of business has also led to increase in split in family businesses in the country over the period. Goenka family and Ambani family are such examples of split in family business in our times. The changing environment of family business in India can be summed up as follows:

| Earlier | Presently |
|---|---|
| Business as family<br>Family wealth and prosperity<br>Growth strategies<br>Expansion and diversification<br>Family succession planning for next generation | Family as business<br>Shareholders' value and prosperity<br>Economic Value Added (EVA)<br>Core and competitive competencies<br>Planning for attraction and retention of professionals |

## Why Family Business?

"When it works right, nothing succeeds like a family firm. The roots run deep, embedded in family values. The flash of the fast buck is replaced with long-term plans. Tradition counts (Facts and Figures: Family Business in the US, *Family Business Magazine).*" A family business provides a range of advantages which other enterprises (non-family businesses) do not. These include but not confined to the following only:

1. **Common Values**: Entrepreneur and his / her family are likely to share the same ethos and beliefs on how things should be done. This will give entrepreneur an extra sense of purpose and pride - and a competitive edge for his / her business.

2. **Strong Commitment**: Building a lasting family enterprise means entrepreneur is more likely to put in the extra hours and effort needed to make the business a success. At the same time, his / her family is more likely to understand that he / she needs to take a more flexible approach to his / her working hours.
3. **Loyalty**: Strong personal bonds, called loyalty, means entrepreneur and family members are likely to stick together in hard times and show the determination needed for business success. Loyalty leads to commitment which gets translated into hard work and perseverance which are the prerequisites of success in any endeavour including business.
4. **Stability**: Purpose provides stamina and stability in efforts. Knowing one is building for future generations encourages and strengthens his / her efforts in terms of long-term thinking and tenacious efforts needed for growth and success of his / her business. Yes, at times it can also produce counterproductive effects in terms of entrepreneur's inability to respond to requirement.
5. **Decreased Costs**: Unlike non-family businesses, members of family business may be more willing to make financial sacrifices for the sake of the business. For example, accepting lower pay than they would get elsewhere to help the business in the longer term, or deferring wages during a cash flow crisis. The family business can also hold down the costs of governance, in terms of special accounting systems, security systems, policy manuals, legal documents and other mechanisms to reduce theft and monitor employees' work habits. This is possible because employees and managers of business are well related and have trust and confidence on each other.

Following is an example of Bajaj family business confirming how family business proves cost-effective:

We may run businesses of different sizes but we have the same standard of living,' says Neeraj Bajaj. 'Rahul runs the Rs 2500 crore Bajaj Auto and Shekhar runs the Rs 200 crore Bajaj Electricals, but they get equal salaries and equal pocket money. Splits take place when there is visible inequality. We take pains to observe absolute equality, and our 15 rules keep us honest. We travel in the same types of cars; we are allowed the same class of air travel; we usually vacation together; thus, we minimise differences and comparisons.

'Every year at Diwali the family members get together and we review the 15 rules by which we run our joint family. These rules relate to what each familymember gets as pocket money, vacation allowance, what women spend on jewellery, and so on. Each year the family members update their allowances under the l eadership of Rahul, who is presently the head of the household after my father Ramakrishna's death. And we meticulously stick to our pocket money.

No exceptions! And I should know because I am currently the treasurer of the family, responsible for managing the family wealth, disbursing funds, filing tax returns and looking after the family affairs (Das 1996).

## Family Business Suffers from Disadvantages too

All is not well with family business. It also suffers from certain disadvantages as mentioned below:

**Risk of Ownership:** Family members hold the impression that the family business will continue to earn profit and, thus, ensure receipt of cash and other benefits on a recurring basis. However, when business either earns less income or incurs loss, receiving cash and other benefits becomes uncertain especially for non-active members. Then they start challenging and questioning the ownership of business to ensure their share in the business cake. This produces various implications for the business like weakens family unity and commitment, conflict surfaces between active and non-active family members and relatives, and businesses' market share starts dwindling and ultimately the business dies out.

**Controlling Ambiguity:** Every entrepreneur wants the control of his/ her business should rest with the closest and trustworthy one. In practice, business control generally rests with the siblings, the minority shareholders have only a minimal control over the business. Minority shareholders normally are given protection of their ownership by having a say in: sale or merger of the company, the issuance of stock to others, borrowing money in excess of a set amount, a major capital expenditure.

**The Subtle Messages of a Buy/Sell Agreement.** We encourage families to put an agreement in place that will make it relatively easy for a shareholder to exit ownership of the business. However, some families believe multiple shareholders will be in place forever. In general experience, this is not the case in 99 per cent of family businesses.

Buy/sell agreements protect the company and its stock, for example, against a shareholder getting divorced and giving an ex-spouse an ownership stake, where the stock must go in case of death, what must happen to the stock in the event of a shareholder declaring personal bankruptcy, and if the stock can be pledged as security for other business investments. Sometimes, a shareholder just wishes to have control of his or her own investments and opts out of the family business. This raises questions like: Are they disappointing their deceased parents? Are the active siblings sending a message to the non-active that they do not trust them or their intentions?

**Inability for Shareholders to Cash Out of the Family Business:** Mostly family businesses lack the financial ability to fund the redemption of stock from one major shareholder. Funds are typically not available, and most owners will refuse to go to the bank for a loan as it might put the company in a poor financial position. Thus, the minority shareholder wanting to cash out either cannot do it or must follow certain company policy, which normally discusses the conditions and timing of a stock redemption.

## Major Challenges Faced by Family Business in India

Although family business has been an integral part of industrial economy of India, it also faces some major challenges but not confined to the following only: *Challenge of Inter-relationships* One of the peculiarities of family business is that the boundaries between work and family are quite intermingled, complex and also multifaceted. Such an inter-related context at times creates three overlapping perspectives that influence the actions and decisions of family business owners (Hoy and Verser 1994: 9-23). These are: (i) The family wants to take care of family members. (ii) The concern for ownership by doing what is in the best interests of family business. (iii) The concern for management by doing what is the best interests of other organizational employees, i.e. non-family employees. How these three overlapping perspectives create challenges for family business can be exemplified with an imaginary example:

Let us consider a fairly common family business situation in which a family member needs a job. From the family perspective, one probably would see this as a chance to help out someone in need of job in the family. From the ownership perspective, one might have concern about the impact of an additional employee on organizational expenses and, in turn, profits. From the management perspective, one might be concerned about the effect of hiring an employee from family on other non-family employees. We find each of these perspectives is valid and justifiable. But the issue is which of the perspectives takes precedence. Remember, these perspectives might not be mutually exclusive all the times, but might be overlapping each other. Nonetheless, there might be situation in which business action or decision is going to be influenced more strongly by one of the perspectives. Here needs the entrepreneurial ability of the family business to properly balance all three perspectives simultaneously in managing the complex and overlapping relationships in running the family business in an effective manner.

## Challenge of Management Succession

Management succession has been found the second major challenge facing the family businesses everywhere in the world including India. Research studies on family business have reported that, on average, only 30 percent of family businesses survive to the second generation, and only 10 percent make it to the third generation (Zimmerer and Scarborough 1998: 17). The statistics is pretty alarming. Then what is the reason for such a sorry and alarming situation? The reason is not difficult to seek. Many entrepreneurs for their own reasons dream of passing on the family business to their children or kins and kiths. But, the human traits such as lack of interest or competence or jealousy usually get into business with their evil effects on business. The consequence is failure of business.

Here the following two excerpts relating to succession in family business seem worth citing:

1. Pulin Garg, the thoughtful Professor at the Indian Institute of Management, Ahmedabad, used to tell his students, '*Haveli ki umar saath saal*' (The life of a family business is sixty years).
2. Thomas Mann, the Nobel Prize winning German writer, expressed the same thought in his great novel *Buddenbrooks*, which is arguably the greatest book about a business family. It describes the saga of three generations of family business: in the first generation the scruffy and astute patriarch works hard and makes money. Born into money, the second generation does not want more money. It wants power; it goes after it with the single-mindedness of a Joseph Kennedy, and Buddenbrook's son becomes a senator. Born into money and power, what else is left for the third generation to do but to dedicate itself to art? So, the aesthetic but physically weak grandson plays the violin. But the signs of decline are visible and that this is end of the Buddenbrooks family.

That madness, i.e. intoxication of power causes damages is very beautifully illustrated in the following Urdu couplet: "Intoxication of liquor leaves you, but intoxication of power continues to grow, takes hold of you, and finally drowns you."

## Sibling Rivalry

One of the challenges family businesses face is sibling rivalry. Why does sibling rivalry surfaces? The main reason for this is the share in family business cake the members get. This happens particularly when business starts flourishing and expanding over the period. The sibling rivalry ultimately culminates to split in family business. As Ramachandran (2009) puts, family businesses are found to split up like amoeba as they grow, and very few of them survive beyond three generations. The reason is sibling rivalry surfaces mainly due to siblings' anxiety to prove their mantle better than the others. Rivalry with each other often amounts to pull each other down at the cost of the organizational resources.

The rivalry further gets fuelled and even complicated when some members of the family in one way or other favour one of the siblings. This further leads to the complication as one of them feels of unjust and undue favouritism. If rivalry is not resolved well in time, it may lead to split in the family business and, thus, may damage the age-old family business. That sibling rivalry destroys family business is very well confirmed by rivalry between Ambani brothers. Here is the story:

The great visionary and astute entrepreneur, Dhirubhai Ambani, who loved to dream big and to attain them, lacked the vision to carve a succession plan for such a giant corporation. He passed in 2002 without providing the company with clear cut succession route. May be that he never thought that even such huge empire will fail short of the aspirations of his two young Ambanis. He failed to understand the strategic importance of planning the succession in advance and in the year 2004; the sibling rivalry in reliance became the most talked story in the business world. Sharp differences between the two brothers started cropping up leading to a nasty seven-month-long ownership row. On the height of rivalry between the brother, on June 18, 2005, after much public dilemmas, Prime Minister and Finance Minister has tried to mediate between two fighting brothers. Mukesh and Anil finally reached an agreement to divide assets after a long drawn battle, split the Reliance Empire to steer ahead their own interests. Following were the split consequences:

Reliance split is a burning case to confirm that family business gets split over ego clashes. Hence presents the biggest challenge for any family

| Step 1: |
|---|
| Split the Ambani family stake in RIL in the 30 : 30 : 40 ratio among the two brothers and Kokilaben. Anil Ambani to relinquish control to Mukesh, who gets full control of Reliance Industries' core oil and gas business. |
| Step 2: |
| Create a special purpose vehicle to house RIL's stake in Reliance Energy and reliance Capital. Anil Ambani to continue heading the two firms. |
| Step 3: |
| In lieu of Anil giving up control in RIL, Mukesh Ambani transfers part of his 45% stake in Infocomm to anil, who now gets to run the venture. |

indulged in business. Just after the split the company slipped in Forbes list. Even if the Reliance does not suffer severely, it certainly devalues status of the family in the society and the trust of the customers and shareholders. If Mr. Dhirubhai Ambani had planned a business envisioning the inherent conflict it could have been another story altogether where both the siblings would have complemented each other with their unique skills and have consolidated the empire created by their father into a well established and cared family business not just another business.

We have seen split in family business due to differences and ego clashes among family members during the past ten years among the Modis, the Walchands, the Raunaq Singhs, the Bhai Mohan Singhs and a dozen other joint family firms who have separated (Das 2010). Family business split generally happens with increase in the size of family, or say, joint family. In a way, living in joint families is a bit like life under socialism. Joint family does not work in the long run in the same way that socialism does not work. Joint families require strict equality to succeed. But, because human beings are by nature unequal and they need material incentives to perform, a joint families break up in the end. In such situation, a strong and fair leader can help family business to prolong like Rahul Bajaj in case of Bajaj's mentioned earlier. Bajaj's experience shows that having a family constitution or family rules help to prolong the life of family business on perpetual basis.

There are yet more reasons that make family business ineffective and, in turn, unsuccessful. Flaming (2000) terms these reasons as *'seven deadly sins'* that can run family businesses into the ground or make them less valuable in the market place. These are given in the following Table 1:

**Table 1: Seven Deadly Sins of Family Business**

| Sins | Consequences |
|---|---|
| 1. It's the same old song. | Family members' childhood behaviour and beliefs follow them into the business |
| 2. We're one big, happy family. | The failure to recognize that running a business requires different practices than running a family. |
| They may have become adults, but they'll always be my children. | The parents are unable to accept and treat their grown children as adults. |
| You're not loyal to this family if you insist on being selfish. | The failure is to acknowledge and treat family members as individuals. |
| 5. Father knows best. | Founders usually possess dominating personalities and may be totally consumed by the business. |
| May be it will go away if we ignore it. | Ignoring problems only adds to their destructive potential. |
| Tell me about your childhood. | Children often enter the business before resolving childhood issues, which can affect the way that may work. |

Besides, Indian family businesses also have some weaknesses that make them ineffective. Following are the four most important ones as reported by Das (1999):

| |
|---|
| 1. An inability to separate the family's interest from the interest of the business. |
| 2. Lack of focus and business strategy. |
| 3. Short-term approach to business, leading to an absence of investment in employees and in product development. |
| 4. Insensitivity to the customer, largely because of uncompetitive markets, but resulting in weak marketing skills. |

No doubt, there are challenges and pitfalls that make family business suffer. But it doesn't mean that family business cannot run effectively. There are ways that family businesses can do to be effective and successful. We are going to look at this important topic next.

## Business Succession Planning

We all know that sooner or later, every one retires from service, business or even from life. But retirement from business is not just a matter of deciding not to go to office anymore. It is, in fact, much more than that. The paramount question that arises on retirement from business is what happens to the business after one retires from the business. Who is going to manage the business when one no longer works in the business? How will ownership be transferred? Will one business carry on or will sell it? Business succession planning seeks to address and manage these vital issues involved in family business by setting up a smooth transition between there owner-leader and the future one of the family business.

Let us begin with defining the term 'succession planning.' Some people term 'succession planning' as 'multi-generational planning' or 'replacement planning.' Be it called by any names, succession planning means planning for succession or making preparations on who will succeed thc owner-leader of the business. Succession planning is a process for identifying and developing family members with the potential to succeed the key role of owner-leader in the business. According to Charan, Drotter and Noel 92001), succession planning is concerned with developing the second order owner-leader to run the family business.

Research studies report that only about 30 per cent of family businesses survive into the second generation, 12 per cent are still viable into the third generation, and only about 3 per cent of all family businesses operate into the fourth generation or beyond. Such trend supports the age-old saying, 'shirt sleeve to shirt sleeve in three generations (Carlock and Ward 2001). The obvious question is why does this happen? More often than not, the lack or failure of a solid business succession planning is to blame to this sorry situation. Since evidences indicate that good succession planning makes the family business survive and thrive generation after generation and absence of it derails the business down and die out. Hence, there is a need for solid succession planning in family business to make the business perpetuate through generations. However, as much succession planning is significant for family business is not so simple. It requires thorough thinking and solid preparations to which we turn our attention subsequently.

There is substantial body of literature on the subject of succession planning. However, the first work on this topic was done by Walter Mahler (1973) in his book entitled 'Executive Continuity.' In fact, Mehler who was highly influenced by peter Drucker was responsible in the 1970s for helping to shape the General Electric succession process which became the gold standard of corporate practice. Later, other researchers (Kesler 2002: 32-44, Goldsmith and Carter 2010) expanded the succession strategies developed by Mehler and recommended for a process owner for talent and succession management in business firms.

As mentioned earlier, family businesses face unique situations and, in turn, challenges that set them apart from the typical business. Foremost among them is maintaining a fine balance between business and family, that is, making decisions and undertaking actions that will honour the family values as well as benefit the business. An instance of imbalance would be, for example, if a father were to pick his oldest son to take over his business, simply because he is the first-born, when the youngest son is clearly the more competent for the job / business. In nutshell, business succession planning needs to be done with serious thinking. Following are some of the important steps involved in making a successful succession planning for a family business:

**1. Make a Solid Case for Succession Planning:** Remember people do not resist changing, they resist to be changed. Therefore, if one wants to influence family members' opinions about business succession, s/he wants first to make a strong case for succession planning. Convince the family members, with real life examples, the need for and significance of having succession planning for ensuring the smooth and effective running of family business generation after generation. Give the family members' facts and figures like nearly 90 per cent of small enterprises are family-owned, but only 30 per cent of them succeed into the second generation, while 15 per cent make it to the third generation, and only 3 per cent reach to the fourth generation. Thus, convince them that the lack of succession planning is to blame this sorry state of family business.

The fact remains that having a solid succession plan is like having a good insurance policy for the perpetual continuity of family business through generations. Educate and help family members understand the value of putting a succession plan into place well in time. Here the views of Jamshed J. Irani expressed about introducing organizational change seem worth citing to appreciate the significance of planning for succession well in ahead: "*Change when you are still strong and when change appears unnecessary – do not wait for the day when you have no option but to change.*"

**2. Prepare an Exit Plan:** Clarify in advance under what circumstances the succession plan will take effect: whether on retirement or unplanned departure or changing financial situations. These question help determine what the succession plan should detail most. Keep in mind that both early-exit and late exist of the owner-leader have advantages as well as disadvantages for family business.

**3. Identify the Successor:** Identifying the right successor is one of the most significant steps in succession planning. The business successor should be identified by competence, not by any other considerations and compulsions. One way to do so is to first identify the qualities or attributes a successor must possess to succeed the business. The family member who possesses the maximum of so identified attributes should be selected for business succession.

**4. Grooming and Developing the Successor:** Once a successor is identified, s/he needs to be groomed and developed to assume the headship of the business. It can be done through various ways like giving on-the-job training, working under mentors and advisors, and delegating some authority to the successor much before the actual passing on of the baton takes place. Of course, grooming more than one member to become the successor of business is not a bad idea, but at times it may create confusions and complexities leading to strenuous succession battles. Business history is replete with evidences, like the recent one of Ambani brothers, that extreme succession battle may cause a split in the family business. Yes, some may not consider the split as a bad thing considering the fact that the split between Ambani brothers led to a dramatic increase in the value of their individual holdings in the erstwhile family business.

## How to Family Business More Effective?

One way to find out effective ways to run family business will be to discover the best practices of successful family businesses. Following are the most important ones:

1. **Focusing on business, not family needs:** Although a family business entrepreneur may feel obligations to take care of family problems of one type or other. S/he should not use business as

employment agency for family members. Neither should s/he use business funds for family purposes (Anonymous 1998: ENT3). Ultimate focus of running family business should be family as business, not business as family.

2. **Ploughing back of profits in the business:** Profits earned by family business should not be used for meeting family requirement, but should be reinvested in the business to further strengthen and sustain it in the market place.
3. **Using caution with family**: Be cautious about the implications of hiring family members in the business to avoid likely conflicts and confrontations among the family members.
4. **Delegating authority or decision taking**: A family business entrepreneur should delegate decision taking to those who are competent and capable of making right decisions. This gives more time to entrepreneur to concentrate on business issues involving more serious thinking and visioning. The family entrepreneur who makes all decisions by himself and does not delegate to others is viewed as control freak. Such entrepreneur does not get wholehearted and willing cooperation and support from others.
5. **Viewing Big and Broader Picture**: Family business entrepreneur should view big and broad, that is, s/he should consider others' interests as well while running the business. In other words, the entrepreneur while running business should strike a fine balance among three broad perspectives of family business: family, ownership, and management, also lumped together as the *'3-Circle Model'* of family business.
6. **Planning for Management Succession**: Because family business runs for a long period of time, hence there is always a need to have a good management succession plan in place to carry on the business effectively. While planning for management succession, entrepreneur should keep six factors into consideration: (i) the role of the owner during the transition; (ii) family dynamics; (iii) income for family members employed in the business and shareholders; (iv) business conditions during transition; (v) treatment of long-term and loyal employees; and (vi) tax consequences (Brothers 1996: S11). Evidences suggest that each of these factors affects the choices made during the transitions and influence whether the outcome is smoothing, functional, and effective. In case no family member wishes to join the family business, then the decision is to be made to transfer the family business to some non-family member. In such case, the owner needs to address a key question is ownership –

what type and how much ownership, if any, will be retained by the family? In nutshell, the main thing in either case, i.e. transferring the business to family member (s) or transferring to non-family member(s) is planning well in ahead. So to say, the entrepreneur should not wait until something happens and then forced to take rush and ill-advised actions and decisions. Here the views of Jamshed J. Irani expressed about introducing organizational change seem worth citing to appreciate the significance of planning (succession) well in ahead: "*Change when you are still strong and when change appears unnecessary – do not wait for the day when you have no option but to change.*"

7. **Prepare the Family Constitution:** The family constitution also called 'family rules,' in simple sense, refers to dos and don'ts dos in the business. It elaborates about the good governance practices to be practiced in the family business. Like corporate and political governance, family governance facilitates the smooth running of family business. It maintains harmonious and cordial atmosphere in the family and business. We have already mentioned earlier how Bajaj family through its fifteen family rules or call it family constitution, has been running successfully for generations. Similarly, austerity and the lack of visible symbols of inequality, among other rules, have helped Murugappa family (one of the few old Chettiar families that is still together) in running family business successfully over the generations. Here one such instance is worth citing. It is for austerity and equality reasons, the young Vellayan, who runs some of the TI companies, was refused an air-conditioned car some years ago. The rule or logic was if the old patriarch, M. M. Aunachalam, did not have an AC car, how could Vellayan? Obviously, for the sake of equality and uniformity, Vellayan had to learn to sudue his ego to the bigger family cause.

Following is an example of 'The Family Constitution' of a growing family business in infrastructural field: G. M. Rao Infrastructure Limited (GMRIL):

## The Family Constitution*

Sitting across a number of his borrowers during his days at Vysya Bank – in which he also owned a sizeable stake that he sold to start GMR Infrastructure – G. M. Rao watched a number of family businesses fail because of deep divisions between members of families who borrowed from his bank. "At that time, I decided that it would be one of the first things I took care of when I started GMRIL," he says. And thus the family constitution was born. The constitution is more than just a succession plan – Rao is just 60 and a decade away from retirement as group Chairman – it is a model of governance that applies to all his companies and how they are run. It lays down a code of behaviour that applies to all family members – his two sons (Kiran Grandhi and G. B. S. Raju) run key parts of the group along with his son-in-law (Srinivas Bommidala).

The next chairman of the group will be selected by a three-member constitution board; if no decision is made, then a deadlock trustee will make the final decision. The constitution is an elaborate document –it runs into over 150 pages and lays down entry and exit procedures for family members, and a dispute resolution mechanism, should the need arise.

Spouses are the part of the family council too, and the members of the family go on annual treats as part of the constitution's requirements. In the next few months, says Prasad M. Kumar, executive director of the GMR Group – he played a key role in the initiation and drafting of the document.- the family constitution will be legal document once all family members finish signing it; the equivalent of taking an oath of office.

***Source: *Business World*, 21 June 2010, p. 35.**

It is found that an entrepreneur is generally worried about ensuring that his or her business not only survives, but also thrives to nurture the next generation. Then, question is how to ensure the same? Some years ago, some researchers (Hunt and Handler 1999) examined the strategies behind successful family businesses. They found that success is generally tied directly to how well a family business manages the five unique resources every family business possesses:

**1. Human Capital:** The first resource is the family's human capital, or "inner circle." When the skill sets of different family members are coordinated as a complementary cache of knowledge, with a clear division of labor, it produces synergy. The result is the likelihood of success improves significantly.

**2. Social Capital:** The family members bring valuable social capital to the business in the form of networking and other external relationships that complement the insiders' skill and knowledge sets.

**3. Parent Financial Capital:** The family firm typically has parent financial capital in the form of both equity and debt financing from family members. Such a family relationship between the investors and the managers reduces the threat of liquidation.

**4. Survivability Capital:** The family business must also manage its survivability capital, that is, the family members' willingness to provide free labor or funds in time of urgency so that the venture doesn't suffer from the two and, in turn, does not fail.

**5. Lower Costs of Governance:** The family business must manage its ability to hold down the costs of governance. In non-family firms, these include costs for things such as special accounting systems, security systems, policy manuals, legal documents and other mechanisms to reduce theft and monitor employees' work habits. But, a family business can minimize or eliminate these costs significantly because employees and managers of business are well related and have trust and confidence on each other. If these family resources are clearly delineated and judiciously leveraged into a well-coordinated management strategy, the chances for success of family business greatly improve.

Ramachandran (2009) has identified ten dimensions of a family business which are interrelated between succession planning and conflict resolution and ownership structure. It is the synergy created by the interaction and reinforcements of these dimensions that help family businesses to perpetuate. He terms them the 'Ten Commandments of Family Business.'

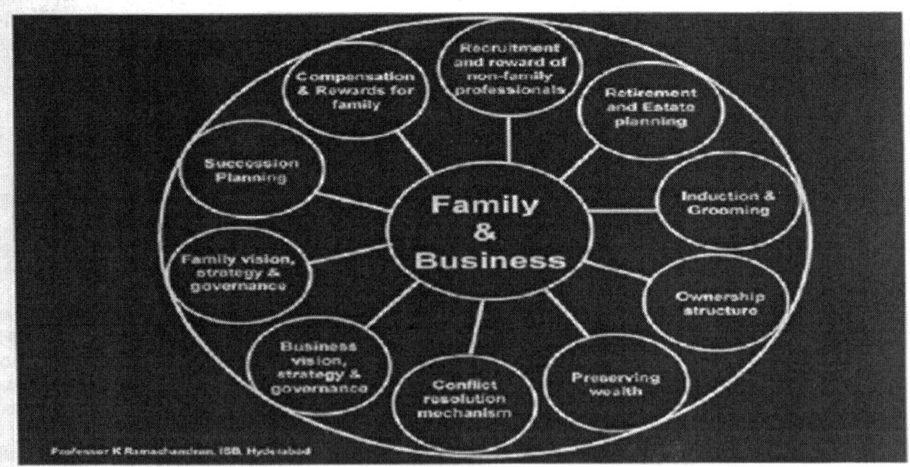


**Figure 2: Ten Commandments of Family Business**

## Concluding Remarks

There is evidence to believe that like family as a root-unit of social system, family business has also been the seedbed for business and industrial development all over the world including India. The greatest advantage of family business is that when it works right, nothing succeeds like a family business. It has contributed and will always contribute significantly in terms of production, employment, income, and exports of the economies. However, running of family business has not been so simple. It's successful running is so sensitive and complex that, as expressed in the Chinese proverb, it needs to be governed as one cooks a small fish – very gently. Evidences are galore to refer to confirm that the success or failure of family business depends on interrelationships, kinship relationship, role and place of family members, management succession, and family council /constitution. More favourable these key factors are, more are the chances for the success of family business and *vice versa.* Thus, family businesses need to strengthen themselves in these matters as quickly and effectively as possible.

## References


1. Anonymous (1996): *The Economist,* 9 March.
2. Anonymous (1997): India's Fifty Business Families, *Business Today,* 22 August.
3. Anonymous (1998): How to Avoid a Dysfunctional Family Business, *Business Week Enterprise,* March 2.
4. Brothers, P. (1996): Succession Plan Vital for Family Business, *The Cincinnati Enquirer,* December 19.
5. Carlock, R. S. and J. L. Ward (2001): *Strategic Planning for the Family Business: Parallel Planning to Unify the Family and Business,* Palgrave, New York.
6. Charan, R., S. Drotter and J. Noel (2001): *The Leadership Pipeline: How to Build the Leadership Powered Company,* Jossey-Bass, San Francisco.
7. Das, Gurucharan (1996): *Interview with Neeraj Bajaj,* 27 February.
8. Das, Gurucharan (1999): The Problem, *http//*www.india-seminar.com
9. Donnelley, R. G. (1964): The Family Business, *Harvard Business Review,* XLII, 4.
10. Dutta, Sudipt (1997): *Family Business in India,* Response Books, New Delhi.
11. Flaming, Quentin J. (2000): *Family Baggage Out of the Family Business,* Simon & Schuster.
12. Goode, W. J. (1982): *The Family* (Second Edition), Prentice-Hall, Upper saddle River.

13. Hoy, F. and T. G. Verser (1994): Emerging Business, Emerging Field:
14. Entrepreneurship and Family Firm, *Entrepreneurship Theory and Practice,* Fall.
15. Hunt, James and Wendy Handler (1999): The Practices of Effective Family Firm Leaders, *Journal of Developmental Entrepreneurship,* Volume 4, No. 2, Fall/Winter.
16. Kesler, G. (2002): Why the Leadership Bench Never gets Deeper: Ten Insights about Executive Talent Management, *People & Strategy,* Volume 25, Number 1.
17. Lee, J. (2004): The Effects of Family ownership and Management on Firm Performance, *S. A. M. Advanced Management Journal, Volume 69, Number 4.*
18. Litz, R.A. (1995): The Family Business: Toward Definitional Clarity, *Family Business Review,* 8 (2).
19. Mahler, W. and W. Wrightnour (1973): *Executive Continuity: How to Build and Regain an Effective Management Team,* Dow Jones-Irwin, Homewood II.
20. McCulloch, S. (2004): Economic Dominance Through Bloodliness, *Families in Business,* May-June, No. 14.
21. Piramal, Gita (1998): *Business Legends,* Viking, New Delhi.
22. Ramachandran, K. (2009): *Indian Family Businesses: Their Survival Beyond Three Generations,* Working Paper, Indian School of Business, Hyderabad.
23. Roy, Rajeev (2008): *Entrepreneurship*, Oxford University Press, New Delhi.
24. Sampath, D. (2001): *Inheriting the mantle-Management of Succession and Transition in Indian Family Business*, Response Books, New Delhi. Sue, Birley (1986): Succession in Family Firm: The Inheritor's View, *Journal of Small Business Management,* July.

# 6

# An Array of Environment for Intrapreneurship Development: An Empirical Study of Some Selected Companies in Lucknow, India

***Abstract***

The global economy is creating substantial changes for organizations and industries throughout the world. These changes make it necessary for business firms to carefully examine their purposes and to devote a great deal of attention to selecting strategies. These strategies pursue the levels of success that are highly probable to satisfy multiple stakeholders. In response to hyperglobalized changing economic environment, many established companies have restructured their operations in meaningful ways. This research gap induces the authors to undertake the present study. For primary data some companies have been selected randomly in Lucknow, India with the sample size of forty. We used the sophisticated statistical model Principal Component Analysis (PCA). Results of this analyzed study based on factor analysis, indicate the four important factors considered by the respondents when developing intrapreneurship such as: (1) Technically skilled labour force, (2) Layout of the organizations, (3) Knowledge of the market and (4) Availability of Secrecy.

## Introduction

The new century is seeing corporate strategies focused heavily on innovation. This new emphasis on entrepreneurial thinking developed during the entrepreneurial economy of the 1980s and 1990s. Today, a wealth of popular business literature describes a new "corporate revolution" taking place owing to the infusion of entrepreneurial thinking into large bureaucratic structures.

Continuous innovation (in terms of products, processes, and administrative routines and structures) and an ability to compete effectively in international markets are among the skills that are increasingly expected to influence corporate entrepreneurship which is envisioned to be a process that can facilitate firms' efforts to innovate constantly and cope effectively with the competitive realities that companies encounter when competing in international markets. Entrepreneurial attitudes and behaviors are necessary for firms of all sizes to improve and flourish in competitive environments. In recent years the subject of intrapreneurship has become quite popular, though very few people thoroughly understand the concept. Most researchers agree that the term refers to entrepreneurial activities that receive organizational sanction and resource commitments for the purpose of innovative results. Thc major thrust of intrapreneuring is to develop the entrepreneurial spirit within organizational boundaries, thus allowing an atmosphere of innovation to prosper.

## Literature Review

Many companies today realize the need for cooperate entrepreneuring. Articles in popular business magazines (Business Week, Fortune, Success, U.S. News and World Report) are reporting the infusion of entrepreneurial thinking into large bureaucratic structures. In fact, Peters (1997) devoted entire sections to innovation in the corporation. Quite obviously, business firms and consultants or authors are recognizing the need for in-house entrepreneurship. Pramodita and James (1999) defined corporate entrepreneurship as a process whereby an individual or a group of individuals, in associations with an existing organization, creates a new organization or instigates renewal or innovation within the organization. Under this definition, strategic renewal (which is concerned with organizational renewal involving major strategic and or structural changes), innovation (which is concerned with introducing something new to the market place), and corporate venturing (corporate entrepreneurial efforts that lead to the creation of new business organizations within the corporate organization) are all important and legitimate parts of the corporate entrepreneurial process.

Fariborz (1991) noted that corporate innovation is a very broad concept that includes the generation, development, and implementation of new ideas or behaviours. An innovation can be a new product or service, an administrative system, or a new plan or program pertaining to organizational members.

According to Burgelman (1983) the intrapreneurship approach to entrepreneurship advocates that innovation can be achieved in existing organizations by encouraging people to be entrepreneurial. Further, the entrepreneurial success depends upon the awareness and ability of key managers (Entrepreneurs) to explore and exploit the environmental opportunities.

On the other hand, Shaker (1991) observed that corporate entrepreneurship may be formal or informal activities aimed at creating new business in established companies through product and process innovations and market developments. These activities may take place at the corporate, division (business), functional, or project levels, with the unifying objective of improving a company's competitive position and financial performance. William and Ari (1990) have stressed that corporate entrepreneurship encompasses two major phenomena such as: (1) new venture creation without existing organizations and (2) the transformation of organizations through strategic renewal. Cunningham and Lischeron (1991) attempted to give key people freedom to think them as entrepreneurs. Hence, intrapreneurship is a “Team” model whereby individuals asked to work together in solving problems and creating opportunities.

Based on the literature reviews, various studies have been done, and it is clearly revealed that a detailed study has not yet been conducted in Indian context, especially in Intrapreneurship development. This research gap determined the authors to undertake the present study.

The *objectives* of the research are as follows:

1. To examine necessary factors for the favourable environment for intrapreneurial development.
2. To identify the factors which are determinant of favourable environment for entrepreneurial development?

## Material and Methods

### Sampling Design

The sample for this study consisted of companies in Lucknow city in India. A purposive sampling technique was used to select the organizations. Initially researchers identified forty companies, then, decided to distribute questionnaires among each company to the Managing director.

### Data Collection

Primary and secondary data was used for the study. Primary data was collected through the written questionnaire following direct personal interviewing technique. The secondary data was gathered from journals, books, magazines, etc.

### Measures

The questionnaire was administered among managing directors in companies. The questionnaire was designed by the researchers as a seven item scale from strong disagreement (-3) to strong agreement (+3) adopted to identify key favorable environment indicators. In this study, "Factor Analysis" model (*Principal Component Varimax Roated Factor Analysis Method*) has been used to group the indicators. Final ranking of the indicators has been made on the basis of mean scores.

## Results and Discussions

To identify underlying potential dimensions of the key favourable environment for intrapreneurship development used in the current study, responses of the participants were subjected to *factor analysis method.* Before applying factor analysis, testing of the reliability of the scale is very important as it shows the extent to which a scale produces consistent results if measurements are made repeatedly. This is done by determining the association in between scores obtained from different administrations of the sale. If the association is high, the scale yields consistent result, thus it is reliable. *Cronbach's Alpha Scale* is the most widely used method. It may be mentioned that its value varies from 0 to 1 but, satisfactory value is required to be more than 0.6 for the scale to be reliable (Malhotra, 2002; Cronbach, 1951). In the present study, we, therefore, used Cronbach's alpha scale as a measure if reliability. Its value is estimated to be 0.898. If we compare our reliability value with the standard value alpha of 0.6 advocated by Cronbach (1951), a more accurate recommendation Nunnally and Bernstein (1994) or with the standard value of 0.6 as recommended by Bagozzi and Yi's (1988) we find that the scales used by us are highly reliable for data analysis.

After checking the reliability of scale, we tested whether the data so collected is appropriate for factor analysis or not.

The appropriateness of factor analysis is dependent upon the sample size. In this connection, *Kaiser – Meyer- Olkin (KMO)* measurement of sampling adequacy is still another useful method to show the appropriateness of data for factor analysis. The KMO statistics varies between 0 and 1. Kasier (1974) recommends that values greater than 0.5 are acceptable. Between 0.5 and 0.7 are mediocre, between 0.7 and 0.8 are good, between 0.8 and 0.9 are superb (Field, 2000). In this study, the value of KMO for overall matrix is 0.756 (For details please see table 1), thereby indicating that the sample taken to process the factor analysis is statistically significant.

**Table 1. Kaiser - Meyer- Olkin (KMO) Bartlett's Test**

| | | |
|---|---|---|
| Kaiser-Meyer-Olkin Measure of Sampling Adequacy. | | .756 |
| **Bartlett's Test of Sphericity** | Approx. Chi-Square | 358.123 |
| | df | .120 |
| | Sig. | .000 |

*Source: survey data*

Bartlett's test of Sphericity (Barlett, 1950) is the third statistical test applied in the study for verifying its appropriateness. This test should be significant i.e., having a significance value less than 0.5. In the present study, test value of Chi – Square 358.123 is significant (as also given in Table 1) indicating that the data is appropriate for the factor analysis.

After examining the reliability of the scale and testing appropriateness of data as above, we next carried out factor analysis to identify the key favourable for intrapreneurship development. In order to do this, we employed *Principal Component Analysis (PCA)* followed by the *Varimax Rotation, (Generally, researchers' recommend as Varimax).* Statistical Package for Social Science (SPSS) software (version 13.0) was used for this purpose. Four variables were extracted from the analysis with an Eigen value greater than 1, which explained 69.091 percent of the total variance (For details please see Table-2).

**Table 2. Total Variance Explained**

| Component | Initial Eigen Values | | | Extraction Sums of Squared Loadings | | |
|---|---|---|---|---|---|---|
| | Total | % of Variance | Cumulative | % Total | % of Variance | Cumulative % |
| 1 | 6.658 | 41.610 | 41.610 | 6.658 | 41.610 | 41.610 |
| 2 | 2.113 | 13.207 | 54.817 | 2.113 | 13.207 | 54.817 |
| 3 | 1.249 | 7.809 | 62.626 | 1.249 | 7.809 | 62.626 |
| 4 | 1.034 | 6.465 | 69.091 | 1.034 | 6.465 | 69.091 |
| 5 | .917 | 5.732 | 74.823 | | | |
| 6 | .813 | 5.082 | 79.905 | | | |
| 7 | .639 | 3.996 | 83.901 | | | |
| 8 | .588 | 3.672 | 87.573 | | | |
| 9 | .529 | 3.307 | 90.880 | | | |
| 10 | .387 | 2.421 | 93.301 | | | |
| 11 | .295 | 1.844 | 95.146 | | | |
| 12 | .245 | 1.529 | 96.674 | | | |
| 13 | .193 | 1.207 | 97.881 | | | |
| 14 | .157 | .983 | 98.864 | | | |
| 15 | .107 | .666 | 99.531 | | | |
| 16 | .075 | .469 | 100.000 | | | |

*Source: survey data*

## Extraction Method: Principal Component Analysis

One method to reduce the number of factors to something below that found by using the *"eigen-value greater than unity"* rule is to apply the *Scree Test* (Cattell, 1966). In this test, eigen-values are plotted against the factors arranged in descending order along the X-axis. The number of factors that correspond to the point at which the function, so produced, appears to change slope, is deemed to be the number of useful factors extracted. This is a somewhat arbitrary procedure. Its application to this data set led to the conclusion that the first four factors should be accepted. Within this solution, Factor 1 had fourteen items with their primary loading on that factor, one item and two items had their primary loading on Factor 2 and Factor 3 respectively, but Factor 4 did not contain any primary loading.

It is worth mentioning out here that factor loading greater than 0.30 is considered significant. 0.40 is considered more important and 0.50 or greater is considered very significant. The rotated (Varimax) component loadings for the four components (factors) are presented in Table 3. For parsimony, only those factors with loadings above 0.50 were considered significant (Pal, 1986; Pal and Bagi, 1987; Hair, Anderson, Tatham, and Black, 2003).

**Table 3. Principal Component Analysis - Varimax Rotation Factors of favorable environment for Intrapreneurship development**

| Indicators | Indicators | | | |
|---|---|---|---|---|
| | Factor- I | Factor- II | Factor- III | Factor-IV |
| Layout of the organization | .853 | | | |
| Intrapreneurial participants | .805 | | | |
| New project meetings | .743 | | | |
| Informal communication | .613 | | | |
| Mentality of the employees | .556 | | | |
| Knowledge of the market | | .807 | | |
| Encouraging the actions | | .725 | | |
| Reward of the personnel | | .616 | | |
| Team work | | .556 | | .523 |
| Availability of the Secrecy | | | .793 | |
| Innovative ideas | | | .719 | |
| Environment for creativity and diversity | | .573 | .609 | |
| Identification of the potential entrepreneurs | | | .568 | |
| Technically skilled labour force | | | | .824 |
| Sponsoring the intrapreneurial projects | | | | .701 |
| Taking actions | .528 | | | .533 |
| **% of Variance** | **41.610** | **13.207** | **7.809** | **6.465** |
| **Cumulative percentage of %** | **41.610** | **54.817** | **62.626** | **69.091** |

*Source: survey data*

**Factor-I: Layout of the Organizations –** This factor was represented by five variables with factor loadings ranging from .853 to .556. These were: layout of the organization, intrapreneurial participants, new project meetings, informal communication, and mentality of the employees. This competency accounted for 41.610% of the rated variance.

**Factor-II: Knowledge of the Market** – Four variables with loadings ranging from .807 to .556 belonged to this factor and they included knowledge of the market, encouraging the actions, reward of the personnel and team work. Furthermore, although the variable "team work" was loaded fairly high on Factor-IV as well, because of its higher loading and greater relevance it was also included in this factor. This factor explained 13.207% of the rated variance.

**Factor-III: Availability of Secrecy** – This factor comprised four variables, namely: the availability of secrecy, innovative ideas, environment for creativity and diversity and identification of potential entrepreneurs. Factor loadings of these variables ranged from .793 to .568. Although the variable "environment for creativity and diversity" was correlated fairly high with Factor-II as well, considering its higher loading and importance it was included in Factor-III. A variance of 7.809% was explained by this factor.

**Factor-IV: Technically skilled Labour Force** – This last factor consisted of three variables relating to the technically skilled labour force. These were: the technically skilled labour force, sponsoring the intrapreneural projects and taking actions. Their factor loadings ranged from .824 to .533. The variance explained by this factor amounted to 6.465%. Furthermore, although the variable "taking actions" was loaded fairly high on Factor I as well, because of its higher loading and greater relevance it was also included in this factor.

Ranking of the above four factors in order of their importance, along with mean, is shown in *Table-4*. The importance of these factors, as perceived by the respondents, has been ranked on the basis of their mean values.

**Table 4. Ranking of Factors according to their Importance**

| Factors | No. of. Variables | Mean | Rank |
|---|---|---|---|
| Factor 1: Layout of the Organizations | 05 | 2.60 | 2 |
| Factor II: Knowledge of the Market | 04 | 2.28 | 3 |
| Factor III: Availability of Secrecy | 04 | 2.23 | 4 |
| Factor IV: Technically skilled Labour Force | 03 | 2.73 | 1 |

*Source: Survey data*

*According to table 4, the ranking evinced the following order:* (1) technically skilled labour force, (2) Layout of the organizations, (3) Knowledge of the market, (4) Availability of Secrecy from 2.73 to 2.23.

## Conclusion

Through an empirical investigation, this study has identified four factors as key favorable environment for intrapreneurship development which is determined in companies based at Luknow (India). The dominant factors are: (1) Technically skilled labour force; (2) Layout of the organizations; (3) Knowledge of the market and; (4) Availability of Secrecy.

## References

1. Bartellet,M.S., *Tests of Significance in Factor Analysis*, British Journal of Statistical Psychology, 1998 Vol. 3, pp. 77-85.
2. Bhatnagar R. P., Kumar Y., *On the Evaluation of Structural Equation Models*, Journal of the Academy of Marketing Science, 1998, Vol.16 (1), pp.74-95.
3. Bansal , R.A., *Corporate Entrepreneurship and Strategic Management: Insights from a Process Study*, Management Science, 1983, Vol. 29, pp. 1349-1364.
4. Cattell,R.B., *The scree test for the number of factors*, Multivariate Behavioural Research, 1986, Vol 1, pp. 245-276.
5. Cronbach,L.J., *Coefficient Alpha and the Internal Structure of tests* , Psychometrik*a*, 1991, Vol. 6(3), pp. 297-334.
6. Chopra,J.B., Mathews , J., *Defining Entrepreneurship*, Journal of Small Business Management, *1991, Vol.* 29 (1), pp. 44 – 61.
7. Firdaus , D., *Organisational Innovation*: A Meta Analysis of Determinant and Moderator, Academy of Management Journal, 1991, Vol. 34,pp. 355- 390.
8. Field,A., *Discovering Statistics Using SPSS for Windows*, 2000,Sage Publications, London.
9. Hair,J. et al. *Multivariate Data Analysis*, Pearson Education, Delhi, 5e, 2003.
10. Kaiser,H.F., *An Index of Factoral Simplicity*, Psychometrica, 1974, Vol. 39, pp. 31-36.
11. Malhotra,N.K. Marketing Research: An Applied Orientation, 2000, Pearson Education Asia, New Delhi, India, 3rd edition.
12. Nunnally , J. C., Bernstein. *Ira Psychometrics Theory*, 1994, McGraw – Hill, New York.
13. Pal,Y.A., *Theoretical study of Some Factor Analysis Problems* and

Pal,Y. and Bagai, O.P.A *Common Factor Bettery Reliability Approach to Determine the Number of Interpretable Factors*, a paper presented at the IX Annual Conference of the Indian Society for Probability and Statistics held at Delhi, University of Delhi, India, 1986, 1987.

14. Peters,T., *Liberation Management, 1997,* New York: Alfred A. Knopf, 1992); and Tom peters, The Circle of Innovation, New York: Alfred A. Knopf.
15. Pramodita,S.,James,J.C., Toward a Reconciliation of the Definitional Issues in the Field of Corporate Entrepreneurship. Entrepreneurship Theory and Practice, 1999, pp. 11-28.
16. Shaker,A.Z., *Predictors and Financial Outcomes of Corporate Entrepreneurship*: An Exploratory Study, *Journal of Business Venturing,1991, Vol.* 6, pp. 259-286.
17. William,D.G., Aniket G., *Corporate Entrepreneurship,* strategic *Management Journal (special issue),1990, Vol.* 11, pp. 5-15.

# 7

# Trends in Youth Entrepreneurial Orientation and Perception in Degree Level Colleges in Nagaland

***Abstract***

Attitude towards entrepreneur, entrepreneurial activity and its social functions are determinant factors for college students to decide upon an entrepreneurial career. According to existing literature identifying entrepreneurial intention in students' mindset bears uncertainty and yet remains a mystery in entrepreneurial research. Therefore the paper addresses explanation of students' attitudes, orientation and intention towards entrepreneurship, their personal characteristics and future plans in connection with entrepreneurship as their career choice.

## Introduction

In an economy where employability in government jobs and public sector units have reached a saturation point, choosing a career on entrepreneurship is an emerging alternative solution of unemployment problem confronted by thousands of students graduating every year in the country. Entrepreneurship offers a viable option for job creation in the market. Research on youth entrepreneurship addresses some of the socio-psychological problems and delinquency that arise from joblessness and promotes innovation in youth.

However, despite this attention, there has been no systematic attempt to look at it from a youth angle. Nagaland, one of the North Eastern states of India is plagued by insurgency and backwardness faring low in economic development parameters. Despite being resource rich with flora and fauna, tribal handlooms and handicrafts, artefacts, forest resources and tourist attractions, it remains underdeveloped. With a registered unemployment of 54,045 in December, 2009-10 (Annual Administrative Report) 1 in Nagaland, this issue is assuming rapid dimensions taking a toll on the economy. The pilot study substantiates the claim that people are inclined towards government sector jobs and there are few takers for entrepreneurship. The reason for the choice remains unclear. The current research focuses on such deviations from student standpoint. Recently, Nagaland has shown good growth of young entrepreneurs. Does that affect the young students? It seeks to find their future plans in case they start business, the kind of business activity they will be interested; the factors that impacts on student mindset on entrepreneurial intentions; problems young entrepreneurs encounter to set up business, etc. To get to the root of the problem of lack of entrepreneurial intentions among the Naga youth, the study tries to explain whether there exist some correlations between the streams they undertake and their intentions on choosing a career. Various studies conducted in developed and developing country (also see GEM report on women entrepreneurs) establishes asymmetric gendered relationship. Taking a cue, one of the research questions posed was to test the differences in male and female student entrepreneurial intentions and judge differences if any. Organizations catering to the North East like the Indian Institute of Entrepreneurship (IIE), Micro Small and Medium Industries Institute (formerly SISI), North Eastern Council (NEC) and North East Development Finance Corporation (NEDFi) supports and sponsors entrepreneurial endeavour. In spite of the support system, the intention rests at the minimum level. Another puzzle that often has repercussions in the entrepreneurial parlance is the primary “born or made” question and whether training or education affects student intention. This paper examines the association between streams and the resultant choice of the entrepreneurial vocation.

It is often disputed that entrepreneurship is inborn and there are certain communities that has acquired talent in risk taking, uncertainty bearing and innovation. Schumpeter (1934) has argued that entrepreneurship and innovation are interdependent. Creativity and innovation drives entrepreneurship followed by idea generation. Authors have agreed that there are primary responses and instinct inherent in an entrepreneur. In India, it is observed that Marwaris, Parsees and Gujaratis have survived the vagaries of entrepreneurship and acquired name in individual and corporate entrepreneurship globally. However in the North Eastern region of which Nagaland is a state fails to adhere to the theory. The people seldom respond and react to the wide opportunities offered to them by the state or nature. In this context, it is thought opportune to conduct research on the young students on the verge of passing out from the educational institutions to judge their mindset on the entrepreneurial intentions. The study also examines their inclination if any, on any specific business activities. Entrepreneurship is in fact a multidisciplinary combination of explanations to obscure and unknown behaviour in individuals. It usually adheres to a socio economic and socio psychological construct to explain complex entrepreneurial intentions.

## Hypotheses

H1: There is no significant difference between students from different stream on entrepreneurship as a career.

H2: There is no significant difference between gender and their perception of entrepreneurship as a career.

H3: There is no significant difference between students in their inclination towards specific business activities stream wise.

## Methodology

The study is empirical and descriptive based on primary data collected from college students in Dimapur, Nagaland. Dimapur district forms the universe of the sample size since it represents the whole of Nagaland because of the increasing economic development and also is its commercial centre (Dimapur Municipal Council2). A structured questionnaire consisting of 20 item-wise questions specially designed to examine their socio economic and socio psychological mindset in their entrepreneurial orientation and perception.

Sample includes students currently enrolled in degree final year of arts, science and commerce streams. Initially, a pilot study was undertaken in a college with students both from commerce and arts stream. For the current study, 104 students from 7 out of 16 colleges were selected in

Dimapur district, out of which 9 questionnaires were rejected due to inconsistency in result. 95 student respondents were selected, (Arts-29, Commerce-39, Science-32) based on stratified and simple random sampling method. The female and male students formed two strata and sample selected is simple random method designed to meet the objectives of the study. In the questionnaire, close and open ended as well as multiple choice questions with ranking systems were designed. Simple statistical tools of average, percentages, comparisons and cross tabulation are used to analyze the data. To test the hypothesis, the non parametric Chi Square (X2 ) test is used. Analyses are made based on using cross tabulations. For rank, dichotomous scale is used.

## Review of literature

Youth entrepreneurship has been viewed by educators and employers as an alternative means for acquiring skills and attitudes necessary for entering the workforce (Tweeten, 1992; Bishop, 1991). (Sexton and Bowman-Upton 1991). Entrepreneurship is the process of identifying opportunities, gathering resources, and exploiting these opportunities through action. Entrepreneurship development has made a positive impact on economic development in any type of economy. Lately, young educated students are taking much interest on entrepreneurship development. Various researches are taking place to study the factors what contributes a person to pursue entrepreneurship. Kolvereid, ystein Moen, (1997) compares the behaviour of business graduates with a major in entrepreneurship and graduates with other majors from a Norwegian business school. The results indicate that graduates with an entrepreneurship major are more likely to start new businesses and have stronger entrepreneurial intentions than other graduates. Clement K Wong & Poh-Kam Wong (2004) a comprehensive study on the attitudes of undergraduates toward entrepreneurship in Asia. High level of interest, inadequate business knowledge and perceived risk were found to be significant deterrents. Dell Mcstay,(2008) made a quasi-experimental research showing that exposure to entrepreneurship education has a positive effect on students' self-employment intentions and that universities are in a position to shape and foster entrepreneurial intentions. ( Rajendran2007) In a study with 62 students studying in B.com final year, M.com first year and M.com final year in J.N.R. Mahavidyalaya, Port Blair.

Majority students preferred job as a career option. 94% of the students' respondents preferred entrepreneurship as a career because of business background. Levenburg and Schwarz (2008) made a study with 142 business students in India and US to find out the impact of culture, education and environment on entrepreneurship among the youth. In recent years, Indian students seem to have significantly higher level of interest in starting new ventures than their US counterparts. Gerry, Marques and Nogueira (2008) Exploratory study, with a sample of 640 undergraduates regarding their future employment preferences; particularly establishing their own enterprise.

"Gender, risk, factors related to profession/employment choice and academic training were found to significantly affect students' interest in and motivation for starting their own business." Volkman and Tokarski(2009) on student attitudes to entrepreneurship investigates the image which university students have of entrepreneurs and entrepreneurship, which looks at the situation in Germany, Romania, Latvia, Italy and Austria. Significant differences but also have common features to the image of entrepreneurship and attitudes in the five countries. Bhandari (2006) A study with Faculty of Commerce and Management Studies at Jai Narain Vyas University, Jodhpur, India on what they intended to do upon completion of their college education: start their own business (become entrepreneurs) or work for someone else. Results of factor analysis, six variables (to lead other people, to be my own boss, to put my innovative ideas into practice, determination, personal challenge and nonbusiness education) were found to relate to the dependent variable. Bureau report, Zee News Limited (2006) Interviewing a reputed NGO in Nagaland called Entrepreneurs Associates and some officials of NEDFi reported that it is not only the state government but the educated unemployed who have realized that opportunity in public sector have reached saturation point in Nagaland and the only alternative is entrepreneurship development among the Nagas who depends on non-Nagas for all forms of business and trade. (Spors, 2007) A case study on few Universities in US about giving importance on entrepreneurship to the college students concluded that many are bolstering their courses and extracurricular activities for aspiring entrepreneurs and helping students create business before graduation. (Khanka 2007) Opting for self-employment career requires some specific traits like risk taking attitude, achieving attitude, enterprising, hardworking; a course on entrepreneurship development... at the secondary level was considered relevant to prepare students for self employment and to become an entrepreneur. (Kamaraj and Muralidaran 2005) With liberalization and global competition being the governing societal paradigm, the concept of young entrepreneurs is receiving closer attention from government and society. "The existing curriculum does not prepare the students to opt for self-employment and entrepreneurial career."(Upadhyaya 2006) So what are those entry barriers in entrepreneurship ...root cause of entrepreneurship development? Perception of youth towards entrepreneurship as career option... lack of policy framework and strategy to create enabling environment for entrepreneurship...If, in case they take up, what kind of business activity would they prefer to pursue. Culture that is positive towards entrepreneurship- reflects in social acceptance of entrepreneurial careers, respect for new business success and positive media coverage-tends to increase participation in starts-ups" (GEM, 2003). In Naga culture, entrepreneurship is a new phenomena and it is notable that, younger generations are creating a positive environment for entrepreneurship. (Chizokho Vero, Eastern Mirror, 2006). "Colleges used to ignore their student's business aspirations. Now, they are trying to nurture them". (Spors, 2007). (Venesaar , Kolbre and Piliste 2006) made a study on students' attitudes based on their own opinions about motivations to start in business, the statements about their entrepreneurial characteristics and behavioral habits connected with business relations and organizations the research results showed most of them do not want to start business after graduation, but postpone this to a more distant future.

From the above literature we get to see that this type of research has been done in India as well as abroad, but mostly on commerce or business students. The uniqueness of this study is that it attempts to compare entrepreneurial intentions with different study streams in student's decision to become entrepreneurs and also compare the interest towards entrepreneurship between male and female students. It also seeks to make gender wise comparison of different business activities they would like to venture upon. Nowadays, many institutions are offering more entrepreneurship programs to motivate and equip students to become successful entrepreneurs. An effort is made to study as to whether the students are interested to have such basic business courses in their degree curriculum. What would be the reason to prefer entrepreneurship as a career and factors that influence to take up business? Gry A. Alsos, Espen J. Isaksen & Erika Søfting,(2006) study based on "Ajzen's (1991) theory of planned behaviour to explore the influence of experience from youth enterprises on entrepreneurial intentions among upper secondary pupils. Pupils with such experience were found to be associated with more positive attitude to entrepreneurship, more positive subjective norm related to entrepreneurship as well as stronger perceived behavioural control, than pupils without such experiences."

## Testing of Hypothesis

H1: There is no significant difference between students from different stream.

*Table 1*

*Students' future plan and Stream of Study*

| Stream of study | | Future Plan | | | | | Total |
|---|---|---|---|---|---|---|---|
| | | Business | Job | Further Study | Get Job & then study | Furtherstudy & then business | |
| Arts | Count | 0 | 8 | 14 | 2 | 0 | 24 |
| | % within stream of study | 0.0% | 33.3% | 58.3% | 8.3% | 0.0% | 100.0% |
| | % of future plan | 0.0% | 47.1% | 37.8% | 14.3% | 0.0% | 25.3% |
| | % of total | 0.0% | 8.4% | 14.7% | 2.1% | 0.0% | 25.3% |
| Commerce | Count | 6 | 2 | 10 | 8 | 13 | 39 |
| | % within stream of study | 15.4% | 5.1% | 25.6% | 20.5% | 33.3% | 100.0% |
| | % of future plan | 60.0% | 11.8% | 27.0% | 57.1% | 76.5% | 41.1% |
| | % of total | 6.3% | 2.1% | 10.5% | 8.4% | 13.7% | 41.1% |
| Science | Count | 4 | 7 | 13 | 4 | 4 | 32 |
| | % within stream of study | 12.5% | 21.9% | 40.6% | 12.5% | 12.5% | 100.0% |
| | % of future plan | 40.0% | 41.2% | 35.1% | 28.6% | 23.5% | 33.7% |
| | % of total | 4.2% | 7.4% | 13.7% | 4.2% | 4.2% | 33.7% |
| Total | Count | 10 | 17 | 37 | 14 | 17 | 95 |
| | % within stream of study | 10.5% | 17.9% | 38.9% | 14.7% | 17.9% | 100.0% |
| | % of future plan | 100.0% | 100.0% | 100.0% | 100.0% | 100.0% | 100.0% |
| | % of total | 10.5% | 17.9% | 38.9% | 14.7% | 17.9% | 100.0% |

*Source - Independent field survey 2009*

H2: There is no significant difference between gender and entrepreneur as a career.

**Hypothesis1**: The calculated value of Chi Square is higher than the significance value (see appendix I.a). Therefore the null hypothesis is rejected and it is concluded that there is a significant difference between students from different stream in taking up entrepreneurship as a career. From Table 1 we have observed that students are not keen to take up

*Table 2*

*Students' future plan Gender-wise*

| Gender | | Future Plan | | | | | |
|---|---|---|---|---|---|---|---|
| | | Business | Job | Further Study | Get job & then study | Further study & then business | Total |
| Female | Count | 3 | 10 | 19 | 9 | 10 | 51 |
| | % within Gender | 5.9% | 19.6% | 37.3% | 17.6% | 19.6% | 100.0% |
| | % within Future Plan | 30.0% | 58.8% | 51.4% | 64.3% | 58.8% | 53.7% |
| | % of Total | 3.2% | 10.5% | 20.0% | 9.5% | 10.5% | 53.7% |
| Male | Count | 7 | 7 | 18 | 5 | 7 | 44 |
| | % within Gender | 15.9% | 15.9% | 40.9% | 11.4% | 15.9% | 100.0% |
| | % within Future Plan | 70.0% | 41.2% | 48.6% | 35.7% | 41.2% | 46.3% |
| | % of Total | 7.4% | 7.4% | 18.9% | 5.3% | 7.4% | 46.3% |
| Total | Count | 10 | 17 | 37 | 14 | 17 | 95 |
| | % within Gender | 10.5% | 17.9% | 38.9% | 14.7% | 17.9% | 100.0% |
| | % within Future Plan | 100.0% | 100.0% | 100.0% | 100.0% | 100.0% | 100.0% |
| | % of Total | 10.5% | 17.9% | 38.9% | 14.7% | 17.9% | 100.0% |

*Source: Independent field survey 2009*

entrepreneurship after their graduation as most of the students plan to go for higher studies. Stream wise, commerce students show higher percentage of taking up business in future, than science or arts students. Thus, there is a relationship between study stream and a person's intention to start a business in future or to pursue it after graduation.

**Hypothesis2**: The calculated value of Chi Square is higher than the significance value (see appendix I.b). Therefore the null hypothesis is rejected and it is concluded that there is a significant difference between male and female in taking up entrepreneurship as a career. Male student respondents are more interested than the female counterpart in choosing entrepreneurship as a career and to start business. During the course of questionnaire it was also seen that female students were reluctant and hesitant to fill up the questionnaire.

**Hypohesis3**: There is a significant difference between students in their inclination towards specific business activities stream wise (see appendix 1.e). Gender wise the differences is comparably less.

## Analysis and Interpretation

### Students on becoming entrepreneur:

From Table 3 it is observed that commerce student respondents are more interested to become entrepreneurs in future with the percentage as high as 82.1% and 45.8%, 68.8% respectively for arts and science students respondent. However, overall the scenario is not bad as, 68% of the respondents elicited positive response. Secondly, when asked about their future plan after finishing their degree, 48.7% of the commerce respondents wanted to be in business or to continue their studies and later be involved in it. Whereas, 100% of the arts students were not interested on taking up entrepreneurship when given a choice to what they plan to do right after their degree, most of them were either interested in opting for jobs or for further study. The science respondents showed 25% positive response on taking up entrepreneurship. It is seen that students are interested on taking up entrepreneurship (as per Chi-square test in appendix I. c) as career if given proper motivation and guidance, which is not possible unless the environment is positive on entrepreneurship for young graduates. From

*Table 3*

*Students interest on entrepreenurship with stream of study*

| | | Stream of study | | | Total |
|---|---|---|---|---|---|
| Interest | | Arts | Commerce | Science | |
| No | Count<br>% of Total | 13<br>13.7% | 7<br>7.4% | 10<br>10.5% | 30<br>68.4% |
| Yes | Count<br>% of Total | 11<br>11.6% | 32<br>33.7% | 22<br>23.2% | 65<br>68.4% |
| Total | Count<br>% of Total | 24<br>25.3% | 39<br>41.1% | 32<br>33.7% | 95<br>100.0% |

*Source: Independent field survey,2009*

the kind of environment how they are been brought up from home, school, culture, society, government policy and the perception on entrepreneurship.

## Future plan after the degree course

Most of the students after graduation wanted to go for further studies, (See Table 1 and Chart 1) the figure as high as 38.9%, for jobs-17.9%, business-10.5%, get job and study- 14.7%, further study and then business-17.9%. As for commerce students because of their study curriculum having entrepreneurship as a subject they are more open to the idea of business as career then the other two streams. It is also observed that Commerce student respondent had more business background with 40.2% then Science-33% and arts-24.7%, which leads to the question that parent's occupation, have direct or indirect impact on students choosing their career.

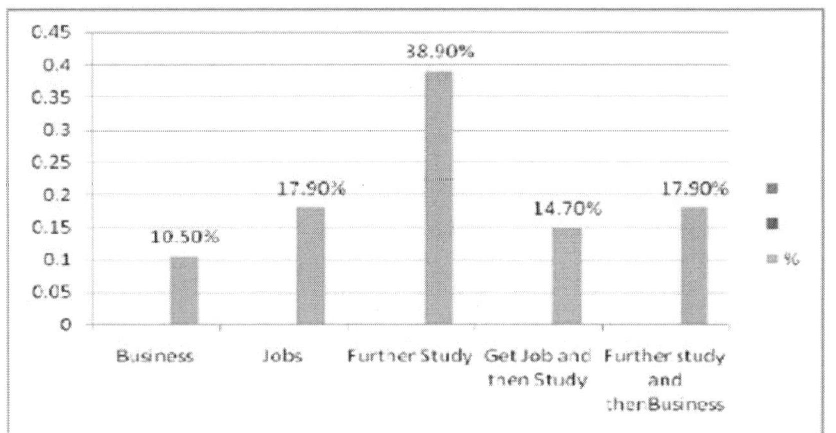


Chart 1: Students future plans after degree course.

## Gender and entrepreneur

Gender wise, the percentage is high on their interest in becoming entrepreneurs 68.4% and 31.6% for male and female respectively (See Table 4).Gender wise, it was observed that male and female decision did not differ much on choosing business activity, though both male and female tend to reject certain businesses- like none of the male respondents choose boutique as an option or female on choosing meat business and motor parts. The Chi-square test also proves that both male and female students are interested to take up entrepreneurship in Appendix I.d.

Results of preferences (out of 21- listed) are:

| | |
|---|---|
| 1st preference | Female (Import and Export-22%) |
| | Male (Import and Export- 34.7%) |
| 2nd preference | Female (Boutique- 16%) |
| | Male (Restaurant-15.9%) |
| 3rd preference | Female (Restaurant – 14% &Clothing- 14%) |
| | Male (Resort/ Hotel- 13.6%) |
| 4th preference | Female (Travelling Agency- 16%, Shopping Malls- 16%) |
| | Male (Agricultural Products – 15.9%) |

*Table 4*

*Students' interest on entrepreneurship gender-wise*

| Interest | | Gender | | Total |
|---|---|---|---|---|
| | | Female | Male | |
| No | Count<br>% of | 20<br>21.1% | 10<br>10.5% | 30<br>31.6% |
| Yes | Count<br>% of | 31<br>32.6% | 34<br>35.8% | 65<br>68.4% |
| Total | Count<br>% of | 51<br>53.7% | 44<br>46.3% | 95<br>100.0% |

**Student and Basic Business Course**

Student respondents from all streams on their response on whether they wish to have a basic business course is high as shown in table 5 with, Don't know- 20.6%; No- 10.3% and Yes- 66.00%. This indicates that majority of the students would want to have such course in their degree curriculum and hence education institution and government should encourage such subject and programs for the under graduate students.

*Table 5*

*Students' wish to have a basic business course*

| Wish to have a basic business course | | Stream of Study | | | Total |
|---|---|---|---|---|---|
| | | Arts | Commerce | Science | |
| Don't know | Count | 8 | 4 | 8 | 20 |
| | % of Total | 8.5% | 4.3% | 8.5% | 21.3% |
| No | Count | 3 | 4 | 3 | 10 |
| | % of Total | 3.2% | 4.3% | 3.2% | 10.6% |
| Yes | Count | 13 | 31 | 20 | 64 |
| | % of Total | 13.8% | 33.0% | 21.3% | 68.1% |
| Total | Count | 24 | 39 | 31 | 94 |
| | % of Total | 25.5% | 41.5% | 33.0% | 100.0% |

*Source: Independent field survey 2009*

## Students' view on entrepreneurship related problems

Out of the 10 listed problems given in the questionnaire which young entrepreneurs face, the highest ranking four are:

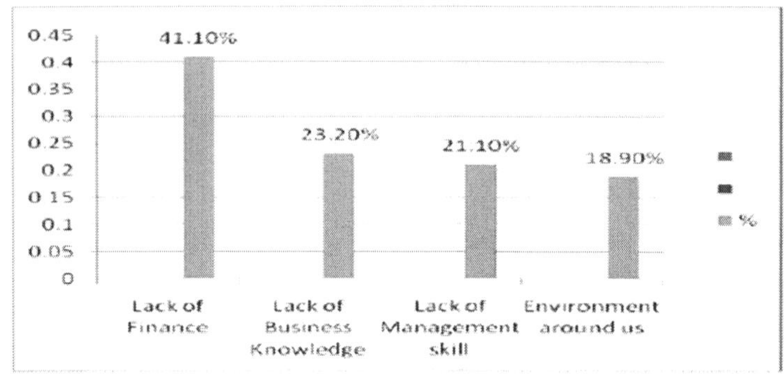


Chart 2: Students view on problems faced by young entrepreneurs

### Students view on factors determining to become entrepreneur

Among the factors mentioned (see table 6), having a business background showed greater influence in determining a person to become entrepreneur the reason would be the experience gained by their parents are percolated down and also it is easier to continue an existing business then to start a new enterprise. The next factor close to that are those who are interested and want achievement in life. These are kind of people who are more challenging and are ready to take a step further. Then the next significant factor is those who want to be master and work on their own terms. Here, it is observed that person determining to be entrepreneur wants to be independent and does not like to work under anybody. Other factors did not have much importance and were considered insignificant for analysis.

*Table 6*

*Factors determioning students to become entrepenuers*

| Factors | % |
|---|---|
| Having a business background | 30.8 |
| They are interested and want achievement | 27.6 |
| Wants to be master and work on their own ter | 23.4 |
| Parents influence and support | 8.5 |
| Having a wealthy family | 5.4 |
| Resort when Government jobs fail | 4.3 |

## Students' Opinion

From Table 7 it can be concluded that unemployment problem can be solved because entrepreneurs employ oneself and others too, which also helps in removing unemployment in the society. There is also a culture difference where government job is considered more superior than business and as such people remain unemployed in search of job. In Nagaland, entrepreneurship is a new concept and during the last few years it has witnessed fresh graduates starting business enterprise taking entrepreneurship to another level. The top 4 respondents' opinion on the basis of 8 listed according to the rank are:

## Students' Recommendations and suggestions

Among the 9 listed Recommendations and suggestions, the highest ranking 4 are:

*Table 7*

*Students' view on entrepreneurship*

| Rank | Opinion | % |
|---|---|---|
| 1st | Entrepreneurs employs oneself and others too | 33.6 |
| 2nd | Help in removing unemployment problem in our society | 29.8 |
| 3rd | Instead of being unemployed searching for government jobs employing oneself is more productive | 18.1 |
| 4th | Entreprenuership is relatively a new subject and as such young people are afraid to venture into it | 18.5 |

*Table 8*

*Students' recommendation and suggestions*

| Rank | Reccomendation and suggestions | % |
|---|---|---|
| 1st | Government should encourage the young entreprenuers by providing grants and financial help | 36.3 |
| 2nd | Training on entreprenuership and strategic management should be organised to motivate youth | 22.3 |
| 3rd | Banks shoul provide loans at low interest to aspiring entreprenuers | 21.3 |
| 4th | Parents should encourage their children when they show interest in being an entreprenuer | 20.1 |

There is a huge scope for entrepreneurship development if the government takes some steps to encourage the young aspiring entrepreneurs by giving some incentives, proper training and programs to motivate the youth. Many a time, young people do not take up business due to financial problems and getting a bank loan becomes difficult and hard. On the other side, most of the parents in Nagaland do not prefer their children to opt for business which is evident that most of the trade are owned and run by other non-Naga communities. For some parents, they are hesitant to support entrepreneurial activities of their children financially for the risk and uncertainty involved in it. The awareness on entrepreneurship is very less and as such people do not know the potentiality and the economic benefit they would gain.

## Future research on the topic

i. It would be interesting to make a study from existing successful entrepreneurs - Do commerce background students make better entrepreneurs than their other peers?

ii. Why entrepreneurship as a subject is incorporated only in commerce curriculum, because with entrepreneurial quality, a person can excel more in any other field too.
iii. A cross study can be made on how cultures or regional customs & traditions and upbringing have an influence upon a person on becoming an entrepreneur.

## Conclusion

The study shows that student's curriculum does have impact pursuing entrepreneurship, as commerce stream students are more inclined than the other two streams which do not have entrepreneurship as a subject in their academic curriculum. It is to be added that none of the students have ever attended any program that trains young people to start their own business. In response to whether they like to have a basic business course, 66% gave positive reply. Despite the employment problem and a booming career in Nagaland, students were found to be less interested to become entrepreneurs. Among the study streams, commerce students tend to show higher interest next to science, while arts students showed little interest. While gender wise, male students shows higher level of interest than females but both of their percentage on interest in entrepreneurship is high as 77.3% and 60.8% for male and female respectively which explains that with proper guidance and motivation it will help the students to become entrepreneurs with a difference to change the society's biggest challenge-that is unemployment.

## Notes

1. The Annual Administrative Report 2009-2010 of Department of Employment & Craftsmen Training, Nagaland under Labour & Employment Department with the main function to maintain the Live Register of Jobseekers of the State by enforcing the Employment Exchanges Compulsory Notification of Vacancies (CNV) Act, 1959.
2. Dimapur Municipal Council, records trade registers and licence registers operating in Dimapur.

## References

1. Kolvereid, Lars & Moen, Øystein (1997). Entrepreneurship among business graduates: does a major in entrepreneurship make a difference? Journal of European Industrial Training, 21, 4: 154-160

2. Wang.K, Clement & Wong, Poh-Kam (2004). Entrepreneurial interest of university students in Singapore. Technovation, 24,2: 163-172
3. Mcstay, Dell (2008). An investigation of undergraduate's student selfemployment and the impact of entrepreneurship education and previous entrepreneurial experience. Ph.D thesis, Submitted to School of Business, Bond University, Australia, 26 May
4. Rajendra. G (2007). Entrepreneurship development among commerce students- a study. . Small Enterprise Development, Management & Extension Journal, 34, 4: 23-32.
5. Levenburg,Nancy.M & Schwarz, Thomas.V.(2008). Entrepreneurial orientation among the youth of India: the impact of culture, education and environment. The Journal of Entrepreneurship, 17, 1: 15-35
6. Bhandari, Narendra .C.(2006). Intention for entrepreneurship among students in India. The Journal of Entrepreneurship, 15, 2: 169-179.
7. Spors, Kelly.K. (2007). Entrepreneurship 101. The Wall Street Journal, March, 2007.
8. Bureau Report. (2006). Social Entrepreneurship Literature Review. Zee News Limited: 13-14.
9. Vero ,Chizokho ,(2006).New crop of banking wizards. Eastern Mirror, August 10, 2006.
10. Khanka, S.S. (2007). Entrepreneurship Curriculum in Secondary Vocational Education: Its Rational and Implementation. Small Enterprise Development, Management & Extension Journal, 34, 4:17-22
11. Kamaraj, J.M.Arul, Muralidaran, K.(2005). Motivation for Entrepreneurial Opportunities . Small Enterprise Development, Management & Extension Journal, 32, 3:51-54
12. Upadhyaya, Ranjan. (2006). Transforming Youth's Perception in Entrepreneurship. E-mail, July 31.
13. Government of Nagaland, Annual Administrative Report, Department of Employment & Craftsmen Training (2009-10), 5.
14. Tweeten, K. (Ed.). (1992). Youth entrepreneurship: Be your own boss. North Dakota State University. (Eao1-FCX01).
15. Bishop, J. H. (Ed.). (1991). Taking charge: Learning economics through entrepreneurship. Reading, PA: Pennsylvania Council on Economic Education.
16. Sexton, D. L., & Bowman-Upton, N. B. (1991). Entrepreneurship: Creativity and growth. New York: Macmillan.

17. Venesaar, Urve, Kolbre, Ene & Piliste Toomas (2006). Students' Attitudes and Intentions toward Entrepreneurship at Tallinn University of Technology. Working Papers in Economics. School of Economics and Business Administration,Tallinn University of Technology (TUTWPE), 97- 114
18. Gerry Chris, Marques Susana Carla, Nogueira Fernanda (2008).Tracking student entrepreneurial potential: personal attributes and the propensity for business start-ups after graduation in a Portuguese university. Problems and Perspectives in Management. 6 (4): 45-53.
19. Volkmann.K.Christine, Tokarski Oliver Kim (2009). Student attitudes to entrepreneurship. Management & Marketing. 4(1):17-38
20. Alsos.A.Gry, Isaksen.J.Espen, Softing Erika (2006). Youth Enterprise Experience and Business Start-Up Intentions. Paper presented at 14th Nordic Conference on Small Business Research Stockholm. 11-13 May 2006.

8

# Role of Socio- Economic Status, Secondary & Engineering Level Education in Development of Entrepreneurial Attitude & Activities of Technical Undergraduate Students


### *Abstract*

Significance of institutions of higher education augment manifold when it is able to produce not only skilful and employable human resource but also help develop attitude among its students to opt entrepreneurship as a career choice. Institutions of education system are distinctive place of knowledge transfer and innovation which help towards nurturing entrepreneurial activities. While in India such entrepreneurial activities by institutions of higher education are not common yet, in Russia and China factories and firms are owned and operated by higher education institutions (Agarwal, 2009). An attempt has been made with the help of this paper to know the entrepreneurial attitude of the students at undergraduate engineering level belonging to Uttar Pradesh Technical University. This research aims to find the role of education at secondary and engineering level towards the promotion of familiarity about entrepreneurship as a career choice and also the amount of interests in the students to take up this career. 206 students from different engineering branches are tested using the Entrepreneurial Attitude Orientation scale. Results show that significant difference exists between the thinking of female and male students towards entrepreneurship. The research identifies that students are not aware much about entrepreneurship. The respondents, who have gone under this study, have revealed that education system, so far, has hardly been helpful in developing awareness about entrepreneurship. Irrespective of societal and parental pressure of getting the good job, today's generation is willing to take entrepreneurship as a career choice, provided they get proper guidance and awareness.

**Entrepreneurs and innovations**, worldwide, are considered to be the engine of a nation's economic growth. Almost every stabilized government in the world has kept this issue as one of the main agenda in its policies and plan documents. US Council on Competitiveness (1998) in its report argues that 'The nation that fosters an infrastructure of linkages among and between firms, universities and government, gains competitive advantage through quicker information diffusion and product deployment'. In the green paper on entrepreneurship- EC Commission-2003 (Michie, et al., 2002), the EU Policy Objectives have been to make the EU the 'leading knowledge based economy in the World' *(Lisbon Council)* and key issue for the EU is to build *a* 'climate in which entrepreneurial initiative and business activity can thrive'. Schools, colleges and universities have major responsibility to stimulate innovative and entrepreneurship led economic growth.

Advance developments in software and manufacturing engineering have opened up many applications of technology in day to day life of mankind and businesses. These developments in turn are creating lot of job opportunities as well as the possibilities of converting nascent ideas into a viable business and thus making an individual into an "Entrepreneur".

Significance of institutions of higher education augment manifold when it is able to produce not only skilful and employable human resource but also help develop attitude among its students to opt entrepreneurship as a career choice.

Institutions of education system are distinctive place of knowledge transfer and innovation which help towards nurturing entrepreneurial activities. While in India such entrepreneurial activities by institutions of higher education are not common yet, in Russia and China factories and firms are owned and operated by higher education institutions (Agarwal, 2008).

The objective of this paper is to identify the entrepreneurial orientation of male and female undergraduate engineering students. This research is particularly taken up to study the influence and contribution made by Indian education system on the students with regards to the awareness about the entrepreneurship and developing inclination towards entrepreneurship as a career option. The research also tries to relate the thinking of those students who have come from business background towards entrepreneurship. Difference in the thinking is also examined between the students, who have come from families having a business background and those who don't. Thus this study examines orientation and thinking of undergraduate engineering/technical students about entrepreneurs and entrepreneurship. Based on the primary data, following hypotheses are tested;

(a) There is no significant difference between the thinking/orientation of female and male students about entrepreneurship.

(b) There is no significant difference between the thinking/orientation of female and male students about entrepreneurship (when both group belong to a family where a business is being run by a member known to them).

(c) There is no significant difference between the thinking/orientation of female and male students about entrepreneurship (when both group have never come in contact with a business person personally known to them). Besides these hypotheses response of students are also examined for different dimension on entrepreneurship.

**Methodology:** Descriptive survey method was employed to conduct the study. The population under study comprised of the undergraduate engineering/technical students studying in engineering colleges in Meerut. The sample was drawn on the basis of stratified random sampling to get the proper representation of male and female students. Meerut is a well known educational hub in Uttar Pradesh particularly known for engineering colleges and is situated near Ghaziabad and Noida. This region of Uttar Pradesh is known for some reputed engineering institute affiliated to Uttar Pradesh Technical University.

The distinguishing feature of these institutes is that none of these belong to Government aided institutions. The admission to these colleges is carried out with the help of state level entrance examination with ten percent of the seats kept reserved for the management quota. Many institutes are the centre of excellence in them and incorporate students from different strata of society.

The availability of the management quota seats, adds different dimensions to the demographic factor of the colleges and a good population of students exist in these colleges who either have parents doing some business or they know someone running business close to them. Thus sample was collected from different branches of the engineering courses keeping in mind that there should be a good representation of male and female students. The sample was basically taken from final and pre-final year students.

Final sample design consists of 88 girl students and 118 boy students. The demographic characteristic suggested that out of 88 girl students, 32 belonged to the group having some business/entrepreneurial person known to them and 56 belonged to the other group. Similarly out of 118 boy students, 55 belonged to the group who knows someone close in their family doing a business and 63 belonged to the other group (having no business interference).

An Entrepreneurial Attitude Orientation (EAO) scale was developed and administered to the students. The questionnaire consisted of 38 items. All the items were scored on five point scale. Total score of this scale is considered for the assessment of the entrepreneurial orientation. Initially EAO scale was administered on a group of students and 3 items were deleted from the scale after item analysis. Thus the final scale consisted of 35 items. Along with these 35 statements, some more statements were asked for the response from the students to judge their understanding about the entrepreneurs and entrepreneurship and the demographic characteristics of students.

The t test was used to test the significance. Important items of the EAO scale are also examined separately to judge the orientation/thinking of students belonging to different categories. Students understanding about the entrepreneurs and entrepreneurship are explained with the help of pie diagram.

**Analysis and Results:** The sample comprises of male and female students and for applying 't' test, these two groups are further categorised into two group i.e. Category *Ent* and Category *NEent*.

**Category *Ent*** denotes group of those students (male and female) who have or have had some business exposure.

**Category *NEnt*** denotes group of those students (male and female) having no business interventions whatsoever.

't' test was conducted on the responses of EAO Scale and following results were drawn:

**Table-1**

**Table 1: Comparison of Female and Male students on EAO Scale (total and for category *Ent* and *NEnt*)**

| t test for total Female and total Male | | | | | |
|---|---|---|---|---|---|
| **Group** | **N** | **M** | **Variance** | **t-Value** | **Level of Significance** |
| Female | 88 | 111.20 | 165.13 | -3.47 | Significant at .05 level df=204 |
| Male | 118 | 117.36 | 149.7 | | |
| **t test for Female (Category *Ent*) and Male (Category *Ent*)** | | | | | |
| **Group** | **N** | **M** | **Variance** | **t-Value** | **Level of Significance** |
| Female (Category Ent) | 32 | 111.88 | 160.76 | -1.83 | Insignificant |
| Male (Category Ent) | 55 | 117.04 | 160.04 | | |
| **t test for Female (Category *NEnt*) and Male (Category *NEnt*)** | | | | | |
| **Group** | **N** | **M** | **Variance** | **t-Value** | **Level of Significance** |
| Female (Category *NEnt*) | 56 | 110.82 | 170.19 | -2.95 | Significant at .05 level df=117 |
| Male (Category *NEnt*) | 63 | 117.63 | 142.95 | | |
| **t Test for Females (Category *Ent* and Category *NEnt*)** | | | | | |
| **Group** | **N** | **M** | **Variance** | **t-Value** | **Level of Significance** |
| Female (Category *Ent*) | 32 | 111.88 | 160.76 | 0.37 | Insignificant |
| Female (Category *NEnt*) | 56 | 110.82 | 170.19 | | |
| **t Test for Males (Category *Ent* and Category *NEnt*)** | | | | | |
| **Group** | **N** | **M** | **Variance** | **t-Value** | **Level of Significance** |
| Male (Category *Ent*) | 55 | 117.04 | 160.04 | -0.26 | Insignificant |
| Male (Category *NEnt*) | 63 | 117.63 | 142.95 | | |

EOA Scale is administered to the students and then the scores earned are tabulated and calculated for the various categories of students as desired by the research. For the first hypothesis, score for the total female and male are used and t test is applied. The value of t test comes out to be -3.47 which is significant at .05 levels. The mean score of male is greater than the female representing more favourable entrepreneurial orientation in male students.

Thus the finding suggests that-"There is significant difference between the thinking/orientation of female and male students about entrepreneurship".

Further the scores were arranged and segregated for the two different group- Category *Ent* and Category *NEnt* of male and female students. Mean, standard deviation and variances were calculated and the value of t was identified. The values in Table-1presents following results:

When male and female students belonging to Category *Ent* are tested, it is found that the difference (-1.83) at .05 level is not significant. The value once again shows that male students have higher orientation/ thinking towards entrepreneurship.

When female and male students are compared for the Category NEnt, significant different (-2.5 at .05 level) exist. Female students belonging to Category *NEnt* have low orientation. We further tried to compare the male and female students belonging to the two categories and it was found that there is no significant difference in the orientation towards entrepreneurship within the same group of students. The distinguish feature that emerged out of this comparison is that the female students belonging to category *Ent* have greater orientation than the female students belonging to Category *NEnt*, but there is opposite scenario for the male students, where Category *NEnt* has high orientation than the Category Ent male students. So, following results are drawn:

I. There is significant difference between the thinking/orientation of female and male students about entrepreneurship.
II. There is no significant difference between the thinking/orientation of female and male students about entrepreneurship (both group belonging to Category Ent).
III. There is significant difference between the thinking/orientation of female and male students about entrepreneurship (both group belonging to Category NEnt).
IV. There is no significant difference between the thinking/orientation of female students belonging to Category Ent and female students belonging to Category NEnt.
V. There is no significant difference between the thinking/orientation of male students belonging to Category Ent and male students belonging to Category NEnt.

Students were also asked some straight forward questions to judge their understanding about entrepreneurship and the responses were analysed with the help of pictorial presentation. This analysis was conducted only on those students who belong to Category *Ent*. It is assumed that such students have greater exposure of business and they are more aware about the intricacies of running a business. Thus the understanding or thinking of male and female students belonging to Category *Ent* is analysed here.

Figure-1, Figure-2

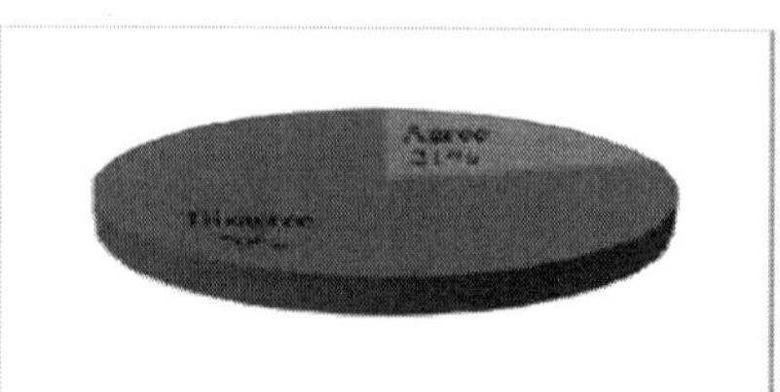


**Fig.1: No Difference between a Businessman and an Entrepreneur?**

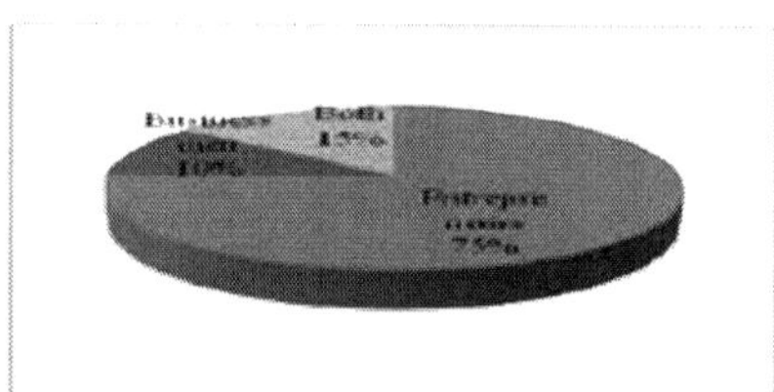


**Fig.2: Who is more Innovative: A Businessman or an Entrepreneur?**

Figure 1 suggests that 21 percent of the students feel entrepreneurs and businessmen are the same and think of them as synonymous to each other while others disagree.

On the innovative index 75 percent of the students feel that entrepreneurs are more innovative (Figure-2).

Figure-3, Figure-4

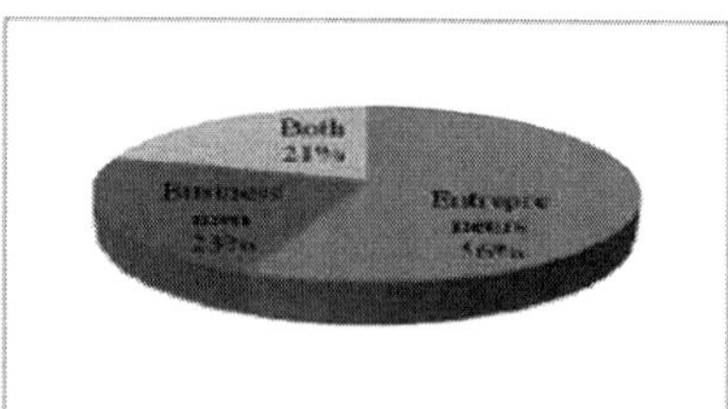


**Fig. 3: Who takes more risk?**

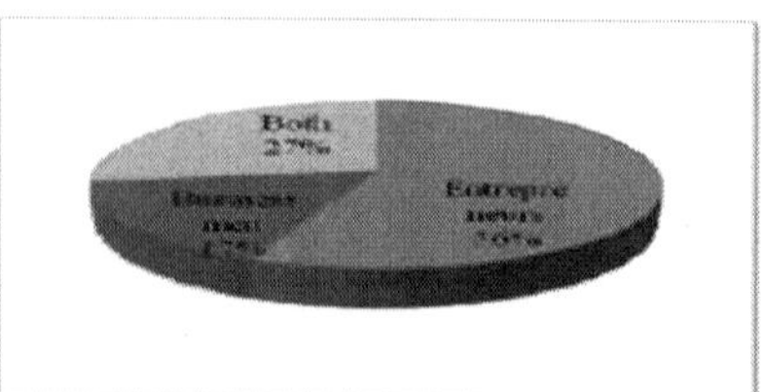


**Fig. 4: Who creates more value for the society by his work?**

Figure 3 shows clear polarisation among the students on their thinking about the risk taking capacity of businessmen and entrepreneurs. 56 percent assumes that it is an entrepreneur who takes more risks other 44 percent think it is either business man or both businessmen and entrepreneurs.

Figure-5, Figure-6

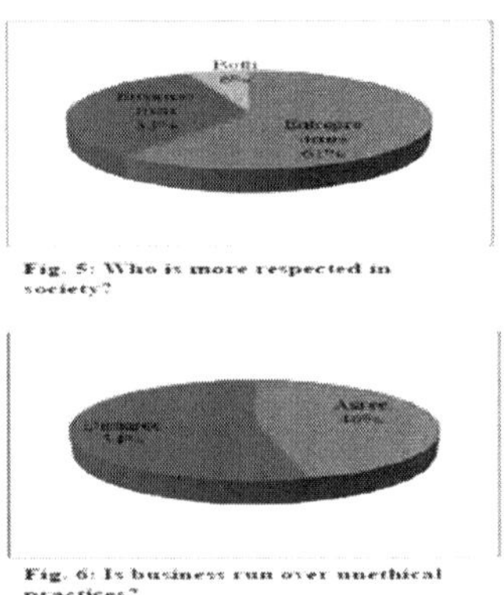

Fig. 5: Who is more respected in society?

Fig. 6: Is business run over unethical practices?

61 percent of the students think that entrepreneurs are more respected in society, while 33 percent feel that businessmen are respected more and 6 percent feel both are equally respected(Figure-5)

Nearly half of the students feel that business is run over unethical practices (Agree: 46 percent; Disagree: 54 percent. Figure-6)

Figure-7, Figure-8

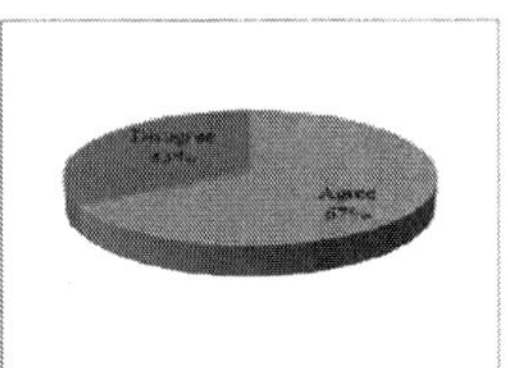


Fig. 7: Are Red-Tapism and Corruption main hindrances?

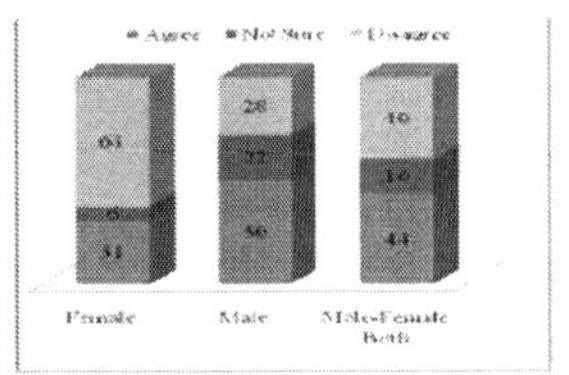


Fig. 8: I will definitely start a business as my parents are running one.

When enquired about red-tapism and corruption, 67 percent of the students agree that these factors are the main hindrances in establishing, starting and running a business (Figure-7).

**Table 2**

**Table 2: Item wise analysis of EAO Scale**

| Statements | Background | Male-Female | Agree (%) | Dis-Agree (%) |
|---|---|---|---|---|
| I have never been taught about taking Entrepreneurship as a career option. **Result:** *Students under study are not very convinced that they have been taught about career in entrepreneurship, as the sample is equally divided on agree and disagree scale.* | Category *Ent* | Female | 56 | 44 |
| | | Male | 34 | 56 |
| | | F-M | 42 | 52 |
| | Category *NEnt* | Female | 58 | 42 |
| | | Male | 62 | 36 |
| | | F-M | 61 | 38 |
| My parents will appreciate me more if I score good marks to get a high profile job rather than thinking of doing some business to earn more money. **Result:** *Students across each group convincingly agree that getting a good job is still the priority in their respective society.* | Category *Ent* | Female | 69 | 31 |
| | | Male | 78 | 19 |
| | | F-M | 75 | 23 |
| | Category *NEnt* | Female | 74 | 26 |
| | | Male | 67 | 29 |
| | | F-M | 69 | 28 |
| My experience suggests that owning a business does not fetch much appreciation in society. **Result:** *Young generation students do agree that businessmen are respected in society, but the degree of agreeability reduces significantly among the students having some business background.* | Category *Ent* | Female | 31 | 56 |
| | | Male | 31 | 63 |
| | | F-M | 31 | 60 |
| | Category *NEnt* | Female | 16 | 84 |
| | | Male | 12 | 83 |
| | | F-M | 13 | 84 |
| Starting a business is fraught with so much risk that it is always safe to go for job oriented studies. **Result:** *Most students are convinced on the risk factors in business, but many also feel that the risk is not as hefty as it is perceived. A good percentage of students have opted their disagreement on this issue too.* | Category *Ent* | Female | 63 | 38 |
| | | Male | 66 | 31 |
| | | F-M | 65 | 33 |
| | Category *NEnt* | Female | 58 | 42 |
| | | Male | 45 | 50 |
| | | F-M | 49 | 48 |
| I have learnt that there is a shortage of infrastructural support to start a business. **Result:** *Maximum population, without any hesitation, agree that there is a shortage of infrastructural support. This may be due to the below average awareness about entrepreneurship process on the part of students.* | Category *Ent* | Female | 88 | 13 |
| | | Male | 72 | 22 |
| | | F-M | 77 | 19 |
| | Category *NEnt* | Female | 79 | 21 |
| | | Male | 52 | 40 |
| | | F-M | 61 | 34 |

**Table 2 Contd.**

| Statements | Background | Male-Female | Agree (%) | Dis-Agree (%) |
|---|---|---|---|---|
| Entrepreneurs are very important individuals for economy of countries as various media claims: **Result:** *63 to 81 percent of the sample students believe that entrepreneurs are important for the development of economy.* | Category *Ent* | Female | 81 | 6 |
| | | Male | 72 | 28 |
| | | F-M | 75 | 21 |
| | Category *NEnt* | Female | 63 | 26 |
| | | Male | 79 | 21 |
| | | F-M | 74 | 23 |
| I Have come across the word "Entrepreneur" during my education so far. **Result:** *88 to 97 percent of the students agree that they have come across the word "Entrepreneur" during their study.* | Category *Ent* | Female | 88 | 6 |
| | | Male | 97 | 3 |
| | | F-M | 94 | 4 |
| | Category *NEnt* | Female | 95 | 5 |
| | | Male | 90 | 2 |
| | | F-M | 92 | 3 |
| I fully understand the concept and meaning of Entrepreneurship. **Result:** *Though high percentage of the sample claim to have awareness about Entrepreneurs but conceptual knowledge declines among all the class of students.* | Category *Ent* | Female | 69 | 19 |
| | | Male | 72 | 22 |
| | | F-M | 71 | 21 |
| | Category *NEnt* | Female | 47 | 42 |
| | | Male | 86 | 10 |
| | | F-M | 74 | 20 |
| I think that my education in technical field has developed inclination towards owning a business in future: **Result:** *Students having no business background response more favourably toward this question compared to the other group.* | Category *Ent* | Female | 44 | 31 |
| | | Male | 56 | 38 |
| | | F-M | 52 | 35 |
| | Category *NEnt* | Female | 74 | 16 |
| | | Male | 64 | 29 |
| | | F-M | 67 | 25 |
| I intend to pursue higher education as it will give me better job opportunities. **Result:** *Wide gap exists between male and female students on the importance of higher education. Female see higher education as an important mean to get good job than anything else.* | Category *Ent* | Female | 100 | 0 |
| | | Male | 66 | 28 |
| | | F-M | 77 | 19 |
| | Category *NEnt* | Female | 95 | 5 |
| | | Male | 60 | 36 |
| | | F-M | 70 | 26 |
| Do you think that higher education will give better understanding about business environment and increased inclination towards owning a business: **Result:** *Female population is more convinced that higher education will increase understanding about business.* | Category *Ent* | Female | 94 | 6 |
| | | Male | 75 | 25 |
| | | F-M | 81 | 19 |
| | Category *NEnt* | Female | 89 | 11 |
| | | Male | 71 | 26 |
| | | F-M | 77 | 21 |

**Table 2 Contd**

| Statements | Background | Male-Female | Agree (%) | Dis-Agree (%) |
|---|---|---|---|---|
| I consistently think about earning good money even at the cost of certain risk. **Result:** *Result shows that males are more motivated and are willing to take risks to earn good money as compared to their female counterparts.* | Category *Ent* | Female | 63 | 38 |
| | | Male | 72 | 25 |
| | | F-M | 69 | 29 |
| | Category *NEnt* | Female | 58 | 42 |
| | | Male | 76 | 21 |
| | | F-M | 70 | 28 |
| I do not find myself comfortable with the understanding of financial terms and financial/economic scenario of the country. **Result:** *There is clear divides between male and female. Male students think themselves better conversant with financial terms than the female counterparts.* | Category *Ent* | Female | 56 | 31 |
| | | Male | 19 | 75 |
| | | F-M | 31 | 60 |
| | Category *NEnt* | Female | 26 | 74 |
| | | Male | 26 | 74 |
| | | F-M | 26 | 74 |
| It will be a foolish decision to quit a job and start a business. **Result:** *Majority of the male students do not think quitting job and taking up business is a silly decision. Though female students also think on the same line, but the percentage is not that much prominent.* | Category *Ent* | Female | 44 | 56 |
| | | Male | 9 | 91 |
| | | F-M | 21 | 79 |
| | Category *NEnt* | Female | 32 | 68 |
| | | Male | 7 | 83 |
| | | F-M | 15 | 79 |
| I am fully convinced that only those individuals start a business who have such backgrounds. **Result:** *Results show that major percentage feels that the sole reason for starting a business is not poor academic records.* | Category *Ent* | Female | 31 | 69 |
| | | Male | 22 | 75 |
| | | F-M | 25 | 73 |
| | Category *NEnt* | Female | 26 | 74 |
| | | Male | 31 | 64 |
| | | F-M | 49 | 48 |
| I would make my children aware about entrepreneurship as a career options. **Result:** *Majority of the students agree to make their children aware about entrepreneurship as a career option.* | Category *Ent* | Female | 94 | 6 |
| | | Male | 78 | 13 |
| | | F-M | 83 | 10 |
| | Category *NEnt* | Female | 63 | 26 |
| | | Male | 79 | 17 |
| | | F-M | 74 | 20 |

When asked about starting a business as their parents are running one, 63 percent of female students showed poor interest while only 50 percent of male students showed interest in taking plunge into business. 22 percent of the male students were not sure about their chances of taking up the business while 28 percent of the male students showed their disinterest in running a business (Figure 8).

**Item wise analysis and Inferences:** Item wise analysis is done and presented in Table-2. Inferences are drawn on the basis of item wise response submit by the students.

**Discussion and Conclusions:** Many studies have been done analysing individuals on their attitude towards taking up entrepreneurship as a career option. Most of the studies are generally based on the Mc Celland's theory of motivation and are generally concentrated on the factors which may help develop the entrepreneurial abilities among individuals. The present study has been conducted for analysing the awareness about entrepreneurship among undergraduate engineering students and their thinking about the opportunities that exist in entrepreneurship and what is their readiness about taking entrepreneurship as a career option. This research also tries to judge the general understanding of the students about entrepreneurship. That is where the role of education and family background comes into picture towards developing entrepreneurial orientation in students.

The result shows that significant difference exists between the orientation/thinking of male and female undergraduate engineering level students towards entrepreneurship. Male students have high thinking about entrepreneurship than female students. The difference is more prominent and significant when Category *NEnt* male and female students are compared. Within the same group of male and female students, difference is insignificant between Category *Ent* and Category *NEnt* students. Thus it is concluded that within the group of male and female students, there is more or less similar thinking towards entrepreneurship whether students have some business background or not. It can be concluded that though students coming from a business background are more likely to become a businessman but overall their thinking about entrepreneurship does not differ significantly from those students who do not have any entrepreneurial background. In the case of male students, individual belonging to Category *Ent* have shown lower orientation as compared to their Category *NEnt* counterparts. Refusal of taking business as a career option by the students coming from the business background further reinforces such conclusion. Only 33 percent of the female students and 50 percent of male students are willing to go into business field irrespective of the fact that they are grown up in business families.

The study has revealed that general understanding of students regarding concept and meaning of entrepreneurship is not very clear. It can be said that only 50 percent of the research population has some clear understanding about the meaning of entrepreneurship. It is found that students are not much exposed to the meaning of entrepreneurship during their family and educational life cycle. Further, students have accepted that they feel business is run over unethical practices, there is lack of infrastructural support and they lack understanding of the business and financial terms (particularly female students); these factors are de-motivating among the students. These students also agree that, though higher education will lead to better understanding of business environment but they are likely to pursue higher education to seek good job opportunities as that will please their parents more than anything else.

Analysis of various statements suggest that respondent think entrepreneurship is a risky affair, still they are ready to take this opportunity if it comes their way. The orientation of students towards entrepreneurship can be said to be positive and if given better exposure during their studies and changed mentality of the parents and family, it may lead to expansion of entrepreneurs in society. The research finding can be stretched further to conclude that thinking about entrepreneurship among young generation population is fast changing and they see entrepreneurship as a respected career to take up. They are ready to experiment and take risk for the better growth and prosperity.

Our education system and media can play important role towards development of such attitude. It is found in the study that students coming from CBSE have better understanding about entrepreneurship. Personal interview with some of the students belonging to CBSE has revealed that they have studied entrepreneurship during their course curriculum at school level.

The higher education system in India has also, by and large, ignored the paradigm shift brought about by NCF 2005 (Kumar, 2009). The admission procedures for the first year at college have remained as rigid as they were, further reinforcing the rigidity of the class XII examination. This situation is going to discourage children from utilising the wider range of subject options available in class XI and XII. NCERT has introduced new subjects like heritage crafts, creative writing and translation, computer and communication technology, human ecology and family studies, but there are few takers of these courses. Such education style produces students who are focused on a targeted path. Average Indian students are generally hard-working but they lack research orientation. On the other hand education at the average American University relies heavily on self-discovery, reflection, open ended questions and analysis (Niketa, 2008).

These concerns have also been raised by National Curriculum Framework (NCF- 2005) (Kumar, 2008). It poses three key challenges:

Linking the child's life at home with learning at school, discouraging rote learning and moving beyond the textbook. Procedural simplicity to start a business is a great motivation factor for entrepreneurs. Table 3 shows the ranking of the various countries on the factorwhere it is easy to start a business and where not?

**Table 3**

**Table-3: Where it is easy to start a business-and where not?**

| Easiest | Rank | Most Difficult | Rank |
|---|---|---|---|
| Singapore | 1 | Niger | 174 |
| New Zealand | 2 | Eritrea | 175 |
| Hong Kong, China | 3 | Burundi | 176 |
| United States | 4 | Venezuela | 177 |
| United Kingdom | 5 | Chad | 178 |
| Denmark | 6 | Congo, Rep. | 179 |
| Ireland | 7 | Sao Tome, Principe | 180 |
| Canada | 8 | Guinea-Bissau | 181 |
| Australia | 9 | Congo, Dem Rep | 182 |
| Norway | 10 | Central African Rep | 183 |

**Source: Doing Business 2010** (period June 2008 through May 2009)

**http://www.doingbusiness.org/economyrankings/** (accessed on 08 May 2010)

Engineering students or the students undergoing professional education have the best building blocks to become full grown entrepreneurs. There is need to change and revise our course curriculum to support such attitude. Young generation, as the research suggest is ready to accept entrepreneurship as a career option but they are generally not aware about the opportunities that exist and the governmental supports and organisation that are working towards the promotion of entrepreneurship.

Increase in awareness about entrepreneurship can help students making up their mind to get involved into entrepreneurial activities. Irrespective of societal and parental pressure of getting a good job, today's generation is willing to take entrepreneurship as a career choice, provided they get proper guidance and awareness. Our system, should, just not rely on identifying entrepreneurial abilities in the individuals which come by birth, but try to develop these abilities gradually and consistently throughout the life till they are ready to become entrepreneurs.

## References


1. Agarwal, R.(2008). Adopt a Life Cycle approach, *Education Times*, New Delhi, 18 Aug 2008, p-11
2. Michie, J. et al. (2002) *'Investing in Innovation: A strategy for science engineering and technology'*, DTI, HM Treasury, DFES July 2002 http://www.cambridgemit. org/object/download/2508/doc/ RINET%20Hughes.pdf.(accessed on 2 October 2009)
3. Niketa Kumar, Education Times, New Delhi, 17 March 2008, p-10 US Council on Competitiveness (1998) Going Global: The New Shape of American Innovation. Washington September, www.isc.hbs.edu/ .../ Council_on_Competitiveness_1999.pdf (accessed on 12 December 2009).

# 9

# Entrepreneurial Sense Among Professional Students

***Abstract***

It is a normal preference of people to pursue their career in the field of their study. Many literatures have been published stating people who ventured outside their academic areas also did well in their entrepreneurial activities. Good entrepreneurship as though requires think out of the box concept. In this paper, the authors have tried to find out two facts. First, are the students of professional courses interested to set up their own firms? Second, among the students interested to open their own firms, how many of them are ready to do it in field of business which they have not studied as a part of their academic education. The results of the study are challenging and exciting, which are interpreted and discussed.

## Introduction

It has become a normal thought of many learned professionals that entrepreneurship is important aspect for the development of nation. However, literature records state a very low percentage of people are involved in entrepreneurial works. Our country is going through many challenges like joblessness, poverty, corruption, etc. In such a scenario entrepreneurship may be considered to play an important role for the economic growth of our country. Even though many jobs are outsourced in India and China mostly, a large number of business prospects are available in these countries as well.

Many professionals accept the fact that there has been a lot of increase in our country's economic development. But there is a lot of gap between the development of academic talents coming out of academic institutions and the country's economic progress. This means that there is very less application of academic output which can be planted for the growth of the nation resulting in unemployment of the educated professionals. Also joblessness among professionals having professional degrees is increasing and professionals with proper expertise are still in demand.

This situation needs to be improved soon to develop our nation. Our country wants a large number of entrepreneurs to get advantage of the various business chances and to become the creators of new jobs. Literature records predict that by the year 2015 there will be around 12 crore people finding jobs which includes 8 crores finding their first jobs. To fight this challenge of unemployment new entrepreneurs are very highly required.

Our country's government tries to consider the people in their 20s to be prospective future entrepreneurs and job givers. There are many institutions in our country including the central and state government which gives priority for the development of entrepreneurship and small scale industries in the form of various incentives and assistances. As entrepreneurship is felt to be very important for growth of individual as well as nation, the aim of this paper is to study the interest of students of professional courses in setting up their own firms.

## Background

Entrepreneurship can be considered as a new factor for the economic growth for developing as well as developed countries. It is a process of getting advantage of the various chances available keeping in minds the risks and indeterminate situations by optimizing resources to create useful output. Much acclaimed for being the basis of innovation, entrepreneurship delivers the advantages of increase in the economic obverse, creation of job opportunities lessening unemployment. Kuratko (2007) defined entrepreneurship in a way that included the attributes like enthusiasm to take evaluated risks, the talent to form an effective team, optimize resources, business plan and finally to have a proper vision.

Entrepreneurship should consist of two things. First one being the existence of beneficial prospects and the next one is creative individuals. In academics, entrepreneurship is taught as being a process from which various opportunities can be taken, how to visualize an opportunity and risks involved, resources required and its optimization. Also it teaches some of the skills necessary and strategies used for being a successful entrepreneur.

It has become an accepted fact that entrepreneurial activity should be encouraged for the economic development of any nation. One way to encourage entrepreneurship is to provoke people to grow out to be entrepreneurs and provide them the proper training to become the owner of firms. Students who have completed professional degree courses can be thought to have good level of knowledge in their area. They can be taught how to use their knowledge to identify and build new opportunities and processes which can generate revenue and create jobs for others.

## Entrepreneurship and students of professional degree courses

The researchers have tried to collect the secondary data (using literature survey) of the professional degree students' intention in pursuing entrepreneurship as a career option. Bhandari (2006) wanted to get the intent of a team of students of university in India once they finished their education in college. He findings were that only two factors viz. luck and leadership skills among 18 other independent factors had important associations with the reliant variable of starting own business.

Leadership skills, aim to be one's own boss and proper inventive plans which could be implemented, self challenges and education apart from business were the attributes which would impact entrepreneurship. Prof. G.S. Popli in his paper titled "A Study Of Entrepreneurial Orientation & Inclination For Entrepreneurial Carrier Of Management Students In India: An Empirical Analysis", most of the students would like to take up jobs instead of starting their own firm. The reason they gave was job security and regular income. Furthermore, his results showed that the students were hesitant because of risks involved, finance problem and social status. The students also wanted a subject on entrepreneurship in their course curriculum along with financial and other form of support from the government and other financial institutions.

Ardichvili (2003) tried to recognize the challenges of a success entrepreneur, knowledge required for being alert in a given business opportunity. One should be alert enough for being successful in an entrepreneurial activity. The success level increases after the level of alertness increases. But the increased alertness depends on several factors like past experience, knowledge, environmental situations, etc.

Similarly in the paper titled "Examining the Entrepreneurial Attitudes of Business Students: The Impact Of Participation In The Small Business Institute" the authors have examined that the people who successfully completed the course on entrepreneurship had impact on the entrepreneurial attitudes. The completion of the SBI course impacted the attitudes of men and women in a different manner.

Their results indicated that students who participated in entrepreneurship education are able to help in improving the entrepreneurial attitudes among female students minimizing the gender gap. They also suggested that experiences in educational environment are very useful for the development of encouraging attitudes towards entrepreneurship.

## Discussions and Suggestions

It could be seen from the above literature survey that there is entrepreneurial intention among the students of professional courses. We believe that this study would help the educationalists in spreading the spirit of entrepreneurship among professional degree students thereby creating many successful entrepreneurs.

Furthermore one could conclude that getting good support is helpful in becoming an entrepreneur compared to personal interest. So if these professional degree students are provided with good information and support there are higher chances that they would become successful entrepreneurs. We mean support in terms of finance, guidance, motivation, etc. Students who want to have a trial of their entrepreneurial activity can be allowed to conduct the entrepreneurial experiment in the campus with a limited financial support. This would boost the entrepreneurial interest among many students, in addition to the participating ones.

Our study mainly focused on the entrepreneurial intention among the professional degree students. The results from this research can work as the base for future study and prove to be a value addition for the economic development of the nation. Also our study shows that to know the factors responsible for entrepreneurial intention among professional degree students, it requires a planned effort and proper process modeling.

## Conclusion

This paper tried to find out two facts. First, are the students of professional courses interested to set up their own firms? Second, among the students interested to open their own firms, how many of them are ready to do it in field of business which they have not studied as a part of their academic education.

But the literatures found so far supported to get the answer of the first fact. No literatures exist to answer the second fact. The literatures which supported the first fact gave out a mixed response. Some stated that entrepreneurial education helps students in becoming successful entrepreneurs, while some denied this fact.

The literatures which supported the first fact gave out a mixed response. Some stated that entrepreneurial education helps students in becoming successful entrepreneurs while some denied this fact. Also some literatures stated that even though some students thought about starting a business, most of them prefer to do jobs after completion of their degree and pushed back the plan of starting their firm to some distant future. The students who had good leadership and motivational skills intended to start a business soon and vice versa.

The findings of this study show that there is requirement for heightening the impact of academic institutions in increasing the entrepreneurial conduct of the students of professional degree students by giving them knowledge regarding sensing an opportunity, visualizing the pros and cons of the opportunity and finally starting the business. The curriculum structure should also incorporate subjects related to entrepreneurship. In addition to this, the government should also take initiatives to increase the entrepreneurial intention among the students of professional degree students.

## References

1. Prof. G.S. Popli, "A Study of Entrepreneurial Orientation & Inclination for Entrepreneurial Career of Management Students In India: An Empirical Analysis".
2. A.A. Refaat, "Fostering Entrepreneurial Intention among Engineering Students".
3. Hessel Oosterbeek, Mirjam C. van Praag, Auke IJsselstein, "The Impact of Entrepreneurship Education on Entrepreneurship Competencies and Intentions".

4. Urve Venesaar, Ene Kolbre, Toomas Piliste, "Students' Attitudes and Intentions toward Entrepreneurship at Tallinn University of Technology".
5. Michael L. Harris, Shanan G. Gibson, Sherrie R. Taylor, Todd D. Mick, "Examining The Entrepreneurial Attitudes Of Business Students: The Impact Of Participation In The Small Business Institute"
6. Mohammad Ismail, Shaiful Annuar Khalid, Mahmod Othman, "Entrepreneurial Intention among Malaysian Undergraduates".
7. Jan Lepoutre, Wouter Van Den Berghe, Olivier Tilleuil, Hans Crijns, "A New Approach to Testing The Effects Of Entrepreneurship Education Among Secondary School Pupils".
8. Wei Li, "Entrepreneurial Intention among International Students: Testing A Model Of Entrepreneurial Intention".
9. Wang, C. & Wong, P. (2004), Entrepreneurial interest of university students in Singapore, Technovation, 24 (2), 161-172.
10. World Economic Forum. 2009. Educating the next wave of entrepreneurs: Unlocking entrepreneurial capabilities to meet the challenges of the 21st Century. Geneva, Switzerland: World Economic Forum.
11. Wilson, F., Kickul, J., & Marlino, D. 2007. Gender, entrepreneurial selfefficacy, and entrepreneurial career intentions: Implications for entrepreneurship education. Entrepreneurship Theory and Practice, 31(3): 387-406.
12. Baron, R. A. 2008. The role of affect in the entrepreneurial process. The Academy of Management Review (AMR), 33(2): 328-340.
13. Aronsson, M. 2004a. Education matters-but does entrepreneurship education? An interview with David Birch. Academy of Management Learning and Education, 3(3): 289-292.
14. Goplalkrishanan (2004), "Unleashing Indian Entrepreneurship -1: The changing mindset", The Hindu-Business Line, Internet Edition, Chennai.
15. Bhandari, N (2006), "Intention for Entrepreneurship among students in India", Journal of Entrepreneurship, Vol.15, No.2.

# 10

# Edupreneurs and Their Challenges and Opportunities in the Field of Engineering Education

***Abstract***

The main objective of this investigation is to classify the challenges and opportunities for an edupreneur (an entrepreneur in education sector) in the Engineering educational sector to be engaged and resolved. The case of one of the reputed engineering institution at Coimbatore, Tamil Nadu, India was studied and analyzed. Extensive feedback and their aspiration reference points were documented from all the stack holders of this educational enterprise. We are juxtaposing and contextualizing the case in hand with new Indian reality, emerging world order and irresistible global market place. Views of some educationists in the field of engineering education were also sought to gain more insight into the issue. It was observed that the challenges and opportunities that institutions face at different stages of growth considerably varies and the way such challenges would be met decides success and reputation of the organization. This paper attempts to be a guideline for edupreneurs and is of much relevance to those entrepreneurs who venture into the field of higher education.

## Introduction

India's Economy has grown by more than 9% for three years running, and has seen a decade of an average 7%+ growth. This has reduced poverty by 10%, but with 60% of India's 1.1 billion populations living off agriculture and with droughts and floods increasing, poverty alleviation is still a major challenge.

During this period of stable growth, the performance of the Indian service sector has been particularly significant. The growth rate of the service sector was 11.18% in 2007 and now contributes 53% of GDP. The industrial sector grew 10.63% in the same period and is now 29% of GDP. Agriculture is 17% of the Indian economy. Growth in the manufacturing sector has also complemented the country's excellent growth momentum. The growth rate of the manufacturing sector rose steadily from 8.98% in 2005 to 12% in 2006. The storage and communication sector also registered a significant growth rate of 16.64% in the same year. At this juncture, it is worthwhile to look at various factors that ensured the constant supply of skilled labour force to match the requirement. Due to rapid technological change, participative management and employee empowerment, global competitions and other workplace innovations have created a demand for a highly skilled engineering workforce.

One of the professions that have been mostly sought-after during this period is engineering. According to The Institution of Engineers, Australia, engineering is a profession directed towards the application and advancement of skills based upon a body of distinctive knowledge in mathematics, science and technology, integrated with business and management and acquired through education and professional formation in an engineering discipline. Engineering is directed to developing and providing infrastructure, goods and services for industry and the community. With the tremendous development of basic sectors like infrastructure, services etc., and the need for engineers have been increasing in an enormous scale. Engineering is the most preferred post school (after 10 plus 2) career option in India today. It is evident from the fact that, the engineering entrance examination coaching market in India amounts to a staggering sum of Rs.10,000/- crores every year. Moreover, Indian students are creative, innovative and scientifically inclined. When it comes to mathematics and the physical and biological sciences, Indian schoolchildren are ahead of their counterparts in other developed countries. As such, there has been in incredible growth in India in the number of institutions for higher learning that foster engineering courses. There were only 20 universities and 500 colleges in India at the time of independence. According to the Annual Report of Department of School Education & Literacy, Department of Higher Education, Government of India (2007-2008), presently there are 416 universities and 20,677 colleges fostering higher education in India. As per Gross Domestic Product Data of Reserve Bank of India, one can expect that the total number of engineers required in an economy, to be related to the size of population. If supply and demand for engineering graduates is to be balanced, it is expected that the number of engineering graduates required would depend upon the growth of the economy and the population.

The aforesaid status of developments in educational field leads to the following assumptions based on supply chain of human capital for positive engagement. These opportunities nationally and internationally can be seized only with educational-training interventions and help stay focused, productive and positive for the humanities.

1. Massive capacity in engineering colleges needs to be created for manning the growing Indian economy
2. Capacity creation is necessitated for maintaining cost arbitrage to engage Global market place
3. Pervasive and ubiquitous technology systems needs to be leveraged for quality arbitrage
4. More than 80 % of manual activities need to be automated in Indian domestic market
5. Huge opportunities in the markets in European union and African continent
6. India is caching up with China to become the next manufacturing hub of the world
7. Demographic advantage of India needs to be leveraged to tap markets of east Asian countries
8. Process and product innovation in the realm of energy, education and healthcare
9. Indian frugal mind set needs to be reinvented and reoriented for national productivity

On the other hand, this booming growth in the number of technical institutions has led to particularly acute issues and concerns for the engineering sector, wherein colleges struggling to hire adequately qualified faculty, graduates failing to find employment and regulators under pressure to improve standards.

According to Rao, U.R. (2003) a serious situation has arisen in recent years because of the mushrooming of a large number of private technical institutions and polytechnics. Barring some exceptions, there is scant regard for maintenance of standards in majority of the newly built institutions of higher learning. The rapid growth of engineering institutions has not only led to surplus numbers of engineering graduates, but also a dramatic shortage in qualified faculty. According to a study cited in the Rao report (2003), an additional 10,000 doctorate holders will be needed by 2008 to adequately staff engineering faculties across the country. Another study estimates that the Ph.D. shortfall is as high as 26,000 (based on a desired student-faculty ratio of 1:15) with an extra 30,000 master of technology graduates needed to fill vacant lecturer positions. The Hindu (2008) stated that although the existing colleges are providing good infrastructure facilities and adhering to the AICTE and university norms, the ever increasing number of private engineering colleges has, however, given rise to concerns about the quality of infrastructure and the standard of education. Over the past five years, at least 10,000 seats in self financing engineering colleges have had no takers annually due to poor quality of infrastructure and the academic ambience.

Above mentioned facts leads to the assumption that the challenges that are involved in venture creation in the field of higher education especially engineering, are numerous. This study is an attempt to conceptualize various such challenges that an edupreneur would face during the institutionalization of an engineering college. The specific case study along with the experiences of some senior educationists has led to the demarcation of challenges being faced by an edupreneur in the field of engineering higher education into three categories namely Initial stage, Growth stage and Sustainability stage. The challenges being faced in these difference stages are of varying degrees and are dealt with as follows.

## Initial Stage

New venture creation in the field of higher learning especially in the field of engineering requires sufficient funding to support initial growth. Following are the major challenges that an edupreneur would face in the initial stages of establishment of a new engineering college. This stage may last up to 4 years since inception.

### *Infrastructure*

Adequate infrastructure is one of the basic foundation on which further reputation of the college is built up. Good infrastructure speaks for itself about the kind of emphasis respective management team places on creating a conducive teaching and learning environment. Moreover, aesthetic design in commensuration with philosophy behind venture creation would add more value to brand building of the institution. In this perspective, the infrastructure has to match with the vision of the institution in all aspects so that it reflects the aspiration of the edupreneur. For e.g. in this case, the buildings have been built with a simplistic and traditional way because it is being run by a charitable institution.

The greatest challenge that the management would be facing at this point of time is adequate funding. Infrastructure being a capital investment, it requires heavy financial support to cater for the needs of the students. This has been very much visible in institutions wherein core engineering branches have been taught that requires heavy investment in machines, laboratories, workshops etc.

***Competent Faculty***

Another challenge that edupreneur would face at the initial stage is the availability of competent faculty to handle classes for different branches of engineering. One of the ways to improve the reputation of the college at the initial stage to attract competent faculty who can in turn attract better students to opt for studies in that college. In the initial stages of any engineering college, there would be reluctance on the part of efficient faculty to take up job in start-up institutions as they consider it to be less challenging.

However, this phenomenon remains as a challenge even in the growth stage. Faculty being a category of employees who generally prefer stability to risk taking, it remains as a great challenge to attract competent faculty at this stage. The availability of efficient faculty at this stage is a matter of concern as there would be fewer takers amongst faculty for a career in a start-up.

There are various ways through which this problem can be tackled. One of the methods is to offer a conducive growth environment for new faculty wherein faculty enjoys more freedom in terms teaching the subjects. Another way to attract best faculty is to provide motivation through financial incentives.

Provision of best compensation in the industry is most likely to attract faculty in the middle level to switch over from other institutions in the locality. Yet another way to attract competent faculty is to invite like-minded people through social network who share similar life-goals that of the edupreneur.

### *Brand Building*

Another challenge that an edupreneur would face in the initial stage would be that of brand building. A new engineering college needs to prove the fact that it is the right place for learning. This brand building is an important factor in the process of growing further and lays the foundation for an upward growth. In fact, the above mentioned factors like good infrastructure and competent faculty would itself provide a brand building for the college. However, it is to be noted that such brand building exercises need the careful selection of medium of communication. The medium of communication could be word-of mouth campaign, advertisement in leading newspapers, hoardings at important places in the city etc.

## Growth Stage

An engineering college will enter this stage once its reputation reaches a level wherein students prefer to identify themselves with brand name of the college. Along with the growth, number and magnitude of the challenges that an edupreneur is likely to face will also escalate. Following are the challenges that would come up at this stage of the life cycle of engineering colleges. This stage has a life span of about 10 years spreading from nearly 5th year of inception to the 15th year.

### *Growing Need for Expansion*

As the reputation of the college grows up in the market, it is more likely to attract greater number of students to opt for various courses. Since profit maximization is also one of the functions of an edupreneur, there arises a need to increase the number of intakes at this stage. With the increase in the number of students, there arises a need to expand the institution qualitatively and quantitatively. Qualitative expansion of an engineering college denotes provision of better competent faculty and other amenities allowed for students.

At this stage, there should be a continuous expansion of faculty fraternity not only by inclusion of other competent faculty but also by promoting those who have helped the organization to attain this growth who can take on the pressures of this growth stage with high morale and enthusiasm. Apart from the qualitative expansion mentioned above, quantitative expansion by way of better infrastructure and other allied facilities need to be brought out at this stage. This stage will therefore necessitate heavy financial investment on infrastructure in order to match up with the growth.

### *Corporate Relations Activities*

One of the key components of engineering education is its proximity to immediate employment. In the growth stage, it might be experienced that alumni of the respective college started working in various organizations of repute and the industry world start feeling the quality of various engineering colleges through these ambassadors. At this point of time, it is imperative that a healthy relationship is being building between various corporate who hire fresh engineering graduates and the college. One of the ways through which the reputation of the college would be analysed at this stage would be the performance of its alumni in the industry. A better liaison with various corporate at this stage would enable the college to project a clear picture about itself in the industry. At this stage, special emphasis must be placed on inviting various industry specialists to get involved in activities like guest lecture, faculty development programme, students' workshop etc.

### *Emphasis on allied activities*

With the institutional growth, engineering education should not remain as the only focus by the management of the college. With the influx of students with better caliber, there arises a need to equip students to pursue their passion in other field than engineering alone. At this stage, special training may be organized to facilitate students to take up other competitive examinations like Common Admission Test (CAT), Graduate Record Examination (GRE), and Graduate Aptitude Test in Engineering (GATE), Civil Services Examination, and Service Selection Board (SSB) etc. Activities pertaining to these areas would enthuse lot of students with different aspirations in life to join the college and pursue their passion while getting engineering education. Apart from the above, special emphasis might be placed in imparting training on various skills that would enhance the employability of engineering students.

## Sustainability stage

Once the college has established itself with a good brand name in the market, the sustainability stage arises. At this stage, efforts should be initiated to elevate the college to a higher institutional level wherein it creates an image worth adoring. Following are the challenges that an edupreneur likely to face at sustainability stage.

### *Research Oriented Education*

At sustainability stage, the institution has to grow beyond an engineering college status. It should promote research oriented education at this stage. In other words, it has to create a name in annals of those institutions which can produce highest quality talent. In order to achieve this status, edupreneur needs to take the institution at par with some of the best in the world. It needs to enter into Memorandums of Understanding with various other universities of repute for collaborative research programme through which both its faculty as well as students get benefited through exchange programmes. Such MoU will further the reputation of the institution in the market which can again result in attracting some of the best talents to take up various course in the institution. Such collaboration would culminate further consolidation of the institution in the market.

### *Higher level of interaction with Industry*

At this stage, there arises a need to have a better relationship with the industry. The performance of alumni must have already brought in good name for the institution in the industry circle at this stage. As a result of this development, the bargaining power of the institution would rise considerably whereby various corporate would prefer to associate their name with the institution at this stage. Industry experts should be invited to interact with students more frequently and be allowed to participate in the academic administration of the college so as to provide industry perspective into the curriculum development. Such invitation would further strengthen the relationship between industry and the college and would most likely to result in various activities by the industry ranging from running industry specific electives to infrastructural development through sponsorship of facilities in the college. Such collaborations would be mutually beneficial ones and would result in creating better image of the institution amongst industry giants.

### *Social Responsibility*

After having reached sustainability stage, it is the time for the edupreneur to contribute heavily to the society which has helped to grow the institution. Some of the activities that can be taken up at this stage are the adoption of weaker sections of the society, higher level of scholarships for underprivileged sections, reward for talented students etc. This would again develop the brand image of the institution in the eyes of society. By virtue of this commitment, it would attract some of the highly talented like-minded people to join hands with the institution in the national building process.

## Conclusion

In nutshell, the challenges that an edupreneur would likely to face are varying at different stages of the institutional development. This study has brought about a number of such challenges which can ensure steady growth in institutional building process. Following is conceptual model that sprung off this study.

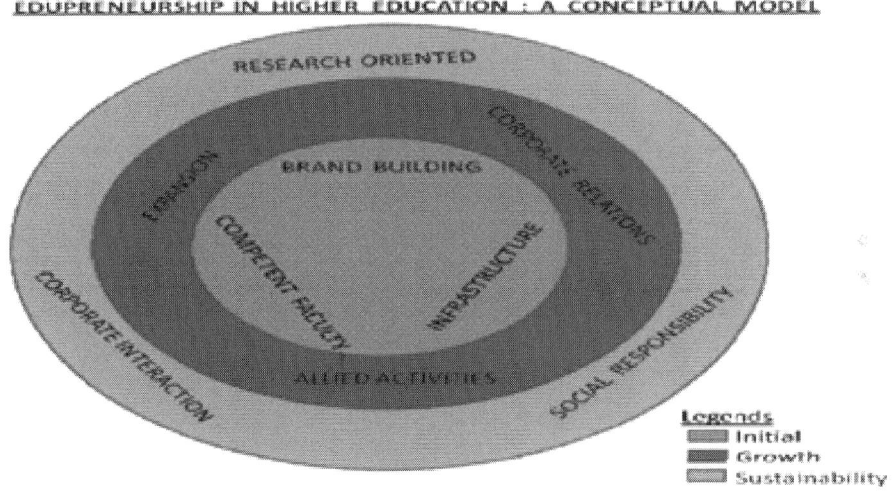


Based on the above conceptual model the following suggestions have been made under this study.

1. Provide students with all modern life style facilities which make the environment a learning friendly one.
2. Scaling up the operation is the key for making the operation cost effective and synergic.
3. Enroll 20% of students from developing nations and 2% from developed Anglo- Saxon countries for understanding their market and cultures.

4. The above said venture shall be under companies act or Public Private Partnership model envisaged by AICTE in its latest notification.
5. Mobilize finance from high network individual, banks and public offer.
6. The project shall be under social entrepreneurship to suit the comfort level of establishment and people at large.
7. Invest in people, technology artifacts and tools for the emerging Learning paradigm than existing teaching –learning paradigm.
8. Design the campus to facilitate entrepreneurship activities and incubation centers for startups.
9. Business model shall be training and education in general and niche areas of engineering pivoting on problem based learning for value creation.
10. Revenue shall be from endowments from various countries, industries and federal government.

## References

1. Reserve Bank of India (1999), "*Gross Domestic Product Data",* available at http://rbi.org.in/scripts/AnnualReportPublications.asp (accessed on 10 Feb 09).
2. Rao, U., R., (2003), "*Revitalising Technical Education*", AICTE Review Report, AICTE, Delhi.
3. The Hindu (2008), on-line edition, Jul 10, 2008, available at http://www.hindu.com /2008/07/10/ stories/2008071057790100.htm (accessed on 28 Dec 2008).

# 11

# Talent Management Challenges for the Entrepreneurs in Post- Tumultuous Times


**Abstract**

The industry today continues to face complex challenges:

- Increasing production to meet surging demands.
- Accessing newer and sustainable markets.
- Managing decline of saturating products in some areas.
- Talent Management : Hiring and retaining talents.
- Accelerating the development of existing technical professionals.
- Operating in increasingly remote and challenging areas.
- Exploiting new technologies available to the industry.


## 1. CHALLENGES during the tumultuous times

- Financial Crisis.
- Business downturn.
- Political turmoil & instability.
- Resource Shortage.
- Industrial inaction, Social unrest, etc.
- To create employment opportunities, working environment, learning & growth avenues, compensation and retention strategies.

## 2. The Solutions for success could be to follow the entrepreneurial way

- Cost control measures to be continued.
- Key Groups (Task forces) of Employees to be formed.
- Process Efficiency to be emphasised by technological upgradation.
- Providing honest information to the employees to keep them engaged.
- Management consulting to be encouraged for subject expertise.
- Maintaining fine balance of commitment, conjecture, cost-efficiency, communication and competition in the culture.

## 3. The Conclusions

Of all the challenges of Post-tumultuous times, the talent of acquisition, assimilation, as well as management of **Talent** has emerged to be the most difficult to tackle. There are insufficient professionals with the entrepreneurial experience to make autonomous decisions on critical projects across the key areas of our business, across all sectors. This fact slows the potential for a safe increase in output considerably.

The corporate world just had a sigh of relief with a recovery from one of most dreaded recessions. But, then the board roams were still grappling with the continued and complex challenges of:

- Optimizing production to meet surging demands.
- Continuously exploring and accessing newer and sustainable markets.
- Constantly managing decline of saturating products in some areas.
- Managing Talents: Hiring, upgrading and retaining talents.
- Accelerating the development and optimally leveraging of existing technologies.
- Operating in increasingly remote and challenging areas.
- Exploiting newer processes as well as techniques available to the industry.

However, the industry has yet to recover completely from the huge downturn that has posed a lot of challenges earlier during those tumultuous years. There are less chances that anyone of us have not been affected by all or atleast some of the following issues, during the difficult times:

- Financial Crisis.

- Business downturn.
- Political turmoil & instability.
- Resource Shortage.
- Industrial inaction, Social unrest, etc.
- Low employment opportunities,
- Disturbed working environment,
- Lesser avenues for learning & growth,
- Restricted and lower compensation and
- Difficult retention strategies.

The same can be best represented by the RISK MATRIX shown in fig.1

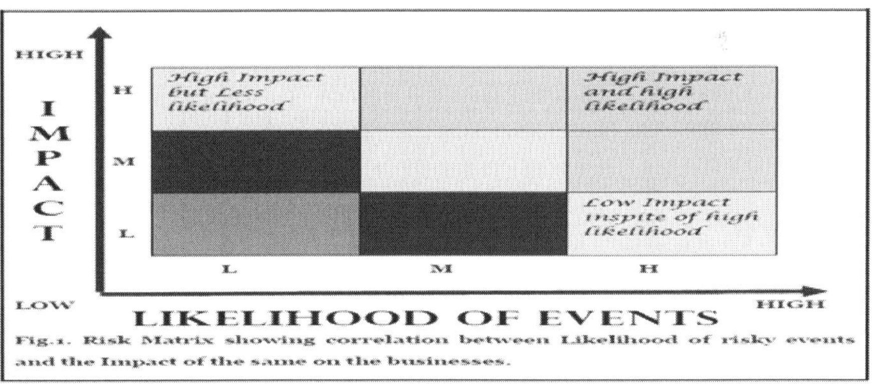

Fig.1. Risk Matrix showing correlation between Likelihood of risky events and the Impact of the same on the businesses.

As described in the fig.1 , in the post tumultuous times, it requires for entrepreneurs to decide and classify the likelihood / probability of various events that can create problematic business situations and assess the impact of each of this

Some of the lessons that Entrepreneurs have learnt from the bad times are startling and will be mostly permanent. They are:

(a) The Entrepreneurs would be avoiding fasting or feasting approach, forever.

(b) Entrepreneurs would be more strategic in our decision making and check whether it makes long term commercial sense.

(c) They would continuously strive to build trust, credibility and brand worthiness which is sustainable during any such crisis.

(d) All Entrepreneurs would appreciate the ill-preparedness before, during and after the recession. Check the gaps and make themselves more capable to face future challenges.

**The Solutions for success could be to follow the entrepreneurial way**

- Cost control measures to be continued.
- Key Groups (Task forces) of Employees to be formed.
- Process Efficiency to be emphasised by technological upgradation.
- Providing honest information to the employees to keep them engaged.
- Management consulting to be encouraged for subject expertise.
- Maintaining fine balance of commitment, conjecture, cost-efficiency, Communication and competition in the culture

Entrepreneurs, today, have the great advantage of being able to follow a trail blazed during the past experiences. To be sure, this is a path fraught with a plethora of stress. However, it is possible to convert that trauma into bundles of positive energy within a developing business. This is possible if one is ever vigilant in maintaining the "Five **C's**" of Talent Management as the platform from which to adapt. Adapting the Organisational systems to this Five C Talent Management platform to is the first step to building a partnership that will last and succeed:

## 1. Change Management

A major hurdle most entrepreneurs might like to overcome but are struggling all along is the ability to acquire and retain talent capable of changing circumstances, processes, systems, technologies, markets and resources to their advantage. The least of all, not resisting but adapting to the changes, that happen in the environment. It becomes important that entrepreneurs nurture and develop talents attuned to change themselves and others. It will ensure the redundancy at bay and many half-opportunities converted into assured business avenues.

## 2. Crisis Handling

Crisis is not necessarily related to a resource crunch only. It could be about limited or saturated markets, it could be about finding out newer and sustainable products, it could be about discoveries and innovations, it could be about the speed, competitiveness or collaborations. It is the ability of the talent within an organisation to handle and manage these crisis situations, makes all the difference!! It calls for entrepreneurs to foster such talent or task forces that stand up tall in these hours of crisis.

## 3. Competence based thinking and action

Competence has become the buzz word for remaining competitive and successful. It is the ability to think and act a cut above the rest, an ability to rise above the situation. Competence should therefore form an integral part of all thought processes and action points that an entrepreneur undertakes in order to create his venture successful. It is of prominence that he creates competencies that build and define paradigms and strategies for success. The entrepreneur creates mechanisms to channelize, develop and reward such competencies within the organisational framework. The organisational systems should be competency driven, generating a sense of fulfillment and enrichment.

## 4. Commitment - Care /Engage genuinely / be sensitive to needs

When asked about why you would leave the current organisation in a random survey, 72% of the interview candidates, quoted organisational commitment to be the single most factor, forcing them to think in the different direction. When further asked to elaborate, the following three points emerged as one of their major points of agony. Either they felt

a. The organisation has stopped caring for them, showing concern for them as an individual or

b. They are not meaningfully engaged or are not perceived to be engaged.

c. No one in the organisation is sensitive to their requirements on the job, their skill up gradation needs and career aspirations.

## 5. Credibility

The organizations fulfilling social, financial and stakeholders' responsibilities and accountabilities are considered to be credible, respected and well managed. One of the important pre-requisite for the organisation to be credible is its ethical governance. The management and practices have to be transparent, free from vested individual interests of the people at the helm of affairs and stakeholder focused. There have been innumerable examples and researches done on the subject and all the researches point at the fact the ethically governed corporate / institutions / organizations are the most preferred ones as employers. The employees consider it as a matter of pride and high honour to introduce themselves as part of an ethical organisation. A fair amount of credibility can also be achieved by the organisation by being socially responsible. By ensuring that society is equally benefited by the existence and development of the organisation, the later benefits by earning a reputation of a socially responsible organisation.

The above 5 Cs of talent management success leads to achievement of the following objectives, creating greater amount of stability, scalability and sustainability of the organizational systems:

Talent to run an enterprise, at right cost and levels of expertise.

Talent to grow the company.

Talent to get an edge in the market.

Once the systems get established, stabilized and built in the right framework, enhancement of "psychic income" is bound to happen. The following action points would ensure the focus on success of Talent Management:

## Action points for Talent Management

- **Analyse Needs at Organisational level**

Understand your Organisational strategy, markets and priorities. The constraints, needs as well as gaps in the organisational systems are to be identified and analysed. The options for solutions are to be developed.

Organisational elements needed to achieve strategic are to be defined and thereby an organisation structure is to be created, which is competitive and sustainable in highly dynamic scenario.

- **Analyze skills needed for your strategy**

Most of the modern organizations have realized the importance of and started working on their skill inventories. The requisite skill-sets are being identified and work profiles are being prepared, anticipating work programmes, project milestones and strategic outcomes. Depending on the skill-set requirements and availability of professionals, the acquisition is carried out. Steps would include identifying key positions, map job positions, identify pivotal roles, develop job descriptions, create initial templates for each job to the industry requirements and review job descriptions with selected stakeholders.

- **Align compensation programs**

Today's organizations are getting anxious about what compensation is paid next door. The compensation range that appears most competitive and attractive easily becomes obsolete before the turn of the Fiscal year or before the same can be budgeted. Therefore, more and more emphasis is being laid on compensation measures which are successful in sustaining the interests of the employees for the long term, viz. ESOPs / Long-term bonuses / Performance Linked Incentives, etc. and some non-tangible perks including sponsoring family vacations, tour programmes clubbed with holidays, flexi-timings, innovative work modules, etc.

- **Buy, borrow, steal but acquire**

The biggest challenge has become the availability of competent talent pool. Demand has far surpassed the supply and the rift is getting wider, with the time. The middle management supply is further scarce and scary. (Fig. 2) Acquiring the right mix of skill has become so very critical and vital; it becomes less important from where and how you get them.

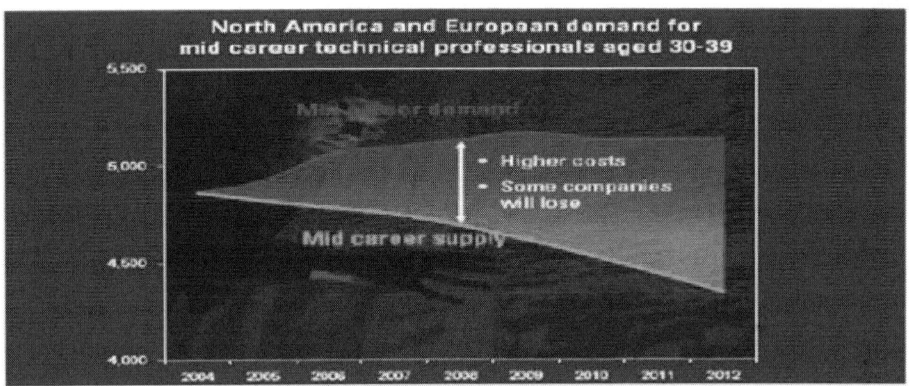


(Fig. 2) Midcareer Supply Demand-Supply Gap Scenario.

The biggest challenge has become the availability of competent talent pool. Demand has far surpassed the supply and the rift is getting wider. Acquiring the right mix of skill has become so very critical and vital; it becomes less important from where and how you get them. In industry, with the growing scarcity of talent, it becomes imperative to not only get the best talent pool but also to keep the existing talent sufficiently challenged and engaged. Inducting the right person at the right time in the organization has become a thing of the distant past. Today getting an almost right person, at any time seems to be the mantra.

The world population today is touching a throttling number of over 6.5 billion but yet the most common complaint heard around among all the CEOs is that they do not have enough competent people. Worse, they do not have much clue, how and where to get them.

- **RETENTION has no alternatives**

Retention is not just about getting your people stay with you but also harnessing, nurturing and creating vast skill and knowledge bank alongwith a huge experience pool, making these the competitive advantage into the ever changing equations of business. The mechanisms of employee retention are multifold some of them are:

(a) Job Challenges,
(b) Growth, learning, value-add opportunities.
(c) Fair and competitive Compensation
(d) Abilities, Aspirations and Engagement being taken care of.
(e) Culture of caring, sharing and fun.
(f) Work-life balance
(g) Identification with values, culture and brand.

- **Promote student awareness**

It has been a well-established fact that world-over the problem of ageing workforce is taking a toll on the availability of dynamic, experienced and competent workforce. There is more number of people retiring in last couple of decades than those inducted afresh. As a result there is a strong likelihood of current and future imbalance (Fig.3 )

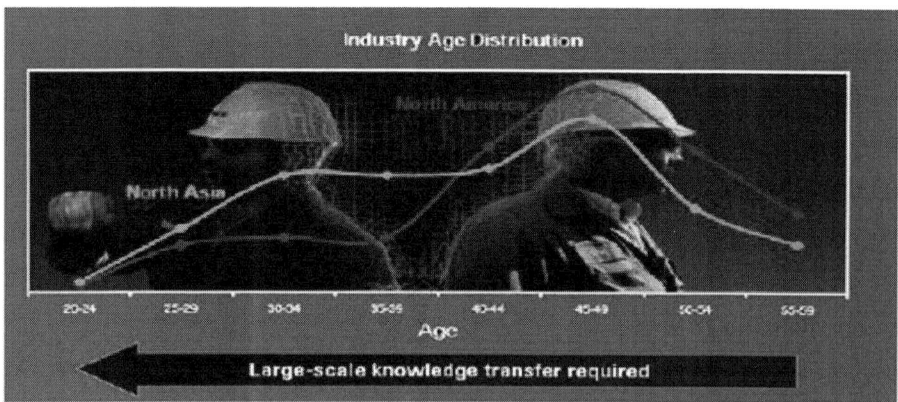


**(Fig. 3) Industry Age Imbalance Scenario**

"Catch them young" is the most effective way of identifying and planning a long-term talent management strategy for the organization. Students will be able to quickly raise up to the fast changing demands of the industry and hence it is advisable that the organizations take special interests in awareness campaigns and orientation drives to induct students even at a level above freshers. The best method therefore, could be to train and induct younger people while they are graduating, disseminate knowledge and the experience of the seniors, about to retire, before they are not available. This may help the organizations in growing their own 'timber'.

It is imperative to equip them to handle live-wire industry scenarios and situations. It may turn out to be a very handy investment to generate the interest among these young, ignited minds for the dynamics of the industry and thereby get more customized talent pool at the appropriate time.

## The conclusions

Of all the challenges of Post-tumultuous times, the talent of acquisition, assimilation, as well as management of Talent has emerged to be the most difficult to tackle. There are insufficient professionals with the entrepreneurial experience to make autonomous decisions on critical projects across the key areas of our business, across all sectors.

This fact slows the potential for a safe increase in output considerably.

# 12

# Effect of Entrepreneur Network, Behavioral, and Personality Traits on Enterprise Performance: A Study of Rural Artisan Clusters, India


### *Abstract*

This study examines the impact of entrepreneurial network structure (density and centrality), network type (internal network and external network), behavioral attribute (entrepreneurial self-efficacy), and personality traits (extraversion, agreeableness, emotional stability, conscientiousness, and openness) on enterprise performance (subjective performance and sales). The sample consisted of 152 micro and small enterprises in two textile handloom clusters in Madhya Pradesh, India. Hierarchical regression analysis results suggested that centrality, internal network, entrepreneur self-efficacy, extraversion, conscientiousness, and emotional stability together accounted for about 68 per cent in subjective performance. Whereas, centrality, external network, entrepreneur self-efficacy, extraversion, and conscientiousness together accounted for about 53 of the variance in sales. Contrary to the expectation, conscientiousness and emotional stability were negatively associated with Sales. Density, Agreeableness and Openness to experience were unrelated to sales. Results are explained by taking interdisciplinary theoretical support from the theory of social network, cluster theory, entrepreneur cognitive theory and personality trait theory. The research has implications for policymaking, research, and entrepreneurship training and education.

## Introduction

Micro, small, and medium enterprises (MSMEs) sector attracted considerable attention of researchers and policy makers from past few years primary because of its potential to generate employment. There has been steady decline of employment in agriculture from 58.54 per cent in 1999-2000 to 54.19 percent in 2004-05 (Prasad, Mathur and Chatterjee 2007) on the other hand MSME sector has recorded steady growth in employment is increased from 4.48 in 2001-02 to 6.24 in 2006-07 (Kishore 2010). The sector has around 26.1 million enterprises providing employment to around 59 million persons, contributing 45 per cent of the total manufacturing output, and 40 per cent of the total exports of the country. MSME sector has largely unregistered enterprises (73.85per cent) located in rural area (51.77 per cent). Most of the micro and small enterprises are spin-off enterprises where entrepreneurs start venture by getting support from the family and friends in terms of initial capital investment, as labors, emotional support, etc. Thereby reducing risks and increasing the chance of survival. However, limited production, limited access to market, and credit base business activities create asset specificity where these enterprises depend on few suppliers and buyers, increase uncertainty and risk. Besides, competition among MSMEs coupled with incursion of large domestic and foreign enterprises into market has increased the intensity of competition which forced MSMEs to compete at low margin which results in low performance and slow growth.

These adverse circumstances create necessity for micro and small entrepreneurs to have trust based long term strong networks with business partners. Entrepreneurial network is defined as exchange of resources in terms of interdependence between two actors where the actions of each directly affect the outcomes (rewards or punishments) of other (McCallister and Fischer, 1983). The quality of resources and information, speed or degree of trustworthiness as the one that gets exchanged through the network, cannot be the same as exchanged through other means (Shypilov, 2005). These networks develop rapidly if micro and small enterprises are located in a cluster - a geographical proximate group of manufacturing enterprises, suppliers, buyers, and supportive institutions, which share a long history of business, and community experience.

Most of the micro and small enterprises in India belong to traditional industries like handloom and handicraft, which are community and traditional skills based enterprises found in the form of clusters. Examples' are Ludhiana knitwear cluster, Agra leather shoes cluster, Tirupur knitwear cluster, Chanderi (Madhya Pradesh) handloom cluster, etc. Networks in a cluster mobilize technology, knowledge, cooperation, competition, and resources (Nadvi 1999; Schmitz, 1999), which accelerate learning, flexibility (Pietrobelli, 1998), and innovation, resulting low transaction costs, achieving economies of scale, and minimizing risk (Iyer and Toh, 2005), thus increasing performance (Visser, 1999; Gilbert, McDougall, and Audretsch, 2008).

Thus, cluster is redefined as a geographical bounded entity within which entrepreneurs' benefits are embedded in their social networks. However, in a cluster, when everyone knows every other person it increases the number of networks which takes the shape of a web. This increased networked relationship however, has certain infirmities embedded into it. For example, it may lead to restrictions on individual's freedom, create lock-in, develop fierce competition, and transferring obsolete information which adversely affect enterprise performance. Thus, the relationship of cluster and performance can be better understood by incorporating the theory of social network. But, it is ultimately an entrcpreneur who runs an enterprise and forms networks, which likely to have effects of his/her behavioral attributes and personality traits on performance.

An entrepreneur is not able to take advantage of cluster and network unless s/he has belief in his/her capability to successfully perform certain tasks, which is referred as self efficacy (Bandura, 1997). Thus, entrepreneur self efficacy refers to the entrepreneur's belief in his or capacity to perform various business tasks (McGee, Peterson, Mueller, and Sequeira 2009) such as identification of opportunity, formation of relationship, efficient resource management, risk taking (Barbosa, Gerhardt, and Kickul 2007), innovation, marketing, and developing critical human resources (De Noble, Jung and Ehrlich 1999). The concept of entrepreneur self efficacy is rooted in the theory of entrepreneurial cognition which states that the knowledge structures of an entrepreneur is different from others which s/he uses to make judgments involve in decisions making, opportunity evaluation, venture creation, and growth (Mitchell, Busenitz, Lant, McDougall, Morse, and Smith 2002). The Big five personality traits, extraversion, emotional stability, agreeableness, conscientiousness and openness to experience are considered as a robust indicators of personality (Barrick and Micheal

1991, Envick and Langford 2000; Ciavarella et al 2004) thus, likely to have influence on enterprise performance. The big five model provides a comprehensive and parsimonious explanation of various and diverse systems of personality which help to understand the outcomes of an individual (John and Srivastava 1999; Zhao and Seibert 2006). Thus, integrating the theory of entrepreneur cognitive and personality traits give better insight to the relationship of social network and cluster.

The objective of this paper is to identify factors that increase performance and by improving these factors, MSMEs can withstand in growing competitive market. Measurement of performance helps to know the current status of enterprise in the market place (Hansen & Wernerfelt 1989) and inform the entrepreneur about the correctness of business decisions taken. In case of micro and small enterprise, difficulty in obtaining financial records (Dess and Robinson 1984), unavailability of information in public, sensitiveness of entrepreneurs about releasing any performance-related data, and greater risk of error attributable to varying accounting procedures (Wall, Michie, Patterson, and Wood 2004) make financial measures insufficient to indicate their performance (Reijonen and Komppula 2007). Subjective performance measures such as product design and process, flexibility, product and process quality, corporate social performance, reputation, productivity, innovations, and team operations (Richard, Devinney, and Yip 2009) along with financial measure are appropriate method of measuring performance of micro and small enterprises.

## Entrepreneurial Network and Performance

The central proposition of social network theory is that actors' differential positioning within a network structure has an important impact on resource flows, and hence, on entrepreneurial outcomes (Hoang and Antoncic 2003). Network structure is defined as the pattern of direct and indirect ties between actors (Wasserman and Fruast 1994). Some of measures of network structure are network size, network density, network centrality, network range, reciprocity, multiplexity, network intensity, etc. For the study purpose, we have applied size, density and centrality measures of network structure. Network size is the total number of contacts of an entrepreneur (Hanneman and Riddle 2005). More number of contacts in a network structure increase the probability of the entrepreneur to access information and resources (e.g., Burt 2000; Hoang and Antoncic 2003; Scott 2000). Network density refers to the number of ties that the entrepreneur has within the network as compared to the total possible size of the network (Scott 2000; Hanneman and Riddle 2005). Entrepreneurs with high network density means know and known by every other person lead to access of more obsolete information and lack of opportunity. This probably happens because high-density networks may exclude outsiders, put excessive claims on group members, restrict individual freedoms, and downward leveling norms (Westlund and Bolton 2003). Whereas, entrepreneurs with low network density means few networks with others within the group (Grave 1995 as cited in Frazier 2000), indicating towards more diverse networks, thus have wide access to information and opportunities. Centrality measure of network indicates how well connected an entrepreneur is in the overall network structure (e.g. Gnyawali, Jinyu He and Madhavan 2007; Vincenzo 2008).

Centrality indicates an entrepreneur's closeness with network partners in terms of frequency of transaction, quickness, superiority and control of information and resources. Plethora of research have found positive and strong relationship between centrality and enterprise performance (e.g. Bulkley and Alstyne 2008).

However, few studies show negative impact of network on performance (Rowley, Behrens, and Krackhardt 2000).

It is expected that the longer an entrepreneur resides within the proximity of others in a cluster, the more she will be engaged in a trust-based strong networks. Proximity is a definite characteristic of a cluster. Proximity, shared beliefs, and business commonalities between entrepreneur and various business actors (i.e. inputs purchased, technology, infrastructure, buyers, distribution channel, transportation, and production process) facilitate the likelihood of communication and interactions (Hoang and Antoncic 2003) transform into strong networks. It develops trust, lower down transaction cost, reduces risks and uncertainty, thus, positively affecting enterprise performance (Uzzi 1999; Maeerinskas and Pakalnienë 2004; Echols and Tsai 2005). Nadvi (1999) observed that cluster draws strength from being embedded in local social networks which are based on the kinship, family and localness. Social networks act as a mechanism to understand the co-existence of local competition with local cooperation.

They co-operate with each other but certain types of information especially about the marketing information and technologies are not shared among them. Gurrieri and Petruzzellis's (2006) study of Italian cluster suggested that social networking has a greater influence than geographic proximity in facilitating inter-enterprise co-operation in reducing the transaction and communication costs.

Enterprises in Silicon Valley cluster in United States were showed high growth because of higher rate of innovation created by transmitting information and knowledge through networks which were dense, performance-focused, trustworthy, collaborative, and productive exist among the research universities, government, venture capital enterprises, and law enterprises (Castilla, Hwang, Granovetter, and Granovetter 2000). Entrepreneur networks have positive impact on Keiretsu cluster in Japan enterprise's financial performance (Lincoln, Gerlach, and Ahmadjian 1996).

Unlike cluster, a network cannot be confined to a particular geographical boundary. It is observed that cluster enterprises form networks outside cluster referred as non-local or external networks. An increase in a cluster population intensifies competition for resources within the cluster, suppress and innovation, and increase failure (Monge and Contractor 2003). Proximity is no longer a rewarding factor for networking (Schutjens and Stam 2003; Stanley and Helper 2003). Pouder and St John's (1996) stated that social networks might become a source of fierce competition, inertia, fewer opportunities, impair innovation and inflexibility. Uzzi (1996) explained that social network had an inverted U-shaped relationship with enterprise performance rather than a linear relationship. He further explained that embedded or strong networks were more advantageous for entrepreneur but, after a threshold level, embedded networks negatively affect performance and an entrepreneurs formed more arm-length or external networks to access new opportunities. Cluster entrepreneurs were better off in not being too embedded in a particular cluster by forming more of internal networks (Maskell 2001). A cluster entrepreneur use external networks as strategy to identify opportunities and resources beyond the geographical boundaries of cluster (Rocha and Sternberg 2005). External networks reduce dependencies over cluster actors, increase innovation (Nadvi 1999), knowledge and information transformation (Das 2008), exploit power advantages, increase share in existing market, and create new markets (Muscio 2006), upgrading about market demand (Schmitz 1999).

Boschma and Wal (2007) observed that enterprises having external networks enhance knowledge inflow resulting high rate of innovative than enterprises having internal networks. Britton's (2002) study of electronics cluster of Toronto, Canada revealed that external networks were privileged over internal networks with respect to markets, material inputs (basic materials, parts and components and sub-systems/subassemblies), and sources of knowledge (R&D, design and engineering, testing, software, market intelligence). Li and Zhang (2007) studied that at the time intense competition, an enterprise prefers to go for more external networks to increase performance. However, Deacon, Pascal, Schwartz and Teach (2006) found that only cluster showed positive relationship with enterprise performance but social capital had no effect on cluster enterprise performance, indicating that social capital was not associated with cluster. Despite, the plethora of research on cluster and enterprise performance, relationship between social networks and cluster is not clear and thus their relationship remains in a black box (Schmitz, 1999).

## Entrepreneurial self efficacy (ESE) and Performance

Understanding Entrepreneur self efficacy was important, because it affect individuals' willingness to engage in entrepreneurship as well as the behavior of those who are already entrepreneurs (Forbes 2005). Entrepreneurs were found to have a significantly higher self-efficacy than non-entrepreneurs on two distinct aspects of perseverance: perceived control over adversity and perceived responsibility regarding outcome of adversity (Markman, Balkin and Baron 2002).

One of the important features of ESE is that it incorporated personality as well as environmental factors, which increase its robustness and allow researchers to distinguish entrepreneurs from non-entrepreneurs, better understand entrepreneurial decision-making processes, and effectively predict entrepreneurial intentions (McGee, Peterson, Mueller, and Sequeira 2009).

Entrepreneurs who are confident in their ability to achieve high-growth are likely to set challenging growth expectations for their enterprises and persist in their leadership efforts towards the accomplishment of those goals (Baum, Locke, and Smith 2001).

Entrepreneurs with high levels of ESE are more likely to exhibit high level of persistence, concentration, and work satisfaction behaviors thus, likely to enhance performance (Forbes 2005; Hmieleski and Baron 2008). Hmieleski and Baron, (2008) found that in dynamic environments, entrepreneurial self-efficacy exerts positive effects on performance for enterprises led by moderately optimistic entrepreneurs. Sometimes, higher level might cause negative impact in terms of undermining their ability to run enterprise efficiently (Barbosa, Gerhardt, and Kickul 2007). Chandler

(1997) found that entrepreneurial self efficacy did not predict performance. Hmieleski and Corbett (2008) found that entrepreneurial self efficacy had negative moderating effect on the relationship of founder's improvisational behavior with both the performance of their startups and their individual level of work satisfaction, but they found that among founders with high level of entrepreneur self efficacy improvisational behavior had positive relationship with new venture performance.

## Big five personality traits and Performance

The big five personality factors (extraversion, agreeableness, conscientiousness, emotional stability, and openness to experience) have been used to differentiate successful entrepreneurs from unsuccessful entrepreneurs (Antoncic 2009) and likelihood of an individual to become an entrepreneur (Shane 2008). Relationship of entrepreneur's big five traits and enterprise performance however is limited (Ciavarella, Buchholtz, Riordan, Gatewood, Stokes 2004). The trait of extraversion has been found to be positively related to the intensity and quality of social network formed by entrepreneur with suppliers and buyers (Zhao and Seibert 2006), energy levels, positive emotionality, and excitement seeking (Ciavarella, et al. 2004) to make business profitable. (Ciavarella, et al. 2004) observed that high level of emotional stability was preferable for an entrepreneur for long term success of an enterprise. In contrast, Zhao and Seibert (2006) observed that an entrepreneur was preferred with low level of emotional stability which characterized as selfconfident, calm, even tempered, and relaxed. Agreeableness trait showed trustworthiness, cooperative, courteous, forgiving, and flexibility in dealing with others (Ciavarella et al. 2004). High level was preferable but for an entrepreneur it might inhibit one's willingness to drive hard bargains, look out for one's own self-interest, and influence or manipulate others for one's own advantage (Zhao and Seibert 2006). Dependability, industriousness, and efficiency are the basic components of conscientiousness and those high on this factor tend to be hardworking, achievement-oriented, and persevering (Ciavarella et al. 2004) thus, positively affecting performance. Openness to experience is characterized as being intellectual, intelligent, and open to new ideas and experiences, increased the ability of an entrepreneur to innovate, thus was positively related to performance (Ciavarella et al. 2004).

Ciavarella, et al. (2004) observed that among the big fives, only conscientiousness showed a positive relationship with long term venture survival. Openness was negatively associated with venture survival and extraversion, emotional stability and agreeableness were unrelated to long term venture survival. Shane (2008) found that agreeableness was negatively affected the likelihood to become an entrepreneur, because agreeable people were less likely to pursue their own self-interest, more skeptical than others, drive difficult bargains, or use others to achieve their objectives. Antoncic (2009) found that only openness was positively related to technology development.

Neuroticism showed a negative relationship with technology developments and others traits showed non-significant relationship. Zhao, Seibert, and Lumpkin (2010) reported that four of the Big Five personality dimensions were associated with entrepreneurial intentions and entrepreneurial performance, agreeableness failing to be associated with either. These studies suggested that personality factors play a role in the emergence and success of entrepreneurs. One of the major criticisms of Big five model is that it does not cover all the dimension of personality. Saucier and Goldberg (1998) observed that personality dimensions such as fashionableness, sensuality/seductiveness, beauty, masculinity, frugality, humor, wealth, prejudice, folksiness, cunning and luck were potentially beyond big five model. John and Srivastava (1999) observed that despite, its comprehensiveness, it suffers from the disadvantage of low fidelity.

Based on the previous research conducted in the field as well as broad understanding of the factors affecting micro and small enterprise performance, the authors formulated several hypotheses. First, we hypothesised that network density will be negatively related to subjective performance and sales. Second, network centrality will be positively associated with subjective performance and sales. Third, external network will be positively associated with subjective performance and sales. Fourth, internal network will be negatively associated with subjective performance and sales. Fifth, while controlling for density, centrality, internal network and external network, entrepreneur self efficacy will be positively related to subjective performance and sales. Sixth, big five personality traits will be positively related to subjective performance and sales.

## Methodology

### Context

The study was conducted in two textile handloom clusters namely Maheshwar and Chanderi in Madhya Pradesh. Maheshwar cluster is well known for its handloom fabric especially Saari known as 'Maheswari Saari'.

In the year 2009, the cluster produced around 21.36 lakh meters per year with total 1778 working loom running by 5334 weavers achieved a turnover of around ` 20 crore.

Traditional Maheshwar designs were inspired by the designs of local fort, temples, and ghats. Till 1990s only Maru (Shatriya) and Ansari caste were involved in this traditional business. Over a period of time, people from other communities were involved in this business such as Khangar, Sali, Julaha, Manjhi, Kevat, Bhil, Bhilala, Kori, and Koli. The cluster comprises of various factors such as, local yarn supplier, chemical color suppliers, entrepreneurs (master weavers), job workers, cooperative societies, and buyers.

Chanderi, Madhya Pradesh is one of the best known handloom cluster in India famous for its specialty of fine textured fabric of silk and cotton embellished with zari-woven work, minimum weight and transparency. Approximately 60 per cent of Chanderi's population is dependent on weaving. Chanderi handloom produces three types of fabric pure silk, chanderi cotton, and silk cotton.

Chanderi cluster has around 3000 looms and 11000 weavers (as per the 2003 UNIDO cluster development report). The core cluster actors consist of traders, master weavers, weavers, designers, dyers, yarn suppliers and supportive institutions.

## Sample

Data were collected from 152 rural micro and small entrepreneurs located in the textile handloom clusters of Maheshwar and Chanderi, Madhya Pradesh. The researcher administered a survey questionnaire. The survey questionnaire included items capturing subjective performance measures (innovation, product quality, and customer satisfaction), networks with supplier, buyers, competitors, and supportive institutions, entrepreneurial self-efficacy, and big five personality traits. The scaled items were originally written in English and later translated into Hindi, back translation procedure was used to maintain the item equivalence. Each questionnaire took approximately 30-40 minutes to complete. Apart from the survey, in-depth interviews were conducted with few entrepreneurs to gain insights into cluster and network relationship.

All entrepreneurs, in the sample, were male and engaged in handloom business. The age of the entrepreneurs ranged from 22 to78 years with an averagc age of 41 years with a standard deviation of 10.46. Entrepreneurial experience ranged from three to thirty five years with an average experience of 13 years and standard deviation of 8.43. Out of the total entrepreneurs, 53.9 per cent entrepreneurs had an education below 10th grade, 18.4 per cent finished 10th grade, 14.5 per cent finished higher secondary, 10.5 per cent entrepreneurs were graduated and only 2.5 percent entrepreneurs are post graduated. Of all the entrepreneurs, 25per cent had sales below ' 1.79 lakhs, 50 per cent had sales below ' 2.29 lakhs, and 75per cent entrepreneurs had sales below ' 2.82 lakhs. Of the total entrepreneurs 25per cent entrepreneurs had number of employees below 7, 50per cent entrepreneurs had employees below 12 and 75per cent entrepreneurs had employees below 25.

## Measures

### Objective measures of performance

Current year sales (2009-10) had been used as an indicator of financial performance. Sales represents net revenue generated from billing customers, reduced by discounts and return allowances (Powell, Koput, Smith-Doerr, and Owen-Smith 2000). Although, sale growth instead of sales is a good predictor of financial measure but, researchers had selected sales as an indicator because of non-existence of past financial sales records. Entrepreneurs did not keep record of their transactions so that it was extremely difficult to get past data.

Therefore, based on the raw figures given by entrepreneurs, current year sales were calculated. Sales arguably sufficient performance measures especially for micro and small firms because of its relative insensitiveness to capital intensity and degree of integration (Lechnera, Dowlingb, and Welpe 2006).

### Subjective Measure of Performance

The subjective measure of enterprise performance captures the entrepreneur's perception of the enterprise performance as compare to competitors. The scale consisted of 11 items. The scale items sales growth and overall performance were adapted from Dess and Robinson Jr. (1986), quality of products, development of new products, satisfaction of customers or clients, ability to offer competitive prices were adapted from Delaney and Mark (1996). Other items such as, quality of customer service, ability to differentiate products, ability to introduce new product, ability to introduce new ideas into business and ability to introduce new designs and pattern introduced by authors. The respondents were asked to indicate on a 5 point scale of 1 equaling "very poor" to 5 "excellent" the extent to which they were satisfied with different aspects of their enterprises performance compared to competitors within the clusters.

Subjective performance scale showed high reliability (Cronbach á = 0.85). Entrepreneurial self efficacy Entrepreneurial self-efficacy measures the extent to which the entrepreneur believes that s/he is having resources or will be able to access resources to effectively carry out the entrepreneurial activities. The scale consisted of nine items. The scale items, develop new designs and pattern, identify market opportunities, dealing effectively with day-to-day problems and crises items were adapted from Hmieleski and Baron (2008) which was originally developed by De Noble, Jung D, Ehrlich (1999), customer satisfaction was adapted from Chandler (1997), competitive price and financial management were adapted from Barbosa, Gerhardt, Kickul (2007), risk and uncertainty, Inspire, encourage, and motivation of employees was adapted from McGee, Mueller, and Sequeira (2009). The participants responded to the items by indicating their level of satisfaction on a five-point Likert scale; ranging from 1 (strongly disagree) to 5 (strongly agree). Entrepreneurial self-efficacy scale showed moderate degree of reliability (Cronbach á = 0.75).

## Entrepreneur network measures

### *Density*

The measure of density was modified version of density scale developed by Frazier (2008). The scale consisted of 10 items covering closeness, trust and reliability of information with suppliers, buyers and competitors. Few of the items were; 'I trust these people that they will not behave opportunistically', 'I get reliable information'. The participants responded on a five-point Likert scale indicating the extent of agreement (Strongly disagree = 1; Strongly agree = 5) to each of the 10 items in the scale. Density scale showed high reliability (Cronbach á = 0.84).

### *Centrality*

The measure of centrality was modified version of density scale developed by Frazier (2008), consisting of 11 items covering exchange frequency and quickness of resources and information with suppliers, buyers and competitors. The participants responded on a five-point Likert scale (1 = Strongly disagree; 5 = Strongly agree) on items like, 'I frequently exchange resources'. Centrality scale had moderate reliability (Cronbach á = 0.68).

***Network size of internal network***

Internal network size refers to the number of networks maintained by entrepreneurs within the cluster. The respondents were asked to indicate numbers of suppliers, buyers and supportive organizations with whom they networked. To arrive at the total internal network, the sum of suppliers, buyers and supportive organization were taken.

***Network size of external network***

Entrepreneur network size is the number of network outside the cluster. The respondents were asked to indicate numbers of suppliers and buyers with whom they networked outside of cluster. External network was calculated by summing up total number of these suppliers and buyers.

## Big Five personality traits

Researcher adopted the Big Five Inventory constructed (BFI) by John, Donahue, and Kentle (1991) containing 44 items. The reliability of BFI is alpha (.83) (cited in John and Srivastava, 1999). BFI was frequently used in research because of its simplicity and less time consuming nature. BFI uses short phrases based on the trait adjectives served as the items core to which elaborative, clarifying, or contextual information was added and avoids some of pitfalls such as ambiguous or multiple meanings and salient desirability. Four items, artistic interests, cooperation with others, easily distract and sophisticated in art, music or literature were dropped from the list of 44 items. Extraversion scale consisting of 8 items covering traits like talkative, reserved, energy, enthusiasm, quiet, assertive, shy, inhibited, and sociable, showed moderate reliability (Cronbach á = 0.74). Agreeableness scale consisting of 8 items covering traits like helpful and unselfish, forgiving nature, trusting, cold and aloof, kind, rude and cooperate, showed high reliability (Cronbach á = 0.93). Conscientiousness scale consisting of 8 items covering traits like careless, reliable, disorganized, lazy, perseveres, and efficient showed high reliability (Cronbach á = 0.83). Emotional stability scale consisting of 8 items covering traits like depressed, relaxed, tense, emotionally stable, moody, and calm and nervous, showed moderate reliability (Cronbach á = 0.74). Openness scale consisting of 8 items covering traits like, curious, ingenious, deep thinker, active imagination, inventive, values artistic, and aesthetic experiences, showed high reliability (Cronbach á = 0.88).

## Results

### *Data Screening*

Prior to the analysis all the measures were examined through SPSS (PASW version 18) for missing values, univariate outliers, and normal distribution. To understand the relationship among variables, mean, standard deviation, and correlation were computed which is presented in table 1. Results suggested that density, centrality, external networks, entrepreneur self-efficacy, extraversion, agreeableness, and conscientiousness were positively and significantly related to subjective measure of performance, but internal network was negatively related to subjective performance; means internal networks reduce bargaining power of entrepreneurs, cause low product quality and development thus, adversely affecting performance. Density, centrality, external networks, entrepreneur self-efficacy, extraversion, and conscientiousness were positively and significantly related to sales. Density correlated positively to centrality, external network, entrepreneur self efficacy, conscientiousness, and emotional stability. Centrality, positively related to supportive network, entrepreneurial self-efficacy and conscientiousness. It indicates that entrepreneurs with high level of entrepreneur self efficacy were tend to be more hard workers and efficient and acquired more central position in the network structure, thus have more access to opportunities and positively affecting performance.

Entrepreneurial self-efficacy correlated positively with extraversion, agreeableness, conscientiousness, and emotional stability. Extraversion was positively related to agreeableness and openness. Conscientiousness was positively related to emotional stability and openness. Emotional stability was positively correlated with openness.

To test our hypotheses we subjected the data to hierarchical regression analysis. Value Inflation Factors (VIFs) were calculated to test for multicollinearity among the predictors. The VIFs values were within the level of acceptable limit of five as suggested by Cohen, Cohen, West, and Aiken (2003).

Two sequential regressions with each of subjective performance and sales as dependent variables were tested (see Table 2). In the Model 1 network structure measures, density, centrality, internal network and external network were entered. These predictors together accounted for ($R = 0.50$; $p < .001$) with about 24 per cent of the variance in the subjective measure of performance. Centrality (â = .343; $p <.01$) and external network (â = .332; p <.01) made unique significant and positive contribution. Internal network (â = -.171; p <.01) made significant but negative contribution to subjective performance. Therewas no unique contribution of density. This supported our second and third hypotheses that centrality and external networks positively affect subjective performance. Internal network was negatively associated with subjective performance, confirmed fourth hypothesis. However, did not find any significant relationship of density with subjective performance, thus not supported out first hypothesis.

In the Model 2, entrepreneur self-efficacy, extraversion, agreeableness, conscientiousness, emotional stability and openness were added. While controlling density, centrality, internal network and external network, the results showed a significant improvement of overall multivariate relationship (R = 0.825; P < 0.001) and variance (68per cent). Entrepreneur self-efficacy has strong significant contribution (â=0.635; p<.01) followed by centrality (â = 0.222; p< .01), extraversion (â = 0.249; p< .01) positively and significantly contributed to subjective performance. Whereas, internal network (â= -0.168; p<.01), conscientiousness (â= -0.114; p<.05) and emotional stability (â = -0.106; p< .05) all of which made a negative but significant contribution to subjective performance. A significant change in R square of 0.437 at p< .01 was observed.

This confirmed our fifth hypothesis that while controlling for density, centrality, internal network and external network, entrepreneurs' self-efficacy is positively related to subjective performance. In the Model 3 network structure measures, density, centrality, internal network and external network were entered. These predictors together accounted for (R =0.63; p < .001) with about 40 per cent of the variance in sales. Centrality (â = 0.367; p <.01) and external network (â = 0.585; p <.01) made unique significant and positive contribution. There was no unique contribution of density and internal network. This supported our second and third hypotheses that centrality and external networks positively affect sales. However, didn't find any significant relationship of density and internal network with subjective performance, thus not supported out first hypothesis.

In the Model 4, entrepreneur self-efficacy, extraversion, agreeableness, conscientiousness, emotional stability and openness were added. While controlling density, centrality, internal network and external network, the results showed a significant improvement of overall multivariate relationship (R = 0.728; P < 0.001) and variance (53 per cent). Entrepreneur self-efficacy has strong significant contribution (â=0.372; p<.01) followed by centrality (â = 0.294; $p < .01$), external network ((â = 0.441; $p < .01$), extraversion (â = 0.144; $p < .05$) positively and significantly contributed to sales. Whereas, conscientiousness (â= -0.136; $p < .05$) was negatively but significant contributed to sales. A significant change in R square of 0.131 at $p < .01$ was observed. This confirmed our fifth hypothesis that while controlling for density, centrality, internal network and external network, entrepreneurs' self-efficacy is positively related to sales.

## Discussion & Conclusion

We had set out to examine the impact of entrepreneurial network density, network centrality, internal network, external network, entrepreneurial selfefficacy, and personality traits (extraversion, agreeableness, emotional stability, conscientiousness, and openness) on enterprise performance measured in terms of subjective performance and sales. And, also integrate the network theory, self efficacy theory and theory of personality in explaining cluster effect on enterprise performance. Being located in a cluster does not guarantee higher performance for enterprises. There are other two important factors namely network and entrepreneur's behavior and personality traits which affect cluster enterprise performance. Network mobilizes cluster benefits to enterprises. An entrepreneur is a significant part in the process of achieving higher performance especially in micro and small enterprises, so there is high chance of influence of his or her behavior and personality on performance. First, we hypothesized that network density will be negatively related to subjective performance and sales. However, this hypothesis was not supported. Second hypothesis that network centrality will be positively associated with subjective performance and sales supported by hierarchical regression. High centrality provides more and quick access to fine grained information, thus positively affect performance. The result is in line with Powell, Koput, Smith- Doerr, and Owen-Smith (2000), Gnyawali, Jinyu He and Madhavan (2007), and Vincenzo (2008). Third hypothesis was supported that external network will be positively associated with subjective performance and sales. The result is in line with Li and Zhang (2007). External network increase innovation rate, expand market, increase bargaining power, and decrease dependencies, thus positively affect performance. Fourth hypothesis was partially supported that internal network will be negatively associated with subjective performance and sales.

Internal network showed significant negative relationship with subjective performance only. Internal network reduce bargaining power and transfer more obsolete information where entrepreneur not able to access information on current market demand, thus negative affect performance. Fifth, hypothesis was that while controlling for density, centrality, internal network and external network, entrepreneur self efficacy will be positively related to subjective performance and sales also supported. The result is in line with Baum, Locke, and Smith (2001), Barbosa, Gerhardt, and Kickul (2007), and Hmieleski and Baron, (2008). High entrepreneur self efficacy increases entrepreneur's capability of doing various business tasks, thus positively affecting performance. Sixth hypothesis that big five personality traits will be positively related to subjective performance and sales was partially supported.

Only extraversion was significant and positively related to subjective performance and sales indicating that entrepreneurs who are more extraversion tend to form more networks especially external networks to seek out new opportunities, thus positively influence performance. In contrast of prediction, emotional stability and conscientiousness were significant and negatively associated with subjective performance and only conscientiousness was significant and negatively associated with sales. Agreeableness and openness were not related to subjective performance and sales which was against the hypothesis. In cluster, availability of sufficient number of suppliers and buyers, long term network, repeated transactions, reduce transaction cost and risk, facilitate timely delivery of payment, and develop high level of satisfaction which make entrepreneurs less industrious and efficient however, these increase performance. Emotional stability was negatively associated with the performance indicating that entrepreneurs have high level of emotional stability tends to achieve higher profit by expanding business require to form more external networks, large capital investment, etc., resulting increasing in transaction costs, risks, anxiety, impulsiveness, and vulnerability, thus negatively affect performance. While entrepreneurs with low level of emotional stability are risk adverse, calm, satisfied, and self confident positively affect performance.

## Implications

Implications of this study are three fold. First, personality traits have implication for investors who are looking for financing new startups, for supportive services, and for entrepreneurs who want to evaluate themselves for success of their own enterprises (Ciavarella, Buchholtz, Riordan, Gatewod, and Stokes 2004). Second, however, internal networks are important but increasing number of competitors and buyers reduce margin of entrepreneurs which lead towards slow growth of enterprises. Long term suitability in market, requires an entrepreneur to form external networks with outside buyers and suppliers.

Formation of external networks should not be limited to their number but focus should be more on the quality of external networks (Schmitz 1999). Integration of internal and external networks implies a market power for the cluster as a whole (S-Olivery and Albors-Garrigo´ Sz 2007). Government mostly provides supportive networks in terms of financial and training however, government need to support theses micro and small entrepreneurs by linking them with buyers and suppliers. Third, increasing capability is essential to survive in competitive market. Motivational training specifically design for micro and small entrepreneurs increase their capability in terms of management skills, learning, and opportunity identification,.

## Limitations & Directions for future research

This study has certain limitations. First, network data were collected from entrepreneurs only which might cause biasness in network measures. Second, networks are dynamic in nature and study was a cross sectional, so their might a chance of not predicting the true effect of network on performance. Third, network is an investment which incurs certain cost and by including cost, net effect of network on performance can be measured. The study does not included cost of network. Nevertheless, there are other factors also that affect cluster enterprise performance, require future research. The presented study was exclusively based on handloom clusters which were very old, traditional skilled and community based cluster, comparative studies between old and emerging cluster, manufacturing cluster and traditional skilled cluster, successful and unsuccessful cluster bring more insight about factors affecting performance. Cluster and network both are dynamic in nature so longitudinal study is more appropriate to understand the evolution, factors lead to formation and decline of cluster and network, etc.

## References

1. Antoncic, Bostjan (2009) "The Entrepreneur's General Personality Traits And Technological Developments", *World Academy Of Science, Engineering And Technology*, 53, pg. 236
2. Bandura, Albert (1997). Self efficacy: The Exercise of Control. New York: W. H. Freeman Barbosa, Saulo Dubard, Megan W Gerhardt,

Jill Richard Kickul (2007). The Role of Cognitive Style and Risk Preference on Entrepreneurial Self-Efficacy and entrepreneurial intensions. *Journal of Leadership & Organizational Studies*, 13, pp.86-104.

3. Baum, J.A.C., Calabrese, T., Silverman, B.S. (2000) "Don't Go It Alone: Alliance Network Composition and Startups' Performance in Canadian Biotechnology", *Strategic Management Journal*, 21: 267–294. Boschma, Ron A and Anne L J ter Wal (2007) Knowledge Networks and Innovative Performance in an Industrial District: The case of a footwear district in the south of Italy", *Industry and Innovation*, May, 14: 2, pg. 177
4. Barrick, Murray R and Mount, Michael K. (1991) "The Big Five Personality Dimensions and Job Performance: A Meta-Analysis", *Personnel Psychology,* Spring, 44:1, pg. 1
5. Britton J. (2003) "Network structure of an industrial cluster. Electronics in Toronto", *Environment and Planning A*. 35:6, pp.983-1006
6. Bulkley, Nathaniel and Marshall Van Alstyne (2008) "An Empirical Analysis of Strategies and Efficiencies in Social Networks", October. Retrieved on 17/11/2008 from www.chicagogsb.edu/research/workshops/orgsmarkets/ docs/bulkley-strategies.pdf
7. Burt, Ronald S. (2000) "The Network Structure of Social Capital", *Research in Organizational Behaviour*, July, 22, pp.1-89
8. Castilla, Emilio J., Hokyu Hwang, Ellen Granovetter, and Mark Granovetter (2000) "Social Networks in Silicon Valley", Retrieved on 17/8/2009 from web.mit.edu/ecastill/www/publications/CastillaExtract.pdf –
9. Chandler, Gaylen N. (1997) "Founder Self-Efficacy and Venture Performance: A Longitudinal Study", *Academy of Management Proceedings*, pg. 98
10. Ciavarella, Mark, A, Ann K. Buchholtz, Christine M. Riordon, Robert D Gatewood, and Garnettt S. Stokes (2004) The big five and venture survival: is there a linkage?, *Journal Of Business Venturing*, 19, pp.465-483
11. Das, Keshab, (2008) "Fostering Competitive Clusters in Asia: Towards an Inclusive Policy Perspective", working paper no. 437. Retrieved on 12/8/2008 http://www.ide.go.jp/English/Publish/Download/Vrf/pdf/437.pdf
12. Deacon, Jonathan, Vincent J. Pascal, Robert G. Schwartz, and Richard D. Teach (2006) "Firm Development In Cluster Zones: A Multi-Country Study Related To Marketing At The Entrepreneurship

Interface", Paper presented at the 10th Annual Research Symposium if the Academy of Marketing Special Interest Group on Entrepreneurial and SME Marketing www.ciber.gatech.edu/workingpaper/2005/007-05-06.pdf

13. DeNoble, Alex, Sanford Ehrlich, Gangaram Singh (2007). Toward the Development of a Family Business Self-Efficacy Scale: A Resource-Based Perspective. *Family Business Review*, XX: 127-140.
14. Dess, Gregory G and Richard B Robinson Jr (1984) "Measuring Organizational Performance in the Absence of Objective Measures: The case of the privatelyheld firm and conglomerate business unit", *Strategic Management Journal,* Jul- Sep, 5:3, pg. 265
15. Echols, Ann and Wenpin Tsai (2005) "Niche and Performance: The Moderating Role of Network Embeddedness" *Strategic Management Journal,* 26, pp. 219– 238
16. Envick, Brooke R. and Margaret Langford (2000) "The Five-Factor Model Of Personality: Assessing Entrepreneurs And Managers", *Academy of Entrepreneurship Journal,* 6:1, pg. 11
17. Forbes, Daniel P. (2005) "The Effects of Strategic Decision Making on Entrepreneurial Self-Efficacy", *Entrepreneurship Theory and Practice*", September, pg. 599
18. Frazier, Barbara J (2000). The influence of network characteristics on information access, marketing competence and perceptions of performance in small rural business, thesis submitted to Michigan State University.
19. Gilbert, Brett Anitra, Patricia P. McDougall, and David B. Audretsch (2008) "Clusters, Knowledge Spillovers And New Venture Performance: An Empirical Examination", *Journal of Business Venturing*, 23, pp. 405–422
20. Gnyawali, Devi R., Jinyu He and Ravindranath Madhavan (2007). Impact of Coopetition on Enterprise Competitive Behavior: An Empirical Examination. *Journal of Management*, 32: 507-530. Retrieved on 06/03/2009 from http://papers.ssrn.com/sol3/papers.cfm?abstract_id=1001873
21. Gurrieri, Antonia R. and Luca Petruzzellis (2006) "Local Networks to Compete in the Global Era:The Italian SMEs Experience", November, Fondazione Eni Enrico Mattei. Retrieved on 12/05/08 from http://www.feem.it/NR/rdonlyres/02A9648E-D180-451E-852D- 8CFBB8F2306/2156/13406.pdf
22. Hanneman, Robert A. and Mark Riddle (2005) "*Introduction to Social Network Methods*". Riverside, CA: University of California, published in digital form at http://faculty.ucr.edu/~hanneman/

23. Hansen, Gary S and Birger Wernerfelt (1989) "Determinants of Firm Performance: The Relative Importance of Economic and Organizational Factors", *Strategic Management Journal*, 10:5, pp. 399-411.
24. Hmieleski, Keith M. and Robert A. Baron (2008). When Does Entrepreneurial Self- Efficacy Enhance Versus Reduce Firm Performance? *Strategic Entrepreneurship Journal*, 2:57–72. Hmieleski, Keith M. and Andrew C. Corbett (2008). The contrasting interaction effects of improvisational behavior with entrepreneurial self-efficacy on new venture performance and entrepreneur work satisfaction. *Journal of Business Venturing*, 23: 482–496.
25. Hoang, Ha and Bostjan Antoncic (2003) "Network-Based Research In Entrepreneurship A Critical Review", *Journal of Business Venturing,* 18, pp. 165–187
26. Iyer, Sriya, Michael Kitson, and Bernard Toh (2005) "Social Capital, Economic Growth and Regional Development" *Regional Studies*, November, 39:8, pp. 1015–1040
27. John, Oliver P. and Sanjay Srivastava (1999) "The Big-Five Trait Taxonomy: History, Measurement, and Theoretical Perspectives", University of California at Berkeley, To appear in L. Pervin and O.P. John (Eds.), Handbook of personality: Theory and research (2nd ed.). New York: Guilford (in press). http://uoregon.edu/~sanjay/pubs/bigfive.pdf.
28. Kishore, Jugal (2010) "MSME –The Growth Engine of Indian Economy", Speech by Sr. Vice President,IIA, delivered in the Seminar "MSME –The Growth Engine of Indian Economy" organized by IIA in Meerut on 25-4-10 http://iiaonline.in/doc_files/growth%20engine.pdf
29. Lechner, Christian, Michael Dowling, and Isabell Welpe (2006) "Enterprise Networks and Enterprise Development: The Role of The Relational Mix", *Journal of Business Venturing*, 21, pp. 514– 540.
30. Li, Xinchun and Shujun Zhang (2007) "Entrepreneurial Networks, Firm Resources, and Performance". Paper presented at first Asian conference on family business at international school of business (ISB). Retrieved on 11/10/2007 from www.isb.edu/.../ManagingFamilyBusinessinChina.pdf
31. Lincoln, James R, Michael L. Gerlach, Christina L. Ahmadjian (1996) "Keiretsu Networks and Corporate Performance in Japan", *American Sociological Review*, February, 61:1, pp. 67-88
32. Macerinskas, Jogaila and Akvilë Pakalnienë, (2004), "The Impact of Embeddedness on The Economic Performance of Enterprises",

*Ekonomika.* Retrieved on 11/03/2008 from www.leidykla.vu.lt/inetleid/ekonom/67(1)/straipsniai/str6.pdf

33. Markman, Gideon D. Robert A. Baron and David B. Balkin (2005) "Are perseverance and self-efficacy costless? Assessing entrepreneurs' regretful thinking", *Journal of Organizational Behavior,* 26, pp.1–19
34. Maskell, Peter (2001) "Towards a knowledge-based theory of the geographical cluster", *Industrial and Corporate Change,* December 1, 10:4, pg. 921
35. McCallister, Lynne and Claude S. Fischer (1983) "A Procedure for Surveying Personal Networks", in Burt, Ronald and Michael Minor (ed.). *Applied Network Analysis.* Beverly Hills: Sage publication.
36. McGee, Jeffrey E., Mark Peterson, Stephen L. Mueller, and Jennifer M. Sequeira (2009). Entrepreneurial Self-Efficacy: Refining the Measure. *Entrepreneurship Theory and Practice,* 33:965-988.
37. Mitchell, Ronald K., Lowell Busenitz, Theresa Lant, Patricia P. McDougall, Eric A. Morse, and J. Brock Smith (2002). Toward a Theory of Entrepreneurial Cognition: Rethinking the People Side of Entrepreneurship Research. *Entrepreneurship Theory and Practice,* 27:93-110.
38. Monge, Peter R. and Noshir Contractor (2003). *Theories of Communication Networks.* New York: Oxford University Press Muscio, Alessandro (2006) "Patterns of Innovation in Industrial Districts: An Empirical Analysis", *Industry and Innovation;* September, 13:3, pg. 291
39. Nadvi, Khalid (1999) "Shifting Ties: Social Networks in the Surgical Instrument Cluster of Sialkot, Pakistan", *Development and Change,* 30, pp.141-175.
40. Pietrobelli, Carlo (1998) "The socio-economic foundations of competitiveness: An econometric analysis Italian industrial districts", *Industry and Innovation,* December, 5:2, pg. 139
41. Pouder, Richard, St John, and Caron H (1996) "Hot spots and blind spots: Geographical clusters of firms and innovation", *Academy of Management. The Academy of Management Revie,* October; 21, 4; pg. 1192
42. Powell, Walter W., Kenneth W. Koput, Laurel Smith-Doerr, and Jason Owen-
43. Smith (2000) "Network Position and Enterprise Performance: Organizational Returns to Collaboration in the Biotechnology Industry", working paper. Retrieved on 12/10/2008 from www.stanford.edu/~woodyp/Rso1.pdf

44. Prasad, C S, Vibha Mathur, and Anup Chatterjee (2007), "*Sixty Years of The Indian Economy 1947-2007" Volume II.* New Delhi: New Century Publications.
45. Reijonen, Helen and Raija Komppula (2007) "Perception of Success and Its Effect on Small Firm Performance", *Journal of Small Business and Enterprise Development*, 14:4, pp. 689-701
46. Richard, Pierre J.,Timothy M. Devinney and George S. Yip (2009). Measuring Organizational Performance: Towards Methodological Best Practice. *Journal of Management*, 35: 718-804.
47. Rocha, Hector O. and Rolf Sternberg (2005) "Entrepreneurship: The Role of Clusters Theoretical Perspectives and Empirical Evidence from Germany", *Small Business Economics*, 24, pp.267–292
48. Rowley, T., Behrens, D., Krackhardt, D. (2000) "Redundant Governance Structures: An Analysis of Structural and Relational Embeddedness in the Steel and Semiconductor Industries", *Strategic Management Journal*, 21, pp.369–386.
49. Saucier, Gerard and Lewis R. Goldberg (1998) "What Is Beyond The Big Five?" *Journal of Personality*, 66:4, pp.498-524
50. Schmitz, Hubert (1999) "Global Competition and Local Cooperation: Success and Failure in the Sinos Valley, Brazil" *World Development*, 27:9, pp.1627-1650
51. Schutjens, Veronique and Erik Stam (2003) "The evolution and nature of young enterprise networks: A longitudinal perspective", *Small Business Economics,* September, 21:2, pg. 115
52. Scott, John (2000). *Social Network Analysis: A Handbook.* London: Sage publication
53. Shane, S (2008) "Entrepreneurship and the Big Five Personality Traits: A Behavioral Genetics Perspective, Western Reserve University, Cleveland, Ohio
54. Shypilov, Andriy Victor (2005). Bringing the firm back in: Firm-specific characteristics and the relationship between network position and performance. Ph.D., University of Toronto (Canada), 172 pages; AAT NR07755. http://proquest.umi.com/pqdweb?index=0&did=1014314401&SrchMode=1&sid=2&Fmt=6&VInst=PROD&VType=PQD&RQT=309&VName=PQD&TS=1286159075&clientId=73173
55. S-Olivery, Jose´ Luis Herva´ and Jose´ Albors-Garrigo´ Sz (2007) "Do Clusters Capabilities Matter? An Empirical Application of the Resource-Based View in Clusters", *Entrepreneurship & Regional Development*, 19, pp. 113–136.

56. Vincenzo, Farina (2008) "Network Embeddedness, Specialization Choices and Performance in Investment Banking Industry, MPRA Paper No. 11701, posted 21. Retrieved on 18/11/2008 from http://mpra.ub.uni-muenchen.de/11701/.
57. Visser, Evert-Jan (1999) "A Comparison of Clustered and Dispersed Firms in the Small-Scale Clothing Industry of Lima" special issue of *World Development*, 27: 9
58. Uzzi, Brian, (1996), "The sources and consequences of embeddedness for the economic performance of organizations: the network effect", *American Sociological Review,* August, 61:4, pg. 674
59. Uzzi, Brian (1999). Embeddedness in the making of financial capital: How social relations and network benefit enterprise seeking finance. *American Sociological Review*, 64: 481-505.
60. Wall, Toby D; Jonathan Michie; Malcolm Patterson; Stephen J Wood; et al (2004) "On The Validity Of Subjective Measures Of Company Performance", *Personnel Psychology,* Spring, 57:1, pg. 95
61. Wasserman, S. and Faust K. (1994) "Notation for social network data". Retrieved on 11/02/2009 from www.soc.umn.edu/~knoke/pages/Notation_for_Social_Network_Data.doc
62. Zhao, Hao and Scott E. Seibert (2006) "The Big Five Personality Dimensions and Entrepreneurial Status: A Meta-Analytical Review", *Journal of Applied Psychology*, 91:2, pp. 259-271
63. Zhao, *Hao , Scott E Seibert, G T Lumpkin* (2010) "The Relationship of Personality to Entrepreneurial Intentions and Performance: A Meta-Analytic Review", *Journal of Management*, March, 36: 2; pg. 381

**Table 1: Correlation, Means & Standard Deviations of all Variables (N= 300)**

| | 1 | 2 | 3 | 4 | 5 | 6 | 7 | 8 | 9 | 10 | 11 | 12 | 13 | 14 | 15 |
|---|---|---|---|---|---|---|---|---|---|---|---|---|---|---|---|
| 1.Subjective performance | 1 | | | | | | | | | | | | | | |
| 2.Sales01 | .565 | 1 | | | | | | | | | | | | | |
| 3. Age of the Entrepreneur | .035 | .070 | 1 | | | | | | | | | | | | |
| 4.Entrepreneur Experience | .306 | .210 | .613 | 1 | | | | | | | | | | | |
| 5.Educational level | .189 | .244 | -.095 | .005 | 1 | | | | | | | | | | |
| 6.Density | .163 | .353 | .034 | .100 | -.075 | 1 | | | | | | | | | |
| 7.Centrality | .299 | .427 | -.007 | .111 | -.023 | .652 | 1 | | | | | | | | |
| 8.Internal networks | -.174 | .069 | -.033 | -.102 | -.166 | .065 | .092 | 1 | | | | | | | |
| 9.External networks | .354 | .501 | .173 | .315 | .320 | .130 | .061 | -.341 | 1 | | | | | | |
| 10.ESE | .722 | .553 | .109 | .319 | .222 | .263 | .290 | -.194 | .421 | 1 | | | | | |
| 11.Extraversion | .438 | .151 | -.040 | .122 | .006 | .041 | .072 | -.030 | .010 | .273 | 1 | | | | |
| 12.Agreeableness | .233 | -.018 | .022 | .017 | .026 | .020 | .039 | -.056 | -.035 | .114 | .352 | 1 | | | |
| 13.Conscientiousness | .207 | .149 | .068 | .113 | .045 | .149 | .136 | -.122 | .129 | .315 | .085 | .033 | 1 | | |
| 14.Emotional stability | .047 | .109 | .072 | .014 | .003 | .154 | .103 | .045 | .030 | .130 | .014 | -.016 | .258 | 1 | |
| 15.Openness | .078 | .045 | .045 | .000 | .036 | .074 | .018 | .018 | .028 | .077 | .199 | .061 | .143 | .232 | 1 |
| Mean | 31.68 | 2.55 | 41.26 | 14.24 | 1.85 | 47.97 | 38.78 | 7.02 | 7.65 | 35.12 | 30.43 | 24.55 | 28.69 | 29.42 | 26.64 |
| S.D. | 5.53 | .85 | 9.85 | 9.08 | 1.03 | 5.24 | 4.79 | 4.92 | 8.49 | 3.92 | 3.67 | 3.24 | 3.84 | 4.09 | 4.29 |
| Cronbach Alpha | .85 | - | - | - | - | .84 | .68 | - | - | .75 | .74 | .93 | .83 | .74 | .88 |

Bold significant at the level of .01(2-tailed)
Bold and italic significant at the level of .05 (2-tailed)

**Table 2 Hierarchical Regression Model**

| Predictors | Subjective Performance | | | | Sales | | | |
|---|---|---|---|---|---|---|---|---|
| | Model 1 | | Model 2 | | Model 3 | | Model 4 | |
| | Beta | VIF | Beta | VIF | Beta | VIF | Beta | VIF |
| Density | -.147 | 1.952 | -.100 | 2.042 | -.041 | 1.952 | -.001 | 2.042 |
| Centrality | .343** | 1.852 | .222** | 1.937 | .367** | 1.852 | .294** | 1.937 |
| Internal networks | -.171* | 1.379 | -.168** | 1.445 | .117 | 1.379 | .107 | 1.445 |
| External networks | .332** | 1.354 | .033 | 1.703 | .585** | 1.354 | .441** | 1.703 |
| ESE | | | .635** | 1.721 | | | .372** | 1.721 |
| Extraversion | | | .249** | 1.326 | | | .144* | 1.326 |
| Agreeableness | | | .028 | 1.164 | | | -.083 | 1.164 |
| Conscientiousness | | | -.114* | 1.315 | | | -.136* | 1.315 |
| Emotional stability | | | -.106* | 1.140 | | | -.029 | 1.140 |
| Openness | | | .025 | 1.130 | | | -.071 | 1.130 |
| R | .494** F (4,147)= 11.887 | | .825** F (10,141)= 30.091 | | .632** F (4, 147)= 24.397 | | .728** F (10,141)= 15.885 | |
| $R^2$ | .244 | | .681 | | .399 | | .530 | |
| $R^2$ Changed | .244** | | .437** | | .399** | | .131** | |

** Significant at the level of .01(2-tailed)
* Significant at the level of .05 (2-tailed)

# 13

# Entry Barriers to Entrepreneurship: A Perception Study of Management Students

***Abstract***

Management education has been at the vanguard of higher education in India. With the booming economy and ever increasing job opportunities, MBA has become the most preferred post graduate degree in the country. The only area of concern is that management institutes are creating more job seekers than job creators. Entrepreneurship is still not being considered as a serious career option by most of the management graduates. This poses a serious problem for the long term sustainability of Indian economy. The top notch management institutes in the country have already started responding to this issue in a major way. But there no signs of any serious attempt made by the second and third tier institutes in this direction. These institutes cater to the maximum demand of management education in the country. This paper proposes to throw some more light on this issue. The paper proposes to get an insight in the perception of management students with respect to entry barriers to entrepreneurship. The results will highlight the social and economical factors that support or hinder the virtue of entrepreneurship in management graduates. The findings of the study would help in recommending certain changes in the pedagogy of management courses so as inculcate the virtue of entrepreneurship in management graduates.

## Introduction

The recent global financial crises and subsequent emergence of economies out of it proved the point that the future of global economy would lie in Asia. India and China, along with a set of emerging economies, are all set to be the future economic powerhouses. The internal consumption stories are the biggest strengths of both these economies. However, the going is not going to be smooth for either of them. A wide range of policies and support environment has to be kept in place, pretty soon. One of them is the area of entrepreneurship. Although, both these economies have a large pool of young workforce, the major problem is that most of these people tend to become job seekers. If private enterprises are unable to grow and generate employment, a major portion of this young workforce will have to struggle for employment.

Thus it is very important for policy makers to create an environment which is conducive towards the growth of entrepreneurial activity. This will have a strong bearing on the social, cultural and economical environment.

Universities in one form or other, have always played a major role in shaping the direction of civilizations. The young minds can be nurtured and energies can be directed for the betterment of the entire society. Since in the recent times, youths are diverted strongly towards management courses, a management institutes(autonomous or university affiliated) is a best place to inculcate the virtues of entrepreneurship in the youth of the nation. Since managements students are well versed with various aspects of business, they can easily be diverted to self employment. This converts job seekers into job creators.

Although, the leading institutes in country have made substantial efforts in this direction, the major chunk of university affiliated colleges is far behind. This paper is an attempt to understand the factors that affects the perception of management students towards entrepreneurship. The paper proposes to use the findings to recommend changes in the pedagogy and mindset of educators so as to inculcate the virtue of entrepreneurship in management students.

## Literature Review

A wide range of literature was available on defining entrepreneurship. It is the process of creating a new business/venture with some element of novelty (Rumelt, 1987). It is also defined as the process of identifying market opportunities and re allocation of resources to pursue the opportunities (Kirzner, 1977; Schumpeter, 1934). The person who is involved in this process of coordinating and allocating resources to create profits is defined at Entrepreneur(Vesper, 1980). Another view of entrepreneur is as a person who seeks to improve the organization through change initiation (Mintzberg, 1973).

An extensive research has been done in the area of identifying traits of an entrepreneur. The first attempts of research to identify the personality traits of entrepreneur can be summarized as

- Need for Achievement (McClelland, 1961)
- Locus of Control and Risk taking propensity (Brockhaus, 1980)
- Tolerance of ambiguity (Schere, 1982)

McClelland(1961), had further associated three behavioral traits namely, assuming personal responsibility for figuring out solutions, setting goals and taking calculated risk to attain them and demanding concrete feedback regarding performance, with the high need of achievement. Taking anticipated risk as a predictor, the results that people with more risk taking propensity tend towards being entrepreneurs, was also validated (Douglas and Shepherd, 1999). Soft skills have also been identified as an important characteristic of an entrepreneur (Dash and Dhayani, 2005). These soft skill's include innovativeness and creativity, good analytical skills, communication skills, consistency, hard work, trustworthiness, teambuilding and high level of confidence. Two scales on entrepreneurship were also available to the author on entrepreneurship, namely, Entrepreneurial quotient(EQ) and Entrepreneurial Attitude Orientation (EAO) (Huefner et al., 1996).

Policy makers all around the world have always been focusing on attaining self sustaining economic development. With the recent global financial crises, the urge to figure out newer means of self sustaining development has become even stronger. Entrepreneurship plays a major role in this. It creates new jobs, improves lifestyle of people by bringing innovation to market and thus increases economic efficiencies (Shane and Enkataraman, 2000). Given the kind of growth, both economic and population, that countries like India and China are witnessing, entrepreneurship will have to play a major role in both these economies. India is expected to become an economic powerhouse in the coming decade provided it can ensure appropriate preparation of its next generation (Huetter, 2007). IIMs have been at the vanguard of inducting entrepreneurship in their students. According to a study jointly conducted by IIM-A and Tianjin University of Finance, 63% of Indian was found to be considering entrepreneurship as a favorable activity (Belew, 2006). According to the survey of Hindu-Business Line, India is the second most entrepreneurial country, next only to Thailand. India traditionally, had its own share of excellent entrepreneurs and the mindset is again re-emerging in India (Gopalakrishnan, 2004). Indian youths are more focused on participating in the country's future and growth then on crying foul about poverty, politics and social systems. The proof of this lies in the fact that an increasing number of students at IIMs are rejecting high salaries from multinationals and opting to become self employed. Inspite of these signs of improvement, there is a long way to go.

Although there are a number of studies conducted globally for entrepreneurship, Indian context has to be viewed differently. Type of culture, like individualist and collectivist, has a direct impact on need for independence and economic security. This in turn affects the motivation towards entrepreneurship in a significant manner (Abbey, 2002; Herron and Sapienza, 1992). A similar study was conducted with the same result on entrepreneurial intentions among Indonesian and Norwegian students (Kristiansen and Indarti, 2004). In India a study was conducted by Bhandari (2006) on entrepreneurial intentions of university students in India, in which he concluded that out of 18 independent variable only 2(namely, luck and desire to lead others) variables showed a significant relationship with entrepreneurship. Shuman et al.(1987) had attempted to study the impact of educational background on entrepreneurial activity. A comparative study of attitude of graduates from business background and from employee background towards entrepreneurship was also done by Peter and Jean(1989). Thus, more or less, it can be generalized that students who come from a background of family business, tend towards taking up entrepreneurship (Krueger, 1993). The impact of various demographic factors like age, gender, educational level, entrepreneurship in friends and relatives and number of courses taken in entrepreneurship was also studied by Chen et al. (1998). However, there are studies that point out that lack of support is the primary reason for entrepreneurship not to prosper. Entrepreneurship has grown slowly in India because of lack of funding(Huetter, 2007). The government policies in India regarding small business are too complex to understand and this leads to stifling of the environment for small entrepreneurs.

On the other side, Venture capitalists have always given more emphasis on the personal characteristics of entrepreneurs then on the other factors

(Shepher, 1999). Research has also shown that human resources are more instrumental compared to environmental factors while setting up a new venture (Rotefoss and Kolveried, 2005). It has been observed that if an individual is made to believe that he or she possess the right set of skills, then the chances of that individual taking up entrepreneurship increases ( Boyd and Vozikis, 1994; Krueger and Brazeal, 1994; Chen et al., 1998; Golden and Cooke, 1998) In a nutshell it can be summarized that there only exists a limited and diversified understanding of factors and the decision process that leads a person towards entrepreneurship (Markman et al., 2002). It is also evident that there is a lack of empirical research in the area of motivation to take up entrepreneurship (Kuratko et al., 1997). With this context in background, the following paper proposes to provide empirical evidence towards the perception of management students towards entrepreneurship. The prime focus of the paper remains to identify the factors that hinder the process of management students taking up entrepreneurship.

## Objective of the Study

The primary objective of this research study is to understand the factors that are most likely to hinder the process of management students taking up entrepreneurship. The purpose is to identify such factors and then recommend changes in pedagogy so as to inculcate the virtue of entrepreneurship in more number of management students. The perception of the students would also be analyzed for any differences on basis of demographic variables.

## Hypothesis

1. H0: The perception of students towards entrepreneurship is independent of the Gender
2. H0: The perception of students towards entrepreneurship is independent of the family income
3. H0: The perception of students towards entrepreneurship is independent of the specialization opted in the management course
4. H0: The perception of students towards entrepreneurship is independent of there being a family business

## Research Methodology

122 final year MBA students (55 from GH Patel PG Institute of Business Management, Sardar Patel University and 67 from B K School of Management, Gujarat University) were choose on a convenience basis for

the study. Top 3 institutes affiliated to GCET(Gujarat) in the state of Gujarat were identified for the study. Major chunk of the students are part of university system. Therefore, the best three institutes in this category(on basis of student's preference while taking admission) were chosen for the study. Due to unfavorable circumstances, Faculty of Management Studies, M S University could not be included in the study. A five point likert scale[Strongly agree(1) to Strongly disagree (5)] was used for the questionnaire. 22 statements were generated and classified on basis of various factors generated from the literature review. The statements were jumbled up in the questionnaire.

**Findings**

**Table 1: Factors related to risk propensity**

| Statement | Mean | Std. Dev. |
|---|---|---|
| Fear of losing face if the business does not succeed | 1.8795 | 0.7561 |
| Lack of courage | 2.3547 | 0.5248 |
| High risk involved of loosing invested amount | 1.5423 | 0.8001 |
| Lack of job security | 1.765 | 0.7995 |

*Source: On basis of primary data collected*

*Mean value would range from 1 to 5 (1 being the most important and 5 being least important)*

The findings of Table 1 are in accordance to the literature review regarding risk taking propensity being an important trait of an entrepreneur (Brockhaus, 1980). The responses have been in the range of agree to strongly agree. Even the deviation is on the lower side, indicating that more or less all students agree to these factors. Statements, 'Fear of losing face......' and 'Lack of courage' have a bit higher means may be because of social stigma associated with the statements. However, it can be assumed that entrepreneurs do have a higher risk taking propensity. Although one cannot be trained to take higher risk, but a fair amount of counseling may

**Table 2: Psychological factors related to entrepreneurship**

| Statement | Mean | Std. Dev. |
|---|---|---|
| I am too young | 2.1789 | 0.7886 |
| I have no passion for entrepreneurship | 1.9542 | 1.4523 |
| I am Not the GUY for entrepreneurship | 1.9112 | 1.5023 |

*Source: On basis of primary data collected*

be useful in increasing the risk taking propensity of the students. A good amount of interaction with successful entrepreneurs too may help in this area.

*Mean value would range from 1 to 5 (1 being the most important and 5 being least important)*

The findings of Table 2 reflect the psychological aspects of student's perception about entrepreneurship. Students strongly feel that they do not want to take up entrepreneurship primarily because either they are too young or they don't have the required passion for it. The Idea of building something new and novel does not enthuse the students. This can be related to the need of achievement as a trait of entrepreneur (McClelland, 1961). Generally entrepreneurs have the zeal and passion to create something new and these characteristics plays an instrumental role in their success. This is what venture capitalist looks forward to before funding a new entrepreneur (Shepher, 1999). However, this is an area where neither training nor counseling can be of any use. It is an innate desire that a person would be born with, according to the author.

**Table 3: Factors related to training for entrepreneurship**

| Statement | Mean | Std. Dev. |
|---|---|---|
| Lack of entrepreneurial exposure | 1.541 | 1.1112 |
| Lack of appropriate training to handle various functions of a new business | 1.758 | 1.023 |
| Lack of required skills, knowledge and insight | 1.6895 | 0.9875 |
| High competition in the intended area of business | 2.145 | 0.9012 |
| I Cannot manage business without partners whom I trust | 2.1356 | 1.0254 |
| I am Not confident about working with business partners because of different opinion or working style | 2.2254 | 1.1245 |
| Being a female, I may not be able to single handedly manage a new business | 2.0354 | 0.7865 |

*Source: On basis of primary data collected*

*Mean value would range from 1 to 5 (1 being the most important and 5 being least important)*

The findings of Table 3 primarily highlight that student's perception ranges from strongly agree to agree on factors which are related to operating the new venture. Whether they start independently or in partnership in whatever area, their main contention is about their ability to run the new venture. Their apprehension ranges from lack of skills and knowledge, tough competition to trusting their business partners. This is in accordance with the recent literature that entrepreneurs should possess fairly good amount of soft skills (Dash and Dhayani, 2005). These factors can be positively affected by imparting appropriate training to the students. Making them to work in group projects will help them in becoming confident about working in groups and team building. Involving students in projects and activities related to entrepreneurship and other aspects of business will give them the necessary confidence that they can take up entrepreneurship. Events like *Business Baazigar* organized by BBA faculty, M S University are a case in point. This training will increase the chances of students taking up entrepreneurship (Boyd and Vozikis, 1994; Krueger and Brazeal, 1994; Chen et al., 1998; Golden and Cooke, 1998)

**Table 4: Factors related to Family support**

| Statement | Mean | Std. Dev. |
|---|---|---|
| My family needs me to immediately support them financially | 4.4462 | 0.412 |
| Pressing need to repay the education loan, if taken | 3.548 | 0.548 |
| No compassion/support from family | 2.869 | 1.213 |
| Bad experience of relatives/friends in entrepreneurship | 3.121 | 0.997 |

*Source: On basis of primary data collected*

*Mean value would range from 1 to 5 (1 being the most important and 5 being least important)*

of family on shaping the perception of students towards entrepreneurship is reflected in the findings of Table 4. Mean values range from Disagree to strongly disagree, with a very small deviation. This means that family issues generally fail to have a huge impact on perception towards taking up entrepreneurship. This may be true partly because most of the students would be from well to do families, thus no immediate responsibilities towards financially supporting the family. As the sample is drawn from the institutes which fall amongst the top 3 in the state, the 122 selected students are one of the best in the state. Since these students are a sincere and mature lot, the bad experiences of friends and relative in entrepreneurship may not necessarily deter the entrepreneurial intentions of the students. The other point worth noting is that on the statement regarding the compassion and support of family, the responses is a bit biased towards agrees. The deviation is also quite wide, indicating that there are a number of students who are very strongly influenced against entrepreneurship by their families. This may be justified by the fact that the previous generation was born and brought up in an economy which was largely dominated by public enterprises. Student's parents would not have witnessed an environment which was conducive to the growth of private enterprise. This may lead to parents forcing the students against entrepreneurship. However, a fair amount of counseling may prove useful in changing the perception of the students.

**Table 5: Factors related to employment versus self-employment**

| Statement | Mean | Std. Dev. |
|---|---|---|
| More work and responsibilities involved compared to working as an employee | 3.7851 | 0.8215 |
| Lucrative career opportunities in various sectors (as employee) | 1.7231 | 0.8412 |

*Source: On basis of primary data collected*

*Mean value would range from 1 to 5 (1 being the most important and 5 being least important)*

Findings of Table 5 compare the perception of students with respect to opting for a career or being self employed. Students strongly perceive that since they are getting very lucrative job opportunities in the corporate world, they do not look towards entrepreneurship very favorably. Opportunities to manage large companies and projects at a very young age, may lead to students avoiding entrepreneurship at early stage of their career. The other statement regarding more work responsibilities as an entrepreneur does not seem to bother the students too much. Students do not agree to the fact that they don't take up entrepreneurship because they need to take more responsibilities and work harder for it.

**Table 6: Factors related to external support**

| Statement | Mean | Std. Dev. |
|---|---|---|
| Absence of a good Business Idea/Proposal | 3.451 | 1.21 |
| Lack of seed capital to begin business | 1.5423 | 0.7824 |

*Source: On basis of primary data collected*

*Mean value would range from 1 to 5 (1 being the most important and 5 being least important)*

Finding of Table 6 are related to external support that can be provided to assist people in taking up entrepreneurship. Entrepreneurship is defined as the process of identifying new market opportunities and creating something new with an element of novelty (Rumelt, 1987; Kirzner, 1973; Schumpeter, 1934). For this it is necessary to have a good business idea or proposal. Findings suggest that students perceive that getting a new idea is not a major hurdle in the process of entrepreneurship. This can be explained by the fact that in last few years various innovative business models have emerged in countries like India and China. Since the managements students are most likely to be aware of these changes, they may not feel too intimidated by the fact that they may not have a clearly charted out business model. Lack of seed capital to start the business, is definitely a major area of concern for the students. The spread of the responses also is quite narrow, indicating the seriousness of this issue. The problems lie more with the awareness of students than with the availability of seed capital.

There are various government initiatives to promote entrepreneurship and a wide range of venture capitalist, angel investors etc. in the market to provide funding to start up ventures. Micro Finance Industry in India is a big case in point. To overcome this, systematic steps should be taken to make students aware about the sources of capital and may be an official platform can be developed by the management institute which can act as an intermediary between the students and sources of capital. There are many institutes which are using their alumni network to help new students set up their own ventures.

Four hypotheses were also test for independence using Chi-Square analysis. The responses of all the students on all the 22 statements were tested for four independent variables, namely, gender, family income; specialization opted in management course and presence of any entrepreneur in the immediate family.

The finding reveals that there is no significant difference in the perception of male and female students regarding entrepreneurship. The same result holds for the student coming from families with different annual income. But there was a significant difference in the perception of students opting for finance and marketing specialization. It was seen that students opting for marketing specialization were more inclined toward taking up entrepreneurship. This supports the literature in the sense that marketing people tend to have more internal locus of control and a higher need of achievement (McClelland, 1961; Brockhaus, 1980). It was also found that students who had a family business, were more inclined towards entrepreneurship compared to students who did not have a family business. This seems to be quite obvious and is also in accordance with the literature (Krueger, 1993).

## Conclusion

Economic and social well being of all citizens is believed to be the prime responsibility of the state. But, time and again, it comes to the forefront that there is not better mechanism with the state to achieve this goal, other than the free spirit of entrepreneurship. Private enterprises have always proved to be more effective in attaining economic and social goals compared to public enterprises. 5 decades of efforts by public sector banks in India, could not achieve the goal of financial inclusion to the extent at which small MFIs have attained in just few years. Thus for the overall development of economy, spirit of entrepreneurship should be encouraged in the youth. Since management education trains the students on various aspects of managing businesses, it would be easiest to inculcate entrepreneurship in management students. The paper highlights a few areas which hinder or negatively affects the perception of students regarding entrepreneurship. If appropriate changes are made in the pedagogy, and mindset of educators, management education can turn out to be the biggest platform for inculcating the virtue of entrepreneurship in youths.

## References

1. Abbey A (2002), "Cross Cultural Comparison of Motivation for Entrepreneurship", Journal of Business and Entrepreneurship, Vol. 14, No. 1, March.
2. Belew B(2006), "3 No-secrets to Growth to China and India." Dec. 6, 2006.
3. Bhandari N (2006), "Intention for Entrepreneurship among students in India", Journal of Entrepreneurship, Vol.15, No.2.
4. Boyd N and Vozikis G (1994), "The Influences of Self-Efficacy on the Development of Entrepreneurial Intentions and Actions", Entrepreneurial Theory and Practice, Vol. 18, No. 4.
5. Brockhaus R (1980), "Risk-Taking Propensity of Entrepreneurs", Academy of Management Journal, Vol. 23, No. 3.
6. Chen C, Greene P and Crick A (1998), "Does Entrepreneurial Self-Efficacy Distinguish Entrepreneurs from Managers?", Journal of Business Venturing, Vol. 13, No. 4.

7. Dash M and Dhyani U (2005), Entrepreneurship Culture, Allied Publishers Pvt. Ltd.
8. Douglas E and Shepherd D (1999), "Entrepreneurship as a Utility Maximizing Response", Journal of Business Venturing, Vol. 15 No. 3.
9. Golden P and Cooke D (1998), "Entrepreneurial Self-Efficacy: Some Antecedents and Outcomes", Paper Presented at the National Academy of Management Meeting, San Diego, CA.
10. Goplalkrishanan, R. (2004), "Unleashing Indian Entrepreneurship -1 : The changing mindset", The Hindu-Business Line, Internet Edition, Chennai.
11. Herron L and Sapienza H (1992), "The Entrepreneur and the Initiation of New Venture Launch Activities", Entrepreneurship Theory and Practice, Vol. 17, No. 1.
12. Huefner J, Hunt H and Robinson P (1996), "A Comparison of Four Scales Predicting Entrepreneurship", Academy of Entrepreneurship Journal, Vol. 1, No. 2.
13. Huetter B (2007), "India rising" SPIE Professional.
14. Kirzner I (1997) "Entrepreneurial Discovery and the Competitive Market Process: An Austrian Approach", Journal of Economic Literature, 35, 60-85.
15. Kristiansen S and Indarti N (2004), "Entrepreneurial Intention among Indonesian and Norwegian Students", Journal of Enterprising Culture, Vol. 12, No. 1.
16. Krueger N (1993), "The Impact of Prior Entrepreneurial Exposure on Perceptions of New Venture Feasibility and Desirability", Entrepreneurship Theory and Practice, Vol. 18, No. 31.
17. Kuratko D, Hornsby J and Naffziger D (1997), "An Examination of Owner's Goals in Sustaining Entrepreneurship", Journal of Small Business Management, Vol. 35, No. 1.
18. Markman G, Balkin D and Baron R (2002), "Inventors and New Venture Formation: The Effects of General Self-Efficacy and Regretful Thinking", Entrepreneurship Theory and Practice.
19. McClelland D (1961), The Achieving Society, Van Nostrand, New York.
20. Mintzberg H (1973), "The nature of managerial work", New York: Harper & Row.
21. Rotefoss B and Kolvereid L (2005), "Aspiring, Nascent and Fledging Entrepreneurs: An Investigation of the Business Startup Process", Entrepreneurship and Regional Development, Vol. 17, No. 2.

22. Rumelt R (1987), "Theory, Strategy, and Entrepreneurship", Teece D (Ed.), The Competitive Challenge: Strategies for Industrial Innovation and Renewal (pp. 137-158). Cambridge, MA: Ballinger Publishing Co.
23. Schere J (1982), "Tolerance of Ambiguity as a Discriminating Variable
24. Between Entrepreneurs and Managers", Proceedings of the Academy of Management.
25. Schumpeter J (1934), "The Theory of Economic Development", Cambridge MA: Harvard University Press.
26. Shane S and Venkataraman S (2000), "The Promise of Entrepreneurship as a Field of Research", Academy of Management Review, Vol. 25.
27. Shepherd D (1999), "`Venture Capitalists' Assessment of New Venture Growth", Management Science, Vol. 45, No. 5.
28. Shuman J, Seeger J and Teebagy N (1987), "Entrepreneurial Activity and Educational Background", Babson Research Conference.
29. Vesper K (1980), "New venture strategies", Englewood Cliffs, NJ: Prentice Hall.

# 14

# Entrepretrait: Personality Traits as Predictors of Entrepreneurial Orientation among the Students of Higher Technical Education in Iit Roorkee: An Empirical Study

***Abstract***

**Purpose** – The identification of the entrepreneurial personality factors is a significant area of research. Entrepretrait is the study to explore the personality traits as the predictors of the entrepreneurial orientation.

**Design/Methodology/Approach** – A sample above 400 Indian Institute of Technology (IIT) Roorkee students belonging to various courses and years will be collected. There are 10 factors defining the entrepreneurial orientation of the students included in this study.

**Findings** – Factors such as Innovativeness, Locus of Control, Risk taking propensity, Management Skills, Need for Achievement, Tolerance to Ambiguity, Ability to Co-operate, Passion for Business, Positive attitude and Team Worker will be evaluated to identify the entrepreneurial capabilities of IIT Roorkee students. The study will explore how strongly the chosen factors predict the entrepreneurial orientation in the respondents. Statistical analysis will be performed to find out the results and discussion will be carried out in the light of the results.

**Practical Implication** – The study would enable the respondents to identify their strengths and weakness and to grab the entrepreneurial opportunities present for them. For the nation the study will be a great help to improve the employability situation as well as economic growth.

**Originality/Value** – The study is an innovative effort in the campus of IIT Roorkee to measure the entrepreneurial potential among the students on 10 different parameters. The respondents will be from various disciplines and various respective years of their courses.

**Keywords** – Entrepreneurship, Students, Entrepreneurial Orientation, Personality Traits, Innovation.

**Paper Type** – Empirical Paper

## Introduction

Entrepreneurship has been a crucial area of research. Joseph Schumpeter (1934) stated that an entrepreneur is an innovator playing the role of a dynamic businessman who contributes to the economic development. According to Zacharakis (1997) entrepreneurs seek for new opportunities. As India has emerged out to be a land of opportunities, there is a tremendous scope for potential entrepreneurs to flourish. Entrepreneurs are catalyst of economic development and they coordinate and manage the basic factors of production. Entrepreneurs shape business ecosystem by commercializing new technologies, introducing innovation, creating new jobs, opening new markets and creating value for the available resources (Rajeev Roy, 2008). Hannu Littunen (2000) states that becoming an entrepreneur and acting as an entrepreneur are both aspects of learning process. In addition, entrepreneurs tend to underestimate the potential negative sides and overestimate the positive possibilities more than wage workers are likely to do (Baron, 1998; Simon *et al.*, 1999).

Students of higher technical education are now being imparted courses of entrepreneurship and business development. Indian Institute of Technology (IIT) students have demonstrated academic excellence by clearing one of the world's toughest technical exam i.e. the IIT – JEE (Joint Entrance Exam). Exploring the entrepreneurial profile of these students would enable us to predict their bent towards starting up their own business. It would help them to find out their strengths and weakness. The study will be a useful help to improve the employability situation of the nation and ultimately contribute to its economic growth. Lazear (2005) has shown that individuals with balanced and wide skill sets are more likely to become entrepreneurs than those that are focused on one role at work or one subject at school. The students are more interested in turning their hobbies into businesses than continuing an existing and already successful business (Römer-Paakkanen and Rauhala, 2007).

## Review of Literature Review on Entrepreneurial Characteristics

There have been many significant studies regarding the characteristics of an entrepreneur. An entrepreneur has a mind of his own. One of the most important characteristic of an entrepreneur is innovativeness (Tibbits, 1979; Bird, 1989). Casson (1982) includes the ability to take risk, ability to co-operate, management skills and the knowledge of how the market function as the key entrepreneurial traits. Bird (1989) further divides risk into five types. These are economic risks, risks in social relations, risk in career development, psychological and health risks. McClelland (1961) contributed with his need for achievement theory which is highly considered as a strong factor determining the entrepreneurial orientation. Rotter (1966) suggested that the internal locus of control is another determinant of the entrepreneurial bend of an individual.

A successful entrepreneur has to have team work skills to establish a business and should function in relation with other people (Carsrud and Johnson, 1989). An entrepreneur should have a positive attitude and passion for business (Lambing and Kuehl, 2000). Gibbs and Ritchie (1982) states that individuals change throughout life and entrepreneurship is a time dependant concept.

Empirical research has revealed contradictory findings about the role of personal characteristics (Brockhaus 1987; Robinson, Huefner and Hunt 1991).

Greenberger and Sexton (1998) added that need for personal control as another important personality trait. This lack of clarity creates ambiguity. Koh (1996) and Teoh and Foo (1997) cite numerous research studies suggesting that entrepreneurs have a significantly greater capacity to tolerate ambiguity.

## The Methodology

### (1) The Study

**Entrepretrait** is the empirical study to explore the personality traits as the predictors of the entrepreneurial orientation. This study is based on the various factors involved for consideration of entrepreneurial commitments among the students which are as follows:

1. Innovativeness
2. Locus of Control
3. Risk taking propensity
4. Management Skills
5. Need for Achievement
6. Tolerance to Ambiguity
7. Ability to Co-operate
8. Passion for Business
9. Positive attitude
10. Team Worker

## (2) The objectives:

**A.** To study the relationship between academic performance* and factors of Entrepreneurship among the students of IIT Roorkee.

**B.** To study the Entrepreneurship factors and gender differentiation. [**Note**-* indicates academic performance measured above and below 7 CGPA respectively]

## (3) Hypotheses

**HO$^A$** - There is no difference in the entrepreneurial orientation among the students with high and low academic performances.

**H1$^A$** - There is a significant difference in the entrepreneurial orientation among the students for their academic performances.

**HO$^B$** - There is no difference in the entrepreneurial orientation among the male and female categories.

**H1$^B$** - There is a significant difference in the entrepreneurial orientation among the male and female.

## (4) The Sample

The sample was collected from 433 Students (Undergraduates/MBA/M. Tech/PhD) from IIT Roorkee belonging to various courses and years.

## (5) Data Collection

The Likert scale was used in the development of the questionnaire of 30 items from 10 factors (personality traits). Each factor had 3 items. The questionnaire was uploaded on the IIT Roorkee intranet website for obtaining the response (Annexure 1). Respondents were asked to indicate their degree of acceptance with each statement on a five-point Likert scale

(1-Never, 2- Occasionally, 4- Frequently, 5-Always). Some statements were reverse-scored and jumbled with other statements to minimize response-set bias. The answers for the category were exclusive so that the respondent had to state only one choice against an item. Name, gender, CGPA (Cumulative Grade Point Average) were the other details collected from each respondent.

## (6) Data Analysis

The data collected was stored in Microsoft Excel against the details of the respondents. Bar diagrams were made for a graphical representation. The value of the response depicts the level of entrepreneurship orientation and their traits (1-Never, 2- Occasionally, 4-Frequently, 5-Always). The sample size of 433 on a 5 point Likert scale was obtained. The data was analysed using special software named SPSS. Independent two sample z-test feature of SPSS was used on the data collected through the questionnaire from the students of IIT Roorkee.

Table - 1: Demographic Profile of the Respondents

| Gender | Frequency | CGPA | Frequency |
|---|---|---|---|
| Male | 388 | Below 7 | 106 |
| Female | 45 | Above 7 | 268 |
| ---- | ---- | Not Applicable | 59 |
| Sum | 433 | Sum | 433 |

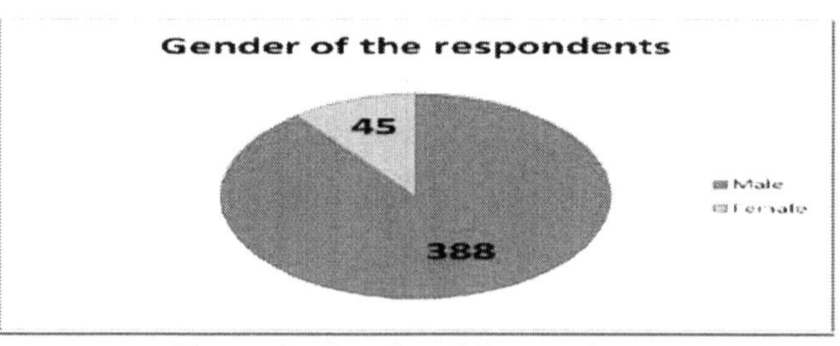


Figure 1 - Gender of Respondents

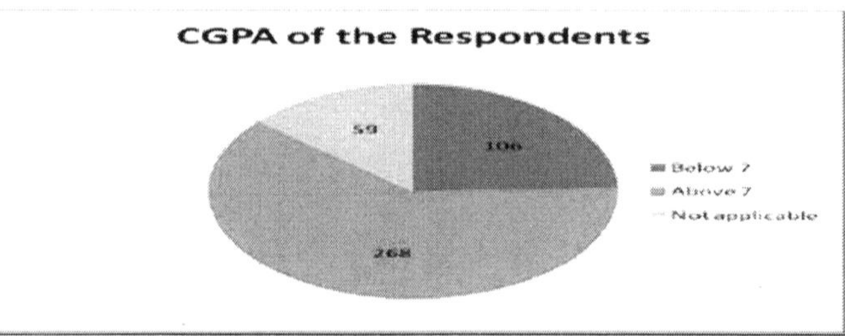


Figure 2 - CGPA of Respondents

## Results and discussions

Here results and discussions are highlighted for both the objectives which has been analysed by using different hypotheses (**HOA, H1A, HOB, H1B**). The Two- Sample Z-test results reveal that there is no significant difference in the entrepreneurial orientation among the students with high and low academic performances. Similarly Two-Sample Z-test results also disclose that is no significant difference in the entrepreneurial orientation among the male and female categories. Therefore **HO B** and **HO A** are found to be valid. Thus, students from IIT Roorkee have the same perception about their entrepreneurial interest regardless of their academic performance and CGPA. Despite the known fact we acknowledge that all the students of IIT Roorkee might consider individual skills and their business interest towards entrepreneurial path to fulfill their competitive career objectives. Finally we should not forget that we have focused on entrepreneurial intentions as the creation of new value within the students of higher technical education.

Future research should be devoted to assessing the other factors which have not been chosen in the study to check the validity above the objectives which are outlined here.

The output bar diagrams are shown which have usual significance from the study.

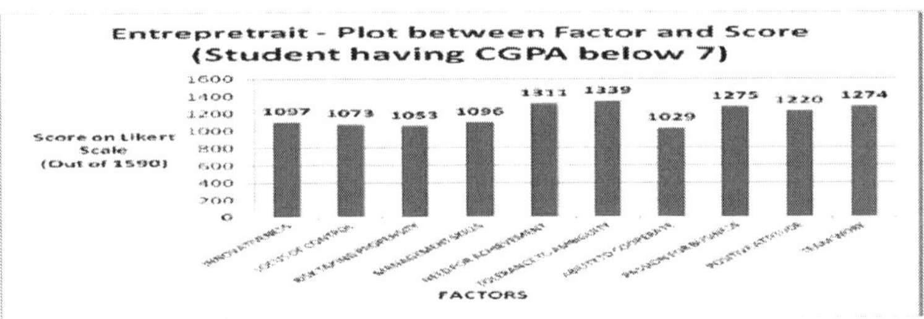


Figure - 3: Plot between factors and score of Students having CGPA below 7

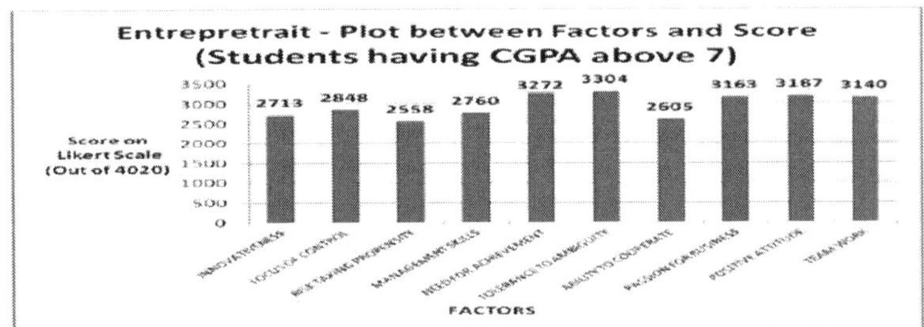


Figure - 4: Plot between factors and score of Students having CGPA above 7

This study revealed that amongst both the group of students having CGPA above and below 7, evens the factors of tolerance to ambiguity and need for achievement is found highest. The factors of risk taking propensity and ability to co-operate are found to be lowest for both the groups. Therefore, the overall score inclusive of all the factors for students with CGPA below 7 comes out to be 74% (11767/15900) which is very close to 73.5% (29550/40200) for students with CGPA above 7. The IIT student belonging to various courses and years are exposed to different extra-curricular activities apart from academics. They have already proved their intellectual capabilities by clearing IIT-JEE at the national level. Thus irrespective of their CGPA, the students exhibit similar entrepreneurial orientation.

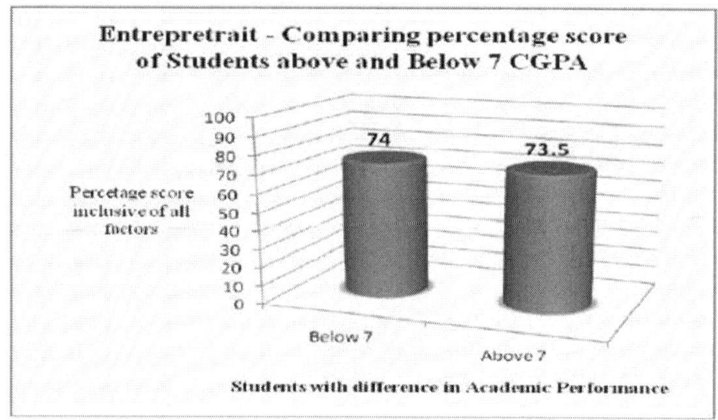


Figure - 5: Comparing percentage score of Students above and Below 7 CGPA

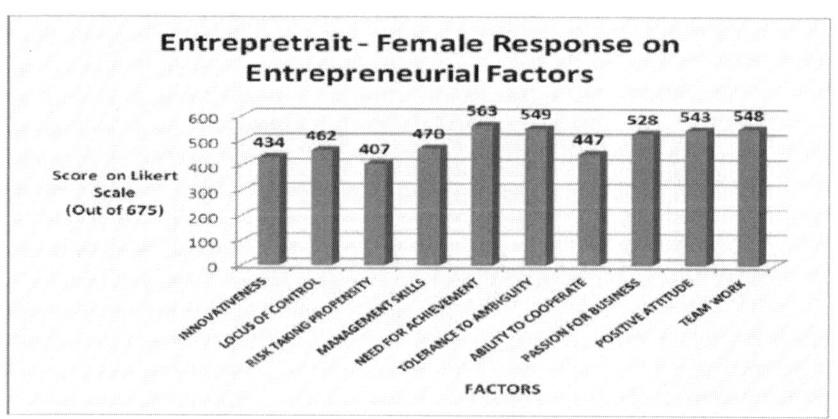


Figure - 6: Female Responses on Entrepreneurial Factors with their score

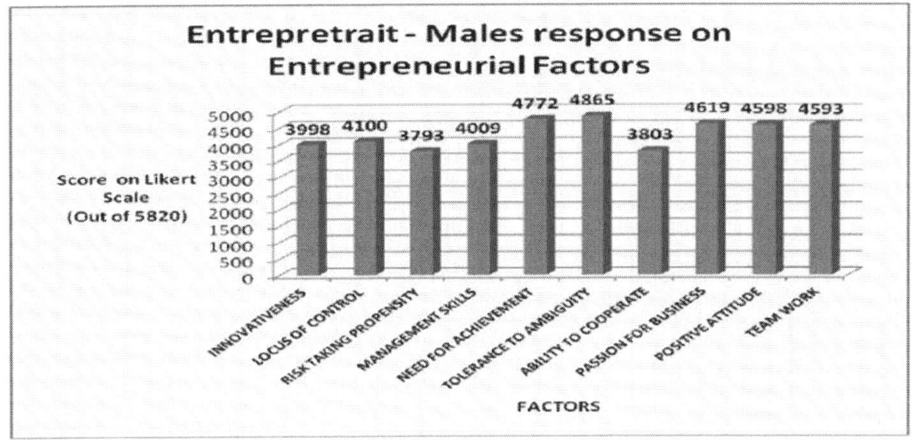


Figure - 7: Males Responses on Entrepreneurial Factors with their score

The study exhibits that amongst both male and female students, the factors of tolerance to ambiguity and need for achievement is found highest. The factors of risk taking propensity, innovativeness and ability to co-operate are found to be lowest for both the groups. The overall score inclusive of all the factors for female students comes out to be **73.33%** (4951/15900) which is very close the **74.14%** (43150/58200) for male students. Hence, the female students of IIT Roorkee show equivalent entrepreneurial potential as of the male students. This can be understood by the reason that the personality development opportunities for both the categories of students are equal in the IIT system.

## Limitations/ Goodness of Findings

1. The sample does not include students belonging to other IITs or other engineering colleges.

2. Within the literature on this subject there is research that both supports and refutes the relationship among the characteristics chosen.

## Implications for the research/area of further research

1. The research could be extended to the other institutes.

2. More characteristics traits can be included in other studies for a better insight towards the different dimensions of the study

## Conclusions

The decision to become an entrepreneur may be possibly considered on voluntary and conscious basis. Therefore, it seems reasonable to analyse how the decision is taken. In this paper authors discovered that entrepreneurial potential among IIT Roorkee students is almost equivalent regardless of the academic performance or gender. The IIT students could generate innovative ideas to start new enterprises or renew existing businesses according to their potential and motivation towards entrepreneurship.

## Acknowledgement

The authors acknowledge and extend thanks to all the students of IIT Roorkee for their contribution to fill up the questionnaire transparently and all aspects discussed during the collection of the questionnaire. Special gratitude is also expressed to the persons who helped directly or indirectly to this research work. Special thanks to Information Management Group (IMG) of IIT Roorkee for their efforts, valuable comments and suggestions.

## References

1. Baron, R.A. (1998), “Cognitive mechanisms in entrepreneurship: why and when entrepreneurs think differently than other people”, *Journal of Business Venturing*, Vol. 13 pp.275-95.
2. Bird, B. (1989), Entrepreneurial Behavior, *Scott, Foresman, Glenview*, IL and London.
3. Brockhaus, R.H. and Horwitz, P.S. (1986), “The psychology of the entrepreneur. In: Sexton, D. L. and Smilor, R. W. (Eds.)”, *the art and science of entrepreneurship*, Cambridge, MA: Ballinger. 25-48.
4. Carsrud, A.L, Johnson, R.W (1989), “Entrepreneurship: a social psychological perspective”, *Entrepreneurship and Regional Development*, Vol. 1, [1], pp.21-31.
5. Casson, M. (1982), the Entrepreneur: an Economic Theory, *Martin Robertson*, Oxford.
6. Hannu L. (2000), “Entrepreneurship and the characteristics of the entrepreneurial personality”, *International Journal of Entrepreneurial Behaviour & Research* – Volume - 6, [6], pp 295-310.
7. Koh, H.C. (1996), “Testing hypotheses of entrepreneurial characteristics”, *Journal of Managerial Psychology*, Volume - 11 No.3, pp.12-25.
8. Lambing, P., Kuehl, C.R. (2000), Entrepreneurship, 2nd ed., Prentice-Hall, *Englewood Cliffs*, NJ.
9. Lazear, E.P. (2005), “Entrepreneurship”, *Journal of Labor Economics*, Vol. 23 No.4, pp.649-80.

10. McClelland, D.C (1961), "The Achieving Society", *Collier-Macmillan*, New York, NY and London.
11. Rajeev Roy (2008), "Entrepreneurship", *Oxford University Press,* New Delhi.
12. Robinson, P.B., Huefner, J. C. and Hunt, H. K. (1991), "Entrepreneurial research on student subjects does not generalize to real world entrepreneurs", *Journal of Small Business Management* Vol. 29 (2), pp. 43-50.
13. Römer-Paakkanen, T., Rauhala, M. (2007), "To be or not to be? The children of business families face the question many times before they can make a decision whether they continue the family business or not", *paper presented at the ICSB 2007 World Conference, Turku School of Business Administration,* Turku.
14. Rotter, J.B (1966), "Generalized expectations for internal versus external control of reinforcement", *Psychological Monographs: General and Applied,* Vol. 80, [1], pp.1-27.
15. Schumpeter, J.A. (1934), "The Theory of Economic Development", *Harvard University Press.* Cambridge, Massachusetts.
16. Simon, M., Houghton, S., Aquino, K. (1999), "Cognitive biases, risk, perception, and venture formation: how individuals decide to start companies", *Journal of Business Venturing,* Vol. 15 pp.113-34.
17. Teoh, H.Y., Foo, S.L. (1997), "Moderating effects of tolerance for ambiguity and risk taking propensity on the role conflict-perceived performance relationship: evidence from Singaporean entrepreneurs", *Journal of Business Venturing,* Volume - 12 pp.67-81.
18. Tibbits, G. (1979), "Small business management a normative approach", *Msu Business Topics*, Vol.4, pp. 5-12.
19. Zacharakis, A. (1997), "Entrepreneurial entry into foreign markets", *Entrepreneurship: Theory and Practice,* No. Spring, pp.23-40.

## Appendix – 1

### Factors wise Items

[**Note:** The items marked as N are negative items which were reverse scored.]

### 1. Innovativeness

1. Do you tend to put forward new ideas and suggest alternative solutions for improvement?

2. Do you like to follow well established routines and practices? (N)

3. I have the ability to generate new ideas/concepts and manifest them from thought into reality.

## 2. Locus of Control

4. I tend to have control over my actions and plans.

5. I am aware of the consequences of my actions and I take firm decisions.

6. I worry about failure/disapproval of others. (N)

## 3. Risk Taking Propensity

7. I take calculated risks and have belief on my actions.

8. I play safe and try to stay away from risky situations. (N)

9. I jeopardize money while not being sure of the outcomes.

## 4. Management Skills

10. I seek for those tasks that require managerial skills.

11. I dislike being bothered with problems. (N)

12. I would speak as a representative of the group.

## 5. Need for Achievement

13. I am willing to do all the tasks necessary for the successful operation of the business.

14. If I want something, I ask for it rather than wait for someone to notice and just give it to me.

15. I am on time for appointments.

## 6. Tolerance to Ambiguity

16. I like trying new food, new places, and totally new experience.

17. I like to change for better even if it takes time and money.

18. I like to be different in a particular way.

## 7. Ability to Co-operate

19. Working independently gives me better results (N)

20. I can easily start up a conversation with an unknown person and enjoy meeting other people.

21. I am a good listener and tend to understand people well.

**8. Passion for Business**

22. I really have the desire to be my own boss rather than work for someone else.

23. I have the desire to stick with the business even in troubled times.

24. I keep myself updated in the fields which interest me the most.

**9. Positive attitude**

25. Even though people tell me it can't be done, I have to find out for myself.

26. I use powerful words in my inner dialogues and keep myself motivated.

27. I endeavour to replace a negative thought into a constructive one.

**10. Team Worker**

28. As an organization, I believe that I trust my team and get on well together.

29. I like to share a common goal in group activities.

30. I can cooperate with people with whom I am less acquaintance.

# 15

# Self-Efficacy and New Venture Success: Testing the Mediating Effect of Polychronicity in Entrepreneurs – A Research Agenda


## *Abstract*

A psychology construct 'Polychronicity' has been introduced to the field of entrepreneurship studies and understanding of entrepreneurial action at its micro level has been initiated by this work. While Self- efficacy has been firmly established in the entrepreneurial intentionality model, the actual action of performing tasks has been less explored for traits, theory and models. This paper hypothesises that entrepreneurs display polychronic behaviour in starting and running of the new venture and that polychronicity mediates between self efficacy and new venture success. It is also explored that polychronicity is beneficial in early stages of a venture and can be detrimental in the later stages.

This study introduces a new construct to the study of entrepreneurship which will find relevance and importance in areas of understanding entrepreneurial traits and new venture success. The paper brings out major descriptions that will have significant implications in studies of various areas of a new venture like new product development, strategy formation and execution and working of team entrepreneurs.

## Introduction

Entrepreneur success appears to drive from two key sources; personal profile and managerial competence of the entrepreneur (Panda 2005, Chivukula et al 2009). Studies have pointed that different propensities may facilitate or impede business owners actions and behaviours. Hence studies of entrepreneurial success indicators have roots in personality traits studies. This paper uses this base and proposes a study to understand determinants of new venture performance through an individual action propensity trait of 'polychronicity' among entrepreneurs.

Polychronicity was first developed by Edward Hall (1959) and has roots in the author's anthropology studies. This has stimulated considerable application in research areas of management especially in the organisation behaviour and psychology field. Hall's study was ethnographic and this study aims to apply this concept to entrepreneurs as a societal group and link this to studies on understanding entrepreneurs as individuals. This concept is a very useful measure to understand how people work in time demanding situations with a requirement to handle or manage multiple roles and demands. This study sees the relevance of applying the construct to entrepreneurs who face such similar situations.

Exploring the most fundamental questions in entrepreneurship of opportunity emergence and entrepreneurial intentionality, Krueger and Brazeal (1994) conclude that there needs to be pre-existing preparedness for these (Chell 2008). Of the two requirements on the preparedness of the individual, perceived desirability of setting up a business is one and Self efficacy is the other.

Self-efficacy has been the fulcrum of traits and behaviour studies of entrepreneurship since the time of development of this construct by Bandura (1986). The combination of perceived desirability and perceived self-efficacy gives a sense of mastery and credibility (Chell 2008). This is the first stage in venture creation leading entrepreneurs to act. Hence self efficacy is at the foundational level of entrepreneur traits theory.

This paper focuses on exploring the linkages between self efficacy and polychronicity as entrepreneurial trait and new venture performance and contributes and adds to the now few initial efforts of bringing in polychronicity as an area within entrepreneurship.

## Polychronicity

Polychronicity is a time use strategy which combines the activities and actors as mentioned above in understanding an individual tendency or preference for engaging in one or more tasks at a time. While polychronicity is a subset of the bigger idea of time management and contributes towards understanding the construct it has now developed as an important construct to study and is finding various application in management sciences. Type A Behaviour Pattern (TABP) links entrepreneur behaviour to polychronicity and distinguishes polychronicity from time urgency as these two form separate sub-components of TABP which are time urgency, achievement strivings, impatience, polychronicity (Ishizaka et al 2001).

In its broadest construction entrepreneurs are individuals who own a company and employ fewer than 500 people. (Bluedorn 2008). Polychronicity, a fundamental life strategy, is the extent to which people (1) prefer to be engaged in two or more tasks or events simultaneously and are actually so engaged and (2) believe their preference is the best way to do things (Bluedorn 2002, 2008). Edward Hall, introducing the concept of polychronicity, described this as a cultural variable involving two ways of organising activities:

(a) Monochronically – involvement in events one event at a time; and

(b) Polychronically – involvement in two or more events at the same time (Bluedorn 1999)

Polychronicity is marked with movement between several tasks and activities and interruptions and unscheduled events between activities is expected and accepted. It is involvement with multiple activities during the same time (Bluedorn 1999).

## Self-Efficacy

Self-efficacy is a key construct in studies on entrepreneurship and has its origin in social learning theory (Bandura 1997, Brice et al 2007). Self-efficacy refers to individuals' conscious belief in their own ability to bring about desired results in the performance of a particular task (Bandura, 1997, Forbes 2005). Self efficacy is an important determinant of human behaviour. Individuals tend to avoid tasks about which they have low self-efficacy and, conversely, are drawn toward tasks about which they have high self-efficacy. In addition, persons with high self-efficacy tend to perform better on tasks about which they hold those beliefs and less well on tasks about which they believe they have low self efficacy. (Forbes 2005)

Many authors have written about the factors that influence one to become an entrepreneur. These factors are combinations of personal attributes, traits, background, experience and disposition (Arenuius 2005; Baron 2004; Krueger et al; Shane et al 2003; Jeffrey et al 2009). It is found that one of the personal attributes, Entrepreneurial self-efficacy (ESE), appears to be a particularly important antecedent to new venture intentions (Barbosa et al 2007, Boyd 1994, Zhao et al 2005, Jeffrey et al 2009). ESE is a strong predictor of entrepreneurial intentions and ultimate action (Bird 1988, Jeffrey 2009). Self efficacy is the differentiator between managers and entrepreneurs (Chen et al 1998). The literature on ESE suggests that higher levels of ESE influence the likelihood of successfully launching a new business (Jeffrey McGee et al 2009)

Self-efficacy is important for entrepreneurs because they must be confident in their capabilities to perform various (and often unanticipated) tasks in uncertain situations (Baum & Locke 2004, Rauch & Frese 2007). In a study involving Meta analysis of entrepreneur's personality Rauch & Frese (2007) found the correlation between personality trait of self efficacy and entrepreneurial behaviour of business creation to be very high. There is a positive link between ESE and newventure performance (Forbes 2005).

Entrepreneurial Self efficacy studies have progressed to the next level of identifying task specific self efficacy under the broad umbrella. As per these there are four sub divisions – opportunity-identification self-efficacy, relationship self-efficacy, managerial self-efficacy and tolerance self-efficacy. (DeNoble et al 1999, Chen et al 1998, Barbosa 2007). Of these managerial self efficacy is associated with getting things done, handling multiple demands and performing various roles.

## Self-Efficacy, Polychronicity and Entrepreneurial performance

Behaviour is a function of the person and the situation (Lewin 1951, Rauch & frese 2007). As a person entrepreneur is strongly self efficacious and polychronicity is situational as well a personal trait.

Schien (1985, 1992) in his work on organisational culture argues that polychromic values are more suitable for small organizations, especially for the early stages of an organisation (Bluedorn et al 1999). This is due to the fact that early stage organizations face complex situations and require complex problem solving and have small teams dealing with large information. Eisenhardt (1989) suggests that large monochronic and small polychronic organizations should be more effective than their opposites.

Entrepreneurs essay multiple roles in the early stages of a venture. They are seen as leaders, managers, inventors etc and are required to perform the tasks associated with stages of growth i.e. organisational systems, sales and marketing, people, production, strategic positioning and external relations (Chell 2008). To do all these entrepreneurs need to possess a wide variety of skills, knowledge and abilities (Shane 2003, Rauch & Frese 2007). The more entrepreneurs preferred to work fast the more polychronic they were. This may be in line with the accepted notion that rapidity- being first to market with a new product or service- is always the best strategy (Drucker 1985, Bluedorn 2008).

A strive for control over external and internal factors is inherent in all and more in entrepreneurs. Control leads to predictability and predictability is a valued possession for businesses and more so for new ventures. The individual stakes of entrepreneurs are high in the new venture. Self efficacy is an individual's belief that he/she can influence outcomes or cause effects in their life situations. Self efficacy beliefs affect human functioning. Entrepreneurs are found to display a high level self efficacy. We propose that the belief that one can control and influence events leads to a tendency to involve oneself in all activities of the new venture to influence a favourable outcome and also to initiate multiple activities at the same time to achieve the desired outcome.

Self efficacy is fundamentally important for an individual to move from a position of entrepreneurial intention to action (Chell 2008). At the threshold of action stands polychronicity. Progress of an entrepreneurial journey from intention to action and self efficacy's presence and effect on the action part needs to be explored. Self-efficacy is very task oriented and task specific construct. It is a belief in an ability to perform a task in unanticipated situations and uncertain circumstances. Polychronicity is the actual action of performing various tasks in such situations and circumstances. Ability and time are the two components of a task that are taken care of by self efficacy and polychronicity measures.

Literature is inundated with self efficacy and its established importance in the intention and conversion of that intention to a venture. We can benefit from stretching this construct to examine its influence on the later stages of action.

Studies of Polychronicity in entrepreneurs will further understanding of 'execution' of an idea or business opportunity and entrepreneur as a manager and leader. Self efficacy is a broad construct and its presence with the individual is assumed to be rather consistent. Polychronicity will measure the actions and modes of actions over the evolutionary period of the organisation. Polychronicity can be a shifting and evolving presence in the organisation while self efficacy can be more consistent factor contributing to various other behavioural outcomes and actions.

The other angle linking entrepreneurs to polychronicity is that entrepreneurs as a group displayed more frequently Type A behaviour than Type B (Boyd & Webb 1982 & Corzine, 1998). Type A Behaviour Pattern (TABP) has been studied as predictor of task performance. The sub-components of TABP are time urgency, achievement strivings, impatience, polychronicity (Ishizaka et al 2001).

A triangulated study of the three areas of self efficacy, polychronicity and entrepreneurship will throw more light on the entrepreneurial behaviour and success factor. The novelty factor of this study is that it will bring to focus the internal functioning of a venture during the early stages and entrepreneur as a manager, leader, and organiser. It also embeds polychronicity as a specific trait to engage in the studies of entrepreneurship. By doing this it addresses lack of specificity in the task performance related personality trait study of entrepreneurs.

## New venture performance

It is useful for practice to know how entrepreneurial personalities are related to venture performance (Rauch & Frese 2007). Multiple measures, objective and subjective, have been used to measure new venture performance. Subjective measures are useful for assessing the broader, non-financial dimensions of performance while objective measures are helpful in measuring financial performance (Stam and Elfring 2008). There have been many objective measures used by studies. Sales growth and profitability measures have been a constant in all these measures (Stam and Elfring 2008, Li and Fernhaber 2010).

This proposed research links the variables to new venture performance. It is proposed that a self-reported sales and net profit year-on-year growth data be used to assess performance. The data can use three year period to measure the sales and net profit growth.

## Hypothesis

An entrepreneur dons multiple hats in the formation and early days of a new venture. He performs the role of an innovator, leader, manager and executive.

He performs all organisational functions of marketing, product development, finance, strategy etc. In the early days of the new venture it is also necessary from a cost and resource angle that entrepreneur plays more than one role and involve himself in all functions and activities of the firm simultaneously. They work under severe time demands, face uncertain conditions and unexpected developments every day. *So entrepreneurs as a group tend to be polychronic.*

If self efficacy is an individual's belief that he/she can influence outcomes or cause effects in their life situations, polychronicity is the propensity or preference of acting with a belief that this preference is the best way of doing something. Polychronicity maybe self efficacy put into action. This stands between the belief in ability to influence course of outcome and the actual outcome of new venture growth. *Hence self efficacy and polychronicity will correlate among entrepreneurs and polychronicity mediates between the self efficacious behaviour of the entrepreneur and the venture performance.*

There are benefits of polychronic behaviour of entrepreneurs during the early stages of a new venture. One single point of decision making, integrated action, clarity of strategy will provide the necessary agility and speed that have been accepted as the areas of competitive advantage for new ventures. However growth of the venture will be slowed if there is only one person handling many critical tasks and everything is centralised with one person. Growth needs delegation and tasks allotted as per expertise and organisational needs. *Hence polychronic behaviour of entrepreneurs diminishes as organizations grow successfully.*

The proposed research model is as below –

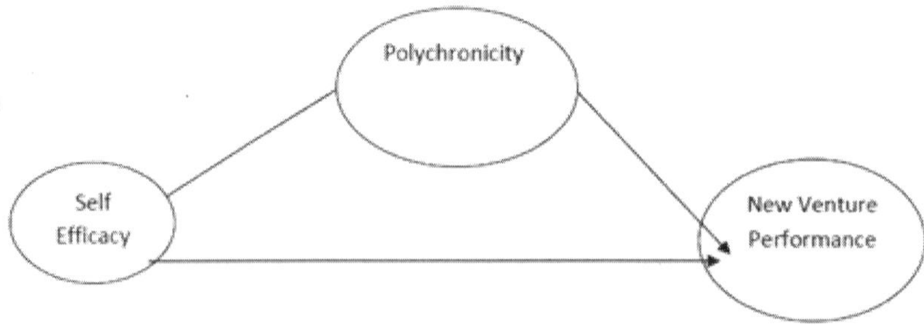


Figure 1: Research framework for testing the mediation effect of polychronicity between Self-efficacy and new venture performance

## Road ahead

### *Measure*

For Self efficacy the 10 point scale developed by Schwarzer and Jerusalem (1986) can be deployed for the study. This scale is a list of ten items on a five point Likert scale. This scale is found suitable for use as this has been tested extensively across cultures. Polychronicity can be measured by the scale developed by Bluedorn et al (1999). This is a ten item scale which can be matched against five point Likert scale. Two widely used scales of Polychronicity are those developed by Kaufmann et al (1999) and Bluedorn et al (1999). The four items of polychronic attitude index scale by Kaufmann is covered by the Bluedorn scale and while Kaufmann scale is used more extensively in consumer research Bluedorn et al's Inventory of Polychronic Values has been developed for measuring dimensions of organisational culture.

### *Sample*

The respondent sample selection is a crucial step in a study. It is recommended that the sample be cross sectional having respondents of approximately 250 entrepreneurs spread across industries. These entrepreneurs can be divided into two groups of venture age 1-3 and > 6 years. The grouping is done to assist the study in understanding early venture and growth situations. The new ventures selected should have an employee size of above 25. This will help understand polychronicity as a personality trait rather than as a necessity. An organisation with very few people will necessitate a polychromic behavior of the entrepreneur and its people. Hence a minimum size of 25 people is a good criterion for the study. The other reason for this proposal is also that new venture survival in the first year for ventures with 25 and above employees is 68% and keeps increasing with number of employees (Timmons & Spinelli 2009). This will ensure covering a sample group of survivors and performers. New ventures failure studies have also reflected that majority of failures occur in the first two to five years (Timmons & Spinelli, 2009). Hence study of ventures above five years will help make useful conclusions about survival and growth. The control variables that can be identified for such a study are entrepreneur's age and prior experiences which can have a bearing on the variables studied. Age has an impact on the behavioural propensities and in the case of polychronicity it can be surmised that it may have a bearing on the dexterity and skill it calls for. Prior entrepreneurial lessons, successes, failures may have altered the behaviour of entrepreneurs. To make the findings easily interpretable the study can control for these two variables and it is proposed that the respondent group consist of entrepreneurs with no prior entrepreneurial experience and be in the age group of 30-40 years.

### *Data collection*

This primary data collection exercise will involve administering the two questionnaires on self efficacy and polychronicity among the sample group. The questionnaires can be personally administered or sent to respondents with a covering note describing the study and with an assurance to keep company specific information confidential. Telephonic follow up calls should be made to all the respondents to ensure higher response rate.

### *Analytical techniques*

It is proposed that statistical technique of mediational regression analysis be used for data analysis, based on the guidelines given by Baron & Kenny (1986). This will be helpful in testing the impact of and presence of polychronicity given self efficacy and further impact of this on the venture growth. This test can be run to also ascertain the relationship between venture growth and polychronicity. For measuring the correlation between self efficacy and polychronicity use of correlation analysis is proposed. Regression and correlation analysis terms refer to techniques used for studying the relationship between two or more variables. The two terms are often interchangeable but correlation analysis involves measuring the closeness of the relationship and regression analysis is used to derive an equation that relates the dependent variable to the independent variable (Churchill et al 2009).

## Implications

Studies in the field of entrepreneurship have always tried to decipher the 'entrepreneur' and understand success of new venture. Early entrepreneurship research focused on finding general traits and motives of successful entrepreneurs (Brockhaus, 1980). Researchers hoped that personality screening could help entrepreneurs avoid personal disappointment and could help nations avoid wasted resources (McClelland, 1965, Baum & Choke 2004). Proposed research will contribute to this quest by exploring a dimension of the personality that can potentially have a significant bearing on how we understand new venture functioning and entrepreneurs as individuals. Earlier works on polychronicity have tended to be job studies relating this personality trait or individual preference of working style to particular jobs like doctors, dentist, salesmen, managers etc. Research in this direction is a step in making polychronicity a part of the literature in entrepreneurship. The findings will have a bearing on the way we understand the actions taken by entrepreneurs and the execution of the idea within the new venture. This can potentially be an independent area and trait to explore amongst entrepreneurs. Polychronicity, while being a personality trait is also a strong link to business outcomes. Self efficacy is concerned with the execution of an action not its outcome (Chen et al. 1998). Polychronicity is an extension of the idea of self efficacy and can be linked to outcomes. Studies on product development, strategic decision making, organisational structure, strategy execution are the areas that can be influenced by the polychronic trait. These are the core functions of early stage ventures that can have a significant bearing on the outcomes for the business. Proposed research will be among the initial few steps taken to integrate this construct of polychronicity with entrepreneurship areas and specifically understand this along with Self-efficacy which has been the backbone of entrepreneur trait studies. That will help bring in a 'How' angle to trait study by linking traits like Self-efficacy to the effects they can have on various functioning of the venture. It will help answer question like how do traits impact actual and specific functioning of tasks of new venture creation, growth and success. Other personality characteristics that have been identified as distinguishing entrepreneurs from non-entrepreneurs are high need for autonomy, independence, dominance, low need for support (Bowman 1985, Murray & MacMillan 1988). Combination study of traits to see how they combine, correlate and contribute to the functioning and performance of entrepreneurs and new ventures can be the way forward continuing from this study. That will advise practice on many core issues and will assist the practitioner find leads to long standing questions.

Such research will contribute towards evoking interest in understanding Indian entrepreneurship in its cultural context as awareness and interest in the field of entrepreneurship grows in India. Culture specific research to understand entrepreneurial personality, action and situation needs to be undertaken to make understanding and practice deeper and relevant. This research will contribute towards taking this important step. This could lead to developing a framework for adapting this to training and teachings in the area of entrepreneurship.

## References


0. Albert Bandura (1997), Self Efficacy: The exercise of control, W H Freeman New York
1. Allen C Bluedorn and Gwen Martin (2008), The time frames of entrepreneurs, Journal of Business Venturing, 23 (2008) 1-20
2. Allen C. Bluedorn, Thomas J. Kalliath, Michael J Strube, Gregg D Martin (1999), Polychronicity and the Inventory of Polychronic Values (IPV), Journal of Managerial Psychology, Vol. 14 No 3 /4, 1999 pp. 205-230.
3. Andreas Rauch & Michael Frese (2007), Let's put the person back into entrepreneurship research: A meta-analysis on the relationship between business owners' personality traits, business creation and success, European Journal of work and organisational psychology 2007, 16 (4), pp. 353-385
4. Bird B (1988), Implementing entrepreneurial ideas: The case for intention, Academy of Management Review, 13(3), pp. 442-453
5. Bjorn Bjerke (2007), Understanding Entrepreneurship, Edward Elgar Publishing Limited, UK
6. Boyd N & Vozikis G (1994), The influence of self-efficacy on the development of entrepreneurial intentions and actions, Entrepreneurship Theory and Practice, 18(4), pp.63-77
7. Brent Bowers (2006), The 8 patterns of highly effective entrepreneurs, DoubleDay, USA Brockhaus, R. H., Sr. (1980). Risk-taking propensity of entrepreneurs, Academy of Management Journal, 23, pp. 509–520
8. Carol Felker Kaufman, Paul M. Lane, Jay D. Lindquist (1991), Exploring more than 24 hours a day: A preliminary investigation of polychronic time use, Journal of consumer research, Vol. 18, 1991
9. Carol Kaufman-Scarborough & Jay D. Lindquist (1999), The Polychronic attitude index: Refinement and preliminary consumer marketplace behavior applications, American Marketing Association Winter Educators Conference Proceedings, Marketing Theory and Applications, Volume 10, 151-157.
10. Chao C. Chen, Patricia Gene Greene, Ann Crick (1998), Does entrepreneurial Self-efficacy distinguish entrepreneurs from managers? Journal of Business Venturing, 13, 295-316
11. Conte J & Gintoft J (2005), Polychronicity, Big Five Personality Dimensions, and Sales Performance. Human Performance, October 2005 18(4), pp. 427-444.

12. Daniel Forbes (2005), The effects of Strategic Decision Making on Entrepreneurial Self-efficacy, Entrepreneurship Theory & Practice, September 2005
13. DeNoble A F., Jung D., & Ehrlich, S. B (1999), Entrepreneurial self-efficacy: The development of a measure and its relationship to entrepreneurial action, Frontiers of Entrepreneurship research, pp. 73-87, Waltham MA: P&R Publications Inc.
14. Elizabeth Chell (2008), The Entrepreneurial personality, Routledge, New York Eisenhardt, K.M. (1989), Making fast strategic decisions in high-velocity environments, Academy of Management Journal, Vol. 32 No. 3, pp. 543-76.
15. Gilbert Churchill, Dawn Iacobucci, D Israel (2009), Marketing Research A south Asian perspective, Cengage Learning, India
16. Hao Zhao, Scott E Seibert, Gerald E Hills (2005), The Mediating role of self efficacy in the development of Entrepreneurial Intentions, Journal of applied psychology, Vol 90, No.6, pp. 1265-1272
17. Janice Barker Corzine & Jacqueline N Hood (1998), Shadow and light: Type A behaviour and conflict handling styles in entrepreneurs, Journal of business and entrepreneurship, October 1998
18. Jeff Brice, Jr., & Barbara Spencer (2007), Entrepreneurial Profiling: A Decision policy analysis of the influence of entrepreneurial self efficacy on entrepreneurial intent, Academy of Entrepreneurship Journal, Vol 13 Number 2, 2007
19. Jeffrey A.Timmons & Stephen Spinelli (2009), New Venture Creation: Entrepreneurship for the 21st Century, Tata Mc-Graw Hill, New York Jeffrey E McGee, Mark Peterson, Stephen L. Mueller, Jennifer M. Sequeira (2009), Entrepreneurial Self-Efficacy: Refining the measure, Entrepreneurship Theory and Practice, Jun 2009
20. J. Robert Baum and Edwin A Locke (2004), The Relationship of Entrepreneurial Traits, Skill, and Motivation to Subsequent Venture Growth, Journal of applied psychology, Vol 89, No.4, 587-598
21. Krueger, N F., jr & Brazeal D.V (1994), Entrepreneurial potential and potential entrepreneurs, Entrepreneurship Theory & Practice, 18(3), pp. 91-104
22. Kyoko Ishizaka, Sandra Marshall & Jeffrey Conte (2001), Individual differences in attentional strategies in multitasking situations, Human Performance 2001, 14(4), pp. 339-358
23. Mary Law, Carolyn Baum & Winnie Dunn 2005, Measuring occupational performance, SLACK Incorporated, USA

24. McClelland, D. C. (1965). N achievement and entrepreneurship: A longitudinal study, Journal of Personality and Social Psychology, 1, pp. 389–392
25. Murray B Low & Ian C MacMillan (1988), Entrepreneurship: Past research and future challenges, Journal of Management, Vol 14, No 2
26. P Arenius & M Minniti (2005), Perceptual variables and nascent entrepreneurship, Small Business Economics, 24(3), pp. 233-247
27. Panda Tapan K & Panda S (2005), Studying entrepreneurial seriousness amid small businesses of Orissa, The Icfai Journal of entrepreneurship development, Vol 2, No.4, pp 10-21.
28. Peter F. Drucker (1985), Innovation and Entrepreneurship, HarperCollins Publishers Inc, USA
29. R Goonetilleke & L Yan (2010), The relationship between monochronicity, polychronicity and individual characteristics. Behaviour & Information Technology. March 2010 29(2), pp. 187-198.
30. Richard C Cuba and Gene Milbourn Jr (1982), Delegating for small business success, American Journal of Small Business, Vol VII, No 2, Oct –Dec 1982
31. R. M Baron & D. A Kenny (1986). The Moderator-Mediator variable distinction in Social Psychological research: Conceptual, strategic, and statistical considerations. Journal of Personality and Social Psychology, 51, pp. 1173- 1182.
32. Romanus Wolter (2006), Trust your team, Entrepreneur, Nov 2006
33. R Schwarzer, & M Jerusalem (1995). Generalized Self-Efficacy scale. In J. Weinman, control beliefs, pp. 35-37, Windsor, UK
34. Saulo Dubard Barbosa (2007), The role of cognitive style and risk preference on entrepreneurial self-efficacy and entrepreneurial intentions, Journal of Leadership and Organisational studies, 2007, Vol.13, No.4
35. Schein, E.H. (1985), Organizational Culture and Leadership, Jossey-Bass, San Francisco, CA.
36. Schein, E.H. (1992), Organizational Culture and Leadership (2nd ed.), Jossey- Bass. San Francisco, CA.
37. Shane S, Locke E.A & Collins, C J (2003), Entrepreneurial Motivation, Human Resource Management Review, 13(2), pp. 257-279
38. Shane and Venkataraman (2000), The promise of entrepreneurship as a field of research, Academy of Management Review, 2000, Vol 25, No.1, pp. 217-226

39. Stephanie A Fernhaber & Dan Li (2010), Entrepreneurship Theory & Practice, January 2010
40. Todd J Maurer & Heather R. Pierce (1998), A Comparison of Likert Scale and Traditional Measures of Self-Efficacy, Journal of Applied Psychology, Vol 83, No 2, pp. 324-329
41. Venkata Ramana Chivukula, Raman K J, Ramachandra Aryasri (2009), Influence of Socio-demographic factors on entrepreneurial attributes and success, South Asian Journal of Management, Oct-Dec 2009, 16;4
42. Wouter Stam & Tom Elfring (2008), Entrepreneurial Orientation and New Venture Performance: The moderating role of Intra and Extra industry social capital, Academy of Management Journal 2008 Vol 51, No 1, pp. 97-111

# 16

# Evaluation of Entrepreneurship Development Preparedness of Tripura Vis-À-Vis Entrepreneurial Framework Conditions

### *Abstract*

It is the entrepreneurship that propels the development of mankind in every forms and focus. It involves the process of transforming creative ideas into commercially viable business. Successful entrepreneurship is a cohesive process of creativity, risk taking, and planning. Germination of entrepreneurship largely depends on the prevailing culture of the society. To develop a positive entrepreneurial culture in any country or any of its region or state, the proper social, political, economical and physical infrastructural support is inevitable.

Against this backdrop, the present paper is an attempt to evaluate the entrepreneurship development preparedness of Tripura in the milieu of Entrepreneurial Framework Conditions (EFC) as referred in the Global Entrepreneurship Monitor Report – 2002. Through analytical discussion, the present paper divulges that although continuous efforts are exerting by the government to promote entrepreneurs in Tripura by conducting Entrepreneurship Development Programmes on regular basis, the prevailing EFC are not synchronizing with that effort to bring the desired outcomes. As such, it is absolutely necessary to improve the EFC of the state to sprout good quality entrepreneurs in large numbers.

## Introduction

Human development and the development of mankind in whatsoever form are basically caused by the spirit of enterprise or entrepreneurship in general. The association between the attributes of the entrepreneurship and economic development is much closer. In fact, the relationship between entrepreneurship and economic development is similar to the relationship between the cause and effect. As such, there is no denying about the fact that it is the entrepreneur who is the prime mover of economic development of any country in one hand and turns the challenges into opportunities for creating new sources of income and employment opportunity on the other hand. Virtually the number, diversity in numbers and quality of entrepreneurs as a whole speak about the level of the socio-economic development of a country in general or any of its regions in particular. The entrepreneurship development scenario in North Eastern Region of India as a whole is still very much gloomy. Despite of huge natural resources as well as potential human resources and consistent effort of the Government for development of entrepreneurs, desired numbers of enterprises are not coming up over the years. In Tripura, both the Central Government and State Government through various promotional agencies are trying to promote entrepreneurial activities by conducting Entrepreneurship Development Programmes (EDPs) on regular basis. However, statistics reveals that the success rates of such EDPs are not at all encouraging. In a study on EDPs in North Eastern States, it has been observed that the success rate of EDPs in Tripura is only 13.2%; which is lowest among the North Eastern States *(Baruah, Sarma, and Mali, 1996)*. But development of entrepreneurs in large scale is the only option before the Government to cope up with the unemployment problem as a result of enduring population explosion in India. Because of the history of India and its multi-cultural composition, it seems impossible to have a Family Planning policy like that of China in the near future. It is likely that India's population will continue to grow, which will consequently worsen the employment situation in the country. Over the past two decades, massive corporate downsizing has led governments around the world to increasingly acknowledge entrepreneurs as a key contributor to new job creation and economic growth. India is not an exception. These events have led the leaders of our country to openly encourage its citizens to embrace entrepreneurship as career by choice. If new ventures are to be considered as engines of growth in an economy, it is therefore incumbent on policy makers to understand the key factors that encourage or impede the creation of start-ups. According to the 2002 Global Entrepreneurship Monitor (GEM), an international comparative research project that aims to benchmark the level of entrepreneurial activities across countries, India ranked 2nd out of 37 nations on the level of entrepreneurial propensity *(GEM Report 2002)*. A salient feature of 2002's GEM India research findings was that while India has emerged as the second most entrepreneurially active nation among the 37 participating nations with a Total Entrepreneurial Activity (TEA) index of 17.9%, it was heartening to note that entrepreneurial activity levels in the country have been consistently on the rise for the past three years from 8.9% in 2000 through 11.6% in 2001 to 17.9% in 2002. It seems the Indian economy has entered a vibrant phase, and it is the responsibility of all concerned to help it in maintaining the momentum. At this juncture, one has to be taken in to accounts about the real ground condition in terms of prevailing entrepreneurial friendly environment of different states of India, particularly the backward states like Tripura. This is for the simple reason that all the states of India must perform to attain the synergy of growth. Against this backdrop, the present paper is an attempt to assess the entrepreneurial preparedness of Tripura in the back ground of *Entrepreneurial Framework Condition* (EFC) utilized by GEM project in Indian or Global context. For the purpose of comparison and assessment of EFC for Tripura, this paper has taken the help of the evaluation study titled *"A critical study of the effectiveness of entrepreneurship development programmes in the northeast"* conducted by Indian Institute of Entrepreneurship, Guwahati.

## Entrepreneurial Framework Condition (EFC) Model

The focal hypothesis of the GEM research project is that the level of entrepreneurial activity in a country has a backward linkage to the quality of the entrepreneurial framework conditions in the country and a forward linkage to the country's economic growth. A simplified version of the GEM Conceptual Model is as shown below with the help of a block diagram. The major area of concern in this regard is what the GEM research calls the "entrepreneurial framework conditions" in

India. As such, many changes are needed in the social, political, economical and physical infrastructure in the country in order to make serious efforts in stimulating entrepreneurship among the youths and thereby overall economic growth in the country.

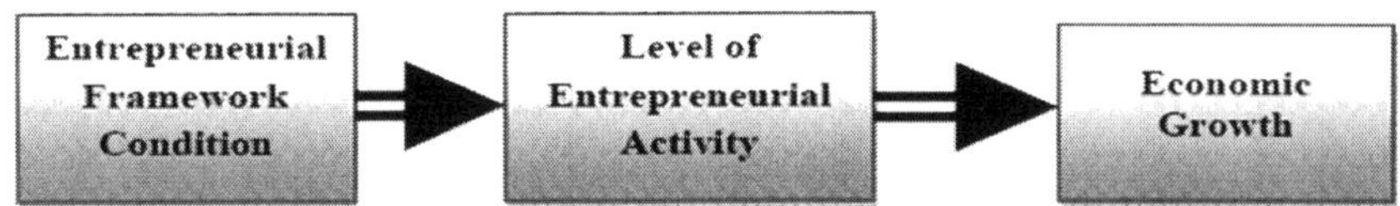


Figure 1: Forward and Backward linkage of Entrepreneurial Activity

The Causal relationships implied in the model are at two levels:

(1) The supportiveness of the entrepreneurial framework conditions influences the level of entrepreneurial activity, and

(2) The level of entrepreneurial activity influences economic growth. At the level of individual states, the GEM research model provides a framework that can be used to ascertain the supportiveness of the state's environment towards entrepreneurship and the level of entrepreneurial activity in the state. In order to assess the supportiveness of entrepreneurial framework conditions in the state of Tripura it is necessary to characterize all the 11 components of EFC in the state specific condition. The 11 components of the EFC are:

1. Financial Support to New Firms
2. Government Policy on New Firms
3. Government Programs for New Firms
4. Supportiveness of Educational system
5. Research and Development Transfer
6. Commercial, Legal and Professional Infrastructure
7. Market Openness and Ease of Entry
8. Adequacy of Physical Infrastructure
9. Appropriateness of Social and Cultural Norms
10. Opportunities for New Venture Creation
11. Entrepreneurial Capacity.

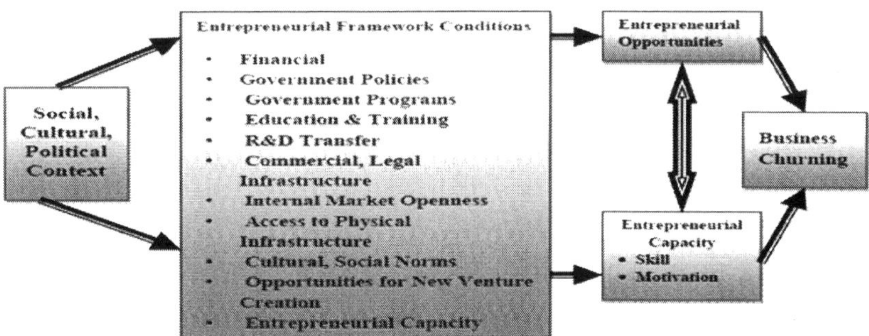


Figure 2: EFC model and 11 Frameworks

## EDP Effectiveness study

To satisfy the twin objectives of growth of small enterprises and employment generation, a massive 212 entrepreneurship development training programme (popularly known as EDP training) were organised during April 1990-March 1996 in the north-eastern region of India with the financial support from Government of India through various financial and promotional agencies. These training programmes aimed at motivating and developing the prospective entrepreneurs of the region in to actual entrepreneurs in the small-scale sector through training intervention and follow-up supports in the proven path of the famous *Kakinada experiment* of David C. McClelland (1966). The EDP trainings (each of 6 – 8 week's duration) were organised in seven states of northeastern region of India by four reputed entrepreneurship development organizations of the country where 5375 participants participated. The major objectives of these EDPs were to

(i) improve the achievement motivation and other entrepreneurial qualities among participants;

(ii) create awareness about the facilities and support system available for enterprise launching;

(iii) special incentives available for setting up enterprises in the north eastern region;

(iv) help the participants to identify projects and formulate business plan;

(v) impart industry knowledge and management skills;

(vi) help the participants in developing linkage with banks and financial institutions and

(vii) Provide counseling support to the participants in launching their enterprise in the post training period.

In short, these 212 EDPs had the common objective of developing the participants of the trainings in to entrepreneurs within a reasonable period. Attempt was made by Indian Institute of Entrepreneurship (IIE) in the year 2000 to ascertain state wise effectiveness of the 212 EDPs and the result were published in the form of study report. Analysis were first made to determine how many of the trainees actually became successful in launching the enterprises i.e. termed as ***doers***, how many of them were on the pipeline i.e. ***dreamers*** and how many of them could not start enterprises and dropped the idea of enterprise launching altogether i.e.

***duds***. It was revealed that out of 2616 respondents who were contacted personally, 569 (21.75%) became the doers, 541 (20.68%) were the dreamers and a large number of trainees i.e. 1506 (57.57%) remained as duds. Out of total 212 EDPs organised in the seven northeastern states a total of 22 EDPs were organised in the state of Tripura where 580 participants were participated. The study found that amongst the seven states, Tripura had the lowest success rate with 13.2 percent "doers" only. The reasons were analyzed also as to why so large number of participants remained "dreamers" or "duds".

## Evaluation of EFC in Tripura

As already stated, the EDP effectiveness study indicated the lowest success rate in terms of new enterprise germination for the state of Tripura. This section of the paper compares the study result against the broad frame work of EFC.

### *1. Financial Support to New Firms*

It is important to be entrepreneur friendly on three components of financial support: (i) availability of debt funds for new/ growing firms, (ii) Venture Capitals as an important source of venture funds, and (iii) public subsidies promoting entrepreneurship. The study found *(Table - 1)* that the dreamers and duds had mostly opined that lack of finance, be it equity or debt, as the major reason for not starting enterprise even after undergoing training.

### *2. Government Policy on New Firms*

There is apparently a marked improvement needed in the government policy on new firms as perceived by the dreamers and duds *(see Table 1)*. Most of the unsuccessful trainees in this dimension have been rated government support below than what they expected.

### *3. Government Programs for New Firms*

The prospective entrepreneur desires that Government provides one top service to them with the facility like incubators, land/ sheds with competent and supportive official manning the support department. However, the study reveals that the new entrepreneurs' expectations were not fulfilled in this respect.

### *4. Supportiveness of Educational System*

It has been well documented that educational system that encourages self reliance, provides information on market economy, gives attention to entrepreneurship, includes entrepreneurship contents in formal course curriculums are bound to germinate more entrepreneurs. Though the study has not highlighted the response of the unsuccessful trainees in this count but this is beyond any doubt that educational curriculums of the state need to be more entrepreneurial to have entrepreneurship as a subject in the primary or secondary level of school education to psychologically mould the young minds to embrace entrepreneurship as career by choice in future rather than searching for a job on completion of formal education.

### *5. Research and Development Transfer*

As in the case of the GEM study report 2002, India, as a whole, is rated lower on this count. The report viewed that though the country has good R&D institutions, it may not necessarily mean that technology is being effectively transferred to enterprises and commercialized. The state of Tripura is not and will not be an exception to the general trend of the country. In fact, Tripura is far lacking in this regard in comparison to the national average.

### *6. Commercial, Legal and Professional Infrastructure*

In general, one could say that Indian new ventures can get suppliers, sub-contractors and services (legal, accounting, banking, etc.) in adequate numbers at affordable prices. Adequacy of suppliers/ sub-contractors for new firms is also an indicator for faster new enterprise germination. The study indicated that a bulk chunk of respondent have reportedly mentioned lack of raw material and complexity of getting legal formalities observed as a major cause towards abandonment of idea of enterprise set-up.

### *7. Market Openness and Ease of Entry*

The GEM report considered India as a high barrier economy, implying that it is fairly difficult for new players to gain entry. The difficulties may arise out of naturally stagnant market conditions *(absence of market dynamism),* which limits the opportunities for new start-up. It may also be due to the unfair practices and machinations of large and established players facilitated by the absence of rigorous laws and/ or their tardy implementation. These are the two aspects expected to prevail in the undeveloped economic condition of the state of Tripura.

### **8. Adequacy of Physical Infrastructure**

New/ growing firm's desires to get utility access in about a month so as stabilize them in the phase of uncertainness. Qualities of physical infrastructure, cheap communication access in about a week are of utmost importance for a new enterprise. The study has indicated that most of the duds had experienced difficulty in getting adequate physical infrastructure while in the process of developing themselves as entrepreneurs.

### *9. Appropriateness of Social and Cultural Norms*

The parameters like culture that is highly supportive of individual success achieved through own personal efforts, culture that emphasizes self-sufficiency, autonomy, and personal initiative, culture encourages entrepreneurial risk-taking, culture encourages creativity and innovativeness, culture emphasizes the responsibility that the individual has in managing his/ her own life have over the years proved to be highly influential invisible factors for promoting entrepreneurship. In fact, experts on entrepreneurship have attributed the entrepreneurial success of some communities of our country like Sindhri, Marwari, etc. towards appropriateness of social and cultural norms of those communities. The study on entrepreneurial effectiveness has indicated that the dreamers and duds of Tripura lacked the support from their families in their endeavor to become entrepreneur.

### *10. Opportunities for New Venture Creation*

As the counties/ regions of the world are moving to globalization, more business opportunities are created. It is therefore perceived that people should see lots of good opportunities for the creation of new firms. If there are more good opportunities for the creation of new firms, then there are people who will be able to take advantage of them. In fact, for India and its states there are more opportunities now since liberalization of economy started almost two decade back. This is particularly true for a bordering state like Tripura in terms of cross border businesses with Bangladesh. It is now easy to get the information required to assess business opportunities. There are plenty of good opportunities to create truly high growth firms. Good opportunities for new firms should have considerably increased in the past five years.

However, on the contrary, the EDP study indicated that the trained entrepreneurs suffered a lot in identification of good business opportunities that have real growth potential. The type of enterprises that the doers selected also indicates that the trained entrepreneurs have not been able to think beyond some petty traditional enterprises.

## *11. Entrepreneurial Capacity*

On entrepreneurial capacity, that is, on whether people in general have the knowledge, skills, experience and attitudes required for starting and managing a new business, the EDP study has not indicated favorable results. About 52.6 percent of the dreamers expressed that they did not feel motivated to start enterprise while about 13.6 percent of the duds felt lack of motivation as the reason for dropping the idea of developing enterprise. Also a sizable number of duds have shown lack of entrepreneurial skill as the reason for not becoming entrepreneur.

**Table - 1**

**Entrepreneurship Development effort in Tripura: Efforts and Results**

| *Parameters* | *Results* |
|---|---|
| Success rate of EDP training : Distribution of Doers, Dreamers & Duds | Doers (10.7%),<br>Dreamers (11.0%), and<br>Duds (78.3%) |
| Reasons for delay in setting up the enterprise after training (Dreamer's view*)<br>* *dreamers had on average 3 reasons for delay* | Problem of finance (100%)<br>Lack of Motivation (52.6%)<br>Government policy (38.1%)<br>Legal formality (31.1%)<br>Marketing problem (32.0%)<br>Non availability of raw material (26.4%)<br>Non availability of land and shed (34.8%)<br>Electricity problem (26.3%) |
| Reasons for delay in setting up the enterprise after training (Duds' view*)<br>* *duds had on average 3 reasons for delay* | Problem of finance (84.7%)<br>Lack of Motivation (13.6%)<br>Domestic problem (12.8%)<br>Fear of Failure (4.0%)<br>Lack of family support (13.8%)<br>Non availability of raw material (10.4%)<br>Lack of entrepreneurial Skill (14.5%) |

Source: *Promoting New Entrepreneurs: Dutta and Mali. 2000*

## Conclusion

The entire process of business development right from conception of an idea to the establishment of a business enterprise is a daunting task. Enterprise germination and taking it to the path of growth has never been an isolated event but the outcome of various macro and micro economic factors involved in the process. The EFC framework provides the understanding of necessary condition needed to prevail for flourishing entrepreneurship. The entrepreneurship development programme (EDP) made efforts on its own way to develop entrepreneurship in different states of the northeast. The low success rate in terms of promoting entrepreneur may partly explain the phenomenon.

That again indicates that given improved EFC conditions the success rate of such kind of EDP training will be optimum. In other words, improving the EFC conditions of the state/ region implies promoting entrepreneurship at a faster rate. With a view to promoting entrepreneurial activities in the state of Tripura, Entrepreneurial Framework Conditions need to be improved to a great extent and as such; the government, policy makers and all other stakeholders may concentrate on this issue to achieve a glorious future of the state.

## References

1. Awasthi, D. M. and Sebastian. J. (1996), "Evaluation of Entrepreneurship Development Programme" Sage Publications, New Delhi.
2. Babbie, J. S. (1990), "Survey Research Methods", 2nd.ed. Wadsworth Publishing Company.
3. Baruah, A. K., Sarma, P., Mali, D. D. (1996): Effectiveness of Entrepreneurship Development Programme – Interim Report, IIE Research Highlights.
4. Block, Z. and Stumpf, S. A. (1992), "Entrepreneurship Education Research: Experience and challenge in The State of the Art of Entrepreneurship", Sexton D. L. and Kasandra J. D. Eds., Boston: PWSKent.
5. Colette, H. and Shane, H. (1999), "European Entrepreneurship Education and Training -The Need for Evaluation", Dundalk Institute of Technology. Conference paper.
6. Curran, J. and Stanworth, J. (1989), "Education and Training for Enterprises: Some Problem of Classification. Evaluation, Policy and Research" International Small Business Journal. Vol. 7 No 2.
7. Draper, N. R. and Smith H. (1981), Applied Regression Analysis. John Wiley and Sons Inc. New York.
8. GEM Report 2002, Babson College, USA
9. Gupta, S.K. (1989), "Entrepreneurship Development: The Indian Case" Journal for Small Business Management, 40(2) 67-69.
10. Mali. D. D. and Dutta, G. (2000), "Promoting New Entrepreneurs". Indian Institute of Entrepreneurship, Guwahati, India.
11. McClelland, D. C. (1966), Urge to Achieve, *Think*, Nov. – Dec.

# 17

# Harnessing the Achievement Oriented Youth for Entrepreneurial Growth

***Abstract***

In spite of the increasing recognition of entrepreneurship as a source of job creation, empowerment and economic dynamism in a globalised world, only a few systematic attempts are made to understand it from perspective of youth. With India all set to reap the “demographic dividend”, young entrepreneurs will be the backbone of economic growth. The focus of the paper is to study the motivations of the youth towards entrepreneurship. The key motivations are studied through a comprehensive literature review on what characterizes youth entrepreneurs followed by a primary research with MBA students as test units.

**Key Conclusions**

1. 80% of the respondents aspired to take up entrepreneurship. Out of those 66.67% maintained that they have a high need for achievement.
2. As per the study, there is no significant relation between gender and entrepreneurial desire.
3. As per the study, there is no significant relation between educational background and entrepreneurial desire.

4. As per the study, there is a significant relationship between a high need for achievement and entrepreneurial desire.

## Recommendations

Entrepreneurship was once the road, less travelled, due to host of external factors. But today, highly motivated youth pursuing MBA in India, do wish to take up entrepreneurship at some or the other time in their careers. Enterprise helps young women and men develop new skills and experiences that can be applied to many other challenges in life. For this, their education should equip them to take on the challenges and enhance their prospects to tread the new road.

Remarkable 20-somethings have changed the way we lead our lives. Numerous entrepreneurs made history by starting out young: Larry Page and Sergey Brin (Google), Steve Wozniak and Steve Jobs (Apple), Kevin Rose (Digg), Chad Hurley, Steve Chen, and Jawed Karim (YouTube), Mark Zuckerberg (facebook), Bruce Livingston (iStockphoto), Matthew Mullenberg (Wordpress)...

Welcome to the new world- one fraught with great challenges and greater rewards, where knowledge is power and businesses run at the speed of thought. No more is the world confined to the proverbial oyster shell with age barriers enchaining daring individuals. The impact of such rapid change is amplified in any young person's life. On a macro- level, the youth are impacted the most by the rapid uncertainties generated by economic, cultural and technological globalization. On an individual level, a young person deals with the transition to adulthood. It is a time when the young face a combination of opportunities for advancement and the greatest challenges.

The present generation of youth is the largest ever in history1. In light of their share, young people are critical stakeholders. Their energy, motivation and vision are essential assets for positive development of the world. A key tool to achieve development is through entrepreneurship. Entrepreneurs are risk bearers, coordinators and organizers, gap fillers and leaders, innovators who assume risks of an enterprise for a return.

At the time when the world is facing an economic downturn, there is an increased recognition of entrepreneurship as a source of empowerment. Global unemployment especially among the youth is a great challenge2. Futurist John Naisbitt (1994)i predicts that as structured employment opportunities decline,

1 According to the United Nations definition, youth constitutes people between the ages of 15 and 24. This makes up approximately 18% of the world population. By this definition, while there are about 1.2 billion young people living in the world today, there will be 72 million more youth by 2025. 2 According to a study by the International Labor Organisation, the global unemployment rate was 6.6 per cent in 2009, an increase of 0.9 per cent over 2007. Young workers were particularly hit hard, with unemployment rate up 1.6 points over 2007 to 13.4 per cent, the largest increase since 1991 entrepreneurial skills will become necessary for youth to compete in the workforce.

Youth entrepreneurship3 needs special attention due to its unique characteristics. Chinguta (2002) asserts that young people are actively involved in running their own businesses in both developed and developing countries.

Shikwati (2009)ii elucidates that youth entrepreneurship is a critical issue especially in the case of developing nations. The youth in developing countries like India are often constrained by the choice between unemployment and hard to obtain public sector jobs. Those who aspire for more must be willing to think creatively and take calculated risks. They have to be prepared to be labeled "black sheep" by their family and peers. Still, the power to shape one's own destiny and to become change-makers gives entrepreneurship an undeniable attraction in these nations.

What Characterizes Youth Entrepreneurs?

*"We were young but we had good advice, good ideas and lots of enthusiasm" Bill Gates, founder of Microsoft, one of the most successful entrepreneurs*

## (1) Personal Characteristics

Lindner and Cox (1998)iii examined the differences between youth entrepreneurs and non-entrepreneurs. Their findings suggest that younger adolescents were more likely to be youth entrepreneurs. Young entrepreneurs tended to rate their organizational, time-management and leadership skills lower than non- entrepreneurs, but were more likely to be involved with community service projects. Chinguta (2002)iv asserts that the level of youth entrepreneurship and self-employment tends to significantly vary according to the age category of youth and gender, with more young men likely to be self-employed than young women. 3 Chigunta (2002) defines "youth entrepreneurship" as the "practical application of enterprising qualities, such as initiative, innovation, creativity, and risk taking into the work environment (either in self employment or employment in small start up firms), by the youth, using the appropriate skills necessary for success in that environment and culture".

## (2) Personality characteristics

Entrepreneurship is affected by achievement motivation (McClelland, 1961)v, risk-taking propensity (Sexton and Bowman, 1985vi; Brockhaus, 1976vii), and locus of control (Brockhaus, 1980viii; Brockhaus and Horwitz, 1986ix). Blanchflower and Oswald (1990)x studied some of the individual traits like entrepreneurial vision, alertness to business opportunities, pro-activity, and risk-taking ability required by entrepreneurs. Begley (1995)xi and Hornaday and Aboud (1971)xii consistently found that the achievement motivation is more prevalent among entrepreneurs as compared to others.

## (3) Cultural environment

The GEM Report 2003 (Reynolds et al., 2003)xiii suggests that cultural environment has an influence on person's entrepreneurial career propensity. In this study, cultural environment was measured with three options: attitudes toward entrepreneurs, acceptance of earning distance, and knowledge of some entrepreneurs.

## (4) Economic environment

It was found that many economic factors affected the level of regional entrepreneurial activity, such as accessibility of suppliers, accessibility of customers or new markets, and high degree of competition among firms (Bruno and Tyebjeexiv, 1982; El-Namaki, 1988xv; Gartner, 1985xvi; Staley and Morse, 1971xvii). More importantly, studies (e.g. Hal, 1990) xviii suggest that, to some extent, a person's rational decisions are the results of his expectations of economic conditions in future. Youth Entrepreneurship in India: Burgeoning Aspirations

*"India is confident again, after how many centuries? The old petulance about foreign successes, whining complaints about imperialist exploitation and the sneaking hunger for the smallest compliment from the feringhee stand replaced by a bright and confident outlook" - Meghnad Desai, Professor of Economics at the London School of Economics*

In India, 'Self-employment' or entrepreneurship was once the road, less travelled, due to host of external factors which put forth excessive entry barriers for start-ups. But now the 'India story' has two noteworthy chapters. The first is that the country holds its ground in the midst of the current global financial crisis.

India has seen 9% growth for 3 years running and a decade of more than 7% growth. This bull-run has reduced poverty in India by 10%xix. Growth had been supported by market-oriented reforms that began in the 1990s. India witnesses huge inflows of Foreign Direct Investment (FDI), rising foreign exchange reserves, Booming Information Technology (IT) and real estate sectors, and a flourishing capital market.

The second chapter is that India is all set to reap the "Demographic Dividend". Nearly half of India's 1.2 billion population falls under the age of 20. Some 22 million belong to the urban middle class and are in a position to influence the economy dramatically as they grow older. Another 100 million or so live in rural India- where young people are aspiring for more.xx The positive economic outlook and widening base of young people signal greater involvement of youth in the Indian economy in the coming years.

## Understanding the Motivations of the New Breed of Entrepreneurs

*"Indians are very entrepreneurial. Everywhere you go, people are selling stuff, even if it is only a pile of spices." Niall Ferguson, Academic historian at Harvard University* With India all set to reap the "demographic dividend" and young entrepreneurs expected to become the backbone of economic growth, I attempted to understand the motivations of this new through a research study to:

1. Explore whether the idea of taking-up entrepreneurship appeals to the youth pursing MBA usually in the age-group of 21-28) in India. If yes, then explore if the willingness to be an entrepreneur is dependent on gender and educational background.
2. Study if there is a relationship between a high need for achievement and the want to be an entrepreneur among the respondents. There is some empirical support for the idea that entrepreneurs have a higher motive to achieve compared to non-entrepreneurs. However, no systematic attempt has been made till now to test this hypothesis in the context of Indian MBA students. The study analyzed their motivations to take-up entrepreneurship using one of most important psychological theories - David McClelland's Theory of Motivation. According to which, regardless of culture or gender, people are driven by three motives:

**1. Need for achievement (nAch):** characterized by the wish to take responsibility for finding solutions to problems, master complex tasks, set goals, and get feedback on the level of success.

**2. Need for affiliation (nAff):** characterized by a desire to belong, an enjoyment of teamwork, a concern about interpersonal relationships, and a need reduce uncertainty.

**3. Need for power (nP):** characterized by a drive to control and influence others, a need to win arguments, a need to persuade and prevail.

The exploratory research was conducted in 2 phases:

(1) A series of expert interviews with young entrepreneurs and eminent faculty on entrepreneurship to design the study and validate the questionnaire

(2) Data collection from test units i.e. MBA students from major cities in India through an online questionnaire based on the 3 needs elucidated above.

We received 46 valid responses. We used Statistical Program for Social Sciences (SPSS) to assess the responses.

## Key Findings

(1) A whopping 80% of the respondents aspired to take- up entrepreneurship. Out of those 66.67% maintained that they have a high need for achievement.

(2) No significant relationship was found between gender and entrepreneurial desire or past educational background and entrepreneurial desire. 4

(3) A significant variation was found between the NAch scores of respondents' who expressed entrepreneurial desire and those who did not, validating McClelland's assertion5.

## Conclusion

The inner spirit of 'need for achievement' is found in abundance among the Indian youth. This shall be the driver for the growth engines in India. Young, energetic and enthusiastic entrepreneurs will continue to induce rapid development in the global economy.

## References

1. Naisbitt, J. (1994). Global paradox. New York: Morrow.

2. James Shikwati (2009), Center for International Private Enterprise, accessed on 25 December 2009 at http://developmentinstitute.org/Member/shikwati_youth/shikwati_entrepreneu rship_plan.pdf
3. Lindner, J.R. and Cox., K J (1998), "Youth Entrepreneurship". Journal of Extension, accessed at http://www.joe.org/joe/1998october/rb2.php on 2 January 2010
4. Chinguta, F ( 2002), "Youth Entrepreneurship: Meeting the Key Policy Challenges" accessed on 20 December 2009 at http://www.fabi.it/giovani/congresso/DOCUMENTI/entrepren.pdf
5. McClelland, D.C (1961).The Achieving Society. Princeton, NJ: Van Nostran
6. Sexton, D.L. and Bowman, N.B. (1985), "The entrepreneur: a capable executive and more",Journal of Business Venturing, Vol. 1, pp. 129-40
7. Brockhaus, R.H. (1976), "Risk-taking propensity of entrepreneurs", Proceedings of the Academy of Management, pp. 457-60 4 Chi Square test results, 5 One way ANOVA results
8. Brockhaus, R.H. (1980), "Risk-taking propensity of entrepreneurs", Academy of Management Journal, Vol. 23, pp. 509-20
9. Brockhaus, R.H. and Horwitz, P. (1986), "The psychology of the entrepreneur", in Scxton, D.L. and Smilor, R.W. (Eds), The Art and Science of Entrepreneurship, Ballinger Publishing Company, Cambridge, MA.
10. Blanchflower, D. & Oswald, A.( 1990). "What Makes A Young Entrepreneur?," Papers 373, London School of Economics - Centre for Labour Economics.
11. Begley, T (1995), "Using Founder Status, Age of Firm, and Company Growth Rate as the Basis for Distinguishing Entrepreneurs From Managers of Smaller Businesses", Journal of Business Venturing. Vol. 10, 249-263.
12. Hornaday, J. and Aboud, J., "Characteristics of Successful Entrepreneurs", Personnel Psychology, Vol. 24., 1971, 141-153.
13. Reynolds, P.D., Bygrave, W.D. and Autio, E. (2003), "Global entrepreneurship monitor 2003: executive report", available at: www.esbri.se/gemglobalreport_2003.pdf
14. Bruno, A.V. and Tyebjee, T.T. (1982), "The environment for entrepreneurship", in Kent, C.A., Sexton, D.L. and Vesper, K.H. (Eds), Encyclopedia of Entrepreneurship, Prentice-Hall, Englewood Cliffs, NJ.

15. El-Namaki, M.S.S. (1988), "Encouraging entrepreneurship in developing countries", Long Range Planning, Vol. 21 No. 4, pp. 98-106.
16. Gartner, W.B. (1985), "A conceptual framework for describing the phenomenon of new venture creation", Academy of Management Review, Vol. 4 No. 10, pp. 695-705.
17. Staley, E. and Morse, R. (1971), "Developing entrepreneurship: elements for a program", in Kilby, P. (Ed.), Entrepreneurship and Economic Development, Free Press, New York, NY, pp. 357-84.
18. Hal, R.V. (1990), Intermediate Microeconomics, W.W. Norton & Company, New York, NY.
19. Indian Economic Overview, Economy watch, accessed on 25 December 2010 at http://www.economywatch.com/indianeconomy/indian-economyoverview. html
20. Bhat, P. N. Mari (2001) Indian demographic scenario 2025**,** accessed on 13 November 2009 at http://iegindia.org/dis_mari_27.pdf

## Readings

1. The Prince's Youth Business International – Youth entrepreneurship: Recommendation for Actions accessed on 12 December 2009 at http://www.youthbusiness.org/PDF/Recommendations for Action. pdf
2. Rock Power Ntumba Kazela (2009), "World Civic Forum 2009 - The Road Map of Youth Entrepreneurship" accessed on 18 December 2009 at http://www.wcf2009.org/program/down/020_S7-I04-3_Rock_Power_N_Kazela.doc
3. Upadhyaya. R (2006), Transforming Youth's Perception in Entrepreneurship accessed on 18 December 2009 at http://www.indianmba.com/Faculty_Column/FC431/fc431.html
4. "How to Change the world": Social entrepreneurs and the power of new Ideas: David Bornstien (2007), Oxford University Press
5. Bremner, B (2006), "Asia's Young Entrepreneurs", accessed on 18 December 2009 at http://www.businessweek.com/smallbiz/content/aug2006/sb20060818_8 86243.htm
6. Sruthijith K K (2010), "India holds to the key success", accessed on 26 January 2010 at http://economictimes.indiatimes.com/India-holds-thekeys- to-success-Niall-Ferguson/articleshow/5496582. cms

# 18

# Trust, Network, and Market: Start-up Strategies of SMEs in Indian ICT industry


### *Abstract*

It is well understood that market plays a determining role with reference to business development. However, the process through which an enterprise identifies and develops a market for its business offering varies contextually and therefore, involves uncertainty. Corporate adopt different strategies, involving innovation and brand-building, in order to address such uncertainty. However, often such strategies are resource-intensive where resource not only involves finance, but also time, and dedicated personnel. It is quite easily understandable that such strategies are seldom affordable for emerging small and medium enterprises (SMEs) which are often resource-constrained. However, what is interesting is that despite such obstacles a large number of SMEs get started on a regular basis and a good number of them do considerable business.

This phenomenon takes a particularly interesting form in new economy which has witnessed mushrooming of new SMEs in the recent years. It is in this context it becomes important to explore the alternative resources that SMEs apply, particularly in the start-up stage, in order to develop a market for themselves and maintain control over it. The current paper attempts to explore the significance of collaboration emerging out of trust and network as an alternative resource. The paper bases itself upon interviews of entrepreneurs in Information and Communication Technology (ICT) industry in India.

Probably there would be little or no disagreement if I claim that initiating and sustaining operation of any business of any scale is contingent on the acclaim received from the market. What is going to be rather more debatable is the process through which an enterprise can create and develop a market for its business. It is true that every business require a unique selling proposition in order to create a space for itself. However, in a competitive market it is often difficult to sustain the use value of uniqueness over a period of time. Corporate adopt different strategies to encounter such a challenge. One of them is to innovate on a continuous basis and thereby retain the uniqueness of business offerings. Another strategy is to engage in a brand-building exercise and thus establish reputation and trust in the market. However, it would be important here to note that often both these strategies are resource-intensive where resource not only involves finance, but also time, and dedicated human resource. These resources are often inaccessible for small and medium enterprises (SME). However, what is interesting is that despite such bottlenecks a large number of SMEs get started on a regular basis and a good number of them do considerable business. This phenomenon takes a particularly interesting form in new economy which has witnessed mushrooming of new small and medium enterprises in the recent years. It is in this context it becomes important to explore the alternative resources that SME start-ups apply in order to develop a market for themselves and maintain control over it. The current paper attempts to explore the significance of collaboration emerging out of trust and network as an alternative resource. The paper bases itself upon interviews of entrepreneurs in Information and Communication Technology (ICT) industry in India.

## Understanding Trust

Over a period of time, trust has emerged as a phenomenon that has attracted significant attention from researchers belonging to different disciplines (see Lewis and Weigert, 1985; Li, 2007b). Trust entails an individual's "expectation about those actions of others which have a bearing on her choice of action, when that action must be chosen before she can observe the actions of those others" (Dasgupta, 2003, p. 312). Such expectation is based on one's knowledge about other actors' disposition, about options available to those actors, about consequences of adopting such options, about actors' ability, and so on (Dasgupta, 1988).

According to Fukuyama, Trust is the expectation that arises within a community of regular, honest, and cooperative behaviour, based on commonly shared norms, on the part of other members of that community. Those norms can be about deep 'value questions like the nature of God or justice, but they also encompass secular norms like professional standards and codes of behavior (1996, p. 26).

Trust is distinct from familiarity and confidence (see Luhman, 1988). Trusting a person means believing that when offered the chance, he or she is not likely to behave in a way that is damaging to others who are trusting her/him. Trust will typically be relevant when at least one party makes itself vulnerable to the other. Higher the level of trust, higher is the likelihood for cooperation.

However, cooperation does not depend on trust alone (Gambetta, 1988). Trust emerges out of reputation and reputation is an outcome of observed consistent behaviour over time. "Reputation is an asset, so people invest in it, in that they forego immediate gains for the purpose of enjoying benefits later" (Dasgupta, 2003, p. 314). Such arguments about trust and reputation may be linked to the writings of early contributors to this field like Mark Granovetter.

The notion of embeddedness advocated by Granovetter emphasizes, ... the role of concrete personal relations and structures (or 'networks') of such relations in generating trust and discouraging malfeasance. The widespread preference for transacting with individuals of known *reputation* implies that few are actually content to rely on either generalized morality or institutional arrangements to guard against trouble ... In practice, we settle for such generalized information when nothing better is available, but ordinarily we seek better information. (1985, p. 490)

## Trust, Network and Business

Researchers in recent times have started focusing on the role of trust in business ventures (see Lane and Bachmann, 1998; Dibben, 2000; Soto, 2006; Welter and Smallbone, 2006). "Virtually every commercial transaction has within itself an element of trust, certainly any transaction conducted over a period of time" (Arrow, 1972 as cited in Dasgupta, 2003, p. 334). In the context of entrepreneurship, there is a close relationship between social network and trust. However, neither trust is an essential precondition for formation of social network, nor vice versa. Rather, presence of one often facilitates the existence of the other (Menning, 1997). Trust plays a critical role in the formation, maintenance, and transformation of interorganizational cooperative relationships (Neergaard and Ulhøi, 2006).

Positive relationship exists between the level of interfirm trust and flow of incoming knowledge spillovers from business partners (Bönte, 2008). Interorganizational trust has a strong and direct relationship with organizational performance. It functions to smoothen negotiation processes and thereby reduce the transaction costs of interfirm exchange. However, high interorganizational trust does not necessarily indicate high interpersonal trust among the people in those organizations. This is because boundary-spanning individuals come and go, whereas the institutionalized structures and processes accompanying interorganizational trust are more stable and enduring (see Zaheer, McEvily and Perrone, 1998).

Every organization is subject to uncertainty emerging out of the behaviour of both market and partner organizations. Firms can attempt to reduce the risk emerging out of partners by shielding their association with legal contracts. However, considering the difficulty of doing so, organizations may have to trust a lot on the moral integrity and goodwill of their partners. Here, trust is a social-psychological bond between two or more partners that provides mutual confidence to both to pursue a relationship in which each may be vulnerable to the other (Ojha, 2002). Trust increases accuracy and quantity of information available to organizational agents. This occurs in proportion with the level of trust between the information provider and information receiver and the actor who bridges a structural hole between the provider and receiver (Droege, Anderson and Bowler, 2003).

In India, depending on the nature of the industry, the basis of trust and the role that trust plays in business vary considerably. For example, in low-end manufacturing and trading business personalized trust based on experience of collaboration, caste connection, etc. play important role. In contrast, higher end business depends more on institutionalized sanctions (formal contracts and bank regulation). However, this is not to say that higher end business does not depend on personalized trust at all. For example, among entrepreneurs in software industry in Chennai there is a striking combination of formal contract and institutionally backed sanctions and incentives, with trust built through personal connections (Harriss, 2002, 2003). John Harriss observes that "... in the new context created by globalization a shift is taking place, depending upon institutional innovation, from a reliance on personalized relationships or 'selective trust' to a reliance on abstract principles and professional codes" (2003, p. 768).

In the discourse over role of social networks in entrepreneurship, discussion about inter-firm alliances has occupied a critical position. Alliances have often been defined as voluntary arrangements that two or more firms get into for the purpose of sharing or co-development of products, technologies, or services. Formation of alliances is often dependent on various forms of social networks.

For example, among small manufacturing firms in the USA, formation of interfirm alliances depend on the social network of executives (BarNir and Smith, 2002). Often initial relationships between business partners lack social relationships. However, with time, some of these business relationships develop into close ties. In an embedded relationship, firms may invest in specialized assets, develop specific knowledge of their partner's plans and problems, and do more than required by the letter of the contract. Such alliance partners may be identified through stakeholders like suppliers (particularly in small firms) and members of board of directors (Cooper, 2002).

Inter-firm cooperation is strongly influenced by various forms of networks (Håkansson and Johanson, 1988; Walker, 1988). In becoming immersed in such networks, the crucial step seems to be establishing the initial intensive linkages, or finding the right niche in the network (Yli-Renko and Autio, 1998). Silicon Valley in the USA is characterized by long-term trust-based alliances between system firms and interdependent but autonomous supplier firms, which emerged out of longstanding tradition of informal information exchange, inter-firm mobility and networking. This is more of a reciprocal relationship where both sides are committed not to take advantage of one another when market conditions change. (Saxenian, 2000).

From the preceding discussion it is clearly understandable that collaboration emerging out of trust and network plays a crucial role in business. What needs to be further explored is the extent to which it can facilitate control over market. It is also important to understand the limitations (if any) of using trust and network as a business strategy. Given that answer to these questions are often context specific it is important that we approach them by use of empirical data. For the purpose of current study primary data was collected from thirty entrepreneurs in the ICT industry located in four Indian cities namely, Mumbai, Chennai, Bengaluru

(Bangalore), and Pune. Data was collected from the entrepreneurs using case study method supported by in-depth interviewing.

Data was qualitative in nature and was processed by generating relevant thematic codes. In order to improve the quality of data, confidentiality was practiced and pseudonyms were developed for all the names available in the data. Each name used in this article is pseudonyms.

During the starting up stage interaction of an enterprise with market takes place through two broad channels, namely, process of identification of business opportunity and procedure of accessing customers. Based on this understanding the current paper would primarily focus itself on these two areas by use of empirical data.

## Networks and Identification of Business Opportunity

Success of any initiative depends on the strength of the guiding idea. One important component of that idea revolves around identification of a right opportunity to take initiative. This is particularly relevant in business enterprises, where it is also referred as 'market opportunity' (Soh, 2003; Ramachandran and Ray, 2006). Therefore, identification of a business opportunity is often considered by many entrepreneurs as the most significant challenge in business. In identification of such 'market opportunity', entrepreneurs' interpersonal relationship with professional colleagues, friends, and family members play an important role.

## Professional Relationships

Developing and maintaining professional relationships is of tremendous importance for any business. Such relationships may include people with whom an entrepreneur has worked as co-worker during her/his career as employee in different organizations. It may also comprise of people who were not co-workers of entrepreneur, but whom the entrepreneur came across through her/his employment career, for example, independent professionals or people working as employee in other organizations with whom entrepreneur's then employing organization had some form of association. In addition, people known to the entrepreneur through various professional associations and meet-ups, where the entrepreneur participated would also be considered here. Professional relationships would also include people whom an entrepreneur came across through her/his own business, for example, customers, financiers, employees, etc. To a large extent, social capital required for business develops out of such professional relationships.

Importance of maintaining professional relationship for developing business was emphasized by a large number of entrepreneurs. To use the words of Gautam Apte, founder of Innovative Web Solutions Pvt. Ltd., "*what's important.... in doing business ... is contacts.... so I think, the critical thing ... is having the contacts and ... keeping in touch with them*". Quite often, informal discussion with existing customers may generate business idea. This was the experience of Rajat Apte, founder of Magnatech Inc. He mentioned, *I had several pharma and biotech companies as customers. And they started talking to me about a general problem they had* ... Then I said I would look into it. The more I looked into it the more excited I got because now you are looking at a real opportunity where you could potentially build a platform and a business around this ... That's when I started thinking in terms of creating [a business around it].

However, it does not mean that discussion with professional colleagues would always help in developing a business idea. This may be useful for incremental business ideas. However, disruptive business ideas are usually non-conventional in nature. Therefore, not everyone can identify its worth. This was the experience of Anil Despande, founder of Tech Writers Inc., a company offering technical writing service. To say it in his words, "I did discuss it with my colleagues. Most of them did not understand what I was talking about".

Social capital emerging out of professional relationships has the potential to become important for all entrepreneurs. However, we found that entrepreneurs from business families, whose family members were strongly involved in their business, were relatively less vocal about its importance. Such entrepreneurs included Ajay Aggarwal, founder of Netware Pvt. Ltd., Amit Sharma, founder of Sindh Infotech Pvt. Ltd., Hitesh Patel, founder of Knowledge Software Pvt. Ltd., and Dinesh Marwari, founder of Ryze Softech Pvt. Ltd.

## Personal Relationships

Just like professional relationships, personal relationships also play an important role in developing business. Personal relationships may include kindred connected directly or indirectly to the entrepreneurs either through blood or through marriage. It may also entail friends of an entrepreneur as well as that of her/his family member(s). This research began with the presumption that ICT is a new industry, and therefore, no entrepreneur would have a family-based network in the same industry. This would mean that every entrepreneur would have to develop necessary networks with her/his own efforts. However, in the process of research I realized that coming from business family background had its own advantage in terms of development of networks, irrespective of the industry the family members of the entrepreneur were involved in. This could happen in multiple ways. Even if an entrepreneur has family members who are involved in an industry different from the one in which the entrepreneur wants to venture into, those family members could still be resourceful for the entrepreneur if they have connection with people from entrepreneur's target industry as friends and/or professional colleagues. Such family members need not necessarily be entrepreneurs. Even as a salaried professional, an individual could possess insider information about an industry.

Ajay Aggarwal, founder of Netware Pvt. Ltd., who is from a business family background, utilized such information for developing his business. He mentioned, *I have an uncle who is ... a very senior US-based IT consultant....* he had come to India at that time. So my father met up ... So my uncle said that this is an opportunity and Internet at that time was just on the horizon or just starting ... So at that time that seemed one industry to get into.

However, family connection, in order to become social capital for business, need not be in the same industry in which the entrepreneur wants to venture in. As a second option, family connection in other industries, particularly industry of prospective clients, could also turn out to be useful. This was quite clear from the experiences of Raj Modi, founder of Softech and Raj Software and Communications, who began his business with development of an accounting software. He mentioned, We are basically from a business community. So we have contacts ... *[My] father had a very good Chartered Accountant friend* ... [I was] speaking to [that] Chartered Accountant, speaking to the person whom you know, [about] whether there is any requirement of this product? ...whether people will buy? ... Because pricing will very much depend on that. What people are willing to pay. Social capital emerging out of family relationships may not always be in terms of social network with people who are well aware about the industry in which the entrepreneur wants to venture in. Social capital may also entail resources evolving out of entrepreneur's relationship with family members who have no connection whatsoever with the industry in which an entrepreneur wants to venture into. Entrepreneurs may identify a business opportunity just on the basis of their familiarity with the everyday activities of their family members.

That is how Hitesh Patel got the idea of starting Knowledge Software Pvt. Ltd.: My wife does a lot of quizzing activities at my children's schools.... like every other quizzer my wife also used to make her notes when she would find an interesting piece of information. She would note it down in a scrapbook at best in an electronic format, let's say in a word document or in an excel sheet, or whatever. Now ... between one quiz and another there would be about a year gap, or six months gap and each quiz, depending on the age group, would require about may be two/three/four/five hundred questions. So you really needed to have a really good database of questions. And they had to be different from the earlier quiz, okay. So, she always had a nightmare, when she had to set a quiz and etc. Because, by the time the quiz came in she would not be able to find where she wrote those questions.... the same problem is also [there] when its electronic filing, okay ... So the only solution was to handle this through a database application.... Then when KBC [Kaun Banega Karorpati – a television programme based on quizzing] came into the country ... I realized that perhaps I would be able to exploit the software that I developed for my wife ... I will let it commercially. So I looked around and I realized that what I wanted to do with the software nobody had done in the world before.... I started building upon this one idea and that idea led me to looking at various areas of life where we as ... individual users create information related to our needs for learning or our needs for entertainment and I realized that I could apply the same philosophy to creating a data software application for vocabulary. Hitesh Patel's experience shows how everyday life problems can give rise to business ideas.

It was observed that entrepreneurs having a family background in business were more vocal about the resource potential of their personal relationships. This included entrepreneurs like Ajay Aggarwal, founder of Netware Pvt. Ltd., Raj Modi, founder of Softech and Raj Software and Communications, Amit Sharma, founder of Sindh Infotech Pvt. Ltd., Hitesh Patel, founder of Knowledge Software Pvt. Ltd., and Dinesh Marwari, founder of Ryze Softech Pvt. Ltd. However, not all entrepreneurs whose family members were involved in business emphasized the importance of their personal relationships. This included entrepreneurs like Pankaj Sen, founder of Advanced Software Systems Pvt. Ltd., Gautam Apte, founder of Innovative Web Solutions Pvt. Ltd., Naresh Ponnaiah, founder of Sunshine Technologies Ltd., and Kirti Harlalka, founder of Knowhow.

That these entrepreneurs did not emphasize the relationship with their family members, even though the latter were involved in business, can probably be explained by the hiatus between the nature of business of these entrepreneurs and that of their family members. As a result of this hiatus, the family members hardly understood the business the entrepreneurs are involved in.

Networking is an activity by which enterprises and individuals obtain potential information about untapped opportunities. However, networking may still be a time-consuming and expensive effort as information is dispersed unevenly among enterprises in the market. Due to disparity in networking strategy, enterprises and individuals may gain differential access to external information about new opportunities. The firms with more efficient networking strategy, having business relationship with large number of firms and being centrally located in an industry network, will secure information before others and thus lead to better new product performance (Soh, 2003; Dyer and Hatch, 2006). A wide variety of research has asserted that the level of innovation/identification of opportunity is directly proportional to the intensity of networking (see Lipparini and Sobrero, 1994; Julien, Andriambeloson and Ramangalahy, 2004; Arenius and Clercq, 2005; Eraydin and Armatli-Köroglu, 2005).

Business networking in the form of alliances is not only a protective mechanism to create benefits of scale, but also an active way of creating entrepreneurial opportunities, and organizing high technology innovation (Moensted, 2007). However, influence of proximity on formation of interfirm network is one field about which researchers have made contradictory observations. 'Technology spillover'-driven innovation in high-technology industry clusters like Silicon Valley in the USA has been influenced by social networks among geographically proximate firms (Cooper, 2002; Saxenian, 2000). Whereas, in Turkey, firms with global networks have higher number of innovations than firms with dense local networks (Eraydin and Armatli-Köroglu, 2005). In Ireland, as well, networking is more likely to involve firms in the international market than firms at lower geographical levels (Andreosso-O'Callaghan and Lenihan, 2008). In Australia, only small manufacturing firms relied more heavily on external knowledge networks as an input to innovation than did large firms (Rogers, 2004).

In Belgium and Finland, individual's education as well as place of residence influences her/his access to network resources and therefore her/his capacity to recognize opportunity. Higher education qualification facilitates entrepreneur's ability to recognize opportunity through increased exposure to 'knowledgeable others' belonging to networks such as alumni organizations. Here, human capital of individual entrepreneur facilitates her/his entry into networks which provides access to information about business opportunities. At the same time, individuals residing in large urban centres are more likely to perceive opportunity compared to individuals residing in rural areas or smaller urban centres due to presence of various organizations like universities, research centres and service providers in those areas, which provide more possibilities to discover and exchange new information (Arenius and Clercq, 2005). Similar observations regarding the link between place of residence and utilization of social network was also made by other researchers (see Kristiansen et al., 2005).

## Network, Trust and Access to Customers

Accuracy and speed of business offerings are critical factors for success in a fast-changing competitive environment. While developing business relationships no one wants to take the risk of working with enterprises whose credibility is 'unknown'. Firms look for strong brand names to be associated with. As a result, new enterprises have to struggle for getting their initial customers. In this context, networks play an extremely important role in any industry. However, membership in networks does not come automatically. Entrepreneurs have to work continuously in order to secure entry into such networks. Getting access to such networks depends upon multiple factors like quality of business idea, reputation, and entrepreneur's networking capabilities (Ramachandran and Ray, 2006). Entrepreneurial founding team members utilize different channels for accessing customers. Some use the reputation of the investors for this purpose.

Some others use their own reputation developed by word of mouth reference, while networking at conferences or through publishing articles in refereed journals (Neergaard, 2005). For some, kins also play an important role as introducers to initial clients (Anderson, Jack and Dodd, 2005). In these contexts trust formation is considered as the primary aim.

## Identification of Prospective Customers

Customers are drivers of any business initiative. Therefore, once the market opportunity is identified, enterprises spend considerable effort in identifying prospective customers. Depending on the nature of business initiative, the processes through which enterprises attempt to identify prospective customers vary considerably. However, broadly it is possible to locate certain considerations that entrepreneurs keep in mind in this process. Customers are often less certain in depending on new companies or new products, due to lack of familiarity with their performance. However, as entrepreneur, one needs to find a way of convincing people, developing trust, and thereby get new customers.

**Reference-based Marketing:** Reference is the process through which the entrepreneur uses another person, who is familiar with the entrepreneur and/or her/his business offering, as referee (see Sengupta, 2010). Role of referee is tremendously valuable in developing trust among people who are unfamiliar with the entrepreneur and/or her/his business offering.

Ajay Aggarwal, founder of Netware Pvt. Ltd., attempted to identify prospective customers by building confidence in their mind. His initial strategy was, "... rather than going as an individual where, as a person, I have to prove my credential ... *take someone who already has the credential....* and take him along as an associate and approach the market." Being in web designing, he decided to design websites for various industry associations, like Builder's Associations of India and All India Rubber Industries Association, at a concessional rate. The idea was that, once he has established a relationship with these associations, it would be rather easier to convince association members to hire him for doing their own web-designing work. This strategy helped Ajay Aggarwal in developing reputation about his work among prospective customers who never knew him personally. Here reputation was developed by using relationship-based social capital that existed between associations and their members.

In case of nascent entrepreneurs, who are yet to develop reputation in the market, social network may play an important role in identifying people whom entrepreneurs would like to approach for job. In such case, relationship may be used as a tool for earning the confidence of the customers. Naveen Jayakumar, founder of Datamagic Pvt. Ltd., plunged into entrepreneurship and then started looking for business opportunity. He got his *initial leads in business through social network of his founding partners*. Kunal Raman, founder of Sharp Technologies Pvt. Ltd., recollected similar memories about his brother who was the founder of the first business venture with which he was associated. He said, ... my brother had to actually walk into lot of companies in Bangalore *through friends*, meet some managers, meet some VPs and then try to get some work ... So *through his relationship*, through his previous work experience *whatever people he knew* he just targeted and then *through known contacts* we got some projects to bootstrap our company.

According to S. Ram, founder of Integrated Software Solutions, as an organization scales up, the role that may be played by personal social networks of entrepreneurs goes down consistently. However, this does not mean that social network becomes unimportant. In his own words, "they still play a part. But that is backed by a strong institutional effort actually.... [building social network] is anyway nonnegotiable. So how do you expand that is the question".

However, there can be limitations of social network as well. This was obvious from the arguments of Alok Dutta, founder of Silicon Networks Pvt. Ltd. He discussed in detail how he used his nationality to get business through Indians working with companies in the USA. He said, ... tons of university students were sitting in the US in those days ... those guys ... were probably sitting in reasonably critical positions in organizations. So you start approaching them as one source.... But the pressure on satisfying that kind of a customer is more than satisfying a total black-box customer.... [Whereas, when you are serving an unknown person] there is no emotional attachment. It's a job, you don't do well they let you go, you do well they come back to you. So clean! Over here, the *emotional aspects come in.* And the *pressure on you is more to do it.* And they have to prove themselves in their organizations. So you havc to prove.... And so you have [to do] much more.

**Reputation, Trust and Attracting Customers:** The findings of this research endorse the importance of reputation in various aspects of business including the process of attracting customers. Reputation in the context of brand depends primarily on the ability of a company to build a public image about the high quality of the company and/or its business offering. Customers' reliance on brand does not depend on their familiarity with the functionaries of the organization that is offering that brand. Neither is it essential for a customer to use a brand in order to rely on it. However, till the time a company and/or its business offering becomes a brand, reputation may develop in two different ways. First, customers may begin to rely on the business offerings of a company either because they have availed it and are satisfied with it, or because their close acquaintances have similar opinion about it. Second, customers may begin to rely on a company because they are familiar with the ability and/or the qualification of the functionaries of the company, particularly its founder. The second factor often becomes more important when a customer is dealing with a new organization whose business offering is yet to attain a reputation in the market. Reputation is closely related with trust, which in this context primarily refers to reliance.

According to Vishnu Krishnaswamy, founder of Techvision, "*nobody gets fired [from their company] for choosing IBM [as vendor]*". This is because IBM, as a company, has now become a brand and, therefore, carries certain inherent reputation. Whereas, depending on a new company always involve some risk for the customers, as the credibility of the company is yet to be established in market. Rajat Apte, founder of Magnatech Inc., said that initial customers are generally individuals or companies who are willing to take the risk. Therefore, in the initial stage, it is necessary to know who the risk-takers are in the target industry. Such risk-takers need not be organizations. They may be individuals in various organizations. According to Rajat Apte, in a technology product industry, one characteristic of these early users of new technology is that, even though they are not completely satisfied with what they are getting, they are confident that they can work with the manufacturers of that technology to take the product to the next level to make it useful for them.

While it is true that the initial customers take risk by depending on a new organization, customers often find a way of mitigating such risk with the help of familiarity with the entrepreneur as a person and/or her/his ability. This was clear from the experience of Gautam Apte, founder of Innovative Web Solutions Pvt. Ltd. One of Gautam Apte's initial customers, who knew his ability personally, decided to trust the reliability of Innovative Web Solutions Pvt. Ltd. because Gautam Apte was the person behind it. Gautam Apte said, See basically ... I started tapping my network and informing [various people I know about] ... what I have [got] to deliver. And if these people are in large companies ... who were already presidents or chairmen of large companies. So now, one example was I approached the president of the last company that I worked for. And he was an American. So I told him well look ... this is what I have. I have started on my own. We have a small team of just four/five people.

This is what we can deliver. And because of my professional record in that company he said hey, you know, *I have seen you perform in our previous company. So as long as it's you handling it I don't have an issue working with you.* So ... [I would] let my VPs know [about you and] work related to this technology, maybe we can get it done through you. So that's how I started.

However, in the absence of initial customer's familiarity with the entrepreneur's ability, an entrepreneur may use her/his educational qualification as well as work experience in a reputed organization to build her/his reputation in the mind of the customer. Pankaj Sen, founder of

Advanced Software Systems Pvt. Ltd., in the initial stage, used these credentials to build confidence in the mind of customers. He said, See at that time when we started a new company we could not sell the company because nobody knows the company. So *I started selling myself.* Right? My skill sets, my experience, my educational experience, and then I said ... I have this experience in LCS [name changed; originally name of an reputed MNC] and other places. This is my background and we can [solve] your Y2K [problem]. We can train your people and all these. And still it was difficult initially. Okay, because people do not just believe the words. So we said, okay, fine, we will test your software for Y2K conformance, [and find] whether it will pass through or not. And we will do it free of cost. And if we really find yes there are problems then it is up to you whether you will give [us a contract to rectify it] or not.

The second part of the argument of Pankaj Sen shows that often educational qualification or work experience is not sufficient to build trust in the mind of the customer. Therefore, it may become necessary to offer free service as sample of ability of the company. Many of the initial customers of Pankaj Sen were these companies for which he did free Y2K testing.

## Getting Initial Customers

Entrepreneurs deploy various strategies for marketing their products and/or services. But no one strategy assures them of getting customers. Getting initial customers is a particularly difficult task. This is because, here, customers are dealing with an entrepreneur whose reputation is yet to be established in the market. This is especially so when an entrepreneur is offering a new type of product/service. This was the experience of Anil Despande, founder of Tech Writers Inc., who offers service in technical writing. He said, I had ... approached quite a few companies. But they were not ready yet for that idea. Many of them thought that they already had good documentation ... many of them thought that people don't read documentation even if you give them.

So it doesn't matter what we give them. They are not going to read it anyway. So why spent something like twenty thousand rupees on getting good documentation written, when it's not going to be read and appreciated at all. Some companies thought that why should an outsider write my documentation. I am the best person to write about my product. And I used to tell them that you are definitely the best person. But then your work is that of a R&D Manager. If you start writing documentation what is the return the company is getting out of your salary. That should not be the idea. So *slowly they started realizing it and then the ... inflow increased.*

There can be different ways of getting initial customers. In many instances it was found that relationship played an important role in getting the first customer. However, initial customers may also come from cold-calling, where the nascent entrepreneur is able to convince an otherwise completely unknown person to become a customer.

The importance of reference in getting initial customers became clear from O.P. Nayar, founder of Accent Tech Solutions. When asked about the importance of reference in getting initial customers, he said, Yeah, see this is very important in the initial days. Because initial days ... word of mouth only can help. You know, initially, you are small company. There are big companies, right? Why should a customer change from an established company to a start-up company as their vendor? So that will happen only if your price is lower. But price alone cannot be the criteria. You got to have the quality and dependability, reliability. All those things are required. So that, you know, if somebody gives some reference it will help you.

A large number of entrepreneurs who had a family background in business used some form of reference in getting their initial customers. Such references came through personal and/or professional relationships. Ajay Aggarwal, founder of Netware Pvt. Ltd., who is from a business family, said that his first customer was through a business contact of a friend with whom he had a relationship at stock market. Same was true for Amit Sharma, founder of Sindh Infotech Pvt. Ltd. and Raj Modi, founder of Softech, and Raj Software and Communications.

Raj Modi's first customer was his cousin's friend. It is not that for getting customers through reference an entrepreneur has to depend only on her/his acquaintances. Contacts established by employees may also be useful in identifying initial customers. This was true for Amit Sharma, founder of Sindh Infotech Pvt. Ltd. Managers in client organizations of Sindh Infotech Pvt. Ltd. were known to managers of Sindh Infotech.

Interviewing Dinesh Marwari of Ryze Softech Pvt. Ltd. was an enriching experience in understanding how family-based social capital facilitates the process of getting customers, as he comes from a family which has more than one hundred years of experience in founding and running large-scale businesses in different industries. He said, I think ... especially starting off from scratch, with zero experience in building a software company the only way you can grow is contacts. You know, if I am a guy that has built a division of ZCS, or MBC, or IBT [all names are changed; originally they were names of large Indian ICT companies] for fifteen years I have over a period of time built relationships and have built a credibility ... there is something to do [with] this experience. But with me with three years experience, may be a bright young chap but the only reason I would give you business is I trust you and I trust your capabilities, not because of your experience or credibility. Because you don't have that. So even till date *most of large clients are relationships of mine* that have been leveraged. *You have to do a lot of networking, you have to do a lot of getting to know the right people and then sort of getting introduced into the right areas.* However, the importance of reference in identifying the initial customers was also visible for entrepreneurs who did not have a family background in business.

Many of those entrepreneurs tried to utilize relationships developed by them in the course of their professional career. This was also true for entrepreneurs having family business background but whose family members hardly participated in their business, for example, Gautam Apte, founder of Innovative Web Solutions Pvt. Ltd., and Kirti Harlalka, founder of Knowhow. Often entrepreneurs began with a reference-based client. Akhtar Hussain, founder of Communication Networks *knew his first client*, who was a customer for the last company in which he was working. He knew that his employer organization was not able to cater to the requirement of this person. O.P. Nayar, founder of Accent Tech Solutions, also utilized the relationships that he developed as a part of his professional career in order to find customers. Even an entrepreneur's ex-employer may become one of the initial clients. This was the experience of S. Ram, founder of Integrated Software Solutions. ICT is one industry which has succeeded in bringing down the importance of geographical distance to a large extent, primarily as result of intensive use of new communication technology. Given this nature of ICT industry, social networks have not remained restricted within the boundaries of nation state.

Transnational networks, particularly with people/organizations located in the USA or Europe, have emerged as extremely important for developing business, even in getting initial customers. This was quite important with reference to ICT industry, as a large number of companies in India target overseas companies as customers. Gautam Apte, founder of Innovative Web Solutions Pvt. Ltd., as well as James John, founder of Spaceage.com testified this. They got their first customers through such transnational networks.

Although initial customers may come through friendship relationships, such customers also need to be convinced about what they are going to pay for. This was quite clear from the experience of Vinay Reddy, founder of Software Consultants Pvt. Ltd. He said that, without ever being part of an industry, he has the ability to understand the requirement of that industry and build a software suitable to that requirement. This is quite useful in convincing a customer about his ability.

First customer is important not only to initiate the revenue flow, but also to get subsequent customers. People and firm are understandably hesitant to be the first customers. Entrepreneurs therefore, often use their social capital to get their first customer. Once there is one customer, it is easy to convince others to become customers for the same product/service as they have the advantage of getting the feedback. Naresh Ponnaiah, founder of Sunshine Technologies Ltd., said, ... once we had the idea, we wanted some early first customers. *So we went back to a friend of ours who is the MD of a very big company....* He is founder of that company.... So I said we have this product and we think this can solve this particular problem for your company. And we want an opportunity to use this product to solve that problem for your company ... next day he gave us an order saying that go ahead and do it and this is my first contribution. So it happened so easily for us so I think we really used that opportunity.... So basically they gave us that opportunity to make ... a finished product. *So once you have that then you have a reference....* [Getting the first customer] I think, its primarily again a matter of trust. That person really knows me as a very good IT person ... anybody who want to go and sell [is asked] do you have customer. Nobody wants to be the first person. Just because this company gave us that opportunity to be the first customer, this made it that much more easier for us to go and tell the second customer that we already have a customer and you are not the first guy.

So in that way it definitely helped. All types of social capital that have been discussed so far were developed through social networks which are based on familiarity existing between two or more persons through either professional or personal life. However, relevant social capital and trust may develop without existing familiarity as well: two completely unknown people may develop a close relationship on the spot because they share special sentiment for or have trust in some third party. The experience of S. Sivakumar, founder of Datainformatics Pvt. Ltd., is illustrative of this. He said that when he and his partners were running around looking for business, they visited an organization. While talking to the person concerned, who was completely unknown to them, it came out that all of them were from the same college. That person was really happy to know that some students from his own college were trying to do something on their own. Therefore, he felt that he should do something for them in order to encourage their initiative. The work was small, but it was a good encouragement for them. In this way *alma mater* can facilitate formation of social capital.

## Conclusion

The preceding discussion brings into light the significance of network and trust as valuable resources for starting up a small and medium enterprise. Broadly we could categorize the entrepreneurial networks into two categories: those emerging out of one's profession and those developing from one's family relationships. However, the difference between these two categories often got blurred. We found that entrepreneurs having a family background in business were more vocal about importance of family relationship than about professional relationship. It was quite clear that even in a new technology industry like ICT entrepreneurs from family business background were at a relatively advantaged position in comparison to the first generation entrepreneurs because of the utility of family-based networks across industries.

However, having a family background in business did not help the entrepreneur all the time, particularly when family members had no understanding of the nature of business in ICT industry.

Identification of a business idea appeared as one field where network plays a crucial role. However, it was also found that with reference to development of business ideas network was more effective in case of incremental business ideas as opposed to disruptive business ideas. Interestingly we found that at times disruptive business ideas emerged out of observation of routine activities of family members. Although network and trust have their own advantages we found them to be expensive at the same time, as information is unevenly dispersed and therefore not easily available. This is particularly true when we take into consideration the time that is required for developing and maintaining trusted relationships. Besides access to different networks like that existing among employees of an organization is naturally restricted and therefore not easily accessible.

We found that networks are crucial in identifying prospective customers and in getting initial customers for new enterprises. References emerging out of networks played a crucial role in these processes. Reference is valuable in developing trust among prospective customers who are otherwise unfamiliar with the entrepreneur and/or her/his business offering. Entrepreneurs adopted various strategies for securing such references. In addition to getting references through personal relationships entrepreneurs also attempted to get them through industry associations. Personal networks had its limitation in getting customers. In addition to being restricted in scope it also entailed considerable liability towards network partners. Therefore, as an organization grew up personal networks used for getting customers needed to be backed by institutional networks and process of brand building.

At an early stage of an enterprise reputation may be developed in different ways. Reference is one among those channels. It may also be developed using educational qualification, work experience of an entrepreneur, as well as by providing free sample of service or product. Another channel for developing reputation is use of embedded networks emerging out of alma mater or work place. On the whole networks and trust play crucial role in facilitating the development of SME start-ups through identification of prospective market and developing control over it. However, it is quite clear that network and trust can only be a facilitator. If the basic components of business are not sufficiently strong just network and trust cannot start-up an enterprise.

## References

1. Anderson, A.R., Jack, S.L. and Dodd, S.D. (2005). The role of family members in entrepreneurial networks: Beyond the boundaries of the family firm. *Family Business Review*, XVIII(2), 135-154.
2. Andreosso-O'Callaghan, B. and Lenihan, H. (2008). Networking: a question of firm characteristics? The case of the Shannon region in Ireland. *Entrepreneurship & Regional Development*, 20(6), 561-580.
3. Arenius, P. and Clercq, D.D. (2005). A network-based approach on opportunity recognition. *Small Business Economics*, 24(3), 249-265.
4. BarNir, A. and Smith, K.A. Interfirm alliances in the small business: The role of social networks. *Journal of Small Business Management*, 40(3), 219-232.
5. Bönte, W. (2008). Inter-firm trust in buyer-supplier relations: Are knowledge spillovers and geographical proximity relevant? *Journal of Economic Behavior & Organization*, 67(3-4), 855-870.
6. Cooper, A.C. (2002). Networks, alliances, and entrepreneurship. In A.M. Hitt, R.D. Ircland, S. M. Camp, and D. Sexton (Eds.), *Strategic*

*enterprise: Creating a new mindset* (pp. 203-222). U.K.: Blackwell Publishers.

7. Cooper, A.C. (2002). Networks, alliances, and entrepreneurship. In A.M. Hitt, R.D. Ireland, S. M. Camp, and D. Sexton (Eds.), *Strategic enterprise: Creating a new mindset* (pp. 203-222). U.K.: Blackwell Publishers.
8. Dasgupta, P. (1988). Trust as a commodity. In D. Gambetta (Ed.), *Trust: Making and breaking cooperative relations* (pp. 49-72). New York, USA: Basil Blackwell Inc.
9. Dasgupta, P. (2003). Social capital and economic performance: Analytics. In E. Ostrom, and T.K. Ahn (Eds.), Foundations of social capital (pp. 309-339). Cheltenham: Edward Elgar Publishing Limited/Inc.
10. Dibben, M.R. (2000). *Exploring interpersonal trust in the entrepreneurial venture.* Hampshire: Macmillan Press Ltd.
11. Droege, S.B., Anderson, J.R. and Bowler, M. (2003). Trust and organizational information flow. *Journal of Business and Management*, 9(1), 45-59.
12. Dyer, J.H. and Hatch, N.W. (2006). Relation-specific capabilities and barriers to knowledge transfers: Creating advantage through network relationships. *Strategic Management Journal*, 27(8), 701-719.
13. Eraydin, A. and Armatli-Köroglu, B. (2005). Innovation, networking and the new industrial clusters: The characteristics of networks and local innovation capabilities in the Turkish industrial clusters. *Entrepreneurship & Regional Development*, 17(4), 237-266.
14. Fukuyama, F. (1996). *Trust: The social virtues and the creation of prosperity.* London: Penguin Books.
15. Gambetta, D. (1988). Can we trust trust? In D. Gambetta (Ed.), *Trust: Making breaking cooperative relations* (pp. 213-237). New York: Basil Blackwell.
16. Granovetter, M. (1985). Economic action and social structure: The problem of embeddedness. *American Journal of Sociology*, 91(3), 481-510.
17. Håkansson, H. and Johanson, J. (1988). Formal and informal cooperation strategies in international industrial networks. In F.J. Contractor and P. Lorange (Eds.), *Cooperative strategies in international business: Joint ventures and technology partnership between firms* (pp. 369-379). Toronto: D.C. Heath and Company.
18. Harriss, J. (2002). *On trust, and trust in Indian business: Ethnographic explorations* (Development Studies Institute Working Paper Series,

No. 02-35). London: Development Studies Institute, London School of Economics and Political Science.

19. Harriss, J. (2003). 'Widening the radius of trust': Ethnographic explorations of trust and Indian business. *Journal of the Royal Anthropological Society*, 9(4), 755-773.
20. Julien, P., Andriambeloson, E. and Ramangalahy, C. (2004). Networks, weak signals and technological innovations among SMEs in the land-based transportation equipment sector. *Entrepreneurship & Regional Development*, 16(4), 251-269.
21. Kristiansen, S., Kimeme, J., Mbwambo, A. and Wahid F. (2005). Information flows and adaptation in Tanzanian cottage industries. *Entrepreneurship & Regional Development*, 17(5), 365-388.
22. Lane, C. and Bachmann, R. (Eds) (1998). *Trust within and between organizations: Conceptual issues and empirical applications.* Oxford: Oxford University Press.
23. Lewis, J.D. and Weigert, A. (1985). Trust as a social reality. Social Forces, 63(4), 967-985.
24. Li, P.P. (2007b). Towards an interdisciplinary conceptualization of trust: A typological approach. Management and Organization Review, 3(3), 421- 445.
25. Lipparini, A. and Sobrero, M. (1994). The glue and the pieces: Entrepreneurship and innovation in small-firm networks.
26. Luhman, N. (1988). Familiarity, confidence, trust: Problems, and alternatives. In D. Gambetta (Ed.), *Trust: Making breaking cooperative relations* (pp. 94-107). New York: Basil Blackwell.
27. Menning, G. (1997). Trust, entrepreneurship and development in Surat city, India. *Ethnos*, 62(1-2), 59-90.
28. Moensted, M. (2007). Strategic networking in small high tech firms. *International Entrepreneurship and Management Journal*, 3(1), 15-27.
29. Neergaard, H. (2005). Networking activities in technology-based entrepreneurial teams. *International Small Business Journal*, 23(3), 257-276.
30. Neergaard, H. and Ulhøi, J.P. (2006). Government agency and trust in the formation and transformation of interorganizational entrepreneurial networks. *Entrepreneurship Theory & Practice*, 30(4), 519-539.
31. Ojha, A.K. (2002). 'Trust' as a foundation for strategic alliances in global software outsourcing. *Vikalpa*, 27(2), 3-12.

32. Ramachandran, K. and Ray, S. (2006). Networking and new venture resource strategies: A study of information technology start-ups. *The Journal of Entrepreneurship*, 15(2), 145-168.
33. Rogers, M. (2004). Networks, firm size and innovation. *Small Business Economics*, 22(2), 141-153.
34. Saxenian, A.L. (2000). The origins and dynamics of production networks in Silicon Valley. In R. Swedberg (Ed.), *Entrepreneurship: The social science view* (pp. 308-331). New Delhi: Oxford University Press.
35. Sengupta, A. (2010). Social capital and entrepreneurship: An analysis of methodological issues. *Sociological Bulletin*, 59(3), 323-344.
36. Soh. P-H. (2003). The Role of networking alliances in information acquisition and its implications for new product performance. *Journal of Business Venturing*, 18(6), 727-744.
37. Soto, H.D. (2006). Trust, institutions and entrepreneurship. *International Research in the Business Disciplines*, Vol. 5, 3-19.
38. Walker, G. (1988). Network analysis for cooperative interfirm relationships. In F.J. Contractor and P. Lorange (Eds.), *Cooperative strategies in international business: Joint ventures and technology partnership between firms* (pp. 227-240). Toronto: D.C. Heath and Company.
39. Welter, F. and Smallbone, D. (2006). Exploring the role of trust in entrepreneurial activity. *Entrepreneurship Theory & Practice*, 30(4), 465- 475.
40. Yli-Renko, H. and Autio, E. (1998). The network embeddedness of new, technology-based firms: Developing a systemic evolution model. *Small Business Economics*, 11(3), 253-267.
41. Zaheer, A., McEvily, B. and Perrone, V. (1998). Does trust matter: Exploring the effect of interorganizational and interpersonal trust on performance. *Organization Science*, 9(2), 141-159.

# 19

# Small and Medium Enterprise (SME) Artisan Clusters: Opportunities and Challenges

***Abstract***

By exploring the challenges and opportunities of SME artisan clusters, this paper departs from traditional research focussed on cluster dynamics. We suggest policy intervention based on the findings of the research by comparing an artisan cluster with a technology cluster. The differences in the two are brought out. The argument is that specific cluster development programmes need to be chalked out taking the help of established organizations as nodal agencies in order to build a vibrant seedbed for future large organizations.

SMEs are the seedbed for a vibrant economy and the future corporate sector. Within the SME sector, an important role is played by the numerous clusters that have been in existence for decades and sometimes even for centuries. This article assesses the challenges and opportunities of artisan clusters differentiating between technology and artisan clusters. The article concludes that cluster membership benefits and shortfalls span a complex 'bundle' of services, ranging from individual support to collective lobbying. Clustering not only gives advantages of scale and scope, but also combines individual and collective benefits in order to mitigate the effects of being small. At the same time, formidable challenges and opportunities have cropped up for the SME sector subsequent to the liberalization of the Indian economy, as well as its closer integration within the global economy. The findings of this study indicate that the biggest challenges are related to finance, skilled management and marketing related challenges and the major opportunities are lobbying and representation and availability of expert advice and information. The 1.3 crore SME units in socialist India contributing to about 8-9% GDP have generated a great deal of interest within India on novel approaches to SME cluster development. With a contribution of 40% to the country's industrial output and 35% to direct exports, the SME sector has achieved significant milestones for the industrial development of India. According to a UNIDO survey of Indian SSI clusters undertaken in 1996 (later updated in 1998), there are 350 MSME clusters. Also, there are approximately 2000 rural and artisan based clusters in India. It is estimated that these clusters contribute 60% of the manufactured exports from India.

The Micro, Small and Medium Enterprises (MSMEs) clusters in India are estimated to have a significantly high share in employment generation. Some Indian SSE clusters are so big that they account for 90 per cent of India's total production output in selected products for example, the knitwear cluster of Ludhiana. Almost the entire Gems and Jewellery exports are from the clusters of Surat and Mumbai. Similarly, the clusters of Chennai, Agra and Kolkata are well known for leather products. However, the majority of Indian clusters, especially in the handicrafts sector are located in rural areas and are very small with no more than hundred workers, so specialised that no other place in the world matches their skills and the quality of their output. This is the case, for example, of the Paithani sarees cluster in Maharashtra. However, only a tiny minority of such artisan clusters are globally competitive.

This paper presents empirical evidence on artisan SME clusters and technology clusters differentiating between them in terms of their challenges and opportunities and evolves a set of recommendations for organised development of SME clusters in India. It focuses on how these processes could be better understood which would allow us to offer a widened view of what may be appropriate to help government agencies when engaging with SMEs in order to develop policy initiatives, which are in line with SME needs and in consonance with successful cluster development.

## Introduction

One of the central purposes of strategy formulation and implementation is the development and sustaining of competitive advantages. The theories in this field are under constant scrutiny and frameworks and analytical models that search to explain the nature of competition among firms abound in the strategy literature. In essence, there is a need for an understanding of why some firms perform better than others while the competitive environment remains the same for all firms.

Although individual firms have been the preferred unit of analysis in strategy literature, today, in a world of alliances and coalitions, competition increasingly occurs between supply chains, networks of firms, or clusters. (Porter, 1998) defines a cluster, whose role in competition has only recently been widely recognised, as a geographical concentration of inter-related firms, specialized suppliers, knowledge producers and research centres, brokers, consultants and consumers, connected in a value producing chain. He further adds that a cluster is a "geographic concentration of interconnected companies, specialized suppliers, service providers, firms in related industries, and associated institutions (e.g. universities, standards agencies and trade association) in particular fields that compete but also cooperate."

Clusters do not develop as a result of the physical proximity between the units. Many persons and organizations can be physically close, and also occur in each other's networks, without leading to the formation of a cluster. For a cluster to be described as existing, certain necessary prerequisites must be present. There must be a certain number of connections between the entities, which are based on functional common interests; there must be a minimum of information regarding this common functional interest, flowing in the connections; there must be a certain amount of expectation of a common result as a function of the connections established and the information flowing through the connections; and in every cluster there must be certain basic common interests and some spontaneously developed interests.

## Literature Review

It was Alfred Marshall who had first recognized the gains of 'external economies' of agglomeration of related industries almost a century ago. Recently, development studies have witnessed a surge of interest in clustering of industrial activities as means for supporting, upgrading and thus generating economic growth in developing countries (Humphrey and Schmitz 2002; Schmitz 1999, 2004). SME clusters facilitate up gradation of SMEs by interactive learning both with local and external sources of knowledge (Beccatini, 1990; Piore and Sable , 1984; Schmitz 1999, Storper 1997). These arise due to general development in the region and due to the demonstrative effect of other units and development of support and complimentary industries. Brussco, 1996; Piore and Sable, 1984; pointed out that such joint actions could be pursued consciously through inter-firm cooperation or through business associations/ consortia etc. In a developed cluster, a lot of seemingly non-economic factors come into play. Beccatini, 1990; and Harrison, 1991 found that competition and cooperation, trust and reciprocity and conscious joint actions were characteristics of such clusters. Trust between organizations has been found to be one of the critical success factors for successful clusters (Batenburg and Rutten, 2003). The local proximity of geographic clusters allow for more frequent face-to-face interaction. This rich medium of communication has been shown to facilitate the building of trust. Thus, collective efficiency could arise out of unplanned (incidental) and through planned (consciously pursued) measures as pointed out by Schmitz (1999). Opportunities of SMEs have been observed in a few earlier studies. Huggins (2000) has found such networking events in clusters to be important elements of SME marketing concerns, and Curran and Blackburn (1994) found some more limited uses made of them in their study of associations and other networking organizations.

SMEs in developing countries are poorly placed to cope with technological change and necessary upgrading. Even in highly industrialised economies they find it difficult to keep abreast of the threat posed by ever-changing technological and market trends. Today, a number of studies find that SMEs are frequently faced with challenges (Bannock et al. 2002; Batra and Mahmood 2001; Brunetti et al. 1998). Matlay (2004), found a relatively high awareness of government initiatives regarding SME clusters but low usage rates among a sample of 600 SMEs. For most developing and transition economies, the common challenges for SMEs typically include financing, overcoming institutional, legal and administrative barriers and accessing network support along with lack of professional management.

## Methodology

In light of the severe scarcity of data related to around 636 SME (industrial) and 6000 artisan/micro enterprise clusters that are estimated to exist in India, this study adopts a field survey on SMEs covering different districts and regions at the grassroots level, so as to unveil the genuine challenges and opportunities of SME artisan clusters by collecting primary data. The collection of data was done on the basis of the stratified random sampling method, drawing a simple random sample independently in each category of technological and artisan clusters.

Many of the units were suspicious of the researchers and simply refused to respond. Through some contacts and references, we could survey 30 units each in the textile and handicraft sector. The real insight was provided by experienced and knowledgeable people in each cluster giving us reasons to be satisfied.

Qualitative research procedures were first carried out by the researchers in the form of focus group interviews and depth interviews to gain insights by listening to a group of people and experts from the population and to uncover underlying motivations, beliefs, attitudes and feelings on the subject of study. This formed the basis of the descriptive research that was carried out in this study. The objectives of this study are:

1. To identify the challenges and opportunities of SME clusters

2. To compare the challenges and opportunities of an artisan cluster and a technology based cluster.

The study was conducted in Jodhpur (artisan) and Bhilwara (technology based) clusters. These were chosen because both are typical clusters that have had phenomenal growth. Both primary and secondary data were used for the study. Primary data were collected by direct interview method with the help of a questionnaire. The secondary data came from government publications, statistical yearbook, books and journals, etc. Factor analysis followed by t-test for independent samples were used to analyze the data.

The study examined 29 variables related to cluster opportunities, including finding common ground, importance of discussion, networking and forming alliances, advice and consultancy from banks and consultants, consultancy from social network, advice from government agencies, training, recruitment, trade missions, bulk purchasing of raw materials, labour pool, group insurance schemes, lobbying and representation, membership of associations, trade fairs and exhibitions, increased clout with state and central government, Information on government support, grants and loans , information on legislation and regulations , information on creditworthiness of clients and suppliers, help with meeting trading standards, help with choice of consultants and advisers, help to meet potential clients and suppliers, other marketing help, help with manager or supervisor training, help with resolving commercial disputes ,influence on training institutions, shared expensive resources of plant and machinery, new product and process development, reduced inventory, improved quality, better access to suppliers, increased availability of complimentary products, better access to public institutions, higher motivation.

The survey examined 21 variables related to the attitude or opinions of owner managers of SMEs with respect to cluster challenges: lack of capital, lack of control over corruption , limited access to institutional credit, lack of foreign direct investment, power failures, poor transport facility , inadequate telecommunication services , load shedding; limited access to market , inability to forecast demand ; lack of standardisation, lack of skilled labour, lack of unskilled labour, narrow specialization among artisans, lack of Entrepreneurial and Managerial (E&M) skills, lack of technological up gradation, lack of awareness of modern methods , lack of creativity, geophysical challenges (geographical remoteness), lack of overall government support and assistance, political environment and other challenges (regulatory challenges).

All these variables were scaled from 1 to 10. A scale from 1 to 3 is considered as 'low'; from 4 to 7 as 'medium', and from 8 to 10 as 'high' value variablc. The data so collected were are analysed by means of SPSS version 13 using standard statistical tools and factor analysis by extracting the principal components using Orthogonal Varimax Rotation that explained the variance in the attributes.

Each group of variables was analysed using varimax rotation with a factor loading of 0.5 or better. The number of factors to be extracted was determined by evaluating the Eigen value scores of 1 or more. Reliability analysis (Cronbach alpha) was calculated to test the reliability and internal consistency of each factor. The results showed that alpha coefficients of the factors were well above the minimum value of 0.50 considered acceptable as an indication of reliability for basic research.

Factors with eigen values greater than 1 were identified and statements with loadings of 0.5 or greater were retained. The structure shown in Table 1 and Table 2 explains the factors and contains all the variables related to challenges and opportunities respectively.

## Major Results

### 1. Respondent Cluster Profile

The study is based on primary data collected from 60 respondents 30 each from a technology and artisan cluster. All respondents were males. The majority of respondent organizations have been in operation for over 10 years. The largest group of entrepreneurs were in the age group of 31-40 years (37%) followed by 41-50 years (27%). 10% of the entrepreneurs were less than 21 years of age.

The Bhilwara textile cluster is well developed with over 400 enterprises engaged in spinning, weaving, processing and trading of textiles with healthy competition leading to rapid development of the cluster. Today Bhilwara is a prominent and leading manufacturer, exporter and supplier of world-class Suitings, Flock Fabrics and Yarn. Its share in the polyester/ viscose fabrics (suiting) sector is around 50 per cent in India. The contribution of the 'Mewar Chamber of Commerce', an association of entrepreneurs of the region is phenomenal.

Textile is a mass consumption item with relatively low and standardized quality. The only innovation is in superficial cosmetics and colours. These are imitated soon after their introduction by the organized sector. The cluster runs not on differentiation but on highly price sensitive competition and hence products from the cluster are compromised in quality to reduce cost. The vertical cooperation in the cluster is reasonably good though strictly price based. There is little horizontal cooperation among units for mutual gains. The main strengths of the industry are huge demand, a large trading network, flexible capacity at the assembly unit level, cost efficiencies of supply chain coordination, substantial employment generation potential and a remarkable entrepreneurial spirit. Major problems in the cluster are price based competition with quality, a victim; lack of managerial training, difficulty in availing institutional credit.

The Jodhpur handicraft cluster has over 500 predominantly artisan based micro enterprises run from their houses, with very limited investment capacity and an immediate survival approach. The business culture is imitation with narrow specialization. With the entire family working in the unit, skills are picked up on the job. With extreme competition, there is extreme mistrust among units.

This is further fuelled by traders as unity among artisans is not in their interest particularly since some of the big players among the traders double up as raw material suppliers. Consequently there is no cooperation even in areas such as purchase of raw material, joint marketing etc. where they distinctly stand to gain. Perennially short of working capital, they are compelled to encash the credit ship of the traders with the raw material supplies for their next round of production. Thus, cooperation among the SME units of the cluster would not be possible until this nexus is broken. Creativity or technological innovation is negligible. With no entry barriers, competition is ruinous. Major challenges of the cluster include lack of finance, lack of information and consulting, lack of standardization, lack of design capability and lack of awareness on modern methods; the strength predominantly being in the artisan skill alone.

## 2. Opportunities

Small and medium-sized enterprises (SMEs) draw on a wide range of resources, internal and external to their business. Their membership of a certain cluster is one such source of external resource. The cluster is a provider of an external source of advice that seeks to provide particular expert knowledge. The suppliers range from the private sector (consultants, banks), through social networks of friends and relatives, to the public sector (such as government advice services). Apart from advice to an SME, clusters have a range of functions offering social opportunities, marketing and collective purchasing, self regulation and lobbying and representation of the interest of the business.

1. Clusters benefit from both competition and cooperation. Competition forces all members of the cluster to improve their efficiencies to control costs and look for ways to enhance their differentiation capabilities. Without this competition to motivate improvements, a cluster will fail. Additionally, there is cooperation among the members of clusters. Much of the cooperation occurs vertically within the supply chain. However, horizontal cooperation occurs whenever there is no direct competition and whenever there is an outside threat to the overall existence of the cluster. Government-backed initiatives at Central and State level in the form of organizations namely SIDBI, NSIC, SIDO and DIC, National Institute of Small Industry Extension Training (NISIET) renamed as National Institute for Micro, Small & Medium Enterprises (NI-MSME) with enactment of MSMED Act, 2006, have sought to promote learning and development in SME clusters, and funding has been consistently available to help SMEs take advantage of these. Several institutions in India also have taken up Cluster Projects besides various government initiatives.
2. The major ones among government and other institutions being Development Commissioner (SSI), Ministry of Small Scale Industries, National Small Industrial Corporation Ltd (NSIC), Development

Commissioner (Handicrafts), Ministry of Textiles, Department of Science & Technology, Ministry of Science & Technology, Textiles Committee of India, Ministry of Textiles, Khadi and Village Industries Commission (KVIC) , Coir Board. Apart from this National Support Institutions include Small Industries Development Bank of India (SIDBI) with their Technology Upgradation Programme, State Bank of India (SBI) UPTECH Programme and National Bank for Agriculture and Rural Development (NABARD). Government provides help in the form of raw material assistance, financial assistance, infrastructural facilities, technological up gradation, handling competition, handling marketing efforts, raising quality standards and promotion of exports.

3. Availability of expert advice and information is also an interesting finding of this research. Importance of discussion and critical reflection in social environment of the cluster appeared to be of great utility and importance to the owner-managers involved in the study.
4. Production, Operations and Marketing is another area that solicits cooperation in SMEs. This includes bulk purchasing of raw materials, increased availability of complimentary products, better access to suppliers, reduced inventory due to vertical cooperation within the supply chain, shared expensive resources of plant and machinery and improved quality. It is surprising to note that the bulk of the exports of the MSMEs in India (more than 95%) consist of non-traditional items manufactured in artisan clusters. The rating for such benefits was more in technology clusters as compared to artisan cluster. Please insert Figure No.1 – Export from SME sector about here.
5. Lobbying and Representation: Enterprises in a cluster have increased clout with state and central governments and do exert influence on policy decisions. This also results in benefits in the form of better access to public institutions, increased clout with state and central government and membership of associations and chambers leading to positive exposure of the SME. Technological clusters have greater benefit on this account.

## Challenges

Although there is a plethora of publicly funded government schemes seeking to promote SME clusters, many of them are perceived to be overly bureaucratic and disconnected from SME needs, driven by government agendas and funding, rather than attention to demand for such opportunities from SME managers. This supply-side mentality has resulted in schemes which fail to connect with the existing small business environment, which is characterised by heterogeneity.

The SME clusters are in pursuit of a multiplicity of objectives. The policy and organisational support tends to be much too simplistic in the context of the complexity and diversity involved in managing clusters.

1. An important finding of this study is the lack of adequate and timely finance and working capital. Despite the cluster opportunities, SMEs are not able to exploit their full potential. Almost 90% of the units are not registered and close to 95% of them do not have access to any kind of formal institutional credit. SMEs are therefore forced to rely more on internal accruals and non-institutional credit. Moreover the share of SMEs in banks total credit flow has declined.
2. Marketing Challenges: These are very commonly perceived challenges by the entrepreneurs of both the artisan and technology cluster. The results show higher ratings for marketing challenges in artisan clusters in comparison to technology based cluster.
3. Infrastructure: Infrastructure facilities in India are inadequate except in some highly developed satellite regions of metropolitan cities. Majority of the respondents rcported frequent power failure, load shedding, poor transport facilities, and inadequate telecommunication services. All the entrepreneurs complained of the problems of power shortage and power breakdowns.
4. Human Resource Challenges: Lack of skilled labour and lack of creativity figure high in the list of human resource related challenges. The skills in an artisan cluster are passed on from generation to generation and there is no facility to train the craftsmen in modern methods and technology.
5. External Environmental Factors: The political environment may act as a constraint in the development of a particular cluster. Geographical remoteness has been rated high as a constraint by both the cluster respondents.

## Results of Independent Samples t-test

1. The comparison of the two independent samples using t-test indicates that there is a significant difference in the artisan and technology cluster competency related to expert advice and information and lobbying and representation; whereas the difference is not significant for production and marketing, social aspects and HR aspects.

2. The comparison of the artisan and technology cluster in their challenges reveals that the two clusters are significantly different in terms of financial assistance, marketing challenges and infrastructure. However they are not significantly different in relation to human resource and external environment factors.

## Policy Recommendations

India having socialism as one of basic concepts in the constitution advocates for balanced economic development of all regions and the populace and therefore strives for sharing the fruits of economic growth with all. The strategy of economic development of any country that formulates programs for removal of poverty by providing large scale employment education and training, capital formation, effective mobilization of resources, balanced economic growth, and equitable distribution of national income with effective involvement and participation of all its citizens in the accomplishment of the goal, cannot neglect strategic policy intervention for SME cluster development.

1. Clusters in India have evolved naturally over a period of time in the preliberalized economic environment. The macro level policies have since changed, and the clusters are finding it difficult to cope up with the changed scenario. The policies have to be tuned to focus on cluster development.
2. There has to be a system for identification of "high potential" clusters for focused support. High potential may be judged based on size and growth potential including exports.
3. Financing agencies need to focus on a cluster approach. This will help them achieve twin objectives of their own business growth and development of the SME cluster. Regenerating SME cluster financing by providing micro finance at reasonable costs will go a long way in making SME clusters domestically and globally competitive and centers of economic growth. Financial support should be provided through banks and financial institutions with local roots. Also cluster nodal forum should provide a credit guarantee to all such borrowings.
4. We can promote a "cooperative model" wherein the cluster members come together to realize collective efficiency more so in artisan clusters where the individual has limited resources. This cooperative model would result in an exchange of best practices of member enterprises.

5. SMEs need their own dedicated representative bodies to push their case forward which includes more than just lobbying. Such an association in the cluster serves as a platform for exchanging ideas, information and generating awareness. There can also be an exchange of best practices and members could work towards evolving a code of conduct.
6. Various factors related to globalization have now rendered implementation of supply chain management an imperative even for the SMEs. The SME clusters need to build competitive advantage thru developing a strong cluster supply chain using local resources rather than concentrating on low cost advantage. For this, we need to assess the current supply chain capability of the cluster constituents and then link that to deliver bottom line results through SCM, competitiveness, order fulfillment, inventory management etc. This can act as a powerful differentiator to significantly improve the competitiveness of the SME cluster.
7. The researcher feels an urgent need to evolve a national level programme for high potential clusters to design, develop and implement self sustaining interventions for improving the competitiveness of the clusters. There is a need to integrate not only information and processes, but also people and technology to advance the market position of the cluster.
8. There is a need for professional institutions and associations that can undertake cluster based local area development, effectively and inclusively in developing and transition economies. Research and academic institutions can adopt a cluster each and play the role of a mentor/ facilitator and act as a nodal institution for all stakeholders related to that cluster.
9. Clusters that are on the survival edge with little inter-firm cooperation and mutual trust need to promote networking for mutual gains and efficiency. This can be done based on the UNIDO approach adopted in Bolivia, Jamaica and Nicaragua. This involves identifying and convincing a critical mass of entrepreneurs on networking for action such as joint purchase, joint marketing etc.; collective assessment of organization, production, technology, quality, skills, work conditions, plant organization etc.( based on self assessment of these as a base); identifying common problems and solutions thereof and gradually identifying strategic projects for implementation. These processes would evolve over time. Such approaches would be relevant in the Indian context also and should be initiated through the nodal institution of the cluster.

## Implications

1. Given the critical role played by the clusters in employment and income generation and in export promotion in some cases, SME cluster development policy initiatives would come through sooner than later.
2. This is in consonance with our ex president's Dr. APJ Abdul Kalam's vision 2020 for the country where India can be proud of having more employment providers than employment seekers.
3. With a fresh imperative towards strengthening the SME sector through implementation of adequate reforms, Indian administration can propel SME economy into a high growth trajectory.

## Conclusion

Every SME can be seen as a unique collection of resources and capabilities whose productive functioning is dependent upon the owner manager's attitude, knowledge and perceptions. They act in the market limited by these perceptions and, sometimes, do not explore their full potentialities. Enlarging these perceptions is a major challenge, both for the SMEs and for the strategists that are responsible for the formulation of industrial and regional development policies.

This study was conducted having as its central purpose the identification of the challenges and opportunities of a cluster and their strategic sustainability and providing suggestions for policy intervention. Since firms are influenced by members of the cluster, SMEs' strategies must be formulated not only from the point of view of individual resources and capabilities, but also taking into account the collective and shared resources and capabilities of the whole cluster. How to manage and co-ordinate this process in an integrated way in both artisan and technology clusters remain a challenge for practitioners and constitute an important area for further empirical research.

The research epitomises that cumulative development and upgrading of resources and capabilities can fundamentally shape the future strategic options of a cluster.

## Limitations of the study

With limited associations in the Jodhpur cluster, the initial going was difficult. The enumerators were looked upon with suspicion. The respondents were from different educational background, some entrepreneurs having scanty educational qualifications and hence we faced some difficulty in interpreting management terms, although simplified to the best of our ability.

## References


1. Bannock, Graham, Matthew Gamser, Mariell Juhlin and Andrew McCann. 2002. *'Indigenous Private Sector Development and Regulation in Africa and Central Europe: A 10 Country Study'*, London: Bannock Consulting, accessed from http://www.dai.com/pdf/ Indigenous Private Sector Development.pdf (on 11 February 2010).
2. Batenburg, R. and Rutten, R. (2003), *"Managing innovation in regional supply networks: a Dutch case of knowledge industry clustering"*, Supply Chain Management: An International Journal, Vol. 8 No. 3, pp. 263-70.
3. Batra, Geeta and Syed Mahmood. 2001. *'Direct Support to Private Firms: Evidence on Effectiveness'*, World Bank Policy Research Working Paper 3170, November, accessed from http:// info.worldbank.org/ etools/ docs/ library/ 86493/ ses3.2_ directsupport.pdf (on 11 February,2010).
4. Becattini, G. (1990*), "The Marshallian district as a socio-economic notion",* in Pyke, F., Becattini, G. and Sergenberger, W. (Eds), Industrial Districts and Inter-firm Co-operation in Italy, OMT, Geneva.
5. Bridges.org (2002), "*Supportingentrepreneurshipin developing countries–survey of the field and inventory of initiative"* available at at:www. bridges . org /entrepreneurship(accessed 2 October,2009).
6. Brunetti, Aymo, Gregory Kisunko and Beatrice Weder. 1998. *'Credibility of Rules and Economic Growth: Evidence from a Worldwide Survey of the Private Sector',* The World Bank Economic Review 12 (3),September: 353–384.
7. Brussco, S., Cainelli, G., Forni, F., Franchi, M., Malusardi, A. and Righetti, R. (1996), *"The evolution of industrial districts in Emilia-Romagna",*
8. CEC (2002), Observatory of European SMEs 2002 /No. 3: Regional Clusters in Europe, Commission of the European Communities, Brussels, available at: www.competitiveness.org/article/archive/ 27/
9. Cossentino, F., Pyke, F. and Sengenberger, W. (Eds), "*Local and Regional Response to Global Pressure: The Case of Italy and its Industrial Districts,*" International Institute for Labour Studies, Geneva

10. Curran, J. and Blackburn, R. A. (1994) *Small Firms and Local Economic Networks: The Death of the Local Economy?* London: Paul Chapman.
11. Eden, C., Jones, S. and Sims, D. (1979), Thinking in Organisations, Macmillan, London.
12. Foss, N. (1997), Resources and Strategy: A Reader, Oxford University Press, Oxford.
13. Harrison, B.(1991*),"Industrial districts:old wine in new bottles?"* Regional Studies, Vol. 26, pp. 469-83.
14. Huggins, R. (2000) *The Business of Networks: Inter-firm Interactions, Institutional Policy and the TEC Experiment.* Ashgate: Aldershot.
15. Humphrey, J.and Schmitz, H. (2002), *"How does insertion in global value chains affect upgrading in industrial clusters?"*, Regional Studies, Vol. 36 No. 9, pp. 1017-27.
16. Marshall, A. (1890), Principles of Economics, Macmillan, London.
17. Matlay, H. (2004), *"Contemporary training initiatives in Britain: a small business perspective"*, Journal of Small Business and Enterprise Development, Vol. 11 No. 4, pp. 4504-13.
18. Nahapiet, J. and Ghoshal, S. (1998), *"Social capital, intellectual capital, and the organisational advantage"*, Academy of Management Review, Vol. 23, pp. 242-66.
19. Porter, M.E. (1998), *"Clusters and the new economics of competition"*, Harvard Business Review, Vol. 76 No. 2, pp. 77-89.
20. Porter, M.E. (1998), *The Competitive Advantage of Nations*, 2nd ed., Macmillan.
21. Porter,M.E. (1998). Competitive Strategies : T*echniques for analyzing industries and competitors.* New York : Free Press p 23]
22. Porter, M. (2000), "*Locations, clusters and company strategy*", in Clark, G., Feldman, M. and Gertler, M. (Eds), The Oxford Handbook of Economic Geography, Oxford University Press, Oxford.
23. Piore, M., Sable, C. (1984), *The Second Industrial Divide*, Basic Books, New York, NY.
24. Schmitz, H. (1995), "*Collective efficiency: growth path for small-scale industry"*, Journal of Development Studies, Vol. 31, pp. 529-66.
25. Schmitz, H. (1999), *"Global competition and local cooperation: success and failure in the Sinos Valley, Brazil"*, World Development, Vol. 27, pp. 1627-50.
26. Schmitz, H. and Nadvi, K. (1999), *"Clustering and industrialization:*
*27. introduction", World development,* Vol. 27, pp. 1503-14.
28. Schmitz,H.(2004), *Local Enterprises in the Global Economy: Issues of Governance and Upgrading,* Edward Elgar, Cheltenham.

29. Schmitz, H. (2007), *"Regional systems and global chains"*, in Scott, A. and Garofoli, G. (Eds), Development on the Ground: Clusters, Networks and Regions in Emerging Economies, Routledge, London.
30. Stewart, J. and Beaver, G. (2004), *HRD in Small Organisations: Research and Practice*, Routledge, London.
31. Storper, M. (1997), *The Regional World: Territorial Development in a Global Economy*, The Guildford Press, New York, NY.
32. Sullivan, R. (2000), *"Entrepreneurial learning and mentoring"*, International Journal of Entrepreneurial Behaviour and Research, Vol. 6 No. 3, pp. 160-75.
33. UNIDO (2000), *"Cluster development and promotion of business development services: UNIDO's experience in India"*, Private Sector Development Branch Working Paper 6, Investment Promotion and Institutional Capacity Building Division, UNIDO, Vienna.
34. Westhead, P. and Storey, D. (1996), *"Management training and small firm performance: why is the link so weak?"*, International Small Business Journal, Vol. 14 No. 4, pp. 13-24.

## Tables and Figures

### Table 1: Cluster opportunity factors

| Factors | Dimensions | Factor Loading | Cronbach Alpha | Eigen Values | Percentage of Explained Variance |
|---|---|---|---|---|---|
| Factor 1 Export advice and Information | D1 | 0.894 | 0.97 | 3.547 | 0.451 |
| | D2 | 0.811 | | | |
| | D3 | 0.762 | | | |
| | D5 | 0.754 | | | |
| | D6 | 0.659 | | | |
| | D7 | 0.573 | | | |
| | D9 | 0.554 | | | |
| Factor 2 Assistance in Production Operations and marketing | D10 | 0.803 | 0.92 | 2.726 | 0.533 |
| | D11 | 0.726 | | | |
| | D12 | 0.625 | | | |
| | D13 | 0.701 | | | |
| | D14 | 0.612 | | | |
| | D15 | 0.628 | | | |
| Factor 3 Lobbying and Representation | D16 | 0.733 | 0.87 | 2.092 | 0.693 |
| | D17 | 0.784 | | | |
| | D18 | 0.812 | | | |
| | D20 | 0.664 | | | |
| Factor 4 Social Aspects | D21 | 0.689 | 0.83 | 1.982 | 0.517 |
| | D22 | 0.571 | | | |
| | D24 | 0.725 | | | |
| Factor 5 HR Aspects | D25 | 0.650 | 0.76 | 2.299 | 0.469 |
| | D27 | 0.664 | | | |
| | D28 | 0.782 | | | |

**Table 2: Cluster challenges Factors Dimensions Factor**

| Factors | Dimensions | Factor Loading | Cronbach Alpha | Eigen Values | Percentage of Explained Variance |
|---|---|---|---|---|---|
| Factor 1 Financial Assistance | E1 | 0.765 | 0.95 | 3.229 | 0.632 |
| | E2 | 0.732 | | | |
| | E3 | 0.814 | | | |
| | E4 | 0.761 | | | |
| Factor 2 Marketing Challenges | E5 | 0.882 | 0.89 | 2.836 | 0.528 |
| | E6 | 0.730 | | | |
| | E7 | 0.727 | | | |
| Factor 3 Infrastructure | E8 | 0.664 | 0.83 | 2.475 | 0.571 |
| | E9 | 0.642 | | | |
| | E10 | 0.782 | | | |
| | E11 | 0.790 | | | |
| Factor 4 Human resource Challenges | E12 | 0.745 | 0.77 | 1.872 | 0.613 |
| | E14 | 0.670 | | | |
| | E15 | 0.582 | | | |
| | E16 | 0.680 | | | |
| | E17 | 0.645 | | | |
| | E18 | 0.736 | | | |
| Factor 5 External Environmental Factors | E19 | 0.870 | 0.71 | 2.004 | 0.434 |
| | E21 | 0.834 | | | |

**Table 3 – Credit flow from organized sector to LOs and SMEs**

| % of credit flow | Large organizations (LOs) | Small & Medium Enterprise (SMEs) |
|---|---|---|
| FY 2001 | 85.8% | 14.2% |
| FY 2008 | 89.1% | 10.9% |

Source: Report of Committee on Financial Sector Assessment (CFSA), 2009

**Table 4: Comparison of Opportunities between Technology and Artisan Cluster**

| Dimension | Organization | N | Mean | S.D. | p value |
|---|---|---|---|---|---|
| Factor 1<br>Expert advice and Information | Artisan<br>Technology | 30<br>30 | 2.06<br>4.10 | 1.132<br>1.230 | .037* |
| Factor 2<br>Assistance in Production Operations and marketing | Artisan<br>Technology | 30<br>30 | 3.35<br>3.92 | 1.222<br>1.038 | .179 |
| Factor 3<br>Lobbying and Representation | Artisan<br>Technology | 30<br>30 | 2.65<br>4.62 | 1.222<br>1.235 | .011* |
| Factor 4<br>Social Aspects | Artisan<br>Technology | 30<br>30 | 2.24<br>2.91 | .996<br>1.014 | .478 |
| Factor 5<br>H R Aspects | Artisan<br>Technology | 30<br>30 | 2.47<br>2.77 | 1.179<br>1.092 | .480 |

*Difference is significant at 95%

**Table 5: Comparison of Challenges between Technology and Artisan Cluster**

| Dimension | Organization | N | Mean | S.D. | p value |
|---|---|---|---|---|---|
| Factor1<br>Financial Assistance | Artisan<br>Technology | 30<br>30 | 3.06<br>2.38 | 1.194<br>1.023 | .005* |
| Factor 2<br>Marketing Challenges | Artisan<br>Technology | 30<br>30 | 4.65<br>3.92 | 1.006<br>1.101 | .014* |
| Factor 3<br>Infrastructure | Artisan<br>Technology | 30<br>30 | 2.65<br>3.23 | 1.250<br>1.217 | .013* |
| Factor 4<br>Human resource Challenges | Artisan<br>Technology | 30<br>30 | 2.65<br>2.62 | 1.019<br>1.115 | .362 |
| Factor 5<br>External Environmental Factors | Artisan<br>Technology | 30<br>30 | 2.47<br>2.77 | 1.314<br>0.923 | .417 |

*Difference is significant at 95%

**Figure 1 - Exports from SME sector**

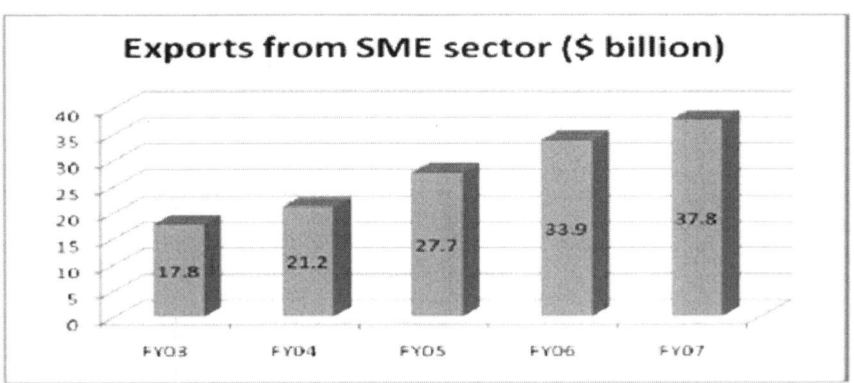


Source: Ministry of Micro, Small and Medium Enterprise website (MoMSME)

**Annexure 1**:

## Cluster Opportunities

(D) 1 Information on government support, grants and loans
(D) 2 Information on legislation and regulations
(D) 3 Information on creditworthiness of clients and suppliers
(D) 4 Help with meeting trading standards
(D) 5 Help with choice of consultants and advisers
(D) 6 Help to meet potential clients and suppliers
(D) 7 Other marketing help
(D) 8 Help with manager or supervisor training
(D) 9 Help with resolving commercial disputes
(D) 10 Bulk purchasing of raw materials
(D) 11 Increased availability of complimentary products
(D) 12 Better access to suppliers
(D) 13 Reduced inventory
(D) 14 Shared expensive resources of plant and machinery
(D) 15 Improved quality
(D) 16 Better access to public institutions
(D) 17 Increased clout with state and central government
(D) 18 Membership of associations
(D) 19 New product and process development,
(D) 20 Membership of associations and chambers
(D) 21 Finding common ground
(D) 22 Importance of discussion

(D) 23 Networking and forming alliances
(D) 24 Higher motivation
(D) 25 Training,
(D) 26 Recruitment,
(D) 27 Trade missions,
(D) 28 Labour pool,
(D) 29 Trade fairs and exhibitions

**Annexure 2**:

## Cluster Challenges

(E) 1 Lack of capital,
(E) 2 Lack of control over corruption ,
(E) 3 Limited access to institutional credit,
(E) 4 Lack of foreign direct investment (FDI),
(E) 5 Limited access to market ,
(E) 6 Inability to forecast demand ,
(E) 7 Lack of standardisation in marketing procedures;
(E) 8 Power failures,
(E) 9 Poor transport facility ,
(E) 10 Inadequate telecommunication services ,
(E) 11 Load shedding;
(E) 12 Lack of skilled labour,
(E) 13 Lack of unskilled labour,
(E) 14 Narrow specialization among artisans
(E) 15 Lack of entrepreneurial and managerial (E&M) skills,
(E) 16 Lack of technological upgradation,
(E) 17 Lack of awareness of modern methods
(E) 18 Lack of creativity
(E) 19 Geophysical challenges (geographical remoteness),
(E) 20 Lack of overall government support and assistance,
(E) 21 Political environment and other challenges (regulatory and bureaucratic challenges).

# 20

# Role of Rural Entrepreneurship in Development of SME sector in Assam with special reference to Nalbari District

***Abstract***

Economic development and entrepreneurship development is closely interrelated. To develop the economic status of a nation the individual must put their efforts towards entrepreneurship development. In Assam, there is huge number of unemployed youth, which is one of the major obstacles for economic growth. There is about 27 lakhs unemployed youth in Assam, which is a major concern for underdevelopment of the economy. No doubt, Assam has lots of human and natural resources and there is ample scope for development in Assam as well as in Nalbari district particularly in the rural areas such as for processing of cereals, fruits, vegetables, milk, meat and other agricultural products like Jute, Ramie etc. So as to make a sustainable economic development it is utmost important to make proper use of the resources available. In this sense, rural unemployed youth must have to take the initiative towards the economic progress through entrepreneurial activities. It is worthwhile to be mention that in the district of Nalbari the rural population is 1110706 (which is 97.59% of total) and urban is 27478 (which is 2.41% of total) as per the census 2001. The literacy rate of rural and urban area is 67.55% and 88.61% as per the census 2001 as against 55.38% and 80.62%

respectively in 1991 in the district. Moreover, entrepreneurs are the driving force behind Small and Medium Enterprises (SMEs).

Therefore, greater emphasis has been given to create awareness among the educated unemployed youth to take initiative to put forward their skills to make them more economic and realistic through entrepreneurship instead of waiting for Government job or searching for Government job after completion of their study.

## Introduction

**Mahatma Gandhi**- the father of the Nation said- "The quality of Life in the village should be same, if not better than that in urban inhabitations. The village people should be ably self-sufficient and self reliant, but also participate in matter of their own development". He emphasized the role of village community in economic development through their active participation in economic activities. In this sense the role of rural entrepreneurship cannot deny for which involvement of every educated unemployed youth in entrepreneurial work is quite important. Assam is a state with abundant resources which is basically an agrarian state. It is a place of proper industrialization which can be groomed if people are willing to work. In fact majority of the people of Nalbari district are dependent on agricultural activities. However, some of the people of the district are engaged in entrepreneurial activities and especially in cane and bamboo products, brass and bell metal products, weaving, fish rearing, poultry farming, piggery etc. In the field of agriculture coconut, banana, mushrooms, seasonable vegetables etc. are cultivated. In the char areas (the south bank of the river Brahmaputra of the district), surplus production of milk could be scientifically managed through the establishment of a processing unit. There are few wholesale milk sellers in the area of Laopara, Bartala who produces various milk products.

Some of the milk products are Ghee, Panner, Butter etc. It has the potential to become the supplier of fish and fish products for entire Assam. Nalbari is also famous for its cultural bent of mind and probably showcases the best theatre talent in its mobile theatre tradition. Geographically the district is close to Bhutan and they form a vast market for any surplus production in the region. So the growth of rural entrepreneurship becomes utmost important especially through Small and Medium Enterprises. To achieve this sustained growth and put a region on the fast track of development, it is important that there should be productive utilization of the resources available, but the question is how to make the best utilization of the resources, the answer could be found in entrepreneurship and in the present scenario it works as the best possible way of self-employment which will ultimately help in generating income for to make them self reliant and to contribute positive role towards economic development. Developing the spirit of entrepreneurship among the youth is important because Government can't provide jobs for all unemployed educated youth. Moreover, after the global meltdown, several big companies had already cut their jobs causing a major concern.

Entrepreneurs are the individuals who have initiated the idea to start entrepreneurship as a career in his/her interested area of work to generate income and help in growing the state to a developed stage. They are born and can be made. Rural entrepreneurship can simply be defined as entrepreneurship emerging in rural areas. The Government sincerely took initiative in the development of rural/village industries since independence. Prior to independence, small industries occupied almost insignificant place to the national economy. The north east has bountiful resources like minerals, agriculture, horticulture, forest, hydropower and human resources etc. To help and motivate the unemployed youth and also for proper utilization of vast resources, taking up entrepreneurial career as an alternative means, a large number of institutions like NSIC, DI- MSME, NEITCO, DIC etc. have been set up in several districts of the states.

From the scenario of population of the district of Nalbari which is given below, it can be said that the rural entrepreneurship will contribute positive aspect towards mobilization of the resources and bring the economy of the state to a better stage. The population of Assam compared to Nalbari district has been shown below:

**Table: 1**

| Particulars | Assam | Nalbari |
|---|---|---|
| Rural Population (No.) | 23216288 | 1121338 |
| Urban Population(No.) | 3439240 | 27486 |
| Total Population(No.) | 26655528 | 1148824 |
| Rural Population (%) | 87.10 | 97.61 |
| Urban Population (%) | 12.90 | 2.39 |
| Literacy Rate (%) | 63.25 | 67.23 |
| Rural Literacy Rate (%) | 59.73 | 66.73 |
| Urban Literacy Rate (%) | 85.35 | 66.73 |

*Source: Statistical Handbook, Assam-2007.*

## Objectives of the Study

1. To find out the potentiality of creating new ventures based on local resources.
2. To identify the need of entrepreneurship as a source of income to reduce the unemployment problem.
3. To assess the market area served by SME sector in rural area.
4. To find out the entrepreneurial awareness among the rural people of the district.
5. To examine the difficulties faced by rural entrepreneurs.
6. To identify the need of Entrepreneurship Development Programme to train, to motivate, to select, and to expand the area of entrepreneurial activities.

## Methodology

In order to meet the objectives of the study, the following methodology were adopted:

1. A set of questionnaire was designed to collect the necessary information. The questionnaires were distributed among the trainees, training personnel, existing entrepreneurs, prospective entrepreneurs, Non- Government Organisation etc.
2. Information's have been collected from block officials to know about Self-Help-Groups and how they are mentoring those groups.
3. Local entrepreneurs were meeting and collected the feedback from them.
4. Some organizations and institutions related with entrepreneurial activities have also been visited to collect secondary data.

## Significance

The district of Nalbari has the potentiality of creating new ventures based on local resources available. There are more than 1000 artisans engaged in bamboo products such as met, sangali, basket, and many more. The area of Tilana from the district is famous for its bamboo products mainly for Japi, in all over Assam.

An achievement has been created in 'Limca Book of Records' on April, 2009 making a 40 feet diameter Japi at Dighalipukhuri, Guwahati within seven days by 20 artisans from Balamugkuchi, Nalbari. They have been rewarded an insurance coverage of Rs.1 lakh by Airtel. In a recently conducted survey in Assam by National Bank for Agriculture and Rural Development (NABARD, which is one the pioneer institute involved mainly in development of rural area), they have been identified 10 sectors in the rural area of Assam which includes sectoral schemes like Agriculture, Fish rearing and processing, Rural Retail Trade, Sericulture and Silk, Small plantation and products, Handloom, Handicrafts mainly Cane, Bamboo and wood products. The development departments like agriculture, Handloom and Textile, Sericulture, Fishery, Veterinary and rural development etc. are to be associated to implement these schemes within a definite time frame. The Govt. of Assam has approved a new industrial policy 2008 extending 100% tax exemption and doubling the capital subsidy given on investment by new as well as existing units. The North East Industrial and Investment Policy (NEIPP) 2007 declared by Cabinet Committee on Economic Affairs (CCEA) were Sikkim and other seven north eastern states in the region and provide Liberal fiscal incentives for 10 years.

Chief Minister of Assam Tarun Gogoi approved the Barbila Beel Tourism project under Pachim Nalbari Development Block in the district and directed the Deputy Commissioner to develop it as a tourist spot under National Rural Employment Guarantee Scheme (NREGS) during the financial year 2008-09. No doubt Govt. has been playing a tremendous role to bring the rural people into proper develop stage, but due to many factors the district is still lagging behind in industrial promotion. Here the significant lies in establishment of new enterprises and to promote the level of existence of the existing enterprises.

## Review of Literature

The whole idea of entrepreneurship has been spread by North East Council (NEC), Shillong in the year 1972. A pioneering initiative was taken by NEC to develop over 5000 entrepreneurs in the north eastern region during seventh Five Year Plan (1985-1990) through training and counseling intervention. This is true that Assam is an agrarian place, so traditional agricultural industries can be established with own initiative to provide goods and services at a lower cost.

The people of the district of Nalbari are engaged in various entrepreneurial activities such as in bamboo products, brass and bell metal products, broom stick, Kouna weaving, fruit processing, agricultural activities, fish rearing , poultry farming etc. Since majority of the people are living in the rural area, so rural entrepreneurship can be considered as an instrument to pick up the growth of rural economy. The emerging industrial scenario of the north east calls for qualitative improvement to be brought about in the complexion of the small enterprise sector with competitive ability and also in the strategies of entrepreneurship development. To achieve sustained growth and put a nation on the fast track of development it is important that there should be productive utilization of resources both human and natural. In this context, entrepreneurship has found greater relevance in the present economic context and looked upon as a solution of some major economic bottlenecks.

## An Empirical Study

The unequal distribution of population and the rural-urban divide have also led to a disparity in the employment opportunities thus affecting the per capita income of the state while schemes like NREGS ( National Rural Employment Guarantee Scheme) & PMGSY ( Pradhan Mantri Gram Sadak Yojana) have managed to increase employment opportunities significantly in Assam, the impact of these two ambitious scheme has been more pronounced in the rural areas and some of the most backward districts of Assam have witnessed reduction in the unemployment problem.

In order to know the prospect and problems of the entrepreneurs in the district, a random selection was done based on certain criteria like population, awareness of the youth, status of the entrepreneurs etc. It also helps to visualize the picture of the industry sector in the study area. Let me give the status of the entrepreneurs which is depicted in the table given below:

**TABLE: 2**

| No. of entrepreneurs | Location | Type | Activity | Income(in Rupees Per month) |
|---|---|---|---|---|
| 10 | Tihu | Service/ Manufacturing | Furniture, weaving, farming etc. | 4000-7000 |
| 10 | Mukalmua | Service | Electrical, stationery etc. | 3500-5000 |
| 5 | Jagara | Service | Engineering works, furniture etc. | 5000-6000 |
| 5 | Mugkuchi | Manufacturing/ Service | Brass and Bell metal products | 6500-8000 |
| 10 | Tilana | Manufacturing | Bamboo products | 10000-15000 |
| 10 | Chatemari | Manufacturing | Weaving | 12000-15000 |

**Source: Field Survey in the district of Nalbari, December-2009.**

From the above information, it is observed that the entrepreneurs are now almost self dependent and satisfactory in terms of their income and even they could provide employment opportunity to the others. When they were asked about their problem, they replied that due to seasonal variation sometimes their income come down and due to financial problem they could not cope up with the market. They supply their products to the city area and in the local market.

It is to be worth mention here that Self Help Groups are extensively introduced everywhere in the rural area of Assam through DRDA. We have visited a few randomly selected blocks in the district to know how far the rural man and women are involved in SHG activity. It has been observed that SHG can be formed both by male and female. The SHG groups were registered in their blocks and they were performed through training, funding categorizing into two steps such as: 1st grading and 2nd grading. In the 1st step they were approved an amount of Rs.25000 out of which Rs.10000 are allowed as subsidy and remaining amount is as financial assistance to the groups which is refundable. If they could disburse as per the terms and conditions, they were inspired for 2nd grading in which they are approved maximum amount of Rs.250000 depending on their projects.

For all the above entrepreneurial activities the groups are need to be monitored through Government officials so that they go ahead in their operation. They still required some training to motivate and overcome the first stage.

## Insitutional Impact

Entrepreneurship can be considered as a backbone of the nation for economic development. It has been well known fact that the level of economic growth of a region to a large extent depends on the level of entrepreneurial activities. The myths that entrepreneurs are born, no more hold goods, rather it is well recognized now that the entrepreneurs can be created and nurtured through appropriate interventions in the form of EDP. In the era of Liberalization, privatization and globalization along with IT revolution, capable entrepreneurs are making use of the opportunities emerging from the evolving scenario. However a large segment of the population, particularly in the industrially backward regions/ rural areas is generally lagging behind in taking the advantage of the opportunities. Therefore, there is a need to provide need base training to such people in order to bring them into mainstream in the ongoing process of economic growth. The steps for entrepreneurship development have now taken countrywide movement. Entrepreneurship Development Programme is now recognized by both Govt. and Non-Government organizations as an extensive usability for proper industrialization. The institutions like State Institute of Rural Development (SIRD), National Small Industries Corporation (NSIC), Development Institute-Micro, Small and Medium Enterprises (DI-MSME), North East Development Financial Institute (NEDFI), Indian Institute of

Entrepreneurship (IIE), District Industries Centre (DIC), etc. are directly or indirectly involved in helping the youth to take up entrepreneurial activities and also in smooth running of their functions. Now a day's NGOs are coming up to explore the knowledge and capability to enhance the productivity of the traditional method of production of the various rural entrepreneurs. They conduct different EDP and awareness camp in their area to become self dependent who are really interested for hard work. The institutional influences in entrepreneurship development in the district have been shown below:

**Table: 3**

**Institutions**

| Institutions /Organization | Name of EDP | Course name | Venue | Year | Duration | Total No. of Participants |
|---|---|---|---|---|---|---|
| DIC, Nalbari | EDP | PMRY training | Office, DIC | 2006-07 | 30 days | 116 |
| DIC, Nalbari | EDP | PMRY training | Office, DIC, | 2007-08 | 30 days | 110 |
| KVIC, Mukalmua | EDP | SFRUTI | Barkhetry Unnayan Samittee, Mukalmua | 2008 (a project of 5 years) | 30 days | 30 |
| NSIC | Cluster Development on Bamboo | Bamboo product | Nalbari | 2007 | 3 days | 135 |
| IIE | Entrepreneurial Education (EE) | Entrepreneurial awareness camp | MNC Ballika Mahavidyaloy | 2006 | 3 days | 75 |

**Source: Offices of the institutions mentioned in the table, Nov-December, 2009**

Besides the above activities performed by institutions, few of the Entrepreneurship Development Training were as follows:

1. Cane and Bamboo thread based training
2. Screen printing
3. Employment cum income generation training based on local resources.
4. Electronic home appliances.
5. Scooter motor cycle repairing
6. Electronic motor rewinding and repairing
7. Common Interested group training
8. Skill development training etc.

**SME Projects sanctioned by NEDFi in the north east India, 2009**

**Table: 4**

| State | 2003-04 | 2004-05 | 2005-06 | 2006-07 | 2007-08 | Total |
|---|---|---|---|---|---|---|
| Arunachal Pradesh | 11 | 21 | 37 | 55 | 16 | 163 |
| Assam | 91 | 129 | 110 | 98 | 66 | 701 |
| Manipur | 8 | 10 | 8 | 15 | 18 | 113 |
| Meghalaya | 19 | 19 | 16 | 14 | 10 | 122 |
| Mizoram | 48 | 5 | 45 | 17 | 1 | 147 |
| Nagaland | 8 | 9 | 8 | 19 | 20 | 119 |
| Sikkim | 12 | 36 | 23 | 27 | 18 | 116 |
| Tripura | 7 | 9 | 38 | 55 | 20 | 142 |
| Total | 204 | 238 | 285 | 300 | 169 | 1623 |

**Source: Effectiveness of State sponsorship and intervention in small and medium enterprises (SMEs): A strategic insight into the working of support variables in the sector: By Borkakoty Aparajita, Goswami Deka Darshana.**

It is fact that development of entrepreneurship has emerged as a national movement due to its strengths to solve the problem of unemployment and poverty. It is against this back ground, several self help employment and antipoverty programmes like PMRY, TRYSEM, etc. involving some entrepreneurial activities were introduced by the Govt. as a tool of bottom up mode of development.

## Limitations

Based on the information's collected, the majority people are in rural areas which is 97.61% and only 2.39% in urban area, the role of rural entrepreneurship can't ignored in providing employment opportunities and in income generation to make them self dependent. The district is industrially very less developed due to improper utilization of the talents of the educated youth. At the same time, it is important to say that Nalbari has relatively higher percentage of educated youth however the education in all fairness does not compare with the rest of the nation, as most of the youth are educated up to the 10th class, which is not of much use. Further the education is mostly in Assamese medium and most of the youth have very poor knowledge of written and spoken English. The trainees among the first generation entrepreneurs, 40% trainees unable to start the ventures as which need to be guided to reach breakeven stage. It is a fact that some unregistered units are also operating their functions. There is a discrepancy between the registered enterprises and the actual existence of the business firms. The reason being that many such enterprises closed down their businesses long back but their registration has not been cancelled in the official registered.

The problems facing in the study area are stated below:

1. Lack of awareness about the scope in entrepreneurship sector.
2. Improper infrastructure facility
3. Poor knowledge of project preparation and financing
4. Lack of technical use in the traditional method of production.
5. Financially very weak
6. Lack of support from outside
7. Fear of competitiveness
8. Fear of failure in the near future
9. Family constraints
10. Fear of terrorism
11. Big time gap between project sanction and implementation
12. Lack of monitoring services.
13. Reduction of land
14. More interested in Govt. jobs etc.

## Conclusions and Suggestions

Entrepreneurs are the ambassador of modern economic system. Realizing the urgent need to generate employment and hasten the rate of industrialization, Assam Chief Minister Tarun Gogoi already announced new industrial policy in the year 2009, which stress the importance on promoting Micro, Small and Medium sized enterprises as the big industrial group too keen on investing in the state.

The AIIDC (Assam Industrial Infrastructure Development Corporation) has been allotted 400 Bighas of land to set up an industrial park on the outskirts of Guwahati which will secure investment inflow amounting Rs. 2000 crore for Assam by the year 2011. Again the development of entrepreneurship depends on the holistic co-ordinate efforts of different departments and professional agencies, financial institutions and entrepreneurs. However it is one sided responsibility of entrepreneurs which have to take right direction to make the unit sustainable. The acceptability of entrepreneurial activities will depend on the positive mindset of the youth. PMRY is another scheme which was implemented in the year 1993 to create and provide sustainable self-employment opportunities to one million educated unemployed youth in the country during the 8th five year plan.

In order to create awareness and to attract suitable persons, the institutions which are mentioned already have conducted meaningful training for the youth. It is necessary to tie up with the development organizations to fulfill the dreams of the entrepreneurs and to help the first generation entrepreneurs to start new ventures in their interested area. It was observed among the beneficiaries that the first aim was to absorb in Govt. service rather than starting enterprises. In this situation the bankers should come forward to help and motivate the skill entrepreneurs by supporting financially in expansion their area. Sometimes the entrepreneurs need to give mortgage to sanction the loan from banks, and as a result real entrepreneurs are not fully supported by banks. Therefore a policy should be framed for easy financing to help the rural entrepreneurs, and then they will come up with full spirit of work. A suggestive role by the institutions must be played which will improve the economic status of the rural masses and remove the economic imbalances between rural and urban. Some suggestions to enhance the quality of the entrepreneurs and to reduce the unemployment problem of the state are enumerated below:

1. Awareness camp weekly/fortnightly, monthly should be held in the rural area.
2. Need base training is necessary to the entrepreneurs in vital area of business operation.
3. Finance is life blood for every enterprise which must be allotted to the needy.
4. More attention should pay for utilization of local resources.
5. Technology must be upgraded as and when necessary.

6. It should be released at an early date doing a survey on the entrepreneurs.
7. Quality products are to be produced by the local producers to attract locality and others.
8. Entrepreneurship courses should be introduced right from primary level of education.
9. EDP training should be given to the educated youth immediately after completion of the study.
10. Create new ideas to motivate the rural people for entrepreneurial career.

Hence, rural entrepreneurship through development in SME sectors can be considered as a vital element to accelerate the movement of entrepreneurs in the nation which will also reduce the unemployment problem and regional imbalances between rural and urban area.

## References

1. Khanka. S.S.; Entrepreneurial Development; S. Chand & Company Ltd, Ram Nagar, New Delhi; 2004.
2. Kalita J.C.; Self- Employment Through Entrepreneurship; Indian Institute of Entrcpreneurship, City Graphics and printers, Ganeshguri Chariali, Guwahati, 2006.
3. Dr. Bhatnagar Bhawna and Budhirja; Entrepreneurship Development and Small Business Management; Vaya Education of India, Darya Ganj, New Delhi, 2009.
4. Mali D. D.; Entrepreneurship Development in North East; Indian Institute of Entrepreneurship; Exclusive Advertising (P) Ltd., Guwahati-1.

# 21

# Networks, Micro and Small Enterprises (MSE's) and Performance in Kenya

***Abstract***

Small and Micro Enterprise in Kenya as well as in the other developing economies are faced with serious challenges in their growth and productivity path. The most appropriate and manageable route to growth and survival lies in networking. This paper examines the role of informal personal networks in determining Micro Small Enterprises (MSE's) success in Kenya. It adopts the network perspective theoretical approach. Empirically, the paper finds that MSE's in Kenya get around market failures and lack of formal institutions through entrepreneurial personal network as a copying strategy in the process of global transformation to bridge the entrepreneurial global divide.

General hypothesis predicting the *'likelihood of MSE's with better network performing better'* is supported by performance models though pro-poor growth is evident with an average business performance. Network strategies to promote small enterprises are recommended to policy makers, donors and actors in the field against those of the failed traditional strategies. However, there are few empirical studies available in this area particularly in less developed countries; therefore further research is necessary in this direction.

## Introduction

It is no doubt that the role of entrepreneurship in the emerging economies such like Kenya cannot be undermined as a number of research in this field has pointed out (G.o.K 1999, McCormick 2009, McPherson 1996). In Kenya, MSE's1 plays a crucial role in the process of development as findings from the 1999 National MSE Baseline Survey show that MSE's activities are contributing to at least 18.4 percent of country's Gross Domestic Product (GDP) and 25 percent of non-agricultural GDP; employing approximately 17 percent of the total labour force from which 64 percent were in the urban employment in 2002 (Karekezi and Majoro 2002). In terms of income contribution, workers in the MSE sector earn an average income per month, which is two and a half times more than the minimum statutory wages in the formal sector. Employment creation in the formal private sector decelerated by 67.7 percent (- from 74.0 thousand new jobs in 2007 to 23.8 thousand new jobs in 2008- ) but employment in the informal2 private sector is estimated to have expanded from 7.5 million in 2007 to 7.9 million in 2008. New jobs created generally in the whole country declined from 485.5 thousand in 2007 to 467.3 thousand in 2008 (G.o.K 2008). Given the importance of this sector in areas of employment creation, growth and poverty alleviation, it is important that it is efficiently managed for effective results within the broader over all objectives. Efficient management has been lacking also due to external factors that are beyond the owner-manager's control.

These factors are inherent in the institutional environment of Kenya which favours larger firms. In addition, ongoing changes in the business environment with regard to globalization of markets act as a further challenge to firms' growth prospects in Kenya. In addition, liberalization of markets has made competition real among firms and only those with a competitive edge can survive. Policy recommendations of the government of Kenya as contained in its 7th National Development Plan on Divestiture and subsequently in Sessional paper No. 2 of 2005, advocates for the government to take the leading role by providing an enabling environment for MSE's market operations. This will require the establishment of infrastructure for access to markets, provision of work site structures, dissemination of market information through networks and innovation amongst other well-known strategies.

With all the above in mind, MSE's are expected to add value to their owners and to the society in general but this has not been the case in Kenya. This is further proved by considering the number of MSE's that manage to grow in terms of sales, profit and assets as well as the number of people it employs. The MSEs' churning rate has been worrying for this sector and as such needs a quick redress by all the stakeholders both in government and private sector (McPherson 1996). While these challenges and drawbacks are real, MSE's Owner- Managers need not to sit back in the short run as these problems persist but should network and come up with various strategic options to address unfavorable conditions so as to secure a more conducive, stable working economic environment within this sector in Kenya. Empirical research has shown that the economic success of MSE's in many countries depends on informal personal networks. Long term business relationships emerge as a result of failures in both market and institutional settings which is characteristic of Least Developed Countries (LDC) countries. MSE's in Kenya get around such market failures and lack of formal institutions by developing relations with the outsiders through a support mechanism provided either by friends, family members, relatives or neighbours. In other cases cooperative relations among groups of MSE's organized in business networks and in associations or local community organizations perform these functions. Prominent examples of such private orderings have been found in the support networks and informal relationships in Europe, America and Asia (Birley 1985, Bryson et al 1993, Burt 2009, Curran et al 1993, Goodman and Bamford 1990, Rabelloti 1995,Steier and Greenwood 2000, Uzzi 2004).The evidence that private institutional arrangements among the MSE's facilitate their performance in many countries fits a theory of the firm that views the enterprise as a collection of contracts and relationships between the firm and various stakeholders from the external environment (Coarse 1937, 1988; Alchian and Demsetz 1972; Williamson 1985)3. Institutional gap left by the government of Kenya has proactively made the MSE's to circumvent the risks involved through informal institutional settings of social networks4. Risks are as well inherent in such arrangements but it is the ideal Mechanisms through which the MSE's can operate under such environment (Birley et al. 1991).In the next section a theoretical concept is developed which features the choice of network variables as drawn from the dynamic network perspective theories or literature on Marketing, Organizational and sociological economics to shed light on how exceptionally high level of poverty can be overcome in Kenya. This recapitulates into the description of the hypothesis then methodology. Lastly the results are discussed on how the network structure impact on MSE's business performance and sustainability and their policy implications.

## Theoretical Concept

To understand network requires a deep understanding of dynamic pattern of networks given that they don't evolve overnight (Venkataraman 1989). With respect to the instrumental role of social capital, we adopt a Marketing Network Model developed by Hakansson and Johanson (1988), which reconciles both Social network perspective (Aldrich, Zimmer 1986, Birley 1985, 1990, Birley, Cromie 1988, Granovetter 1976, 1985, Johannisson 1986, 1987a, 1988 1995b, Uzzi 1996, 1999, Veciana, Clarke 1999) and Resource Dependency Theory (Butler and Sohod 1995; Pfeffer and Salancik 1978, 2003). The Marketing Network Model is an amalgamation of these two distinct theoretical perspectives. The study uses the integrated network theoretical approaches of Marketing Network Model on the argument that, small firms cannot perform better without direct or indirect network relationships hence our hypotheses is formulated on this basis.

Researchers have used different types of theoretical approaches in order to analyze and understand networking and small business performance as there is no single general theory of small business networks. Economic functions can be performed either within the boundaries of hierarchical firms (within the organization) or by market processes that cut across these hierarchical boundaries5; either hierarchies or markets. For small firms, the economic functions and transactions within the boundaries of hierarchical firms are either impossible or extremely difficult because small firms, being small and alone, are inherently lacking in resources thereby causing higher production costs. Market mechanism is also not a better solution because perfect competition6 is far from reality especially in developing countries like Kenya. Perfect competition causes higher transaction costs. Hence, it is clear those small firms find it difficult to perform their economic activities either at the level of hierarchical firm (or bureaucracy) or market. Given this, small firms in developing countries need support to compete and survive in their businesses. Networking is one of the best solutions given in the literature for the development of small firms in LDCs because networking7 lies between the hierarchy (or bureaucracy) and the market (Borg 1991; Jarillo 1988; Thorelli 1986). Hierarchies and markets are regarded as being the polar ends of a variety of governance options (Butler 1991; Williamson 1985). In the network, the logic of exchange differs from the economic logic of market and hierarchy. The logic of exchange of networks considered in this study is that of 'social embeddedness' because ongoing social ties shape actors expectations and opportunities in ways that differ from the economic logic of market behavior (Granovetter 1985, Uzzi 1996). A small firm without networking with its external actors is bound to fail. Networking is the best solution for small firm development (Borg 1991, Donckels and Lambrecht 1995, Gibb, 1993; Johannisson, 1990b; Szarka 1990). At one hand of firm's hierarchy level, firms are too small and thus growth may be hindered by lack of resources. At the market level, on the other hand, transaction costs to obtain necessary resources are extremely high. Therefore small firms have to obtain resources and support from 'outsiders' or external actors. Thus, small firms are dependent on other external actor, which is called 'interdependence'. Hence, to study small firms and entrepreneurship, this research views focal firms within their external environment. Within this integrated model, Resource Dependency Approach examines the behavior of a firm within its environment on the basis of resource dependence meanwhile Social Network Approach looks at how network relationships influence small business performance and its application to the economic phenomena. In addition, Social Network Approach views entrepreneurship as an act of creation and small business as a way of life that is different from the rational economic behavior. As with Social Network Approach, actors and their exchange relationships are very important for small firm development. In this framework, entrepreneurship is seen as an ongoing process of venturing forth through personal networking8 in which actors, resources, exchange relations and activities are the major network elements.

On the whole, there are two major arguments behind the concept of networking. Firstly, since market transactions tend to become costly, firms attempt to overcome transaction costs by networking. Secondly, in order to perform, firms need various kinds of resources. Small firms, in particular, do not have all these resources fully at their disposal. Firms gather these resources from 'outsiders' or, in other words 'external actors'. As most resources are controlled by external actors, a small firm always depends on its outside actors.

Therefore, in order to perform economic activities, firms have to enter into relationships with these external or outside actors thereby forming entrepreneurial networks. Firms being heterogeneous in nature, they face different problems and requirements in different phases9 of their development.

Therefore the firms need different resources and support in different stages of business growth. At the start –up phase the business needs resources but an entrepreneur does not have all the necessary resources needed to start the business. This he can acquire through personal networks (Birley and Cromie 1988, Curran et al 1993, Ostgaard and Birley 1996). Networks are not static; they are dynamic (Birley and Cromie 1988, Butler and Hansen 1991) as relations are continuously constructed and reconstructed during interactions (Grabher 1993:3). It is very common for small entrepreneurs in Kenya to follow evolutionary network model to meet different needs of different phases of entrepreneurship as other writers suggest. At the Entrepreneurial stage or phase, the entrepreneurs discuss with friends, relatives and formal co-workers before they practically start their businesses. Besides, these networks also encourage new entrepreneurs. This is the stage where businesses are developed and social support is sought (Butler and Hansen 1991; Bridge et al. 1998; Larson and Starr 1993). Professional and organizational actors play a very small role in the case of Kenya's MSE's when compared to other phases10 as at the second stage they never engage professionals but make use of friends and relatives to do the professional work for them if any.

## Development of the hypothesis

The study brings forth its three major hypotheses out of which eight subhypothesis are developcd to help us understand fully the impact of networks on micro small enterprises in Kenya. The study seeks to test the following hypotheses:

**Hypothesis 1:** Small firms engage in local, homogeneous networks among themselves to cope with uncertainty and risk.

**Hypothesis 2:** Heterogeneous networks which include non-local partners stabilize performance outcomes.

In this second hypothesis we deal with how the entrepreneur having acquired the resource moves up the hierarchy and his/her problem now is extending his/her market through network thereby he/she gets into by subcontracting with outsiders in the second phase of the businesses. He makes use of the elements of network to carry on his activities by extending his network. Dependent Variable here is performance and sustainability measured in terms of the market expansion or as well profit and sale can be used. But the independent variables to be measured here is the network density of activities of business focused network with regard to money, information and nonmaterial support.

**Hypothesis 3:** Networking with interest groups influences their agenda and actions and therefore benefits small businesses. In this hypothesis it is assumed that an enterprise with more networks relations benefits more than the one with low network density through resource support from outside actors which ultimately help improve their business performance.

Eight sub-hypothesis is set for their analysis and as drawn from the 3 main hypotheses by linking them to the dependent variable of performance measurements. The dependent variable growth is dichotomous (growth, no growth).Growth is used here as a performance indicator given that performance is a relative term.

**Sub-hypothesis (a):** Owners' Membership in various support groups or clubs and societies has a positive impact on the Business' performances;

**Sub-hypothesis (b):** Consultation with family members has a positive impact on the performance of the business;

**Sub-hypothesis (c):** Consultation with friends has a positive impact on the performance of the Business;

**Sub-hypothesis (d):** Use of external consultants is positively related to the performance of the Business;

**Sub-hypothesis (e):** Attendance at seminars' has a positive impact on the business performance;

**Sub-hypothesis (f):** Participation in trade fairs is positively related to business performance;

**Sub-hypothesis (g):** Trade, Exhibition and Fare are positively associated with growth of the firm;

**Sub-hypothesis (h):** Advertisement has appositive impact on the business performance;

At the same time, we also expect; Hypothesis: The relations with other entrepreneurs *(No contact/ Immediate Neighbourhood, Local surroundings .e.g.*

*Village/ Small town/ Wards/ Quarter, District, Regional, Kenya wide, International)* are boosted by other network elements *(memberships in various support groups, clubs and societies, consultation with relative, consultation with friends, external consultation, attending seminars, and participating trade fairs/ exhibition; Advertisement)*; (i & j)

***Dependent Variable***

Performance and sustainability measured in terms of profits terms, Sales made and expansion of the market. Note that these financial indicators are used for growth of the small firms and by extension satisfy the 'if' condition for performance in the small business case. The firm sustainability is achieved when correlation between performance and networks is positive and significant at a given level of significance. Whereby from the good performance an entrepreneur can climb the hierarchy of net works and back forth in a circular manner.

### *Independent Variables*

The independent variables are: social networks, supporting networks, and interfirm networks. For the correlation measures, the study used network densities for social, support, and inter-firm networks. In the case of probability analysis, the study used networks as dummy variables; dummy (social): 1 = if the entrepreneur had social network relations (yes), 0 = otherwise (no); dummy (supporting): 1 = if the entrepreneur had support network relations (yes), 0 = otherwise (no); and dummy (inter-firm): 1 = if the entrepreneur had inter-firm network relations (yes), 0 = otherwise (no).

### *Control Variable*

Before testing our hypotheses, it was important to ensure that the potential effect of the other factors was minimized. Several other enterprise related factors (such as firm and market locations, number of employees, and types of businesses) and entrepreneurial related factors (such as gender, age, place of birth, education, and work experience) were therefore statistically controlled for in the estimations.

## Research Methods

### *The Population and Sample*

The population of this study is Micro small enterprises in Kenya estimated to be

1.3 Million based on the MSEs Baseline Survey carried out by the government of Kenya in 1999 once and has not been carried out again (CBS, K-Rep/ICEG 1999 pp. 17,105). The population frame which targets those small enterprises in the big towns, peri-urban, urban and rural areas was selected on the basis of this research framework and comprised the micro small enterprises in four districts of Kenya based on their location, size and region. Then the research sample was selected from the population frame by using a standard sampling method.

### *The Sampling Method*

A total of 400 firms were sampled through a multi-stage cluster sampling method. Four strata were chosen from eight clusters covering areas; for example, cities; of which Nairobi was chosen to be representative of all the major cities in Kenya, towns; of which Kisumu town was chosen to be representative of all the major town in Kenya having a population above 10,000 people, urban; of which Eldoret was chosen to be representative of all urban areas in Kenya with a population of between 2000 people to 10,000 people, and lastly rural; of which Kakamega was chosen to be representative of all the rural areas in Kenya and the choice of Kakamega was made as informed by the BIOTA4C11 project and the other geographical activities taking place in Kakamega.

From these stratified clusters, 400 MSE's were chosen based on their demographic and economic characteristics with each stratum producing 100 MSE's. A bigger percentage of the total MSE populations of the small enterprises (61 per cent) are concentrated in the rural areas and the type of industry in which most of them are involved in are Service industry (40 per cent) followed by Manufacturing (23.2 per cent). The response rate of the MSE's owner or Managers was impressive with 99 per cent response rate. Due to practical difficulties12 *(money, time, and transport),* we were restricted to this particular number of the sample size despite the immense cooperation received among the entrepreneurs.

**Table I. Type of enterprise and sampling area *(Clusters)***

| | Sampling Area of the respondents | | | | | | | | | |
|---|---|---|---|---|---|---|---|---|---|---|
| | Town | | Urban | | Peri-urban | | Rural | | Total | |
| | n | % | n | % | N | % | n | % | n | % |
| Manufacturing | 45 | 11.2 | 10 | 2.5 | 23 | 5.8 | 15 | 3.8 | 93 | 23.2 |
| Service (Incl. Repair, health and Beauty ,I.T) | 32 | 8.0 | 58 | 14.5 | 41 | 10.2 | 29 | 7.2 | 160 | 40.0 |
| Trade | 9 | 2.2 | 16 | 4.0 | 16 | 4.0 | 18 | 4.5 | 59 | 14.8 |
| Agricultural Processing | 3 | 0.8 | 1 | 0.2 | 2 | 0.5 | 4 | 1.0 | 10 | 2.5 |
| Handicraft | 10 | 2.5 | 8 | 2.0 | 3 | 0.8 | 25 | 6.2 | 46 | 11.5 |
| Food and beverage/Restaurant. | 1 | 0.2 | 7 | 1.8 | 15 | 3.8 | 9 | 2.2 | 32 | 8.0 |
| Total | 100 | 25 | 100 | 25 | 100 | 25 | 100 | 25 | 400 | 100 |

Source: Survey Data (2008-2009)

## Measures of Dependent Variables

### *Variables and Variable Measurement*

Determining the variables to use for such kind of a study is an upheaval task because most of the variables are social relationships. The measurement of social relationships has always been a nagging and unresolved problem (Hall et al. 1977:462). For this study purpose the following general questions13 were asked to the entrepreneurs about their networking activities; for instance- how Sampling Area of the respondents many business partners do you have? Where they are mostly situated? For how long have you been cooperating with your partner firms? For which purpose do you cooperate with other firms? Are you a member of any support group? Who is your main source of input? Who is your main customer? Do you have any subcontracting arrangements for inputs or orders received from clients? How do you set your prices? What are the main methods of advertisement of your product and services? Have you sought and received any formal assistance for any of the above problems for your business in the last 2 years? In order to obtain a better and deep understanding about the external actors and their roles, respondents were given five choices of answers; not important, fairly important, average, important, and very important. Besides, they were also given a choice of two sets of six persons to whom they could turn to most likely for business related advice or any other help. The main aim of this questionnaire was to collect information on the relationships between respondents and these two set of persons.

### *Dependent Variables of the Study*

*Performance and Sustainability:* Based on a review of the literature (Donckels and Lambrecht, 1995; Hansen, 1995; Ostgaard and Birley, 1996) pertinent to the measurement of performance, two objectives of measures of growth were included; sales growth and increase in profitability over a given time period. In addition, market expansion *(Local, regional and national)* is used as a business performance measure. Studies (Johanson and Mattson, 1993) in the field of marketing and international business have identified a positive relationship between network formation and market expansion of small businesses.

Growth of Sale = [{(sale in Current Season – Sale in Previous Season)/ Sale in Previous season}/2]* 100 .................. .................. (i) Growth of profit = [{(Profit in Current Season – Profit in Previous Season)/Profit in Previous Season}/2]* 100 ......... .................. (ii)

However the big challenge facing many MSE's is that the entrepreneurs do not properly keep business records related to their daily business operations due to ignorance14,therefore obtaining financial details for sales and profit is foolhardy.

To overcome this agony for the MSE's in Kenya, the study tried to get the relevant data on sales and profits by asking respondents their perception with respect to last year business performance to that of the current one as expected for next year. To capture this categorically the respondents were asked about whether their sales or profits vary over time on a seasonal15 or monthly basis. The figures got were compared to the performance and sustainability parameters for those particular firms who provided the required information.

***Independent Variables***

**Network Density:** Network density is a very important indicator measure in evaluating entrepreneurial networks in the firms three different phases. It is generally measured as the proportion of ties present out of all-possible ties (Burt 1992; Greve 1995; Duysters 1995). Network densities also can be obtained by dividing the number of existing alliances among actors in the network by the total number of possible links between those actors16. For all the practical reasons, network density is very difficult to exhaustively measure due to geocentricism of human beings (Greve 1995 ;) where only relations that are directly connected to ego are visible as networks are defined from a focal person's perspective.

**Network Size:** The larger the network, the greater is the number of network members who provide emotional support, goods and services. Entrepreneurs with large networks may win both ways; not only do they have more potential providers of support in their networks, but also each number of their network is more likely to be supportive (Wellman and Gulia 1993).Network size was obtained by asking respondents to estimate the number of people or organization with whom they dealt with in business activities, resource support and discussions of their business, information on market, technology and group membership. Therefore, the size of entrepreneurial networks may be one of the most important variables to explain the success of a small enterprise (Aldrich,

Rosen and Woodward, 1987; Hansen 1995; Johannisson 1986; Greve 1995). Entrepreneurs identify product or service ideas, access to markets, information, money and other resources in their environments, and they also gain access to these resources through various members of their networks.

The importance of size is recognized by almost all writers, but there have been significant shifts recently in how the term is used. One usage of size focuses upon the number of ties or links between an organization and outside contacts.

These approaches converge on the basic idea that what matters is the number of links between an organization and its context is that; the greater the number of links, i.e. the more extensive the network, the better for the organization, irrespective of whether the links are direct or indirect (Larson 1992).

### *Control Variables of the Study*

Control variables help us to minimize the potential effect of the other factor that may be considered to affect the outcome of the other variables in a relationship therefore they should be controlled for in the estimation. Previous researches (Donckels and Lambrecht 1997; Sarder, Ghosh and Rose 1997) have suggested several enterprise- and entrepreneurial –related factors that affect growth. Based on the same, the following enterprise-related factors were included as control variables in this study:

1. Service sector are known to be growth oriented and solid in network therefore it was found prudent to include them (Donckels 1995; Lambrecht 1997) than Manufacturing and trade.
2. Firm's size is used as a control variable because previous network studies have found that the larger small enterprises to be more in the growth league (Donckels and Lambrecht 1995; Mohan-Neill 1995). It is therefore important to ensure that the potential effect of the size of a firm is minimized before testing our hypotheses.
3. Firms' location is important for network formation and business performances. Previous studies found that firms that are inside industrial estates are more in the growth league. Those firms have a better potential for networking (Grabher 1993b; Lomi and Grandi 1997).
4. When one analyses the performance of small enterprises and network formation, one can not overlook the possible impact of family workers in the business. Family influence is very strong in small Businesses (Chu 1996; Johannisson 1990a). Mostly they are used during peak and off seasons as unpaid in cash to ease the work pressure. Therefore, the impact of family worker has also to be minimized before testing our hypotheses.
5. The mentioned entrepreneur -related factors have an impact on the growth orientation of a small enterprise and network formation

(Donckels and Lambrecht 1995, 1997). The quality of the network is highly dependent upon given personal skills and attributes (Johannisson 1988: 85).

6. Entrepreneurs who have lower education and highly trained are more likely to be in the growth league (Donckels and Lambrecht 1995) .The same research on network formation points out that there is a causal relationship between network formation, growth, and level of education.
7. Gender composition of networks is significantly different for men and women (Singh and Reynolds 2001). The present study uses these variables as control factors since it is necessary to make sure that the potentially moderating effect of those factors is minimized.

***Model specification***

Given the nature of our data which is, qualitative, binary and categorical, a logit 17 or regression techniques was used to analyze the data. Drawn from logit, an empirical model used to test the effects of network strategies on firm performance and sustainability as we control for other firm and entrepreneurial characteristics is stated as:

$$\Delta Y_{ts} = (Y_{ts_2}) - (Y_{ts_1}) = \alpha_1 + \varepsilon Y_{ts_1} + \gamma Y_{ts_2} + \delta \sum_{j=1}^{3} D_{Strat_j} + X_t \beta + \mu_t$$

Where $\Delta Y_{ts}$ is the growth (yes=1) or no growth (No= 0) of firm ith as measured by the financial performance indicators of $(Y_{ts_1})$ and $(Y_{ts_2})$ denoting sales made by firm ith and profit made by firm ith respectively between the high and low seasons. While D_Strat.j are the network relationship dummy variables of strategies adopted with j=1, 2 and 3 to represent Social network, support networks and business networks respectively and $x_t$ 's representing the explanatory variables of the network elements and the is the error term to capture for all the unobserved and control variables and $\alpha_1$ is the network intercept with $\varepsilon$, $\gamma$, $\delta$, $\beta$ being the network coefficients.

## Data Set Analysis: Empirical Evidence

The empirical results of the regression models for the dependant, independent and control variables are presented here as empirical evidence. Their relationships are traced on how they relate with each other on building the networks for MSE's in Kenya. This is followed by a detailed discussion and conclusions of these findings as to whether the relations exhibited consequently has an impact on the performance, growth and sustainability of the MSE's in Kenya under the given institutional environment. As mentioned before, the dependent variable of the first hypotheses was identified as firm growth and performance (in terms of profitability and in terms of sales) and market expansion (National, regional and local). The firms were divided into three groups (growth, neutral and decline firms) on the basis of the respondents' answers and data availability as Table II below show. From the table, 58.8 per cent of firms report growth category, while 9.8 per cent of them are reported 'not growth'. 31.5 per cent of them are in neutral. In sales term, 40.5 per cent are in the neutral growth category as sales increase in 57.0 per cent of firms.

2.5 per cent recorded sales declining during the two season's periods of high and low (Growth is in financial terms of which in sale terms it is measured by using available records of which most of the small firms do not own record therefore the entrepreneurs' point of view is taken into consideration).

**Table II. Performance of Small Enterprises**

| | in Profitability term % | in sales term % | Major Market location % |
|---|---|---|---|
| Growth | 58.75 | 57.00 | National 20.75 |
| Neutral | 31.50 | 40.50 | Local 45.75 |
| Decline | 9.75 | 2.50 | Regional 33.50 |
| Source: Survey Data (2008-2009) | | | |

Note: The firms were divided into three groups (growth, neutral, and decline firms) on the basis of the respondents' answers and data availability.

In the major market location, 20.8 per cent of the small business represented growth and 33.5 per cent represented a decline with a higher percentage of 45.8 stagnating at a neutral state. The situation can further be understood by considering the market segment in which these enterprises operate be it at the local, regional or National Level. The models of growth in financial terms (Model 1), in sale terms (Model 2) and market expansion (Model 3) are presented in Table III. Entrepreneur-related and enterprise-related factors were used as control variables in all models.

## Table III. Ordered *Logit* Regression Analysis of Business Performance

| DEPENDENT VARIABLE ▶ / INDEPENDENT VARIABLE ▼ | Growth Models† *(Ordered Logit)* Financial | | Market Expansion‡ Model 3 *(Logit)* | | |
|---|---|---|---|---|---|
| (a)Network Elements: | Profit | Sale | Local | Regional | National |
| | Model 1 | Model 2 | | | |
| (i) Membership of a support group (Memb.) | -0.5391474 | -0.412117 | -0.6257845 | 1.127626 | -4.306764* |
| (ii) Consult with Relatives (RltvC.) | 0.1768815 | 0.3213644 | -0.0035988 | 0.2077015 | 4.688457 |
| (iii) Consult with friends (FrndC.) | 0.4204207 | 0.5413413 | -0.7643241* | -2.67127*** | 2.188995* |
| (iv) Sponsor (Spo.) | -0.6301558* | 0.4360656 | -0.7658631* | 1.562125 | 3.946916 |
| (v) External Consultancy (Excon.) | -0.2912984 | 0.2297336 | 0.6087752** | -1.048016* | -0.620859* |
| (vi)Training attendance (Trainat.) | 1.062539*** | -0.8131616** | 0.900166** | -1.385168** | -4.237001*** |
| (vii)Trade Fairs/exhibitions (Exhb.) | -0.8757981* | 0.1488198 | -0.5060612 | 0.7765897 | -4.314818*** |
| (viii) Advertisement linkages (Advert.) | 0.876145** | -0.4422695 | 0.9287112** | -1.136924* | -4.018183*** |
| Local Contacts (LC) | 1.092227*** | 0.2776574 | - | - | - |
| Regional contacts (RC). | 0.0145981 | 0.4474843 | - | - | - |
| Table III. Continued. | | | | | |
| National Contacts (NC) | -1.356309 | 0.5181947 | - | - | - |
| (b)Entrepreneur-related: | | | | | |
| Age (Log form) | -0.2574903 | -0.3141566 | -0.8465496 | 0.4008095 | 5.111433** |
| Gender | 0.4416784* | -0.0293623 | -0.2337811 | -0.1055492 | -4.050044*** |
| Location of the Respondent | -2.06825*** | 0.2434624 | 0.4514045 | 2.635399*** | -4.077537 |
| Educational level | 0.0827355 | 0.0479231 | 0.1825082 | 0.5934178 | 0.5322168* |
| Owner's Period of experience (log form) | 0.1612917 | -0.1033626 | -0.5007559** | -0.0989244 | 5.111433** |
| (c)Enterprise-related: | | | | | |
| Manufacturing Industry (S1) | 0.1445633 | 0.6296169** | -0.2698701 | 0.1677356 | 0.8007031* |
| Service Sector (S2) | -0.077937 | -0.4589423* | -0.4939045* | -1.022068* | 1.368797 |

| < 5 Employees (SE1) | 0.544956 | -0.8335374 | -0.5937174 | 0.632742 | 0.674099 |
|---|---|---|---|---|---|
| > 5 Employees (SE2) | 0.2237928 | -0.1952878 | -0.1158605 | 0.3893944 | -4.110874* |
| Firm's life time (Log form) | -0.0351872 | 0.3125358* | 0.1420394 | 0.493515 | -1.291059 |
| Regular Employees (RE) | 0.0521155 | 0.0197024 | 0.0444308 | - 0.0241193 | 0.056759 |
| Seasonal Employees (SE) | -0.055761* | -0.0009008 | 0.0250711 | 0.0475733 | 0.6124792 |
| **Intercept** | - | - | 4.056091* | - 8.055703* | -56.09511* |
| **Pseudo $R^2$** | 0.1296*** | 0.0692*** | 0.1580*** | 0.2014*** | 0.4893*** |

**Source:** Survey Data (2008-2009) *Note: z-values are in parentheses; N = 386;†Baseline (comparison category) is non-growth group‡ Baseline (comparison category) is Regional market;*** P- value < 0.01-statistically significant at 1%** P- value < 0.05- statistically significant at 5%;*P -value < 0.10- statistically significant at 10%*

The dependent variable of model 1 and 2 are binary choice as 1 for growth, and 0 for otherwise (decline). Model 1 is statistically significant with a moderate goodness of fit as indicated by the value of chi-square (p-value < 0.01, Pseudo R2 = 0.1296). The model tests the impact of network elements on growth. In this model, growth is defined in financial terms of profits (1 = if growth, 0 = otherwise). Model 2 also tests the same impact, but in terms of sales. The second model is also significant at 0.01 levels (p-value < 0.01, Pseudo R2 = 0.0692). Positive relationship between network formation and market expansion of small businesses has been identified by international business and marketing scholars (Johanson and Mattsson 1993). Consequently, in addition to the growth measures (profit and sale), we used market expansion within the seasonal periods as a dependent variable to test our hypothesis. Most of the small enterprises mainly serve the local market. In our multinomial logistic model, model 3, we therefore used regional market as the baseline (comparison category). The baseline (regional market) is very important when the results are interpreted. Our multinomial logistic model is also statistically significant (pvalue <0.01, Pseudo **R2** = 0.2014).

**Table IV. Predicted probabilities**

| DEPENDENT VARIABLE ► / INDEPENDENT VARIABLE ▼ | Growth Models† (Ordered Logit) Financial | | Market Expansion‡ Model 3 (Logit) | | |
|---|---|---|---|---|---|
| | Profit Model 1 | Sale Model 2 | Local | Regional | National |
| (i) Membership of a support group (Memb.) | -0.1219823 | -0.0955673 | -0.1224285 | 0.020988 | - |
| (ii) Consult with Relatives (RltvC.) | 0.041908 | 0.075337 | -0.0007909 | 0.0053108 | 0.0050787 |
| (iii) Consult with friends (FrndC.) | 0.0968764 | 0.1235845 | -0.1817392* | 0.0280143** | 0.0004007 |
| (iv) Sponsor (Spo.) | -0.1427058** | 0.1075258 | -0.1494425** | -0.0272787* | -0.0014332 |
| (v) External Consultancy (Excon.) | -0.0704618 | 0.05534 | 0.1302733** | -0.0763014 | -0.0000402 |
| (vi)Training attendance (Trainat.) | 0.2595442** | -0.1806918** | 0.2135369** | 0.0356637 | - |
| (vii)Trade Fairs/exhibitions (Exhb.) | -0.2155145* | 0.0355592 | -0.1183603 | 0.034191 | - |
| (viii) Advertisement | 0.2133669** | -0.1048577 | 0.2129096** | -0.0445727 | - |

**Source:** Survey Data (2008-2009), *** P- value < 0.01; ** P- value < 0.05; * Pvalue < 0.10 Note: †baseline/ comparison category for growth models (profit and sale) is 'non-growth group'. ‡baseline or comparison category for market expansion is 'regional market'.

Given the difficulties in interpreting the changes in logit, the predicted probabilities were computed to show the marginal effects for all the network elements as Table IV indicates. Half of the sub-hypothesis is statistically insignificant. However we found a positive impact of pro-poor growth for these network formation elements on business performance as expected in the main hypothesis. Meanwhile in terms of firm growth and performance a number of variables are significant e.g. sponsor (14 per cent at $p < 0. 05$), Training and seminar attendance (26 per cent at $p < 0. 05$), Trade fair/Exhibition (22 per cent at $p < 0.1$), advertisement (21 per cent at $p < 0.05$) on profit. Training and seminar attendance is significant (18 per cent at $p < 0.05$) on sales. In terms of market expansion, the following variables are significant; consultation with friends (18 per cent at $p < 0.1$), sponsor (15 per cent at $p < 0.05$), External consultancy (13 per cent at $p < 0.050$), training attendance and seminar (21 per cent at $p < 0.001$), advertisement (21 per cent at $p < 0.05$) on local market expansion. For the case of Regional markets, only two variables are statistically significant with consultation with friends (3 per cent at $p < 0.05$) and sponsor (3 per cent at $p < 0.1$) on regional market expansion. From Table IV, a firm which has membership of a support group is likely to decrease its financial growth as measured by profits by 12 percent as compared to a firm without membership to a support group. In addition, membership to a support group is likely to decrease sales growth by 9.5 percent while it would increase market expansion from local to regional/ national level by 12.2 percent decreasing rate though the variable membership to support group is not statistically significant in all the models. Consultations with relatives increase growth in profits by 4.2 percent. It also increases sales growth by 7.5 percent and in addition would more likely increase market expansion from local to regional/ national by a decreased rate of less than one percent. Consultations with friends would increase profits and sales by 9.7 and 12.4 percentages respectively. This would also significantly increase market expansion by a decreased rate of 18.2 percent at 10 percent level of significance. Sponsors can influence the agenda for actions of the MSE's through increased participation at the local market level characterized by a decline of 14 per cent and are negatively significant at five percent level of significance in order to expand their markets to the national level. In many cases sponsorship are not for profit gains in terms of profitability hence sponsorship has a 14 per cent probability of decreasing MSE's profits at five percent level of significance meanwhile has 11 per cent probability of increasing sales though it is statistically insignificant in relation to sales. In terms of external consultancy, rarely do the MSE's seek for professional consultants therefore it is statistically insignificant and due to this the profit levels are reduced by 7 per cent but sales increased by 6 per cent as markets for the service significantly increases by 13 per cent at 5 per cent level of significance towards the national level. Entrepreneurs that attend training and seminars significantly increase their profits by 26 per cent at 5 per cent level of significance. This is in conformity to other earlier studies carried out by other researchers in the field (Donckels and Lambrecht 1995). Whereas external consultancy has a negative impact on sales by 18 per cent at 5 per cent level of significance. The local entrepreneurs have a 21 per cent probability at 5 per cent level of significance of expanding their markets if they attend seminars and training. In contrast to this is that the MSE's or entrepreneurs who attend trade fairs or exhibition has a 22 per cent probability of realizing decline in profit levels at 10 per cent level of significance and an increase in market expansion by 12 per cent decrease but is statistically insignificant. For advertisement linkages, those MSE's which advertise for their services and products has a 21 per cent probability of registering growth in profits with similar percentage in terms of market expansion locally at five per cent level of significance.

Meanwhile advertisement has a 10 per cent negative impact on level of sales for these MSE's even though it is statistically insignificant. Important to note in this discussions is that marginal impacts on growth on these variables were pro-poor as the details above can indicate which is an attendant problem for the MSE's in Kenya. In addition to the probabilities, partial correlations for network formation variables were estimated as shown in Table V.

**Table V: Partial Correlations Matrix II**

| | Mean | S.D | Memb | RltvC. | FrndC. | Spo. | Excon | Trainat | Exhb | Advert |
|---|---|---|---|---|---|---|---|---|---|---|
| Memb | 0.94 | 0.2378 | 1.0000 | | | | | | | |
| RltvC. | 0.055 | 0.2283 | 0.0610 | 1.0000 | | | | | | |
| FrndC. | 0.0725 | 0.2596 | -0.0106 | 0.1440 | 1.0000 | | | | | |
| Spo. | 0.865 | 0.3422 | 0.0542 | 0.0632 | 0.0540 | 1.0000 | | | | |
| Excon | 0.40 | 0.4905 | 0.1633 | -0.1298 | -0.0708 | -0.1105 | 1.0000 | | | |
| Trainat | 0.8775 | 0.3283 | 0.0661 | 0.0232 | 0.0457 | -0.1476 | 0.1027 | 1.0000 | | |
| Exhb | 0.0525 | 0.2233 | 0.0123 | -0.0568 | -0.0226 | 0.0602 | -0.0778 | -0.0488 | 1.0000 | |
| Advert | 0.7075 | 0.4555 | -0.1162 | -0.0859 | 0.0526 | -0.2219 | 0.2333 | 0.1956 | -0.1197 | 1.0000 |

*Index:(i)Membership of Support Group (Memb.), (ii) Consult with Relatives (RltvC.), (iii) Consult with friends (FrndC), (iv) Sponsor (Spo.), (v) External Consultancy (Excon.), (vi) Seminar & Training attendance (Trainat.), (vii)Trade Fairs/ exhibitions (Exhb.), (viii) Advertisement linkages (Advert), Contacts with Entrepreneurs (EntpC)-Regional Contacts (RC)-Both Regional &National contacts (RC&NC),-National Contacts (NC)‡For control variables refer to 5.1.3*

*Note: p-values (two-tailed significance) are in parentheses. N = 386,*p-value < 0.01,**p-value < 0.05,***p-value < 0.10,† Contact with other entrepreneurs (EntpC) has four categories: 0 = no contact; 1 = only Local contact; 2 = Regional Contact; and 3= only national contact*

From Table V, 94 percent of the firms had membership to support groups, 86.5 percent had a sponsor, 87.8 percent had attended training and 70.8 percent had advertisement linkages. Frequency of contacts on an average by relatives through consultations was 5.5 percent in building the social networks, 7.3 percent for consultations with friends, 40 per cent for external consultations and 5.3 per cent for trade fairs or exhibitions. Looking at the value of the correlations which are below 30 percent, we are assured there is problem of collinearity of the variables.

## Discussion

Network relations are vital and important for small business, in particularly to the small firm as it does not have all resources such as raw materials, capital, machinery, etc. Therefore, small business network researches (Donckels and Lambrecht 1995, Ozcan 1995, Szarka 1990, Uzzi 1999) suggest networking as a necessary strategy in obtaining resources such as gathering information, technology, finance, etc. Besides, building contacts through networks are the fundamental factor in determining the success of any firm (MacMillan, 1993) because through entrepreneurial networks, the entrepreneur can gather information, look for customers and suppliers, and obtain the other resources he needs. As regards contacts with entrepreneurs, network literature suggests that inter-firm linkages may span various levels of aggregation: Firms may be linked only locally, sometimes, interregional or globally (Stabber 1996a). The purpose of this chapter has been to explore the impact of network formation on small business performances. We predicted the positive impact of network formation on business performance. Logistic regression technique was used to analyze the data. The first hypothesis which includes seven sub-specific hypotheses is about the impact of the formation of networks on growth. We tested this hypothesis by using three separate dependent variables. Entrepreneurs with only local contacts (LC) are significantly less likely to be in the growth group. But those who have national level connections are more likely to belong to the growth group. In the case of the market expansion, the formation of networks is positively related to the market expansion. The results conclude that when the market expands beyond the regional border, the influences of the network connections are vital and important for the small entrepreneurs. The second hypothesis is about the network elements and the network relations with regional and national entrepreneurs. We expected the relations with other entrepreneurs to be promoted by the network elements and they are positively related with the formation of networks. However, we fail to identify considerable network relations with international entrepreneurs. At the same time, we found that the small entrepreneurs do not have direct export opportunities. They deal with export market through some link-agents or firms.

Although we expected the second hypothesis that all of the network elements influence network formation, the contact with other entrepreneurs is not significantly influenced by external consultancy. One reason for the lack of significant relationship could be that the relationship between education and contact with other entrepreneurs is positive and significant. Meanwhile, we found that small entrepreneurs who attend seminars and training and participate in trade fairs have a higher chance of developing relations with other entrepreneurs .Consultation with relatives is also very critical as family ties occupy an important role in entrepreneurial networks in Kenya in which social relations are largely built around the family. In such a society, Family members work together in their businesses as well as at home. The family relationship is stronger in rural areas. We found that the rural-entrepreneurs consult and discuss their business matters with relatives more than the entrepreneurs in urban areas do. However, when we defined consultation and discussion with relatives we omitted very close family members if they were partners of their business. In most cases, the close family members are also a part of the businesses. Future research should be conducted in this direction.

Tribal variables should also be included into the overall model. It is also important to study how the other enterprise- and entrepreneurrelated factors such as gender, education, firms' location etc. separately influence on each of the network formation elements. We found that there are some significant relationships between the network formation elements and the enterprise-and entrepreneur -related factors, though they are not very strong relationships. The results show that educated entrepreneurs are more likely to attend seminars, training, advertise and attend trade fairs, join professional and other societies, and contact other entrepreneurs, while they are less likely to discuss their business matters with relatives and friends. Meanwhile, female entrepreneurs discuss their business matters with relatives and friends more than their male counterparts. By contrast, compared to female owners, male counter-partners are looking for more external consultants, attending more seminars, and training, advertise and attend trade fairs. The male entrepreneurs also have more contacts with other entrepreneurs as pointed out above. In conclusion, this chapter analyzed the impact of network formation on the growth of small enterprises in Kenya. We found that network formation is an essential aspect of small business development. Hence networking, therefore, becomes an important element in the growth and performance of small enterprises. However, networking is time-consuming, experience-based, and does not evolve over night. Therefore, the policy makers, small entrepreneurs, donors and others, who deal with the development of small enterprises in developing countries, can use the network formation approach apart from their traditional supporting approach. For instance, supporting institutions should organize network activities for small businesses. Small business owners should also realize the importance of constructing Networks. However, there are few empirical studies available in this area particularly in less developed countries. Therefore, further research is necessary in this direction. Researchers should also deeply consider enterprise- and entrepreneur -related factors when studying networking and small businesses.

## Conclusion

The purpose of the study has been to analyze the role and impact of networks on small business performance and sustainability in Kenya. However, the concept of networks and network analysis cannot easily be explained due to an array of different definitions of network found in the literature and on the other hand, network analysis has been used in different areas of studies by different researchers in different perspectives. In this study, networking has been seen as an effective vehicle for obtaining necessary resources for small enterprises from the outsiders or external environment. The study found that small entrepreneurs who maintain regular relationships with external actors are more likely to be successful in their respective businesses because such relationships provide a constant and reliable source of resources and effective influence on firms. These external relationships are identified as entrepreneurial networks in this study. This study is different from the other studies in the field of small business networking in four ways.

First, current studies largely focus on formal business networks such as alliance. In contrast, the focus of this study is on the entrepreneurial informal network relationships in a less developed country.

Second, most current studies are largely focused on the experiences of developed countries (for example, Birley 1985 (USA), Bryson et al. 1993 (UK), Curran et al. 1993 (UK); Goodman and Bamford 1990, (Italy). Therefore, there was a gap in our understanding of small business networks in developing countries. In particular, small business networks in Kenya have not been studied and some studies which have been done focus on the possibilities of emerging clusters and subcontracting in the industrial estates (McCormick and Pedersen 1996).

Thirdly, this approach also differs from others in respect of the unit of analysis. For example, the industrial estate (holistic approach) has been widely used in the field of small business development in developing countries. This study has employed an individualistic approach (the ego-centered firm) to study small business development within the context of entrepreneurial networks.

Fourth, entrepreneurial networks are always regarded as advantageous for small business success. Apart from various case studies, however, a critical approach was needed in the network analysis in order to assess the importance of networks for small business performance. This study has filled this gap. We believe that this approach is necessary for advancing research on the field of entrepreneurial informal networks beyond general descriptions of the advantages of networks of single case studies. In this regard, the study contributes to network studies in four ways. Firstly, the study analyzed entrepreneurial informal network relationships. Secondly, the recent studies in this area are largely focused on the experiences of developed countries. A very few or no such a study has been available in the field of entrepreneurial networks in developing countries, particularly in Africa. Thirdly, the study used survey research approach to test a number of hypotheses. Overall, this study contributes to the literature by showing how small firms use network relationships to overcome their business bottle-necks, identify new market opportunities and finally to perform their business successfully. The findings of this study will without doubt be useful to the policymakers, business community, researchers, public institutions, financial organizations, donors and supporting organizations of small firms, and social workers particularly in Kenya and the other countries as well.

To sum up, there are some conclusions from the study, but the major conclusion is that entrepreneurial networking can create a successful small firm sector by helping to overcome the lack of resources, the managerial and professional weakness of small firms within a broader supportive external environment.

Owing to lack of resources, small enterprises always need to maintain contacts with their external actors to obtain necessary resources. The actors of social networks and supporting networks are very important for small enterprises particularly in developing countries such as Kenya. Before a new entrepreneur starts his venture, his social network relationships work as an opportunity set.

Then gradually the entrepreneur develops his network relationships with supporting agencies and other firms as well. The study emphasizes the fact that, in order to really succeed in business, small business entrepreneurs must use their own personal networks as well as the inter-organizational networks. To reach the conclusion, we analyzed informal networks of small enterprises in Kenya. We also believe that the results have significant policy implications. This empirical study has further recommended the need for more in-depth comparative studies before generalizing the results.

## References

1. Abeka, E. O. (1995). *Role of State Cooperative Banks and Regional Rural Banks in Supporting Micro and Small Enterprises in Agra District (U.P):Their Perceived Relevance to Non- Financial Business Development Services Offered.* India (U.P) Agra: Unpublished M.A Dissertation at Dr. R. B Ambedkar University.
2. Aldrich, H Rosen, B and Woodward, B.L. (1987). " The Impact of Social Network on Business Founding and Profit: A longitudinal Study" in. In M. C. Wellesley, *Frontiers of Entrepreneurship Research* (pp. 154-68).
3. Aldrich, H. and Zimmer, C. (1986). Entrepreneurship through Social Network. In P. a. Nystrom, *Handbook of Organization design,* Vol. 1, pp. 385 - 408. Oxford University Press.
4. Alchian, H. and Demsetz. (1972). "The Property Rights Paradigm". *Journal of History, 1* (1).

5. Birley, S. (1985). "The Role of Networks in Entrepreneurial Process". *Journal of Business Venturing, 1* (1), 107-17.
6. Birley, S. and Cromie, S. (1988). "Social Networks and Entrepreneurship in Northern Ireland". *Enterprise in Action Conference, September.* Belfast.
7. Birley, S. (1990). *Entrepreneurs Networks: Their Creation and Development in Different Countries.* Cranfield: Cranfield School of Management.
8. Birley, S. Cromie, S. and Myers, A. (1991). "Entrepreneurial Networks: Their Emergence in Ireland and Overseas". *International journal of Small Business, 9(4) pp.* 56-74.
9. Borg, E. (1991). Problem Shifts and Market Research: The Role of Networks in Business Relationships. *Scandinavian Journal of Management, 7* (4), 285-295.
10. Bryson, J. Wood, P. and Keeble, D. (1993). " Business Networks, Small Firm Flexibility and Regional Development in the U.K Business Services". *Entrepreneurship and Regional Development, 5,* 265-277.
11. Burt, R. (1992). *"Structural holes: The Social Structure of Competition".* Cambridge: Havard University Press.
12. Butler, R. (1980). Control through Markets, Hierarchies and Collectives. *Paper Presented to European Group for Organization Studies Conference.* London: Imperial College.
13. Butler, R. (1991). *Designing Organizations: A Decision-Making Perspective.* London: Routledge.
14. Butler, J. and Hansen, G. S. (1991). "Network Evalution, Entrepreneurial Success, and Regional Development". *Entrepreneurship and Regional Development, 3,* 1-16.
15. Butler, R. and Sohod, S. (1995). Joint-Venture Autonomy: Resource Dependence and Transaction Cost Perspectives. *Scandinavian Journal of Management, 11* (2), 159-175.
16. Bridge, S., O'Neill, K., Cromie, S., (1998). *Understanding Enterprise, Entrepreneurship and Small Business.* London: McMillan.
17. Donckels, R. and Lambrecht, J. (1995). "Networks and Small Business Growth: An Explanatory Model". *Small Business Economics, 7,* 273 - 89.
18. Duysters, G. (1995). *The Evolution of Complex Industrial Systems: The Dynamics of Major IT Sectors.* PhD Thesis, University of Maastricht.
19. Carroll, G. R. and Teo , A.C. (1996). On the social networks of Managers. *Academy of Management Journal.*

20. Chu., P. (1996). Social Network Models of Overseas Chinese Entrepreneurship: The Experience in Hong Kong and Canada". *Canadian Journal of Administrative Sciences, 13* (4), 358-365.
21. Curran, Jarvis, R. Blackburn, R. A and Black, S. (1993). "Networks and Small Firms: Construct Methodological Strategies and some Findings". *International Journal of Small Business, 11* (2), 34 - 45. Coarse, R. (1937). *"The Nature of the Firm"*. Economica.
22. DeMaris, A. (1992). *Logit Modeling: Practical Applications* (Quantitative Applications in the Social Sciences ed.). Newbury Park: Sage.
23. Gibb, A. A (1993). Key Factors in the Design of Policy Support for the Small and Medium Enterprise (SME) Development Process: An OVerview. *Entrepreneurship and regional Development, 7*, 1-24.
24. G.o.K /CBS/ ICEG/ K-EP. (1999). *National Micro and Small Enterprise Baseline Survey Results.* Nairobi: Government Printer Press.
25. G.o.K (1965). *Sessional Paper No. 10 of 1965.* nairobi: Government printer Press
26. Goodman, E. and Bamford, J. (1990). *Small Firms and Industrial Districts in Italy.* London: routledge.
27. G.o.K (2008). *Economic Survey of Kenya.* Nairobi: Government Printer Press.
28. Grabher, G. (. (1993a). The Embedded Firm: On the Socioeconomics of Industrial Networks. London and New York: Routledege.
29. Grabher, G. (1993b). "Rediscovering the Social in Economics of Inter-firm Relations". In G. Grabher, *The Embedded Firm: On the Socioeconomics of Industrial Networks"*. London and New York: Routledge.
30. Granovetter, M. (1976). Network Sampling: Some First Steps. *American Journal of Sociology , 81*, 1287-1303.
31. Granovetter, M. (1985). Economic Action and Social structure: The Problem of Embeddedness. *American Journal of Sociology, 91* (3), 481-510.
32. Greve, A. (1995). Networks and Entrepreneurship: An Analysis of Social Relations, Occupational and Background, and Use of Contacts during the Establishment Process. *Scandinavian Journal of Management, 11* (1), 1-24.
33. Hagenaars, J. (1990). *Categorical Longitudinal Data: Log-Linear Panel, Trend and Cohort Analysis.* Carlifornia: Sage Newbury Park
34. Hakansson, H., and Johanson, J., (1988). Formal and Informal Cooperation Strategies in International Industries Networks. In F.

J. Contractor, *Cooperative Strategies in International Business.* Mass: Lexington Books.

35. Hall,R.H. Clark, J.P. Giordano, P. C. Johnson, P.V. and Van Roekel, M. (1977:462). Patterns of Inter-organizational Relationships. *Administrative Science Quarterly, 22*, 457-74.
36. Hansen, E. (1995). Entrepreneurial Networks and New Organizational Growth. *Entrepreneurship Theory and Practice,* 7-19.
37. Jarillo, J. (1988). On Strategic Networks. *Strategic management Journal, 9*, 341.
38. Johannisson, B. (1988: 85). Business Formation; A Netrwork Approach. *Scandinavian Journal of Management , 31* (3/4), 83-99
39. Johannisson, B. (1990b). Economics of Overview-Guiding the External Growth of Small Firms. *International Small Business Journal, 9* (1), 32-44.
40. Johanson, J. and Mattson, L. G. (1993). 'Internationalization in Industrial System: A Network Approach'. In B. P. (eds)., *The Internationalization of The Firm: A Reader.* Harcourt: Academic Press.
41. Johannisson, B. (1987a). Beyond Process and Structure; Social exchange Networks. *International Studies of Management and Organization, 17*, 49-63.
42. Johannisson, B. (1986). "New Venture Creation: A network Approach". In R. R. (eds), *Frontiers of Entrepreneurship Research* (pp. 236-38). Wellesley, M.A: Babson College.
43. Johannisson, B. (1990b). Economics of Overview-Guiding the External Growth of Small Firms. *International Small Business Journal, 9* (1), 32-44.
44. Johannisson, B. (1996): The dynamics of entrepreneurial networks. Frontiers of Entrepreneurship Research, 1996, 253-267.
45. Kallinikos, J., (1995: 122). Cognitive Foundations of Economic Institutions: Markets, Organizations and Networks Revisited. *Scandinavian Journal of Management, 11*, 119- 137.
46. Karekezi, S. and Majoro, L. (2002). Improving Modern Energy Services for African's Urban Poor. *Energy Policy , 30*, 1015-1028.
47. Kenya National Commission on Human Rights (2008): *On the Brink of the Precipice a Human Rights Account of Kenya's Post-2007 Election Violence.* Nairobi: KNCHR.
48. Larson, A. (1992). " Network Dyads in Entrepreneurial Settings: A study of the Governance of Exchange Relationships". *Administrative Science Quarterly, 37*, 76-104.

49. Larson, A, A., and Starr, J. A.,. (1993). "A Network Model of Organization Formation". *Entrepreneurship Theory and Practice, Winter*, 5-15.
50. Lomi, A. and Grandi, A. (1997). The Network Structure of Inter-Firm Relationships in the Southern Italian Mechanical Industry. In M. Ebers, *The Formation of Interorganizational Networks.* Oxford: Oxford University Press.
51. MacMillan, I. (1993). The Politics of new Venture Management. *Havard Business Review* .
52. Maddala, G. (1983). *Limited-dependent and qualitative Variables in Econometrics* (1st. Edition Econometric Society Monographs. ed.). London: Cambridge University Press.
53. McCormick, D. (1996). *Small Enterprise: Flexibility and Networking in an African Context.* Nairobi, Kenya: Longman.
54. McPherson. (1996). Growth of micro and small enterprises in Southern Africa, *Journal of Development Economics, 48,*, 253-277.
55. Mohan-Neill, S. I (1995). The Influence of Firm's Age and Size on its Environmental Scanning Activities, *Journal of Small Business Management.*
56. Murphy, T. J (2000). "Network, Trust and Innovation in Tanzanian's Manufacturing Sector". *World Development, 30* (4 ), 591-619.
57. Ongong'a, J.O. (2010). Kenyan Entrepreneurship: The Emergence and Shaping of the Informal Sector in Kenya, Lambert Academic Publishing.
58. Ostgaard T. A and Birley S. (1996). New Venture Growth and Personal Network. *Journal of Business Research, 36* (1), 37-50.
59. Ozcan, G. B. (1995). "Small Business Network and Local Ties in Turkey". *Entrepreneurship and Regional Development, 7*,265-282.
60. Pedersen, Poul Ove (1999). Flexibility, networks and clusters: strategies of small enterprise development in unstable developing economies in Robert Kappel, Utz Dornberger, Michaela Meier and Ute Rietdorf (Hrsg.) (eds) Klein-und Mittelunternehmen in Entwicklungsländern, *Die Herausforderungen der Globalisierung* : 58 Schriften Des Deutschen übersee-instituts Hamburg (DÜI)
61. Pfeffer, J., and Salancik, G. R., (1978). *The External Control Organizations: A Resource Dependence Perspective.* New York: Harper and Row Publishers.
62. Pfeffer, J. and G. R. Salancik (2003): The External Control of Organizations. A Resource Dependence Perspective. Stanford, A: Stanford University Press

63. Powell, W.W., (1990). Neither Market nor Hierarchy: Network forms of Organiztion. In B. M. (eds), *Research in Organization Behaviour* (Vol. 12, pp. 295-336). Greenwich, CT.: JAI Press
64. Rabelloti, R. (1995a). Is there an "Industrial district Model"? Footware Districts in Italy and Mexico compared. *World Development, 23*, 29-41.
65. Sarder, J. H., Ghosh, D., and Rosa, P.,(1997). The Importance of Support Services to small Enterprises in Bangladesh. *Journal of Small Business Management (JSBM) , 35* (2( April)), 26 - 36.
66. Staber, U. (1996a). The Social Embeddedness of Industrial District Networks. In U. S. Staner, *Business Networks: Prospects for Regional Development.* Berlin, New York: Walter de Gruyter.
67. Steier, L and Greenwood, R. (2000). Entrepreneurhip and the Evolution of Angel Financial Networks. *Organization Studies , 21* (1), 163-92.
68. Singh, S.P. and Reynolds, R.G. (2001). A Gender-based Performance Analysis of Micro and Small Enterprises in Java, Indonesia. *Journal of Small Business Management , 39* (2), 174- 182.
69. Szarka. (1990). " Networking and small Firms". *Journal of International small Business , 8* (2), 10-22.
70. Thorelli, H. (1986). Networks: Between Markets and Hierarchies. *Strategic Management Journal , 7*, 37-51.
71. Uzzi, B. (1996). 'The Socurce Consequences of Embeddedness for the Economic Performance of Organization: The Network Effect; American Sociological Review, , vol.61, pp.674-98. *American Sociological Review, vol.61*, pp.674-98.
72. Uzzi, B. (999). 'Embeddedness in the Making of Financial Capital: How Social Relations and Network Benefit Firms Seeking Financing". *American Sociology Review, 64*, 481-505.
73. Uzzi, B. (1997). 'Social Structure and Competition in Interim-firm Network: The Paradox of Embeddedness'. *Administration Science Quaterly , 42* (1), 35-67.
74. Uzzi, B. & Lancaster, R. (2004): Embeddedness and price formation in the corporate law market *American Sociological Review, 69, 319-344*
75. Veciana, J. M and Clarke, A. M (1996). Theoretical Approaches to Entrepreneurship: The Social network Approach. *European Doctoral Programme in Entrepreneurship and Small Business Management.*
76. Venkataraman, S. (1989). *Problems of Small Venture Start - up, survival and Growth: A Transaction set Approach".* PhD Dissertation, University of Minnesota.

77. Wellman, B. and Gulia, M. (1993). Which Types of Networks Provide What kinds of Social Support? *Paper Presented at the International Sunbelt Social Network Conference.* Tampa.
78. Williamson, O. E (1985). *The Economic Institutions of Capitalism: Firms, Markets, Relational Contracting.* New York: The Free Press.

# 22

# Small and Medium Enterprise (SME) Development in Vietnam

***Abstract***

Vietnam has the potential to emerge as a next Asian giant on the economic map of the world, with its phenomenal GDP growth from the introduction of "Doi Moi" in 1986 through to till recently. This growth is a manifestation of the entrepreneurial spirit of the Vietnamese people and the state. The Small and Medium Enterprises (SMEs) sector is the major driver of this growth. However, the same also faces certain challenges that need to be addressed for a sustainable growth of the Vietnamese economy. The paper explores these challenges and suggests possible changes in current policies. It also highlights measures that can assure growth of the SMEs, which are the major contributors to the private organizations.

Keywords: SMEs, SOEs, Entrepreneurship.

## The Growth Story of Vietnam:

Vietnamese history dates back more than 4,000 years to when the ancient Vietnamese people founded their first nation under the name "Van Lang". The recent history of Vietnam is best characterized as one long, continuous struggle for freedom and independence that was influenced by various cultures. Vietnam's surging economic growth is evident from facts like the consistent GDP growth rate of over 8 % till the recent global recession. This is undoubtedly a result of reforms introduced in the late 1980's, known as "doi moi" – or "renovation" policy allowing the market mechanism to operate and permit the individual ownership businesses. The country maintains diplomatic and economic relations with more than 160 nations and territories, including all the world powers. The country is currently a member of the Association of Southeast Asian Nations (ASEAN), the ASEAN Free Trade Area (AFTA), the AsiaPaper Presented at 9th Biennial Conference held at EDI, Ahmedabad during 16 18 February 2011 Pacific Economic Community (APEC), and the ASEAN – Europe Meeting (ASEM). Vietnam was accepted into the WTO on November 7, 2006 In the country, now the basic economic unit of reference has changed from the commune to the household and families and individuals are being encouraged to set-up small and medium sized enterprises. This fundamental shift towards encouraging private enterprise has now snowballed to a point where the private sector accounts for 26% of the country's GDP and is an important source of new jobs. Living standards have grown more than three times higher than 20 years ago. Initially growth was driven by labor-intensive industries like footwear and clothing. Now, sectors like electronics are coming to the forefront.

Furthermore, from being an important of crude oil, the country now drills for oil offshore and is a net exporter. The nation has also made significant inroads in the spheres of tourism and culture. Vietnam is increasingly being looked upon as a viable and cost effective destination with recent years seeing a spurt in regional and international tourist flows. In the cultural arena, Vietnamese art is booming.

## Vietnam's Economy:

Gross Domestic Product of Vietnam was $ 45.4 billion in 2004, with $ 553 in per capita terms. Vietnam has achieved outstanding success in poverty reduction over the past 15 years. The poverty rate which was 20% in 2001 dropped to 14.3% in 2002 and to under 9% of the population in 2004. It is worth mentioning that its GDP grew at the rate of 7.7% in 2004 compared to 5.4% for East Asia and Pacific, and 3.9% for low-income countries.

## Agriculture and Allied sectors

The country has made impressive progress in the field of agriculture.

Although its share in the GDP has been decreasing over recent years, agriculture still represents an important economic sector, accounting for 21.76% of GDP in 2004.

It also employs nearly 70% of the workforce. Over the past 10 years, agricultural growth has averaged about 4.3% per annum.

## Promising Industrial Sector

Over the past ten years, the industrial sector has grown at an average of 14% per annum. In 2004, it expanded by 16%. The private sector has been playing an increasing role in industrial development in Vietnam. During 2002, about 20,745 new private enterprises were registered with a total capital of about USD 2.37 billion (far higher than the level of new FDI commitments amounting to USD 1.33 billion). Foreign invested firms produced $ 8,045 billion in 2004 accounting for 35.7% of the country's industrial output. Light manufacturing, particularly in food processing, textiles, garment and footwear dominates the sector. Heavy industry located mainly in the north, makes up a modest portion of industrial output.

In an effort to promote its industry, Vietnam has been establishing industrial parks (IPs) throughout the country. Setting up of 11 such parks was licensed during 2004, raising the total number of IPs nationwide to 110 of which 68 have become operational.

## Foreign Trade

The country's exports have grown from $ 5.45 billion in 1995 to $ 19.88 billion in 2003 and $ 26.00 billion in 2004. Similarity, imports grew from $ 8.15 billion in 1995 to $ 25.00 billion in 2003 and $ 31.52 billion in 2004. The main items of export during 2004 were crude oil ($5.67 billion), textiles and garments ($ 4.32 billion), footwear ($ 2.6 billion), seafood ($ 2.4 billion), agricultural products ($ 2.97 billion), forestry products ($ 1.46 billion). For the first time exports of wood products and electric components crossed $ 1 billion each. The major imports in 2004 were machinery, equipment and spare parts ($ 5.12 billion), petroleum products ($ 3.57 billion), iron and steel ($ 2.51 billion). Other major items of imports are textiles, garments, electronic parts, plastic materials, fertilizers, chemicals and pharmaceuticals. Consumer goods account only about 5% of the total import value. In the area of foreign trade, import & export restrictions are being reduced gradually moving away from State monopoly.

Vietnam's main export markets include Japan, the USA, the European Union, China and ASEAN nations. The recent global recession has hurt

Vietnam's export-oriented economy with GDP growing less than the 7% per annum average achieved during the last decade

***Swot Analysis of Vietnam's Economy***

## Strengths of Vietnam's Economy

Vietnam's economy has several strengths, the significant being its growth in GDP which is over 7%. As mentioned earlier, exports have risen from $ 9.1 billion in 1997 to $ 26 billion in 2004, an average growth rate of over 26% a year. This is much faster than other countries of the region. Because of its topography Vietnam's tourism industry recorded an average growth rate of 40% annual from 1991 to 1997. The total number of foreign tourists visited Vietnam in 2004 were 2.93 million helping the country's 40 million-estimated young workforce. With a growth of around 4% a year, 1.5 to 1.7 million new workers enter the job market every year. Till 2004, nearly 397,000 Vietnamese workers were working in 48 countries including Libya, South Korea, Japan, Taiwan, UK, Denmark and France. The country received $ 1.6 billion as remittances from these nonresident Vietnamese during the year 2004. Inflation is controlled and fiscal deficits have been contained to acceptable levels. The growth of gross industry output has been faster, at over 14% a year. The most dynamic sector since the year 2000 when the Enterprise Law was passed has been the domestic private sector. Industry for this form of ownership, which excluded household level activities, has grown nearly 20% a year since 1999. Vietnam has political stability with one ruling party for 30 years. Special efforts of the national leaders to have new policy approaches and innovative policies aiming at enhancing the competition of the economy, restricting public sector and encouraging private sector can be seen clearly through every national congress in 1986.

## Weaknesses of Vietnam's Economy

Till 2003, the annual average capital employed by state-owned enterprises has been 59.53%, by foreign invested enterprises 21.99%, and in non-state enterprises only 18.47% (including 3.58% enterprises having state capital but that are not state-owned). This emphasizes the need to promote indigenous entrepreneurs and domestic entrepreneurship. The other weaknesses include unstable economic structure and slow change of labor structure in comparison with economic structure. The speed of equalizing state-owned enterprises and reforming the banking sector is slower than planned. The competitiveness of the economy has remained low due to number of factors like inadequate infrastructure, obsolete technology, shortage of skilled workers and managerial talent and non-conducive business environment etc. Though statistics show that, Vietnam has achieved outstanding successes in poverty reduction, the definition of poverty is not in line with international standards. At present, anyone who live in rural areas with a monthly income of less than VND 100,000 ($ 6.4 equality) is considered poor in Vietnam while threshold for urban poor resident is less than VND 150,000 ($ 9.6 equality). It is proposed to raise these poverty thresholds to $ 11.5 and $ 14.6 respectively in 2006 – 2010 Plan. The present industrial growth rate has also resulted in regional imbalances and widening the gap between rich and poor.

## Opportunities of Vietnam's Economy

Vietnam is an important market for a wide range of goods and services, particularly capital goods, telecommunications equipment, power generation, aviation and avionics equipment, hotel and tourism, construction, food processing and packaging, textile machinery, transportation, financial and legal services, and consumer products. As Vietnam seeks to meet demands for inputs to build its infrastructure and industrial base, demand will be strong for the future for goods and services in those sectors.

Although, Vietnam has faced too many difficulties and challenges, we cannot deny the optimistic aspects. First of all, becoming a member of economic groups and international organizations such as ASEAN, APEC, WORLD BANK, IMF is a progress step for Vietnam to integrate into the global market. This helps Vietnam to obtain necessary information and to have her voice articulated in regional and international meetings and discussion. Becoming member of such organizations also helps Vietnam gain most-favoured-nation (MFN) status as well as obtain lower tariff for exported goods.

Secondly, signing a bilateral trade agreement with USA has marked an important step to achieve a "normal diplomatic relationship" between the two countries.

This is perceived to be giving domestic suppliers more chance to enter US market with favourable tariffs and other conditions, such as modes of payments. Also the change in ideology and thinking of the authority from blaming external factors into blaming themselves and try to find out a positive resolution should be considered as a big opportunity for the Vietnam economy.

## Threats of Vietnam's economy

Last but not least, Vietnam also faces too many threats. Firstly, the serious reduction in the foreign investment and the aggregate demand was warned by Vietnam Prime Minister as early as on July 30, 1999. One of the reasons for the decrease in total demand is that common people do not have enough money to spend since they are unemployed, especially workers in heavy industries (steel, coal, miner, cement). In these industries, the supply exceeds the demand so significantly that the stocks increase very high.

Secondly, graft and patronage-client relationship has been practiced for a long time in Vietnam. Now, they have become "traditions" and hinder the development of the national economy and other renovation policies. This practice becomes a well-known feature as "business culture" in Vietnam.

Also, the lack of competition and a sense of "Kaisu" ("want to be the best" which help Singapore achieve amazing results) makes Vietnam economy recover more slowly than other countries. In addition to these, overemphasis on directed investments could be a threat to Vietnam's economy.

## Entrepreneurship in Vietnam

Entrepreneurial spirit and many entrepreneurial attempts by hundreds of thousands of ordinary people in Vietnam have cultivated a new wave of economic growth taking advantages of varieties of existing and future opportunities. Until March 2009, in Vietnam, there had been approximately 350000 SMEs, who were basically entrepreneurs. When seeking ways to attain the business freedom and self-reliance for themselves, Vietnamese entrepreneurs have helped change both themselves into more professional business people and the economy into more business oriented- model.

The economic and cultural values of the Vietnamese economy has gained from these entrepreneurship processes are apparently enormous. It is agreeable that entrepreneurship had changed the economic situation to a large extent.

Currently, the private SME sector contributes approx. 40% of GDP to the economy, as reported in the official statistics. As to the industrial output, private entrepreneurship contribution in Vietnam has increased from 24.6% in 2000 to 27.5 %, 37 % in 2003 and 2005 respectively. Therefore, it is worth noting that entrepreneurship activity has also created a majority of new jobs for the country.

Given the critical importance of entrepreneurship, the government of Vietnam, since 1998, has set forth a strategic goal of promoting the number of domestic enterprises to half a million by 2010- a goal that is equivalent to facilitating hundreds of thousands of people to become entrepreneurs and also turning the existing entrepreneurs running small businesses to grow to a corporate level. In this effort of Vietnam, the Government of India extended its support by setting up Vietnam- India Entrepreneurship Development Center (VIEDC) at Hanoi in the year 2006 and transferred its' know-how on Entrepreneurship Development.

## Small and Medium Enterprises (SMEs) in Vietnam

The Agency for Small and Medium Enterprises Development (ASMED) created under the Ministry of Planning and Investment (MPI) is the nodal agency responsible for assisting Ministry of Planning and Investment in performing state management functions in SME promotion and development. It has prepared and finalized SME Development Plan 2006 – 2010. In Vietnam SMEs are defined as those independent business and production establishment that have registered under the current legislation and have registered capital of less than VND 10 billion (about $ 650,000) and have annual average number of permanent employees of more than 10 but less than 300. The SME sector, both in terms of quantity and quality, has contributed to economic growth, job creation, income generation, and has helped mobilize different sources of domestic investment capital for socio economic development. Despite these achievements, the draft SMEs Development Plan has identified some weakness and shortcomings. One such shortcoming was the definition itself which was not clear and too broad based including from household enterprises to state owned enterprises and manufacturing, service and trading enterprises. To further adding to the ambiguity the definition says- "On the basis of the concrete socio-economic situation of each branch or locality, in the course of implementing the support measures and programs, both or either of the above-mentioned criteria on capital and labor may be applied in a flexible manner."

## Features of Vietnamese SMEs

The following statistics in table 5.1 provides a broad picture of SMEs in Vietnam, based on the latest Establishments Census conducted by the General Statistics Office in 2002. For the purposes of this analysis, SMEs have been divided into 3 sub-groups:

1. Micro enterprises: Engaging up to 9 employees
2. Small enterprises: Engaging up to 49 employees
3. Medium size enterprises: Engaging up to 299 employees

**Table 5.1: Establishments and Employment in Vietnam (2002)**

| Vietnam, 2002 | SME | | | | LSE | Total |
|---|---|---|---|---|---|---|
| Establishments | Micro | Small | Medium | Sub-Total | | |
| Number of business establishments (1,000) | 2,660 | 46.7 | 11 | 2,718 | 2.5 | 2,720 |
| Percentage of all establishments (%) | 97.8 | 1.7 | 0.4 | 99.9 | 0.09 | 100 |
| Employment | | | | | | |
| Employment (1,000) | 4,375 | 887 | 1,221 | 6,483 | 1,909 | 8,392 |
| Percentage of persons engaged (%) | 52.1 | 10.5 | 14.5 | 77.3 | 22.7 | 100 |
| Average Size of Establishments | | | | | | |
| Persons engaged per establishment | 1.6 | 19 | 112 | 2.4 | 773 | 3 |

**Source:** GSO Establishments Census (2002), classified as per tentative size groupings.

As per the above table there were 2,720,000 business establishments in Vietnam according to the Establishment Census conducted by the General Statistics Office in 2002. Of these, large enterprises having over 300 employees constituted less than 0.1% of business establishments and created jobs for 22.7% of the non-agricultural labor force. That shows that almost all the enterprises fall under the category of SMEs. Moreover out of these SMEs, the majority being the Micro-enterprises (less than 10 employees) account for 2,660,000 of the total enterprises (97.8%), and employing more than 52% of the non-agricultural labor force. The remaining 467,000 enterprises are small (10 – 49 employees in each enterprise), and 11,000 enterprises are medium (50 – 299 employees in each) account for 2.1% of the total enterprises and together employ 25% of the non-agricultural labor force. It is clearly evident from the data that the base of the pyramid is very large and broad covering large number micro and household enterprises.

The Vietnam economy is long perceived to be agricultural. SMEs there tend to be more labour intensive than large enterprises, and hence create more job opportunities per unit of capital invested. This feature has been one of the most motivating factor s for the government to encourage entrepreneurship. The number of privately held firms is considerably above Limited Liability firms. This explicitly indicates that the small scale business contributes a major chunk of the Private Enterprises.

**Table 5.2: New Business Registrations Since (2000)**

| Year | Total | State Owned Enterprises | One-member Limited Liability Companies | Private Enterprises |
|---|---|---|---|---|
| 2000 | 14.457 | 16 | 0 | 14,441 |
| 2001 | 19.800 | 27 | 0 | 19,773 |
| 2002 | 21.535 | 12 | 59 | 21,464 |
| 2003 | 27,771 | 20 | 98 | 27,653 |
| 2004 | 37,230 | 6 | 125 | 37,099 |
| 2005 | 39,959 | 8 | 292 | 39,659 |
| | | | | |
| Total | 160,752 | 89 | 574 | 160,089 |

**Source:** Business Information Center (Ministry of Planning and Investment), (2005)

The growth in number registrations of SMEs in 2005 is also magnanimously 176 % over the same in the year 2000 from 14,457 to 39,959. Moreover, it must be noted that most of these registrations are by Private Enterprises. The total of registered enterprises before 2000 was 46,770 which rose to 160,089 in 2005 with a phenomenal 242% increase.

In terms of firm classification by economic activities, Table 5.3 shows that SMEs are reported to be concentrated mainly in industry and construction, and services and commerce, these subsectors accounting on average for 85 % of total SMEs during the 1998-2002 period.

**Table 5.3: Classification of Tax-Coded SMEs by Economic Activities**

| Sector | 1998 | | 1999 | | 2000 | | 2001 | | 2002 | |
|---|---|---|---|---|---|---|---|---|---|---|
| | Firms | % of tax-coded SMEs | Firms | % of tax-coded SMEs | Firms | % of tax-coded SMEs | Firms | % of tax-coded SMEs | Firms | % of tax-coded SMEs |
| Agriculture, Forestry and Fishery | 2,453 | 7.5 | 2,750 | 6.9 | 3,273 | 6.5 | 4,071 | 6.1 | 4,903 | 5.8 |
| Industry and Construction | 11,867 | 36.3 | 14,297 | 35.9 | 18,211 | 36.1 | 25,139 | 37.9 | 32,218 | 38.2 |
| Services and Commerce | 15,642 | 47.9 | 19,518 | 49.0 | 24,806 | 49.2 | 31,630 | 47.7 | 39,985 | 47.4 |
| Others | 2,688 | 8.2 | 3,266 | 8.2 | 4,133 | 8.2 | 5,501 | 8.3 | 7,265 | 8.6 |
| Total | 32,650 | 100.0 | 39,831 | 100.0 | 50,424 | 100.0 | 66,342 | 100.0 | 84,371 | 100.0 |

**Source:** Asian Development Bank Vietnam, Preparing the SME Sector Development Program- “enterplan” in association with

**Price water house coopers**

Table 5.3 further shows that the percentage of growth of Agriculture, Forestry and Fishery sector as a percentage of tax coded SMEs has come down from 7.5% to 5.8% from 1998 to 2002 with an absolute number increment from 2,453 firms to 4,903 firms respectively. The reduction in % of tax coded SMEs indicates a shift from the primary sector of Vietnam to other sectors like Industry and Construction which shows a growth from 36.3% to 38% of the tax coded SMEs. Also, the robust growth in the number of SMEs from 32,650 to 84,371 firms must be noted.

## Weaknesses of SMEs in Vietnam

Though the Government recognizes the importance of nurturing Small Enterprises, the SMEs face challenges due to some inherent weaknesses in a small enterprise system. Shortage of capital, which is the foremost driver of any activity, is one of the largest flaws in the system. Most enterprises belonging to the less than 1 billion cadre lack in financial support to expand and mostly run the business functions. Moreover, the profit margins generated are also not so motivating.

After the introduction of "Doi Moi" policy, the competition faced by the SMEs has increased. Shortage of Marketing channels and the lack of knowledge of the same limits the market reach thus affecting the top-line. The shortage of capital adds to the limitation. Only 20% of SMEs sell products in big cities. This may further be broken down to the obsolete machines and equipment. The old technology finds it difficult to compete with the foreign producers with better machinery and capital to enhance the same. About 18% and 5% of businesses in Ho Chi Minh and Hanoi respectively are unable to increase productivity with their own facilities.

The literacy rate of Vietnam is 90%, which is a considerably fair number. However, this does not guarantee the academic qualification for self-dependent economic activity. There lies a large lacuna in the as-is and to-be of the academic standards for the entrepreneurship activities.

There are important cases of small, specialized firms that operate internationally or globally, but in many cases SMEs work within a small economic 'space'. This generally means working within a small geography, but it can also mean a tight linkage to a particular industrial sector or to the supply-chain of one or a small number of large companies

The startups incubating in the economic opportunities lack space for production. They find it difficult to enter into a business and take the underlying risk, mainly due to the risk of survival. Lack of successful example and a general disbelief in entrepreneurship can be the reasons. Moreover, the higher trust of public and employees in SOEs as compared to SMEs can also be a reason for the difficulty. The encouragement from the State is also poor where the State management merely focuses on granting certificates.

## Challenges & Difficulties

### Funds and Credit

Vietnamese economy is in an emerging stage. Most of the SMEs are first-time borrowers with no established track record of creditworthiness and are unable to provide reliable financial records or credible business plans. Lack of public and bank confidence in SMEs leads to reluctance in lending to SMEs, perceiving them as inherently high risk, and lack the skills to undertake proper credit assessment entities. Moreover, banks have a lending preference to SOEs as compared to SMEs due to low recognition of their role in economic development. Lack of a well-defined project appraisal and evaluation system makes financial organization less interested in often start-up SMEs. Collateral focused lending makes it difficult for SMEs to procure capital for starting or expanding their operation. Again, the venture capitalists and stock market being in a nascent stage cannot contribute to financing SMEs. Small available loan sizes and high transaction costs per VND lent make taking credit unattractive.

The process of procuring loan is also very complex. This prevents SMEs from easy and quick access to finance.

It is also observed that the current accounting systems applicable to SME are too complex for small enterprises and there are inconsistencies and incompleteness of certain financial reporting regulations

The legislative system has option to file bankruptcy. However, the lack in transparency and the fear of losing personal reputation there of prevents entrepreneurs to use this facility. The current legislative framework discourages filing bankruptcy. It considers a business bankrupt only when it has suffered losses for two consecutive years to the extent that it is unable to pay its due debts or salaries to employees for three consecutive months, even after it has applied rectifying measures. This is joined by the complex process involved to file bankruptcy. Thus, though available, the option of filing bankruptcy is rarely utilized. Furthermore, there are ambiguities relating to the rights of creditors to file a bankruptcy petition.

## Land

Land is essential for enterprises – both to establish a location from which to operate the enterprise and as the most tangible (and probably the most valuable) asset that can be offered as collateral for a loan. With a complex legislative framework and high associated transaction taxes there is no single land-use registry system covering the whole of Vietnam - making zoning an issue. This results into many informal transactions in the land market significantly impacting the SMEs. The system for land acquisition involving compensatory payments to existing users and site clearance is extremely expensive and time consuming. Moreover, no effective system to use unused land is instated. Non-state SMEs interested in obtaining land most commonly do so by leasing idle land from SOEs. The leasing fees and the taxes payable over and above the high rentals make obtaining land very unattractive. This results in lack of premises for business and production. The complexity with the land use rights and its state limitations are serious problem, particularly for the manufacturing sector. The way that land use rights are managed by the State results in higher land usage costs for SMEs.

As a result of the complexity in obtaining land for production, most industrial SMEs operate from their own home. This results in inefficient production, urban pollution and significant public disturbance.

## Technology

SMEs must be able to meet required technical standards if they are to become sub-contractors to foreign direct investors or reap the opportunities created by Vietnam's planned accession to AFTA and WTO. Technologically Vietnamese SMEs face strong resistance to technology transfer and development as per global standards, majorly due to the regulatory framework that does not encourage SMEs to invest in new technology. Failure to meet such standards will also hit producers for the domestic market who will face increasing competition from higher quality and increasingly cheaper imports.

Limited information about technological availabilities and awareness about the benefits of implementing better technologies prevent the needing firms to opt for such options. Financial limitations also lead to lack of interest in investing in technological development. The regulatory framework barely provides for any incentive for knowledge transfer from consultation organization. Moreover, being in nascent stage, the procedures of import and transfer of foreign technology are very complicated and not customized for SMEs.

Furthermore, associations and technology institutes lack the capacity to support enterprises in the way that they should be supported in order to fulfill the requirements of the world markets. In the context of the economic globalization and the development of the knowledge based economy, the strengthening of enterprise competitiveness is increasingly important for Vietnamese economic development. Recent international experiences show that science and technology have become direct and first production forces and competitiveness of nations depend mostly on science and technology capacities. Advantages of natural resources and cheap labor become less important. Experiences from developed as well as developing countries indicate that universities and research institutes have played a crucial role in applying knowledge into enterprises, and therefore supporting enterprises competitiveness. The existing linkages among industry and technology institutes are very weak. This is acclaimed for the low competitiveness of small and medium enterprises in Vietnam and also considered one of main reasons for failure of science and technology activities as foundation for the shortened industrialization, sustainable development and successful integration in the global economy.

## A Small Market with Weak Competitiveness

Vietnam does not have a separate legal framework limiting or regulating competition between enterprises in the market. This makes it difficult for the SMEs with lesser margins and financial limitations to sustain and even begin production. This completion is elevated by the local large scale producer. The better economic conditions give large scale producer a competitive advantage over SMEs. Although the current legal regimes do ensure fairness of competition between the public and private business sectors, so called “unwritten laws” of discrimination against SMEs still exist strongly in society.

Information about market, opportunity for SMEs, the importance of strategic plan and trade policies are not widely revealed to SMEs by the concerned parties. SMEs have limited access to market information and information. Most information is obtained through the media or by personal contacts of firms, and not through formal channels. Only the more dynamic SMEs tend to get in touch with formal organizations like the SMEs club, the VCCI and the various trade associations for information. As a result, SMEs may face problems of missing out on business opportunities and cooperation or being deceived by their overseas partners due to the lack of reliable information.

Vietnam faces lack of a well-defined export oriented trade policy. Without such policy, learning and technological advance are decelerated. Moreover, the complication in the trade promotion procedures hinders the international market reach of SMEs.

SMEs are still facing many hurdles in relation to tariff barriers. For example, the tax rate on used equipment is normally based on custom officers’ whims, given that the tariff criteria for quality assessment are not clear. Again, export promotional funds and incentives are not available to SMEs. Subsidy policies are offered to SOEs as large exporters. Furthermore, import and export quotas are not easily obtained. This is due to the bureaucratic administrative regime and difficulties in the import-export licensing system that have prohibited SMEs from doing business directly. As a result they are restricted to operating as subcontractors for larger firms and SOEs.

Business people in Vietnam, particularly SMEs, also are affected by prejudiced cultural attitudes that have little confidence in the private sector, and perceive dealing with and being employed in SOEs as preferable to private sector employment. Vietnam's culture has yet to become "pro-enterprise"

## Training and Management Skills

Intellectual capital is the biggest strength of an underdeveloped or developing economy. Vietnam, with its high literacy rates lacks professional training systems for management skills. The government offers some training programs to enhance SMEs managerial skills and professional skills for SME labour.

However, the roles of these supporting agencies are still not specialized enough and too Training have theoretically biased to provide a high quality of advisory and training programs for SMEs. Training programs are not practically focused and are too general. Their low applicability and relevance of training content for the development requirements of SMEs and of the economy is a challenge.

**Table 5.4: Employees employed by SMEs by their education**

| | Total | College | Undergraduate | Master | PhD | Scientific PhD |
|---|---|---|---|---|---|---|
| Total S&T staff | 348.711 | 66.380 | 278.542 | 2.938 | 638 | 213 |
| % SMEs | 46.7 | 45.4 | 46.9 | 49.6 | 66.0 | 53.5 |
| Total R&D staff | 103.696 | 25.113 | 77.961 | 543 | 68 | 11 |
| % total S&T staff | 29.7 | 37.8 | 28.0 | 18.5 | 10.7 | 5.2 |
| R&D staff in SMEs | 45.684 | 10.100 | 35.271 | 264 | 38 | 11 |
| % S&T staff in SMEs | 28.1 | 33.5 | 27.0 | 18.1 | 9.0 | 9.6 |

**Source:** The Linkages Between Universities/Research Institutes And Small And Medium Enterprises By: Nguyen Dinh Cung, Pham Hoang Ha, Phan Duc Hieu, Hanoi, (2006)

R&D works in enterprise sector mainly relate to learning how to operate efficiently the imported technologies rather than to carrying research for technology renovation or product development. This situation is little bit worse in the SMEs as this ratio is generally lower than the average. Thus, the impacts of university education activities on the enterprise sector are further reduced as only small share of graduate people in the enterprise sector carry the R&D works and R&D works mainly relate to leaning the imported technologies.

There is mismatch in the supply and demand for university graduates mainly because the universities' teaching programs do not response to needs of enterprises. For example, engineering studies have a less weight in total university education, and the ratio of engineering to pure sciences students is very low. Consequently, there is comparatively high unemployment rate of university graduates. Moreover, the quality of graduates does not meet requirements of training high-quality S&T human resources

## Information

Right information at the right point in time can be critical for making an informed decision. The complexity in information systems between enterprises and the state management make the flow of information delayed and often inconsistent. As a result decisions like creditworthiness of a startup, new market reach, labour market condition, demand-supply regularity, etc. become a shot in the dark. As observed before, it also prevents the loss making entities to file bankruptcy.

Under the current system, market participants do not know the volumes that have been committed for export until they are loaded on the ship. This makes it difficult for the government and market participants to know the pace of exports commitment. Again, poor labour market information leads to job search still being dependent on personal connections, and information supply constrained by limited media outreach

Most of the SMEs work only on personal relations to fetch the right information. The sources not being authentic or audited lead to a chaotic multi- dimension and multi-source of information system which hinders the processing of information for timely and effective purposes. However, the costs involved with the information provision sources are too high to be affordable by an enterprise startup unaffordable cost for an SME.

## Some Other Difficulties

There is a continuing complexity in the business registration and licensing process. Being a new issue in Vietnam, there are too many unnecessary licenses, problems of management overlap and regulation barriers, particularly when businesses apply for a business license, tax file number or business seal.

Moreover, the limited implementation capacity in the business registration system and non-uniform implementation lead to a chaotic environment for beginners.

There is also observed a lack of proper insurance and other social welfares for SMEs, residence permit and registration, etc. The high risk involved with startups, their financial limitations and lack of information available about their viability makes it difficult for the insurance organizations to develop the ample trust and provide services to the same.

## Challenges Due to WTO

On one hand the introduction of "doi moi" policy has brought foreign investment to the state, while on the other it has also introduced it has brought sophisticated competition to the local producers. This competition is well equipped with better production methods and more supportive legal conditions making it cheaper and better. WTO introduction also tries to enhance the export worthiness of the local producers. However, it brings about a raise in the level of standards required to sustain international competition. This implicitly means technological and managerial up gradations. As stated above, lack of managerial human-resource hinders benefits WTO can bring. The lacuna thus created adversely affects the growth interests of the SMEs.

It is also observed that there is a need for a shift from tactical thinking to strategic thinking by SME owners. This may be attributed to the interest in making long-term strategies to increase sustainability and exploit the opportunities WTO would bring in terms of extended market reach.

## Promotional Policies and measures

### Policies

The Government of Vietnam has formulated the following policies to enhance the support for SMEs and encourage their start-ups and growth:

1. Realizing obstacles against SMEs development from the viewpoint of business scale and globalization impacts.
2. Putting forward non – financial promotion programs, reducing government subsidies, providing programs of training, consultancy & information – sharing, technology and innovation
3. Reducing direct supports and assistances to SMEs

4. Strengthening the role of local authorities to develop SMEs
5. Ensuring the comprehensive promulgation of policies

## Measures

—More Administrative Simplifications (Technology)

As a measure a simplified and more transparent legislative framework for land need to be developed. A single land use registry system covering the whole of Vietnam with a simple and transparent process for the assignment and leasing of land by SMEs from the State should support starting and scaling up of production. Furthermore, land use planning and zoning which ensures stable and simple access to land for SMEs should be useful. A system for land acquisition where the State takes responsibility for land compensation and clearance and reflects the cost in the land rental can make easier flow of information.

Moreover, an effective and transparent system for surveying and bringing back into effective use of unused land allocated for use by state enterprises should enable productivity of available land.

Raising information quality and credibility should better ascertain viability of a new project or a scale-up. A process standardization to collect such information and use the same for credit scoring is inevitable to make the credit and financial services better reachable. Interest subsidies and smoother financial enrollment processes are suggested.

The competition issues may be addressed by developing competitive neutrality between the private and the public sector. This can be enacted upon by instituting an independent administrative supervisory authority led by highly qualified and impartial professionals and provided with strong investigation and sanction powers. Again, international cooperation with foreign competition authorities must be developed to trade-off between the FDI incentives and the incubation for local producers competing with the former.

It is believed that investment in human resource development (HRD) is the best in long term interest of any economy. The growth potential of Vietnamese industrial sector can be further improved by making such investments.

Improving linkages between educational institutes and the industry is required. The programs offered should be customized with respect to the industry requirements. Moreover, Government involvement to incentivize the institutions to provide such knowledge resources can be effective. For the SME growth to reach another level, the aspiring Entrepreneurs also need to be trained to streamline their approach to evaluate and select right options.

—Creation of More Favorable Environment For SME (Partnership)

—Effective Management & Implementation of SME Development Plan

## References


1. Rajkumar Phatate and Sunil Shukla (2006). Feasibility Study Report for setting up Vietnam-India Entrepreneurship Development Centre (VIEDC). *Entrepreneurship Development Institute of India(EDII) Ahmedabad.*
2. Hitoshi Sakai and Nobuaki Takada (2000). Developing Small and Medium- Scale Enterprises in Vietnam. *Nomura Research Institute*
3. Nguyen Dinh Cung, Pham Hoang Ha, Phan Duc Hieu (2006): The Linkages Between Universities/Research Institutes And Small And Medium Enterprises
4. Nguyen, T. H. Alam, Q., Perry, M. & Prajogo, D. (2009). The Entrepreneurial role of the State and SME Growth in Vietnam, JOAAG, Vol. 4. No. 1
5. Vuong, Quan-Hoang and Tran, DungTri, The Cultural Dimensions of the Vietnamese Private Entrepreneurship(2009). *The IUP Journal of Entrepreneurship and Development, Vol.VI, No. 3 & 4, pp. 54-78. The Icfai University Press, September-December 2009*

# 23

# Challenges of Pharmaceutical Entrepreneurship in India: The SME Sector

***Abstract***

Evolution of Indian pharmaceutical industry per se will always revel the fact that growth path adopted by the Indian pharmaceutical industry is having conceptual difference in comparison to the growth pattern of organizations from other developed countries; however pharmaceutical industry is always knowledge as well as research and development driven. Number of Indian registered pharmaceutical companies has grown to approximately 24000 out of which only 250 to 300 companies could make a presence in Indian market by capturing almost 70 per cent market share. Alike other sectors, government could provide enough support to small and medium enterprises of Indian pharmaceutical industry which in return can achieve higher volume of production to meet domestic as well as international demand. A paradigm shift in business model could well be observed while conducting a rave review of literature on entrepreneurship in pharmaceutical industry-SME sector. Present study attempts to evaluate the conceptual framework on pharmaceutical industry-SME sectors modes of organization, resource acquisition, opportunity exploitation along with performance measurement on selected companies from Gujarat. Study is based on literature review along with personal interview for selected entrepreneurs with the help of a structured questionnaire. Further, study focuses on problem areas faced by the sector and outcomes may provide possible solutions to the identified problems and provide adequate inputs to practitioners for a strategic decision making.

## Introduction

As it has been observed and studied by many a researchers including economist, whether developed or developing country and economy, contribution of entrepreneurs are always quite significant. Although as on date no single definition of entrepreneur is globally accepted, yet researchers could conclude at one point that entrepreneurship is a certain set of behaviour observed in an individual or group of people. The word entrepreneur is borrowed from the French language. It is derived from 'entreprendre' meaning 'to undertake'. The word entrepreneur has been used even before 18th century but in recent time and socio-economic structure adequate importance has been perceived for achieving equitable growth or inclusive growth through encouraging entrepreneurship. Many a time it has been quoted that economic development is a matter of resource utilization where human resource included.

Entrepreneurs do undertake the risk of utilization of these resources in a organized way to achieve their set objective. Since independence up to recent time in Indian economy policy changes have taken place time to time where encouragement of entrepreneurship was vital point. Pre-independence industrial scenario was quite different than that of post independence, however various global economic platform could recognize Indian economy as quite closed in nature up to 2005, the product patent regime, scenario have changed and will change further at least in strategic point of view.

Indian economy as well as industry could operate under highly protected environment up to 1990, though the justification of same is a matter of moot interest for researchers. This period could observe departure of many multinational organizations from Indian market but today the situation is just reverse. Even once considered to be superpower of this world recognizing India as opportunity, right or wrong further debate may go on. Under this context when free trade could start since 1990 and after 1st January 2005 because of accepting product patent, Indian economy could take another turn.

Pharmaceutical Industry per se being science driven in other word patent sensitive started reorganizing themselves for finding out a solution for survival and growth. In recent past sell out of Indian pharmaceutical giant RANBAXY, whose growth journey was also from a small enterprise to the present, can validate the point of changing scenario of pharmaceutical sector. While debate was on with the decision of selling out RANBAXY by 3rd generation entrepreneurs, further business development in turbulent economy took place in same line of selling out Nicholas Piramals pharmaceutical formulation business to Abbott pharmaceuticals. In both the cases common point came out because of no new molecule development in their research and development they decided to withdraw from this research driven industry. Published report suggesting that RANBAXY could get approximately Rs 10,000 crores in their sale out deal which is cost of development of a new molecule in R&D that to with ten to fifteen years of research.

Indian pharmaceutical industry could create an impression in global pharmaceutical market mainly in terms of volume of production and excellence in process patent, both are indicator of production excellence. This has been highlighted and recorded many a time that next to United States India is having maximum number of 'US FDA' approved production facilities which is approximately sixty plus in number, again another indicator of strength in production facilities. Analysis of pre to post independence data will always prove the fact that India could meet domestic demand as well as earn revenue through export because of sizeable volume of production.

## Objective of study

Present study has been undertaken with the solemn objective to evaluate challenges of pharmaceutical entrepreneurship in India, in context to small and medium enterprises. In the process of creating organization to achieve objective by utilizing resources there are many a deviations from the expectation of conceptual framework which creates a gap, this gap analysis will be the outcome of this study with a direction to future study too. Pharmaceutical industry can be classified in various ways and to narrow down the study for a focused approach, organizations engaged in manufacturing as well as marketing of pharmaceutical formulation products in other word generic products has been undertaken. Measuring challenges for industry in absolute term is quite difficult so findings have been presented as case-let manner.

## Methodology

In this study data has been generated from both the sources primary as well as secondary. Structured questionnaire has been designed to conduct personal as well as focus group interviews. Attempt has been made to relate secondary data with primary and presented as case-let manner. While conducting interviews of entrepreneurs data extracted from secondary source has been placed for further findings for considering same as industry specific.

## Conceptual Framework for SME

As per the guideline and recommendation of government of India and respective bodies for promotion of small and medium enterprises the conceptual framework for pharmaceutical industry also remains same as for other sector.

There has been major as well as minor changes been observed in policy which has direct as well as indirect impact on pharmaceutical industry too. While analyzing the data and nature of pharmaceutical industry which is always science and knowledge driven focus on regulatory affair has been observed in the framework.

Classification of industry along with nature is based on types of products adopted for manufacturing like formulation; bulk further divisions are also there. While raised the question in individual discussion as well as focus group interview on the increase of number of registered pharmaceutical companies various points came in surface where most important point is profitability and opportunity are the major points of attraction for entrepreneurs in this sector.

However, in conceptual framework during survey on the mode of organization it was quite obvious that lack of concrete planning is missing. Many a time because of government regulation and entrepreneur's past professional experience as chemist in pharmaceutical industry motivated them to initiate or form their present venture. Paradoxical point could well be observed because of capacity utilization of their unit they are surviving but always looking forward for a better opportunity. Capacity utilization in a sense is they have job work for other established companies as a result they can run the show however in job work profitability is low.

## Gap in conceptual framework

Government of India under the development along with encouragement of micro, small and medium enterprises could unfold a framework where turnover along with investment in plant and machinery is a major criterion. Present study could compare the nature of industry and investment pattern along with the government regulations where on a major point during interview a gap could well be observed. In pharmaceutical manufacturing to full-fill the regulation like schedule-M, good manufacturing practices (GMP) along with world health organization (WHO) to upgrade the manufacturing unit we need to consider the further investment part which is much higher than the routine investment.

Further, to meet the need of the customer whether domestic or overseas depending upon type of product that is liquid, solid or injections on packaging front customers will always place the most modern and attractive options. For example in oral capsule form in Indian market there is a popular demand of alualu pack which is depended on availability of a particular machine and further cost is involved in it. Paradoxical point is older manufacturing pattern is replaced by the modern machines which is costly affair for entrepreneurs and in majority of the cases entrepreneurs fail to upgrade their production unit in time. However as quoted in reports production efficiency is always depended on few factors like :

(a) Capacity utilization is a key driver in cost management and production efficiency
(b) Contract manufacturers have lower product margins, resulting in higher conversion costs as a percentage of total sales
(c) Too much variety in product types can lead to under-utilized equipment and diluted management, maintenance and quality focus.

While compared with the entrepreneurs view point they could agree on all three points and they look for expert support on all three to improve their production efficiency. They are with the view point that with their own marketing set-up better profitability can always be achieved which they lack at this point of time.

While conducting focus group interviews as well as personal interviews of some of the entrepreneurs it was quite obvious and evident that primary data generation is quite difficult from them, consequently same became limitation of this study. However from available data following case-lets can be presented without disclosing the identity of the organization as requested by the entrepreneurs. One case-let is presented here by mentioning name of the organization because some published data was available and some could be collected from pharmaceutical professionals.

Present case-lets will provide enough direction for future in depth study which can provide further direction to the problem areas.

## Case-let- 1

Mr. Ravi Saxena (name changed for identity purpose) never had a dream even that someday he will own a pharmaceutical production unit though as small and medium enterprises. With a smiling face he could reply yes sir I own this plant which is producing approximately one hundred products in liquid form of various composition. Surprising to note but he is running the business with required profit though looking for further volume with profit. When enquired we could found that he used to work with the company as employee and had a very good relation with the owner who was the first generation entrepreneur and started this company and Mr. Saxena is also continuing with the same name now.

Initiator as first generation entrepreneur could realize that his sons are not interested to run the business so the most reliable employee of him Mr. Saxena got the offer from him to continue the show. Mr. Saxena though not qualified enough and used to work in the same unit with few hundred rupees salary took the opportunity and took over the charge as owner. After approximately fifteen years of operation which he is managing independently now, with a profit and no liability is worried too for future growth. While interaction with Mr. Saxena who is a very down to the earth personality and to some extent very clear and open in his thought could summarize few points as his problem area. He is worried because of following points:

(a) He could control his operation up to present level single handedly and surviving but worried for further growth because his turnover is less than 1 crore in a year.
(b) His unit is located in a small town of Gujarat where at local level even qualified pharmaceutical professionals are not available while he is ready to offer good remuneration but people are not even ready to accept his offer from nearby bigger towns/cities. He could even share his view that whether, we as professional can help him or not?
(c) Though he can assess the point that he should expand his operation mainly in terms of market and marketing but unable to do so because not having skilled professional with him.
(d) At manufacturing level he is not expanding to other section like oral solids (tablets/capsules) or even injectables because he cannot

control the required marketing expertise. Further, he could upgrade his plant up to schedule-M as per the guideline and planning for GMP (good manufacturing practices) but when asked about why not WHO-GMP? His reply was when he cannot reach up to domestic market fully so why to plan for export as WHO-GMP compliance is pre-requisite for exporting products to other countries.

## Managerial implication and suggestion

On the basis of discussion we had with the entrepreneur (Mr. Saxena) following points could be placed before respective bodies and authorities for future research and consideration. Pharmaceutical business because of profitability is highly attractive but always knowledge driven in nature so authorities must consider followings for their policy framework.

(a) Pharmaceutical sector should not focus only on production front but must provide enough support to entrepreneurs in market as well as marketing front.

(b) Academic research must be supported and encouraged to explore more data to identify problem areas to provide a sustainable growth to the SME sector.

(c) Product selection to positioning must be supported in professional manner as a result healthy competition can be encouraged.

## Case-let- 2

Authors of this paper having sufficient industry exposure in terms of academic research as well as organizational exposure as a result this case-let has been selected on the basis of peculiarity observed on it. Present case-let will further validate the point that we need to support entrepreneurs in a professional manner. In this case-let also because of identity problem names has been changed however required supportive data could be generated for present and future study also.

In Indian pharmaceutical industry rise and fall of regional companies are known to all keeping updated information on sector. Rise of Ranbaxy from scratch to the present level up to sell out to Japanese giant Daichi is a lesson for strategist too. As quoted in story of Ranbaxy by Bhupinder arora in his book Ranbaxy also started journey as pharmaceutical trading house. In this case-let we are presenting a case which is again example how number of registered pharmaceutical companies growing in India? When conducted the interview it was evident that Arora brothers (Name changed) inspired by profitability in pharmaceutical formulation business started their operation sometime in 1980's. Neither they have registered the company nor the products (brands) with trade mark authority but they could arrange for a loan license production arrangement at Gujarat. Loan license arrangement is a production arrangement under another company having entire production facility so here two organizations are in business transaction. Arora brothers could even provide a name to their company as they will market their products in a particular state by promoting products at doctors' level. To promote their company's products (formulations with a specific name) they could recruit some medical representatives who will directly report to them. Pharmaceutical formulations those days even could provide a profit of 400%, while cost of the products are even lowest in India (Table 2) so survival with a small volume was possible for them because of higher profitability. As quoted in the book of Hisrich (entrepreneurship) and types of entrepreneur Arora brothers could fall under as life style entrepreneur though entered in a business where high profitability is there. In loan license arrangement those days regulation was even if you do not produce any product in a particular month you have to pay a fixed amount to the manufacturer for the license. They have to keep an office in that particular town where loan license arrangement has been taken so that was another cost of business. This has been observed many a time in present style of pharmaceutical entrepreneurship entire financial planning is based on credit mainly in backward integration which is another area of detail study. Because of improper financial backup in the case of Arora brothers also after few years of operation they failed to pay even their loan license fee to the manufacturer.

Consequently they had to work for another business model as a result they invited another partner who is the production in charge of the production unit where Arora brothers having loan license. Entire data could be gathered through this person for our present case-let whose name also we have to change for identity purpose. While interviewed the person (Mr. Ravi) he could share the profitability attracted him to the business though not having much idea on pharmaceutical marketing as his core area is manufacturing. From our study even it is clear as per the form of organization entire arrangement is very vague as they cannot approach financial institutions even for working capital because of structure of the organization. Mr. Ravi could arrange some finance from private source in tune of rupees 10 lakhs to boost the operation while took a risk of launching marketing operation in another state with independent control. As Mr. Ravi not having enough marketing experience so too help of another person who is his colleague having some experience of marketing. They launched their marketing operation in a state with a structure of 16 medical representative and 3 area sales manages along with 1 regional managers with a sizeable amount of fixed cost. Because of improper financial planning and back-up operation could survive for six months only and entire marketing operation of the state could collapse, however organization as business entity is surviving till date.

**Learning**

While comparing both the case lets as discussed in brief we can summarize following points:

(a) In case-let one there is financial planning so Mr. Saxena is surviving but looking for professional help for future growth. In case-let two there is a lack of financial planning which is again a professional help Mr. Ravi is looking for to survive in the business.

(b) If further study could be conducted on this sector possibility of finding out too many similar cases like present cases cannot be ignored.

**Case-let- 3**

**Rise of Mankind pharmaceutical and future plan**

Researchers and policy makers must be surprised to believe that in Indian context many organizations could rise up to national level even to some extent created a strong presence in international market while growing from regional shape and size. Ranbaxy, Alchem, Aristo to mention few could grow from a regional level to their present size. Presenting the case-let of Mankind pharmaceutical because their journey as well as growth path is matter of discussion in board room of other companies. Some published reports are available now for this company so comparison with case-let 2 and case-let 1 can provide direction for further research as well as policy framework.

Mr. R.C. Juneja, founder and chairman of Mankind pharmaceutical who is a science graduate started his journey to reach up to present level with a small step in the year 1995 from Meerut. An in depth analysis of available data along with field interaction with pharmaceutical professionals of other organization's will support the idea that Mankind's approach was and always is market driven.

Growth up to present level is summarized in table (3 & 4 ) where it is quite clear that Mr. Juneja and his team had to struggle very hard between

1995 to 2002 that is till the date they became a national company. Strategy adopted by Mankind in initial days is reflecting the fact that being market driven and involvement of entire field force company could record a turnover of Rs.4 crore with 52 people working with them and same turnover could shot up to Rs.8 crore. In the year 2009 they had a revenue of more than Rs.1,250 crore and this year they are expecting a growth in revenue of 30 percent. Unlike other small and medium enterprises who will first focus on production facility, Mankind as started with a very small capital base could do reverse by focusing on market along with marketing while creativity was in central theme. As strategy they tried to serve those markets where others were not operating with very innovative combination of formulations with lowest possible price without compromising in quality.

## Recommendations/Managerial Implication

On the basis of personal interview as well as focus group interview following points came out which can be considered for future study and recommendations even. Interestingly when we compare the report of task force on MSME (Table 1) with three case-lets in this paper along with points came out during interview with entrepreneurs, sufficient similarities could be observed however some of the points should always be considered as topmost priority these are:

(a) Timely and sufficient financial support to upgrade the production facility of the pharmaceutical SMEs so that they can come up to global standard.
(b) Managerial expertise and support to them in terms of training and development.
(c) At marketing as well as development of network SMEs always expect support in organized way.
(d) In the case of capacity utilization of the plant after upgrading the units they always face a problem because always do not have sufficient job work.

## Limitation of this study

Considering the industry size in terms of volume and number, drawing a conclusion with this study will not be academically correct however some of the points are indicators. Apart from data generation because of conservative mindset of entrepreneurs, time and sample size along with required financial support was a limitation but an in depth future study can always be initiated on the basis of present study.

## References

1. Chaudhury, S. (2005). The WTO and India's pharmaceutical industry.
2. Kale, D. & Athreye, S. (2006) Experimentation with strategy in the Indian Pharmaceutical sector.
3. Pradhan & Prakash, J. (2006) Global competitiveness of Indian Pharmaceutical industry: Trends and Strategies.
4. Pradhan, P. J. & Sahu, P.P. (January 2008). Defining the role of government in transnationalization efforts of Indian SMEs- A case study of Indian pharmaceutical industry.
5. Reddy, N. P. (2010). Entrepreneurship text and cases.
6. Report of Prime Minister's task force on micro, small and medium enterprises, (January 2010).
7. Rao, Manohar, J. (2007) , Globalization, technology and competition.
8. Rao, Subba, S.V.R. (1997). Pharmaceutical marketing in India.
9. Ramu, Shiva, S. (1997). Globalization-The Indian scenario.
10. Shahani, R. (2006). Wanted a pragmatic policy. *The Hindu Survey of Indian Industry,* 221-226
11. Smarta, B,R.(1997). Revitalizing the pharmaceutical business.

**Table (1) Major issues concerning the MSME sector**

| Although Indian MSMEs are a diverse and heterogeneous group, they face some common problems, which are briefly indicated below : |
|---|
| • Lack of availability of adequate and timely credit;<br>• High cost of credit;<br>• Collateral requirements;<br>• Limited access to equity capital;<br>• Problems in supply to government departments and agencies;<br>• Procurement of raw materials at a competitive cost;<br>• Problems of storage, designing, packaging and product display;<br>• Lack of access to global markets;<br>• Inadequate infrastructure facilities, including power, water, roads, etc.;<br>• Low technology levels and lack of access to modern technology;<br>• Lack of skilled manpower for manufacturing, services, marketing, etc.;<br>• Multiplicity of labour laws and complicated procedures associated with compliance of such laws;<br>• Absence of a suitable mechanism which enables the quick revival of viable sick enterprises and allows unviable entities to close down speedily; and<br>• Issues relating to taxation, both direct and indirect, and procedures thereof. |

**Table (2) PHARMACEUTICAL PRICES IN SELECT COUNTRIES**

| | Drugs, dosage form and strength | Pack | Price in India (Rs) | Price in Pakistan (Rs) | Price in Indonesia (Rs) | Price in U.S. (Rs) | Price in U.K. (Rs) |
|---|---|---|---|---|---|---|---|
| | Anti-infectives | | | | | | |
| 1 | Ciprofloxacin HCL 500 mg tabs | 10's | 29 | 423.86 | 393 | 2352.4 | 1185.7 |
| 2 | Norfloxacin 400 mg tabs | 10's | 20.7 | 168.71 | 130.63 | 1843.7 | 304.78 |
| 3 | Ofloxacin 200 mg tabs | 10's | 40 | 249.3 | 204.34 | 1973.8 | 818.3 |
| 4 | Cefpodoxime Proxetil 200 mg tabs | 6's | 114 | 357.32 | 264 | 1576.6 | 773.21 |
| 1 | NSAIDs Diclofenac Sodium 50 mg tabs | 10's | 3.5 | 84.71 | 59.75 | 674.77 | 60.96 |
| | Anti-ulcerants | | | | | | |
| 1 | Ranitidine 150 mg tab | 10's | 6.02 | 74.09 | 178.35 | 863.59 | 247.16 |
| 2 | Omeprazole 30 mg caps | 10's | 22.5 | 578 | 290.75 | 2047.5 | 870.91 |
| 3 | Lansoprazole 30 mg caps | 10's | 39 | 684.9 | 226.15 | 1909.6 | 708.08 |

**Table (3) MANKIND'S SUCCESS STORY**

| Year | Expansion and growth |
|---|---|
| 2008 | • Achieved 35% growth<br>• 1st rank all-India as per prescription/ doctor/ month<br>• 4th rank in India & 3rd in north India as per market Analysis<br>• 21 brands at no.1, 14 brands at no 2<br>• 53 brands in top 5 position as per market analysis |
| | |
| 2007 | • Launched Future Mankind, Special Mankind and VetMankind<br>• Acquired Magnet Labs Pvt. Ltd<br>• ChrysCapital become an investor partner<br>• Tied up with Roche Diagnostic for the marketing of product 'Accu-Chek Go' |
| | |
| 2006 | • Established injectable state-of-the-art unit at Paonta Sahib ( Himachal Pradesh )<br>• Group turnover surged up to Rs.512 crore |
| | |
| 2005 | • Launched Lifestar Pharma. Invested Rs.50 lakh to start operations |
| | |
| 2002 | • Company established its operations all over India<br>• Launched new division Discovery Mankind |
| 1995 | • Inception of Mankind Pharma |

Source : Adopted from entrepreneur November 2010 volume 2 issue 3 page 63- 66

**Table (4)**

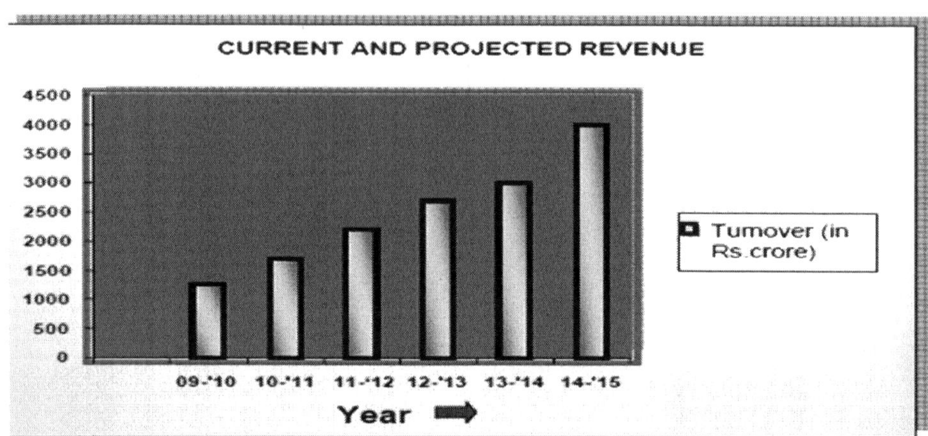


Source : Adopted from entrepreneur November 2010 volume 2 issue 3 page 63- 66

# 24

# Challenges faced by Small Scale Entrepreneurs

***Abstract***

The paper deals with the actual problems faced by the Entrepreneurs in micro and small scale industries; based on facts of author & experience of other entrepreneurs. It is very important to have proper location and partner for setting up a successful unit. If one desires to have the partner, he must have good business standing and should not be a defaulter of any bank. In one case due to financial constraints, a bank defaulted land lord was admitted as a partner and the entrepreneur lost one year to take off his project. In the same case as all R.M and finished market was within 5km radius, he was interested to set unit in the same area. Ultimately he chose to have unit in SIDC As a entrepreneur, he had an advantage of having all infrastructure at best price ; and he got loan facility from nationalized bank Earlier he was forced to go to cooperative bank where cost of interest was very high and had to compromise for inadequate cc limits.

In few cases author observed that working capital was diverted for buying e.g. a house or a car. Majority of entrepreneurs divert the project finance for other purpose. Entrepreneur should postpone such purchases till he starts getting good profits and generate surplus funds. It is also observed that C.A. encourages showing losses, many times it erodes entrepreneur's capital; as a result his growth stops. This observation is in more than 80% cases. Entrepreneur's must learn fast about financial aspect, taxes etc. so that his dependency on consultants should be minimal or he should be in position to analyse the advice of tax consultant and its impact on his business.

In another case, due to inadequate or lower profit margins, entrepreneur could not sustain changes in import policies resulting closing of the plant. According to author no project should be under taken unless and until cost of R.M. or components are 40 to50% of selling price. One entrepreneur decided to expand his existing production in backward area, and he failed due to non availability of skilled and managerial personnel. Further he did not anticipate time taken to disburse the seed capital and other govt. benefits of backward area zone.

The author has noticed failure of entrepreneurs when first time Centre Govt. introduced C.Ex. Concessions to SSI unit in 1978.Hence it is vital for an entrepreneur to have knowledge of direct and indirect taxes. While running a unit entrepreneur comes across various problems in administration, production, marketing, break downs in machinery, quality and delivery of products in time soon & so forth. For efficient management ; building teams, treating the personnel as human beings, having the mission statement, vision, values, strategies, systems, empowerment of employees etc.; is vital but due to ignorance of entrepreneurs on above qualities; they cannot progress. Hence banks must conduct or insist for training to entrepreneurs on these qualities which is the need of the hour.

The paper deals with the actual problems faced by the Entrepreneurs in micro and small scale industries; based on facts of author & experience of other entrepreneurs. It is very important to have proper location and partner for setting up a successful unit. Both things have long term effects. Hence, one has to be very careful while choosing a partner and location of manufacturing unit. As far as partner is concerned, he must have good business standing, experience in the subject, good character and should not be a defaulter of any banks, if he is already running another business. His temperament and nature should match with your temperament. Your weakness should be his strength. as per SWOT analysis. Please get details of his bankers and counter check it with bank branch manager for his status of his banking account. It happened with author that he chose a partner who was bank defaulter unknowingly. He chose that partner only because he was having his own unit and he offered one shed for the project. His shed was out of SIDC. As a result, he could not get any financial assistance from any institute till he decided to get rid of the defaulter partner and he lost his money, time and energy due to delay in the project by more than a year. He also landed in losses and he had to borrow money from his relatives for completion of the project.

For manufacturing plant, location should be as far as possible in SIDC and all major and critical raw materials should be available easily nearby. If majority of components are imported, then it should be near to the port. Cost of transportation is a recurring expense and hence it is very important to have proper location of the plant. Apart from this, the time required to reach the plant should be minimal. This reflects in the inventory cost.

Author put up his unit later on in MIDC for manufacturing Dyes and Textile Auxiliaries. His decision proved very much beneficial to him as all raw materials were available nearby and finished products had buyers in the same MIDC. Cost of transportation and low inventory proved to be beneficial to him. Further, when he had his unit in other industrial estate, he could not get loan from nationalized banks and as a result he had to opt for Co-op bank. The interest rates were higher and Co-op bank was not in a position to give adequate CC limits. Interest is having a long term effect on your project. Hence it is also equally important to have good banker for the project.

At SIDC, all infrastructures such as electricity, water and good roads are available. One can get permeations from various authorities quickly as compared to non SIDC location. In some SIDC, concessions are available for Octroi, Import duty, etc. In backward zone lots of benefits are available such as tax holidays, incentives and subsidies for project. It varies from one state to another state. Hence, it is very important to have proper location based on various factors for viability of the proposed project. At the same time, an Entrepreneur has to check at his end, his ability to implement the project successfully. Particularly for small and medium scale units, it is very difficult to execute the project successfully, as many times they face problems of availability of skilled manpower and senior management positions. The benefits available are disbursed only after completion of project. The entrepreneur should have adequate funds for completing the project. The author had faced similar problems for his export oriented unit in backward zone in Maharashtra State. His calculation based on policy went hay wire and he had to borrow money from the market at very high interest rate and after completion he could not get even a Works

Manager to look after the factory. According to author only professionally managed companies can get benefits from backward zone.

Hence location plays a very vital role for the success of a project. In few cases author observed that working capital was diverted for buying e.g. a house or a car. This is done to justify their status in society. Majority of entrepreneurs divert the project finance for other purposes. Entrepreneur should postpone such purchases till he starts getting good profits and generate surplus funds. Diversion of fund will lead to industrial sickness and put the project in jeopardy.

It is also observed that Chartered Accountants encourages showing losses, many times it erodes entrepreneur's capital; as a result his growth stops. If a unit is making reasonable gross profit, in that case depreciation and other admissible expenses should be debited to the extent that firm makes net profit. This observation is in more than 80% cases. This will increase capital and hence it will help the entrepreneurs to raise funds when ever needed. If balance sheet shows losses, in that case capital erodes and financial institutions will not be willing to finance for expansion, etc. The author had seen that public limited companies manage the balance sheet showing profit for raising fund from public issue for the proposed project. Few of them go to such an extent that they give dividends as well. Entrepreneur's having technical background must learn fast about financial aspects, taxes etc. so that their dependency on consultants should be minimal or they should be in position to analyze the advice of tax consultants and its impact on his business.

Govt. policy changes have a great impact on a running business. In one chemical intermediate manufacturing unit, firm decided to take up an import substitute product for manufacturing. Earlier the unit had suffered heavy losses due to famous textile strike by Dr. Datta Samant in Mumbai in 1981.The firm had taken decision to go for import substitute product and after successful implementation of project, the unit stared recovering from the losses and after 3-4months import duty was slashed down drastically, and his product was no more viable and the company had to suffer heavy losses as they could not market their product as imported product was available at much cheaper price than their selling price. During 80,s many companies had failed, due to frequent changes in import duties and few had prospered.

Author had faced great difficulties due to changes in govt. policies mainly Central excise. He shifted his project to MIDC in 1977 with loan facilities from MSFC and SBI, having his breakeven point of sale of Rs.2.0 lakhs /month. Till Feb 1978, everything was fine even by paying excise duty to the tune of 35%. In 1978, Janata Govt declared concessions in excise duties to SSI unit for the first turnover of Rs.5.0 lakhs-Zero duty. This might have helped many micro and small scale units, but it hampered the unit of author as his breakeven point was high. End users and traders took maximum advantage of this policy to squeeze the entrepreneurs in various manufacturing sector. In case of authors unit, process houses were not willing to buy by paying 35% extra excise duty as others were in a position to supply without excise duty. He had to find various options to keep his unit running healthy such as export and introduction of new products which will not attract excise duty. He stared producing textile auxiliaries without aid of power. For the products manufactured without the aid of power there was nil duty for no limit on turn over. He also developed export market. This cost him more capital which he had borrowed from his friend and relatives. Some big names now in chemical industries had also taken the benefit of manufacturing products without aid of power and made their fortune. It is observed that banks do not give timely assistance to the needy and deserving entrepreneurs. This many times affect malfunctioning of the unit and in a long run, unit becomes a NPA unit. If the bank officers help timely to such units, not only it will help the entrepreneurs but his bank's profit will go up. And therefore it is vital that proper training be given to the bank officers, who are having such discretionary powers, as it will help them to exercise the powers in a proper and efficient manner. Hence it appropriate to train bank officers for effective execution and Leadership qualities. If the financial institutes do not help the entrepreneurs in time, then the entrepreneurs have to raise the money from open market by paying high interest cost. This is the beginning point of distrust between the entrepreneur and the financial institute. In the beginning they spend lot of time in arranging the finance or requesting the bank officer to honor their Cheque. If the problem does not get resolve at this stage, then entrepreneur opts for going for a current account in another bank. Everyone knows that time is money; however this precious time of entrepreneur is being lost for unproductive cause. Over a long period this results in improper functioning of the unit and ultimately turning into NPA unit.

The author was associated as consultant with one unit manufacturing chemical process equipments having turnover of almost 10 cr. The entreprencur was very ambitious and he wanted to expand his enterprise to 100 Crore turnover in the next 3-4 years. The pain areas from author's findings were mismanagement, lack of system, lack of strategy for reaching to the targeted objective, financial indiscipline or lack of financial planning for reaching to target, lack of trained managerial and supervisory staff etc. The entrepreneur had strong desire and ambitions, but he does not want to change and wants to operate his unit in the same fashion. Further, he had some short comings and lacked some of the desired qualities of a successful entrepreneur. He lacked trust level in all areas; which will detract him from his ambition. As informed, he has already landed in financial problems.

Recently, author had come across another such unit which manufactures process equipment. The unit has huge accumulated losses and owner wants to turn it into profits. In this case reason of accumulated losses is lack of factory management, systems and improper marketing which has led to losses. The firm is having good machines, trained manpower and good products having large market. If it is used properly with small financial help, unit can become profit making unit in a year or so.

The author had almost four decades of experience in various fields and he would like to sum up as, most of the units go into losses due to diversion of fund and mismanagement of unit at various levels, improper handling of the labor force. Most of entrepreneurs are not willing to change and have inadequate qualities in them to run the unit. Further 50% units suffer due to not getting timely financial support from financial institutions. He had created at least a dozen entrepreneurs in various fields and all are successful by giving them hard earned advice and guidance. He also concludes as follow-

To have success, entrepreneurs require guidance at three stages-

1. Entrepreneurs starting a new venture: It is very important for them to have a clear idea about their objectives and they must draw a right plan. Research shows that 95% businesses fail in the first attempt. Guidance is required for planning and proper management of available funds. It is often noticed that funds are utilized for unplanned expenses which result in unavailability of funding for the right purpose for which you allocated it.
2. Entrepreneurs who are expanding: They have achieved success already and they are stuck up at a particular turnover for 2 to 3 years. They want to cross this and achieve higher feats and higher targets. At this stage they need a guidance to grow from consultants and their willingness to change.

3. Entrepreneurs who are struggling and riddled with problems: They have landed in problems of various natures like a few-inadequate working capital, production bottlenecks, cash flow problems, etc. This is when one wrong step can decide the fate of their business. They need expert advice to come out of all these problems successfully.

While running a unit entrepreneur comes across various problems in administration, production, marketing, break downs in machinery, quality and delivery of products in time so on & so forth. For efficient management building teams, treating the personnel as human beings, having the mission statement, vision, values, strategies, systems, empowerment of employees etc. is all vital but due to ignorance of entrepreneurs on above qualities, they cannot progress. 80% entrepreneurs are not willing to change their functioning style, do not empower the employees at various levels, not creating trustworthiness with all stake holders etc. Hence, banks must conduct or insist for training to entrepreneurs on these qualities which is the need of the hour. Why banks, because they are the ones who finance more than 75% of the cost of project and have major stake and hence they should take the initiative for proper training to entrepreneurs at various stages.

# 25

# Entrepreneurship and Small Business Survival Techniques: The Indian Experience

***Abstract***

The paper reports on the role of Entrepreneurs in the development of small business survival techniques. It reports on the various ways which small business entrepreneurs help their businesses to survive in the midst of too many small businesses fighting for survival. The paper points out the survival techniques being used by the various entrepreneurs. The paper identifies the following survival techniques used by the entrepreneurs: assessment of the future prospects of an industry, capital build-up and capital adequacy, working capital management, total quality management, the effective use of the Balanced Scorecard Model and coaching. The data for this paper has been collected through observation, textbooks, journals and business analysis newspapers. The paper concludes by advising the entrepreneurs on business diversification and consultation.

## Introduction

In the Business environment, the management team provides the necessary direction to be followed in order to achieve the goals and objectives of the organization. The management team has a composition of three levels, that is, the top level management engaged in the development of strategic techniques, the middle level management who are involved in the development of tactical technique and the lower level management charged with the development of operational techniques. The management team must make sure that they are current in all business activities and should be proactive rather than reactionary.

The management team should be very well vest with the mission, vision, goals and objectives of the company. They have a prima facie task of carefully analyzing the industry to see how it fits into the economy and making a careful review of the functioning of the markets. After completing an analysis of the economy and the overall markets, if the management is convinced that the economy and the markets are attractive from the point of carrying out business activities, the management should proceed to consider those activities that promise good prospects in the business environment.

The purpose of this paper is to high the survival techniques carefully implemented by the small business community in the Indian Sub-continent. The paper starts with a brief introduction, assessment of the future prospects of an industry, capital build up and capital adequacy, working capital management total quality management, coaching and a conclusion. The data for this paper has been collected through observation of the behavior and selling habits of small business owners in small parts of the Indian Sub-continent.

## Assessment the Future Prospects of an Industry

The management, in assessing the future prospects of an industry, should use the following four steps:

(i). Identifying the key factors about the industry in which they are operating or going to operate.

(ii). Conduct a careful examination of the potential Life cycle of the industry.

(iii). Make a careful analysis of the competitive position of the company in the industry.

(iv). Examine the segmentation of the industry and identify all profitable segments

### (i) The process of identifying the Key Factors of the industry

There are various factors which help in determining the future prospects of the industry. They are:

(a). past sales and earnings performance
(b). Permanence situation and growth of the industry
(c). Attitude of the government towards the industry
(d). Labour conditions and performance
(e). Industry share prices relative to industry earnings

**(ii) Past sales and Earnings Performance**

Analyzing the historical performance of the industry is one of the most effective ways to assess the industry. From the data of the past sales and the earnings performance, one has to interpret average levels and stability of performance and growth rates of sales and earnings.

**(iii) Permanence situation and growth of the Industry**

Permanence is a phenomenon related to the product and technology of the industry. Sometimes an industry is eliminated from the market scene because of another replacement industry that diminishes or eliminates the need for the original industry. The factor of permanence assumes considerable importance in assessing the prospects of hi-tech industries.

**(iv) Attitude of the Government**

The attitude of the government towards a particular industry is a very important factor to be considered. The government can help the selected industries in several ways which includes:

(a) liberalizing the industrial licensing procedures and other statutory control

(b) providing liberal financial assistance on soft term

(c) extending a more favorable treatment with regard to direct and indirect taxation and

(d) ensuring adequate protection from external competition by imposing imports quotas and tariffs. Conversely, the government can also initiate various measures that lend to hamper the growth of an industry.

**(v) Labour conditions and performance**

The labour conditions in the industry become more important with the strengthening of the labour unions. In industries which are either labour intensive or capital intensive, if the labour performs crucial operations, the possibility of a strike is an important factor to be reckoned.

## (vi) Industry Share Prices Relative to Industry Earnings

This factor evaluates the share prices of industry relative to the industry earnings. Sometimes in an industry all the factors discussed above may be favorable. The management has a duty to carefully evaluate and then make a decision in view of the organization's plans on how best to achieve its goals and objectives.

The industry trends provide the management team with the momentous to invest in that industry. Good decision making is required. This means that the management must have confidence and competence in what they do. They require conceptual skills, technical skills, leadership skills, human skills, communication skills and in addition they need compass and coaching to develop business survival techniques.

## Capital Build up and Capital Adequacy

The first resource of the company is management. Management has the obligation to arrange and direct the other company resources, like capital, land, and labour. The first thing for management to do is to source for adequate capital for the company. This is the responsibility of management. Top management decides the amount of capital that will be adequate and the sources from which such capital should be raised. The duty of the middle management is to decide on the capital structure of the company. How much of the share capital should be equity shares, how much should be preference shares and how much should be debentures or other stocks. The task of the lower level management is to decide how to raise it at a particular time and when the money should actually be raised and in what proportions. Management should remember that capital management is very important in a company environment. Having too much capital is as dangerous as having very small capital.

**Figure 1: Capital Adequacy Model**

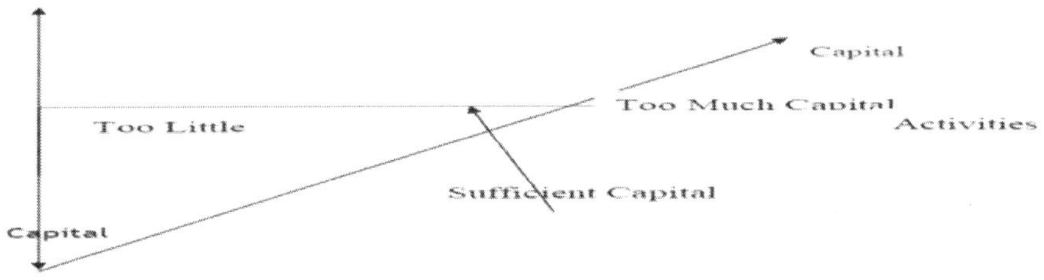

**Source:** Field Analysis (Visemih, 2010)

A company with too much capital creates idle resources. This means that the company is paying dividends and/or interest on capital that is not productive. On the hand, the company may be put in a situation where its capital is very insufficient. In this case, the company will not be working at full capacity. This will lead to poor performance, (see Fig. 1) Any company with insufficient capital will produce a low Marginal Capital Productivity (MCP) on the same footing any company with too much capital will certain produce an equally low Marginal Capital Productivity (MCP). The company with insufficient capital may eventually develop losses, but the company with too much capital may not generate losses. Its performance in the industry will certainly be below the industry average. This is because its capital capacity exceeds the entrepreneurial capacity. There exist an imbalance between the management strength and the capital it controls, (see Table 1).

**Table 1: Capital Adequacy Effect**

| Capital | Management | Consequence |
|---|---|---|
| Too Little | Enough | Low Profit |
| Sufficient | Enough | Low Profit /High Profit |
| Too Much | Enough | Low Profit |

**Source:** Field Analysis (Visemih, 2010)

The capital of a company when insufficient, the management cannot use it to adequately exploit the other resources. The capital must up to level that it can be used with too much sacrifice of quality. However, where the share capital is short, the management team should be allowed to borrow to make for the difference. Borrowing in the form of debt capital or debenture stock will provide the company with balanced capital and sufficient funds to adequately exploit the other resources of the company. Borrowing provides the company with leverage or gearing strategy. A highly geared or levered capital structure is one that is preferred in a booming economic situation. The management team must make sure that they are proactive in forecasting the trend of the economy, so that they can quickly adjust their capital structure to take advantage of the changing economic climate. This implies that where a boom period is foreseen, management should adjust its capital to a highly geared situation and when a depression is eminent the management team should adjust its capital to a lowly geared situation. Using the example in Table 2 and 3, we can find out why the management team should always adjust its capital to suite a particular economic condition.

A company's financial strategy establishes an effective and efficient match between its competences and opportunities and environmental risks. It provides a mechanism integrating the goals of its multiple consistencies. Every entrepreneur should make sure that any strategy selected for implementation is company goal congruent, that is, the company's operating policies. In addition to financial strategies, the company must be involved in innovative research in order to keep the company afloat. Key in the agenda should be research into new products, making sure that new products are introduced with the declining life of other products. Management should develop new unique sales strategies to encourage customers to stay loyal to the company's products. Management must employ competent staff who through their enthusiasm in the work environment will add value to the company's reputation. With a good reputation, the company can withstand competitive forces and other pressures.

Cash flow pressures are normal in a business environment, but must not be ignored, since cash flow is necessary for the survival of the business/ company. In Tables 2 and 3, the figures illustrate the position of a company in two economic periods, under two different capital planning strategies. Looking at the figures in the two tables in absolute terms, one will be tempted to advise the company management to take the lowly geared strategy during good economic conditions. It has a profit after interest of Rs 18,500 against the highly geared strategy with Rs 17,600. However, using the Earnings Per Share (EPS) to the same situation the advice will be different. The good year in Table 1 produces a better EPS than the good year in Table 2. In Table 1, the EPS is Rs 0.352 as opposed to the EPS in Table 3 of Rs 0.23125. The advice therefore, is for the management team to always adopt the highly geared strategy, during good economic times, in order to maximize profits. During bad economic periods the lowly geared strategy should be adopted. The leverage, (capital structure) of a company is highly geared when debt capital is higher than the equity capital. It is therefore lowly geared when the equity capital is higher than the debt capital.

**Table 2: Highly Geared Company Situation**

| S.N | Type of Economic Condition | Capital Structure | | Number of shares @ R1 per share | Profit/(loss) / Interest | EPS |
|---|---|---|---|---|---|---|
| 1 | Bad year with a Profit of Rs 2,000 | Equity<br>3% Debt | Rs 50,000<br>Rs 80,000 | 50,000 shares<br>Nill | Nill<br>Rs 2,400 | Nill |
| | | | | | | |
| 2 | Good year with a Profit of Rs 20,000 | Equity<br>3% Debt | Rs 50,000<br>Rs 80,000 | 50,000 shares<br>Nill | Rs 17,600<br>Rs 2,400 | Rs 0.352 |

**Source:** Field Analysis (Visemih, 2010)

**Table 3: Lowly Geared Company Situation**

| S.N | Type of Economic Condition | Capital Structure | | Number of shares @ R1 per share | Profit/(loss)/ Interest | EPS |
|---|---|---|---|---|---|---|
| 1 | Bad year with a Profit of Rs 2,000 | Equity<br>3% Debt | Rs 80,000<br>Rs 50,000 | 80,000 shares<br>Nill | Rs 500<br>Rs 1,500 | R 0.00625 |
| | | | | | | |
| 2 | Good year with a Profit of Rs 20,000 | Equity<br>3% Debt | Rs 80,000<br>Rs 50,000 | 80,000 shares<br>Nill | Rs 18,500<br>Rs 1,500 | Rs 0.23125 |

**Source:** Field Analysis (Visemih, 2010)

The Capital Build up and Capital Adequacy strategy of business survival implies that the management team should be able to keep the business at a manageable size, which can allow for survival in the future. Business continuity is a concept, buried deep in the mind of every entrepreneur. This is the best survival strategy which keeps small businesses alive. The Indian entrepreneur prefers a small business that is running on a daily target basis.

## Working Capital Management

A company needs both fixed and circulating capital in order to run smoothly. Fixed capital is in the form of fixed assets, such as land, buildings, furniture and fittings, equipment and machinery. The company's capital is always divided into two components, namely: permanent capital and circulating capital. The permanent capital is in the form of fixed assets and circulating capital is in the form of current assets, but minus current liabilities. The management team should avoid the risk of running short of working capital. Working capital to a company is like blood in the human system. In the human system, when blood is short or runs out the system cannot function well and may grind to a halt. The same applies to a company. When working capital is not there or is short, the system cannot function as well as expected.

Working capital therefore is defined as current assets less current liabilities. The components of current assets are: stocks (raw materials, finished goods, and work in progress), debtors, prepayments, marketable securities, bank and cash. The most important item of current liabilities is trade creditors. However, any payables a current nature should be added in order to complete the items of current liabilities.

### (a). Debtors' Management

In order to survive, companies sale on credit. It is a competition strategy design to grow faster than the companies' competitors. It is used as a marketing tool to maintain or expand the company's sales. Trade credit creates a current asset in the form of debtors (book debts) or accounts receivable. A company's investment in accounts receivable depends on the volume of credit sales, the collection period and collection rate. The volume of credit sales should be large, but the collection period should be relatively short. The company needs money to function smoothly. This means that the company requires a high collection ratio. With a high collection ratio, the company is sure of available working capital for smooth operations.

The financial director is the key person who can influence the volume of credit sales and the collection period through a reasonable credit policy. A good credit policy includes credit standards, credit terms, and proper collection efforts. The incremental return that a company may gain by changing its credit policy should be compared with the cost of funds invested in receivables. The company's credit policy will be considered optimum at the point where incremental rate of return (IRR) equals the cost of funds (COF), (see Figure 2). The cost of funds is related to risk; it increases with risk. The important goal of credit policy is to maximise the shareholders wealth; it is neither maximisation of sales nor minimisation of bad-debt losses.

Credit Standards are the various criteria used by the financial entrepreneur to decide to whom credit sales can be made and by how much. Where the company sets poor standards and sells to customers who are not credit worthy, its sales may increase, but its incremental rate of return will not increase. This is because its costs in the form of bad-debt losses and credit administration will increase heavily. The financial director must therefore, consider the impact in terms of increase in profits and increase in costs of a change in credit standards or any other policy variable.

**Figure 2: The Optimum Credit Sales Model**

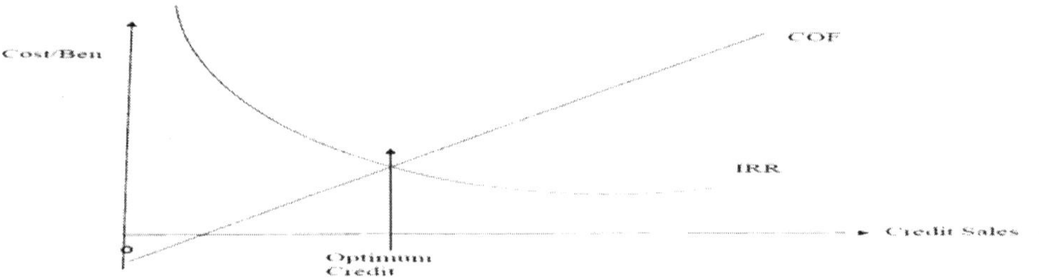

**Source:** Field Analysis (Visemih, 2010)

The conditions for extending credit sales are called credit terms and they include the credit period and cash discount. Cash Discounts are given for receiving payments before the normal credit period. All customers do not pay within the credit period. Therefore, a company has to make efforts to collect payments from customers. Customers should be encouraged to pay fines on overdue accounts.

Collection efforts of the company are aimed at accelerating collections from slow-payers and reducing bad-debt losses. The company should have a credit control officer whose job is to thoroughly investigate each Customer/account before extending credit. He/she should gather information about each customer, analyse it and then determine the credit limit. Customer rating is very important. It provides a basis for decision making on the setting of credit limits for various customers. Depending on the financial condition and past experience with a customer, the company should decide about its collection tactics and other procedures.

Where the company needs money and debtors are not yet due, the financial entrepreneur can obtain money use the help of factoring. Factoring involves the sale of receivables to specialised companies, called factors. Factors collect receivables and also advance cash against receivables to solve the client company's liquidity problems. For providing their services, they charge interest on advances given to clients and some commission for other services.

### (b). Stock Management

In a business environment, companies hold inventories in the form of raw materials, work-in- process and finished goods. Inventories represent investment of a company's funds. The objective of the inventory management should be the maximisation of the value of the company. The company should therefore consider: (*a*) costs, (*b*) return, and (*c*) the risk factors in establishing its inventory policy.

There are three possible motives for a company to hold stocks:

(a) Transaction Motive – this means that the company is holding inventory to facilitate the smooth production and sales operation.

(b) Precautionary Motive – this means that the company is holding inventory to guard against the risk of unpredictable changes in the usage rate and delivery time.

(c) Speculative Motive - helps the company to take advantage of price fluctuations, increases in ordering costs, requisition, placing of order, transportation, receiving, inspecting and storing and clerical and staff services. Ordering costs are fixed per order. Therefore, they decline as the order size increases. Carrying Costs warehousing, handling, clerical and staff services, insurance and taxes. Carrying costs vary with inventory holding. As order size increases, average inventory holding increases and therefore, the carrying costs increases as well.

In a transaction motive situation, the Economic Order Quantity (EOQ) should always be applied, so that costs can be reduced. The company should minimize the total cost (ordering plus carrying). The Economic Order Quantity (EOQ) of inventory will occur at a point where the total cost is at a minimum level.

**The following formula can be used to determine EOQ:**

$$\text{Total Holding costs} = q \times \frac{C}{2} \quad \text{....... Equation (i)}$$

$$\text{Total Ordering costs} = A \times \frac{O}{q} \quad \text{...... Equation (ii)}$$

$$EOQ = q \times \frac{C}{2} = A \times \frac{O}{q} \quad \text{....... Equation (iii)}$$

$$q^2C = 2AO \quad \text{.......... Equation (iv)}$$

$$\therefore \quad q = \sqrt{\frac{2AO}{C}} \quad \text{.......... Equation (v)}$$

**Where:**

*A* is the annual requirement,
*O* is the per order cost, and
*c* is the per unit carrying cost.
2 is a constant

The economic order level of inventory is *q*. *It* represents the optimum inventory policy. The Optimum Inventory Policy optimised when the marginal rate of return of investment in inventory is equal to the marginal cost of funds. The marginal rate of return (*r*) is calculated by dividing the incremental operating profit by the incremental investment in inventories, and the cost of funds is the required rate of return of suppliers of funds. At that point the total holding cost is equal to the total ordering cost of inventory. There are a lot of cost savings to be made in using the Economic Order Quantity Model, (see fig. 3)

**Figure 3: The Economic Order Quantity (EOQ) Model**

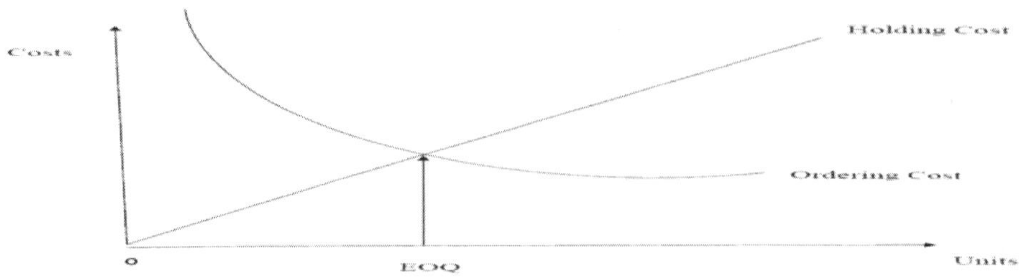


**Source:** Baumol Model

Q is the reorder quantity and Reorder Point of inventory is the level at which the company places an order to replenish its inventory. It depends on the following:

(*a*) the lead time, that is, the time it for an order to be placed and deliveries received, and Holding Cost Ordering Cost Units EOQ Costs

*b*) the usage rate, that is, the lot that can be used within the lead time. The company should maintain a safety stock which serves as a buffer or cushion to meet contingencies. In that case, the reorder point will be equal to: Lead time x Usage rate + Safety stock. The company should strike a trade-off between the marginal rate of return and marginal cost of funds to determine the level of safety stock. This very important, because when stock is short the company will be losing a lot. That is, losing out on production, sales, paying people who are idle, losing reputation and customers.

The Selective Control System of inventory using A-B-C Analysis. According to O'Gorman (2004), the ABC classification is based on Vilfredo Pareto's principles developed during his studies of the population and distribution of wealth in England in 1897. Pareto observed that a large percentage of the total national income was concentrated in a small percentage of the population. As applied to stock, companies, which carrying a number of items in inventory that differ in value, can follow a selective control system. A selective control system, such as the A-B-C analysis or the 80-20 analysis, classifies inventories into three categories, according to the value of the items:

A - Category consists of highest value items, (80% Value and 20% Quantity)

B - Category consists of high value items, (15% Value and 30% Quantity)

C - Category consists of lowest value items, (5% Value and 50% Quantity)

More categories of inventories can also be created. Tight control may be applied for high-value items and relatively lose control for low value items.

### (d) Cash Management Techniques

Cash is a very illusive current asset. Its existence is very important for the survival of the company. Just like company inventory, cash has three motives by which it can account for the survival of the company: There are three possible motives for a company to hold cash:

(a) Transaction Motive – helps in the smooth functioning of activities.

(b) Precautionary Motive – helps in avoiding shortages in cash

(c) Speculative Motive – helps in creating and enhancing shareholder wealth.

Whatever the case, too much cash should not be allowed to lying idle, the opportunity cost of cash is very high and it always exposed to the danger of theft and misuse. Accurate cash forecast provides the management with a very good cash management mechanism. A cash budget is a very good tool to use.

Using a cash budget management will be able to say when receivable due to come in and when necessary payments are going to be made. A cash budget is a cash flow forecast for the ensuing period. It is therefore a detailed statement of anticipated in flows and out flows of cash. It is a master document providing a detailed analysis of cash movements, in and out of the company. It helps to pin point, specifically what time cash will be required to be received or paid out.

This provides cash planning information to management. This means that when a cash shortage is foreseen, management should negotiate a loan well in advance to avoid last minute rush and getting into the hands of loan sharks.

Where a cash surplus is forecast, management should investigate well in advance and put it into a profitable short term investment. No money should be allowed to be idle for too long. Proper cash planning and general resources planning provide a good foundation of all business survival. Planning entails finding out, how much resources are available, who to do what, when to do what, where to do what to what, why to do what and how to do what.

## Total Quality Management (TQM) System

Large numbers of companies today, follow the total quality management (TQM) system which requires companies to adopt the Just-in-time (JIT) and computerised system of inventory management. To maintain total quality and cost effectiveness some entrepreneurs opt for slim organization and downsizing.

They encourage co-operation and teamwork for synergy effect to be enhanced and gives rise to the Balanced Scorecard effect.

## The Balanced Scorecard (BSC)

The balanced scorecard is a strategic planning and management system that is used extensively in business and industry, government, and nonprofit organizations. It is used worldwide to align business activities to the vision and strategy of the organization. It helps in the improvement of internal and external communications and monitors organization performance against strategic goals. It was originated as a performance measurement framework that added strategic non-financial performance measures to traditional financial metrics to give managers and executives a more 'balanced' view of organizational progress and performance. The phrase balanced scorecard was coined in the early 1990s, the roots of the this type of approach are deep, and include the pioneering work of General Electric on performance measurement reporting in the 1950's and the work of French process engineers (who created the *Tableau de Bord* – literally, a "dashboard" of performance measures) in the early part of the 20th century. The balanced scorecard has evolved from its early use as a simple performance measurement framework to a full strategic planning and management system. The "new" balanced scorecard transforms an organization's strategic plan from an attractive, but passive document into the "marching orders" for the organization on a daily basis. Hence, it provides a framework that not only provides performance measurements, but helps planners identify what should be done and how it should be measured. It enables executives to truly measure and execute their strategies for better results. The Balanced Scorecard is defined as "an approach to the provision of information to management to assist strategic policy formulation and achievement" (CIMA, 2002). This model points out that every organization needs a balance between various variables in translating the stated organisational mission into workable operational strategies. To achieve this, the BSC integrates traditional financial measures with non-qualitative issues that are critical in promoting organization's competitiveness. This model's approach is four-pronged introducing three other dimensions in addition to the traditional financial indicators in its evaluation of organizational performance. The additional three perspectives focus on customers, internal business efficiency and innovation and learning issues. The customer perspective identifies and measures the drivers behind the value placed on the organization by customers.

The internal business perspectives strive to improve internal processes to be able to retain current and attract more customers. The innovation and learning perspective looks at how the current processes can be improved to enable organizations to have a competitive edge over their rivals. For organizations to be successful, there must be a balance amongst the identified drivers in each of the four categories. Figure 4 depicts the interaction between the four perspectives.

**Figure 4: The Balanced Scorecard, Translating Strategy into Action**

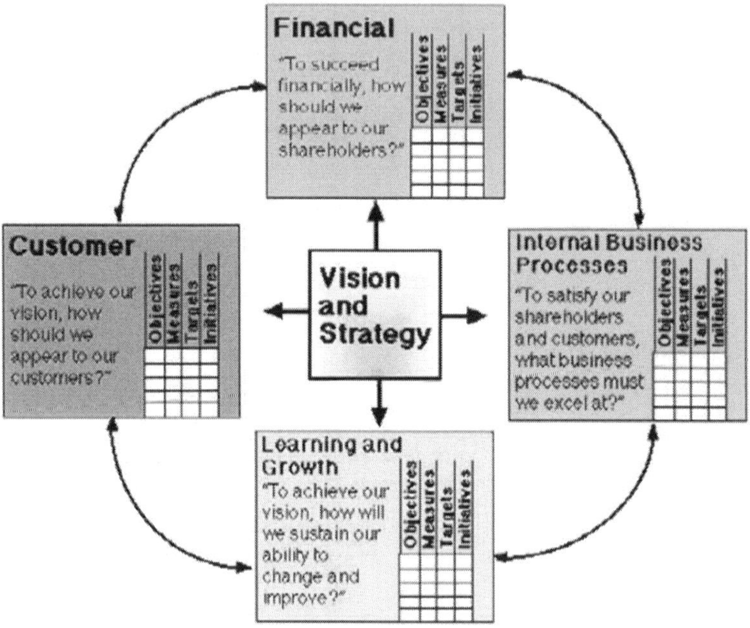

**Source:** Adapted from Kaplan and Norton, 1996.

Essentially the BSC emphasises that the financial results of any organization is a reflection of a combination of several variables whose value should be assessed accordingly as an integral part of the financial reports for purposes of making well informed decisions. As depicted in figure 4, the BSC model recognises the interdependence that exists amongst a number of variables, which influence each other, one way or another and assumes a cause-and-effect relationship amongst the organizations' critical success factors. For example, if the organization's decisions are in tandem with the forces of change and management is able to devise innovative competitive strategies, this will certainly result in improved financial performance and growth.

## Coaching

It is a belief that the entrepreneur should be a multi-skilled person, not a narrow expert. In order to cope well in certain area the entrepreneur must solicit the services of an expert. The entrepreneur needs the services of a Legal Expert, the Accountant, the Financial Analyst, the Human Resource Expert, the Marketing Expert, the Management Information Specialist, the Production experts, the Purchasing Expert and the Research and Development Specialists. These experts provide the entrepreneur the necessary services to enable him keep the business afloat. The survival of the business is in the hands of the experts, who are able to influence the entrepreneur's decision making abilities.

Such people provide advice which enhances the better allocation of scarce resources. No matter how brilliant a entrepreneur is, he must require the services of a coach, especially in a big company environment. Coaches are very important, since they provide specialist advice on specialist areas.

## Conclusion

Business survival is not only about having the resources with which to work, it is also about formulating and implementing policies and business decisions as accurately as possible. Business failure results from lack of approach rather than lack of resources. Diversification is a key strategy of business survival.

Diversification in terms of introducing a variety of products or company-wise diversification carried out by investing in a variety of companies. The company must employ a workforce that will perform as expected, looking at the mission and vision of the company. Teamwork and consultation is greatly encouraged in order to avoid business failure. The management staff must have very good communication skills. They should be very transparent in all dealings, making sure that all the employees should clearly understand what they should do, how it should be done, where it should be done and why it should done and in the stipulated time. Nothing should be left to chance, especially at uncertain times, since fear and ignorance may evolve into gossip which may have a very negative impact on the general performance of the company. Proper information handling will always dispel rumours and bring improved performance. The Management team should always be surgical in their decision making. Making any changes carefully, gradually, and only after much forethought. Get close to big customers. Understanding your customers' business and being regarded as a partner drives loyalty. This also includes conducting loss reviews, because it is very important to find out what is motivating all of your customers' behaviour.

They are the key to growth. Hence, the customer is the King in the business environment. Be very specific about short-term goals. Maintain immediacy in your short-term goal setting and do not plan more than it is necessary. Management must be able to react quickly to any changes in their operating environment.

## References


1. Balanced Scorecard and sustainability, Chartered Institute of Management Accountant Guidelines (2002)
2. Dessler, G. (2002), A Framework for Human Resource Management, Pearson Education, Inc. India
3. Gilbert, J. P., & Schonberger, R. J. (1983). Inventory-based production control systems: A historical analysis. *Production and Inventory Management, 24*(2), 1-13.
4. Gupta, S.K and Sharma, R.K (2007), Financial Management, Theory and Practice, Kalyani publishers, New Delhi, India
5. Kaplan, R. and D. Norton (1996). "The Balanced Scorecard: Translating Strategy into Action", Harvard Business School Press.
6. O'Gorman, B. (2004). The Road to ERP — *Has Industry Learned or Revolved Back to the Start?* Idea Group Inc. Hershey PA 17033-1240, USA, P. 13
7. Olicky, J. (1975). *Material Requirements Planning — The New Way of Life in Production and Inventory Management. New York: McGraw-Hill.*